ALL 63 US NATIONAL PARKS
THE COMPLETE TRAVEL GUIDE

ALL 63
US NATIONAL PARKS
THE COMPLETE TRAVEL GUIDE

FIRST EDITION

VALERIE PONTIFF

PUBLISHED BY TRAVEL WRITER, INC.
CHESTNUT HILL, MASSACHUSETTS

Published 2021 by Travel Writer, Inc.

Cover photography:
Clouds over Longs Peak in Rocky Mountain National Park
by John De Bord/Shutterstock

Cover and interior design:
Megan Katsanevakis, *Hue Creative*, Charleston, South Carolina

Library of Congress Cataloging-in-Publication Data

Pontiff, Valerie Foster

All 63 US National Parks The Complete Travel Guide – 1st ed.

ISBN 978-0-578-90249-4 (pbk.)
ISBN 978-0-578-90250-0 (ebk.)

To Jeff, Oscar, and Audrey

MAP OF ALL 63 UNITED

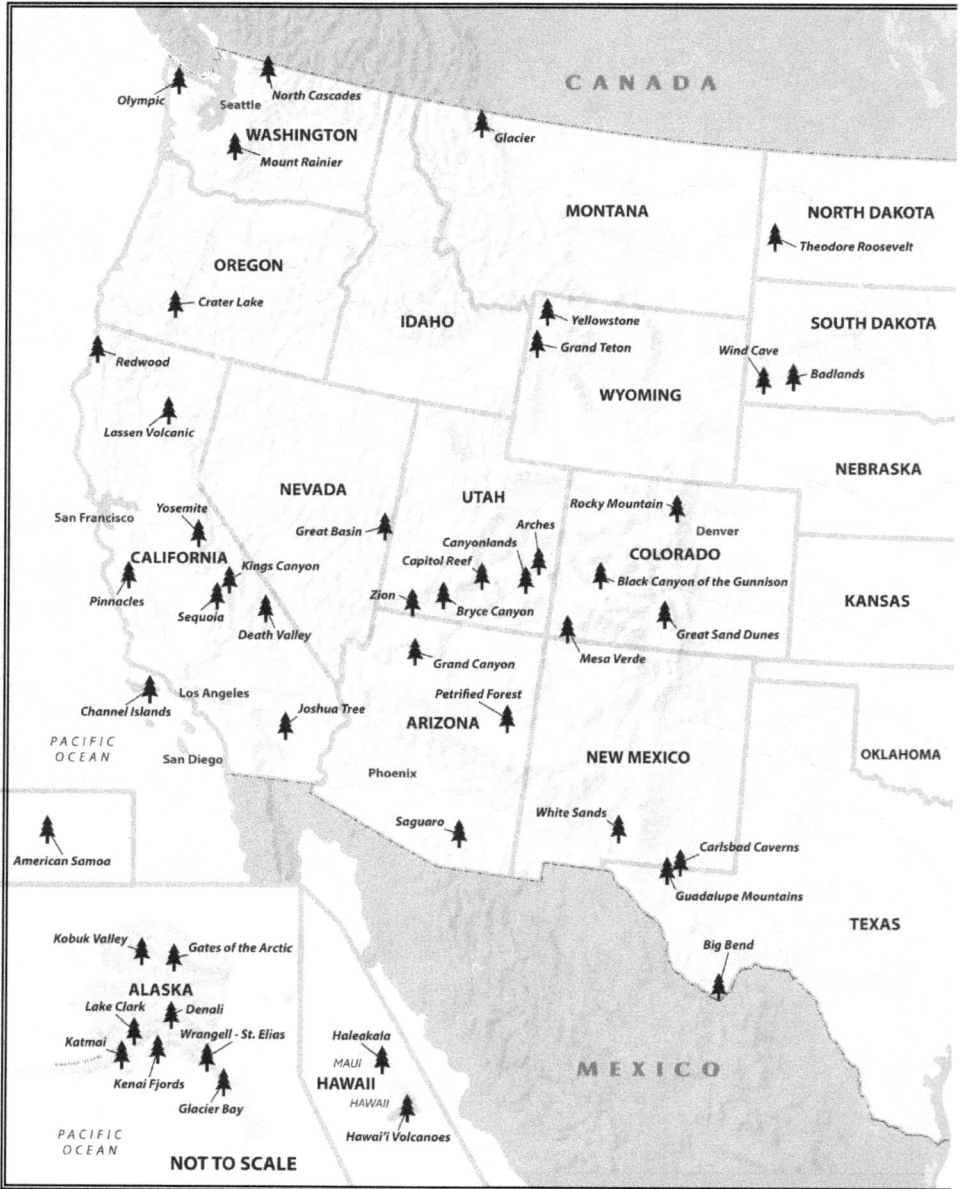

CANADA

Olympic
Seattle
North Cascades
WASHINGTON
Glacier
Mount Rainier

MONTANA

NORTH DAKOTA
Theodore Roosevelt

OREGON
Crater Lake

IDAHO
Yellowstone
Grand Teton

SOUTH DAKOTA
Wind Cave
Badlands

Redwood

WYOMING

Lassen Volcanic

NEBRASKA

NEVADA
San Francisco
Yosemite
UTAH
Rocky Mountain
Great Basin
Arches
Denver
Canyonlands
CALIFORNIA
Kings Canyon
Capitol Reef
COLORADO
Pinnacles
Zion
Black Canyon of the Gunnison
KANSAS
Sequoia
Bryce Canyon
Death Valley
Great Sand Dunes
Grand Canyon
Mesa Verde
Los Angeles
Petrified Forest
Channel Islands
Joshua Tree
ARIZONA
PACIFIC
OCEAN
San Diego
NEW MEXICO
OKLAHOMA
Phoenix
Saguaro
White Sands

American Samoa

Carlsbad Caverns

Guadalupe Mountains

TEXAS

Kobuk Valley
Gates of the Arctic
Big Bend
ALASKA
Lake Clark
Denali
Haleakala
Katmai
Wrangell - St. Elias
MAUI
Kenai Fjords
HAWAII
MEXICO
Glacier Bay
HAWAII
PACIFIC
OCEAN
Hawai'i Volcanoes
NOT TO SCALE

STATES NATIONAL PARKS

CONTENTS

*The wilderness holds answers to questions
man has not yet learned to ask.*

—attributed to midcentury nature photography critic and writer Nancy Newhall

INTRODUCTION

SEEING THE COUNTRY THROUGH the lens of the United States national park system is very special. I hope you will find the park descriptions, maps, and suggested itineraries helpful and inspiring as you explore this beautiful land and create your own memories. There is something for every age and interest in the national parks and few better ways to see the physical diversity of this great country. Happy travels.

A Brief History of the National Park System

European settlers arriving in what is now the United States brought with them a concept of formal boundaries and land ownership. This led to the 13 colonies and ultimately to the 50 states, Washington, DC, and the five populated territories. Delaware was the first state, founded in 1787, followed quickly by other eastern and southern states.

The idea of nationally owned land set aside for recreation began as part of the discussions surrounding the Louisiana Purchase, which was completed in

1803. What is now Arkansas was part of that acquisition. Travel to Arkansas, especially to its hot springs, was popular. Development pressure in the area caused local residents to petition the United States Congress to set aside land that was to be federally owned and free from development. In 1832, Congress set aside 2,500 acres as the Hot Springs National Reservation, and President Andrew Jackson signed the preserving documents into law. Arkansas was admitted as the twenty-fifth state in 1836. The seeds of the United States national park system began here.

It took another 40 years for the idea of preserving large tracts of land to take further hold. The center of this movement was in California's Sierra Nevada Range, specifically in what is now Yosemite National Park and nearby Sequoia National Park. Writer and explorer John Muir was an important historical figure who lived there for several years and wrote about the scenery in nationally syndicated columns. He pushed for preservation of the area, and others soon joined him. In 1864, President Abraham Lincoln signed the Yosemite Valley Grant Act, preserving 39,000 acres in the Sierra Nevada Range. This grant was to the state of California, meaning this was not the first national park.

Land that is now Yellowstone National Park had been on the radar of preservationists since about 1840. Although there were many champions, Ferdinand V. Hayden (now recognized by Yellowstone's Hayden Valley) was the lead cheerleader. He organized a survey of the land in 1871 and helped convince Congress, and ultimately President Ulysses S. Grant, to preserve the area as a national park. President Grant signed the Act of Dedication in 1872 that created Yellowstone National Park. The Yosemite area, by then including Sequoia, came into the national park system in 1890. Through the efforts of explorer Philemon B. Van Trump and tourism promoter James Longmire, Rainier National Park was named the fourth national park in 1899.

President Theodore Roosevelt served from 1901 to 1909 and took the national park system to the next level. During his tenure the Antiquities Act was passed in 1906. This act has enabled nationalization of lands under the auspices of preservation ever since. Before the act passed, Roosevelt added Crater Lake and Wind Cave National Parks. After it passed, he added Mesa Verde National Park and expanded Yosemite. He also used his executive authority to name national monuments. This single-person naming power paved the way for later congressional action approving national parks. Roosevelt's monuments that later became national parks include Petrified Forest, Lassen Volcanic, Grand Canyon, Pinnacles, and Olympic. President Woodrow Wilson formalized the administration of what had become a critical mass of nationally owned recreation land by creating the National Park Service in 1916.

From the midcentury through around 1980, about 20 national parks were added, or one park every four years on average. The parks ranged in geography from Acadia in Maine to Haleakala in Hawaii. Though each park has a founding story, the national mood was broadly supportive. Then came President Jimmy Carter, the rise of the environmental movement, the acceleration of modern-day political polarization, and the November 1980 election of Ronald Reagan. Western states were beginning to flex their states-rights muscles, and environmentalists believed time was short to fully preserve remaining large swaths of undeveloped land.

In late 1978, President Carter named sites throughout Alaska as national monuments. These included to-be national parks Gates of the Arctic, Kobuk Valley, Wrangell–St. Elias, Kenai Fjords, Katmai, and Glacier Bay. On November 12, 1980, six days after Ronald Reagan won the presidential election but before his inauguration, Congress passed and President Carter signed the Alaska National Interest Lands Conservation Act (ANILCA) that converted the just-mentioned national monuments to national parks. The act preserved 43.6 million acres, or over 10 percent of Alaska, as national park land, with limits on natural resource extraction. This action resulted in western states in particular becoming more skeptical of further national park formation within their borders.

Though there have been 15 national parks converted from monuments since the ANILCA, only one park, the National Park of American Samoa, was added outright afterward, in 1993. A multidecade rethink of federal land ownership has been underway in the United States since the 1980s. In 1990 the federal government owned about 28.5 percent of the United States. By 2018, that percentage had dropped to 27.1 percent as some nationally owned land was ceded to the states and Native American tribes. The balance between state and federal ownership of preservation and conservation land is likely to continue, making existing national parks and monuments all the more precious.

RESERVATIONS, PLANNING, AND ACTIVITIES

A good plan today is better than a perfect plan tomorrow.
—World War II hero General George S. Patton Jr.

TO GET A PASS OR NOT

If you are 62 years old or older, it makes sense to purchase an America the Beautiful Pass. For $80, the pass provides lifetime access to all national park properties (63 national parks and approximately 350 other sites) as well as the holdings of five other agencies, for a total of around 2,000 sites. For those younger than 62, Annual Passes are free to active and reserve members of the military, to fourth graders, and to volunteers who meet a certain level of volunteer time per year. Each pass holder can bring up to three other adults; children 15 and under are always free.

For others under 62, the wisdom of getting an Annual Pass for $80 is less clear. The cost to enter most national parks via car with passengers is around $25 for one week. To complicate the decision further, certain park vendors (e.g., private airlines, rafting companies, narrated bus tour providers) add park access fees to the reservation. Additionally, many national parks don't charge a fee at all, or if a fee is charged, often the entrance station is unmanned. This is not an invitation to skip paying a fee but rather an observation that fee collection is spotty in the national park system. Finally, if the pass is lost or stolen, there are no replacements.

VOLUNTEERING IN THE NATIONAL PARKS

Volunteer.gov lists volunteer opportunities by state. In addition, certain national parks have their own volunteer coordinators. An example is Voyageurs National Park in Minnesota, where volunteers have been tracking the loon population each August for years. If interested in volunteering at a specific park, contact the park directly.

TO STAY INSIDE OR OUTSIDE THE PARK

Staying inside the park saves time, while staying outside the park can be less expensive, especially when factoring in the cost of meals.

TO STAY IN A LODGE OR CAMPGROUND

As with so much of life, this is a decision of time versus money, with the overlay of your personal preference for chatting under the stars versus sleeping between four walls.

LODGING AND CAMPING RESERVATIONS

Most lodging and camping can be reserved between 6 and 18 months in advance. Remember that availability to visit some of the most spectacular parks can be very limited during the peak times. If traveling with children, reserving in advance is even more important. Most lodges were built a long time ago with rooms designed to accommodate two people. Scarce rooms with two double beds are reserved quickly.

Camping spaces fill up more slowly, but don't assume that arriving without a reservation will work. The most popular parks have "campground full" signs for much of the peak season and will use active measures to prevent overnight stays by campers with no reservations.

FRONT COUNTRY AND SERVICED BACKCOUNTRY

This is a book for front-country travelers, whether camping or staying in hotels/lodges. In a few cases, a park offers serviced backcountry lodging and meals. Examples include Phantom Ranch at the bottom of Grand Canyon, Denali's four backcountry lodges, Sperry Chalet in Glacier, the High Sierra Camps in Yosemite and Sequoia, LeConte Lodge in the Great Smoky Mountains, and Brooks Camp in Katmai. These are the diamonds of the national park system and reservations must be made well in advance, often on a specific day and hour.

Activities

HIKING

The primary purpose of the national parks is to provide recreational opportunities for all. Walking and hiking are at the top of the list. Most parks have miles of maintained and well-signed trails of varying difficulty, with more hours of trail time offered than you will likely spend in the park.

RANGER-LED TOURS

Many parks have ranger-led talks and tours. Some of these are no cost and happen every day. A great example is the wonderful ranger-led tour series at the compact Hot Springs National Park. Other parks have fewer regular tours, in part because rangers are responsible for resource management as well as hospitality and interpretation. Check the websites and even call the visitor center to find out how often and reliably tours happen.

Fee-based ticketed tours led by a ranger or other subject-matter expert operate at a number of parks. These tours rarely get cancelled and are a tremendous opportunity to spend a nice chunk of time with a subject-matter specialist in a beautiful setting.

FISHING

Some of the greatest fishing in the world is found in America's national parks. For the small price of a fishing license, a collapsible fishing rod, and some flies or bait, visitors can enjoy fishing the parks. If planning to fish, obtain a license even if hiring a guide service.

BIRDING

Because national parks can be quite large and remote, the bird life is often incredible. Some specific parks worth noting are Everglades with its enormous winter resident migratory population, Kenai Fjords with its puffins and other rock-dwelling ocean birds, and Yellowstone with its large pelican colony. Bring your binoculars!

GUIDED TOURS

The national park system has thousands of concessionaire partners—outside companies that operate their businesses inside a national park. Concessionaires offer boat tours, kayaking/canoeing, rafting, horseback riding, covered wagon rides and cookouts, flightseeing, biking, and so much more. These fee-for-service activities and tours can be instrumental in bringing the park alive for visitors. Enjoy them where you can.

HIRING A GUIDE SERVICE

A 2005 study of Yosemite National Park indicated that 70 percent of visitors spent less than nine hours in the park and 50 percent of visitors spent less than four hours. Why? One reason may be that visitors are not comfortable in the outdoors. If that sounds like you, don't shy away from hiring a guide service. Guides provide backcountry and naturalist expertise, encourage children to cheerfully keep going, and enable the group or family to get the most out of all the park has to offer.

I travel light; as light, that is, as a man can travel who
will still carry his body around because of its sentimental value.
—Christopher Fry, English poet and playwright

What to Bring

DAY HIKING

Bring as little as possible. The list here should be enough for a week of temperate lodge/hotel travel. Adjust the clothing recommendations as necessary according to the climate and time of year of your visit.

Day pack small enough to fit under seat on plane	Casual dress (female) or collared shirt (male) for nicer dining
Rain jacket and rain pants	Bug-protecting head net
Hat and gloves	Baseball or other sun hat
Hiking shoes or light boots	Insect repellent wipe-on pads
Water sandals	Lip protection balm and sunscreen (under 3 ounces)
Lightweight wool socks (7 pairs)	One-liter water bottles (2)
Undergarments (7 sets)	Water purifier pills or other filtration
Swimsuit	Flashlight or headlamp
Quick-dry long-sleeved camp shirt	Small plastic bag of minor wound-care supplies
Quick-dry T-shirts (7)	USGS map of the area(s) you will be hiking in plastic protection
Quick-dry pants (2)	Toiletries
Quick-dry shorts (2)	Passport if going to Waterton while in Glacier or Boquillas while in Big Bend
Lightweight fleece jacket	

Since a great day of sightseeing is the point of the trip, consider buying food for lunches in advance. Trail mix minus the melting pieces, dried fruit, and jerky meat are tried-and-true choices. Many parks have camper stores where you can purchase food, but the selection is often lackluster.

CAMPING SUPPLEMENT

With a small investment in camping gear, visitors can access more of the park and save money in the process. Here are some additional things to bring for camping.

Tent	Tent liner/space blanket
Sleeping bag (rated 20–25 degrees for summer camping)	Small propane camp stove
Sleeping bag liner	Packages of dehydrated meals
Long johns (top and bottom)	Long spoons for cooking and eating
Ground pad	Cup
Large fully collapsible duffel bag to store all camping gear listed	Propane and perishable food, purchased after your flight lands

TROPICAL SUPPLEMENT

Six national parks are tropical and water-sport-oriented—the National Park of American Samoa, a small section of Volcanoes in Hawaii, Dry Tortugas off Key West in Florida, the oceanfront portion of Everglades, Biscayne in greater Miami, and the US Virgin Islands National Park on the island of Saint John. Channel Islands National Park, though not tropical, should also be on this list. All of these parks offer good to excellent snorkeling and/or scuba diving. If visually challenged, don't forget to bring contacts or prescription goggles/mask.

BEARS IN THE NATIONAL PARKS

From 2010 through 2020 there have been 28 deaths in the United States and Canada from bear attacks. Of these, five have occurred in the national parks (three in Yellowstone, one in Denali, and one in Wrangell–St. Elias). During that time, there have been over three billion visits to United States national parks. If bears are a concern, consider carrying bear spray, using bells tied to a backpack to alert bears to your presence, and hiking in groups of two or more. When camping in bear country, follow the park's protocols for keeping a clean campsite.

CELL PHONE SERVICE AND WI-FI

Some parks have cell service, though probably not intentionally. Plan to be off the grid and have hard copies of maps and any reservation information for campsites, lodges, and activities. Some lodges have Wi-Fi service for their guests. Often it does not work. Use this special time for a technology sabbatical.

FUEL PLANNING

The distance between gas stations can be vast, and electric car charging options are sometimes nonexistent. Particularly if traveling in remote areas, plan fuel stops in advance.

NATIONAL PARK SERVICE MAPS, USGS MAPS, ALLTRAILS.COM, AND THE HIKING PROJECT

Always stop by the ranger station and get a map of the park and any supplemental maps on offer. For a serious hike, it is critical to also bring paper copies of professional hiking maps in a thick zippered plastic bag or to purchase waterproof, tear-resistant trail maps. The best place to get maps is the United States Geological Survey (USGS) online store. USGS maps include topography, hiking trails, roads, and buildings. As an additional resource, pay the small fee for the AllTrails app, which provides a stripped-down version of USGS maps and simpler trail viewing. The Hiking Project is similar to AllTrails but crowd-sourced. Both provide great information for pre-trip planning. An app on a phone, though, should never be your only trail map.

HOW THIS BOOK IS ORGANIZED

The national parks are presented moving roughly west to east in the Lower 48 states, with the three Pacific Island parks and eight Alaskan parks at the end. Parks are grouped together based on geography and proximity to major transportation hubs. The appendix includes contact information for lodges, campgrounds, visitor centers, and activities. The specific cost of lodging, camping, and activities are not included.

RANKING THE PARKS

EACH NATIONAL PARK EXPERIENCE is unique. A top park for one visitor may seem lackluster to another. Here is a brief summary and ranking of each park based upon my experience.

RANKING	PARK	OBSERVATIONS AND SUGGESTIONS
1	Yosemite (California)	A year-round park with lush valleys, splendid peaks, stunning alpine meadows, gorgeous lodges, and an extensive network of serviced backcountry camps for hiking in comfort. This park has it all.
2	Glacier (Montana)	The crown of the continent, Glacier is compromised only by its limited season. Large wildlife, glacier-fed lakes and rivers, and sky-high peaks make this park a must. Some of the best hiking in the country, and a road leading to Canada's adjacent Waterton Lakes National Park.

3	Yellowstone (Wyoming/ Montana)	The hot Yellowstone Caldera makes this place so unique. Abundant life teems throughout the park. Raging steam vents, roaring rivers, deep canyons, and pristine mountains yield an unforgettable experience. Famous lodges, endless camping, and fun activities like covered wagon rides through buffalo country make Yellowstone an international destination.
4	Great Smoky Mountains (Tennessee/ North Carolina)	A four-season park serving the developed southeastern US, this park supports the highest number of visitors in the national park system. With a backcountry lodge, extensive camping, and gorgeous hikes among its lakes, rivers, peaks, and valleys, there is plenty to do. Preserved historic buildings add a special twist, making this park a star for both education and recreation.
5	Olympic (Washington)	Four lodges, abundant camping, a 33-mile round-trip hike to the lowest-elevation glaciated mountain in the United States, rugged Pacific coastline, four old-growth rain forests, and breathtaking alpine lakes and meadows make this park almost unbeatable. The catch? Bathed in cold rain much of the year, the season is short to enjoy this special place.
6	Grand Canyon (Arizona)	Sweeping vistas, miles of flat and steep hiking, historic hotels, ample camping, mules, biking, rafting! This is a spectacular park but with an unforgiving travel season. Cold winters and hot summers make late spring and early fall the time to go. The North Rim is less crowded than the South Rim.

7	Grand Teton (Wyoming)	Jagged, distinctive mountains reflected in pristine Jackson Lake make a perfect backdrop for boating, fishing, and horseback riding. Endless trails with lakes, waterfalls, and meadows, coupled with the easy-to-raft Snake River, make this animal-rich park a must. A bonus? Extensive groomed cross-country skiing trails in the winter.
8	Acadia (Maine)	A trip back in time to when summer was a verb. Rugged Maine coastline, historic cottages, Rockefeller-funded carriage lanes perfect for bicyclists, and Cadillac Mountain with its sweeping views of the Atlantic. Add historic gardens, an iconic lighthouse, and a mailboat to an outpost island. Acadia is a national treasure.
9	Rocky Mountain (Colorado)	Elk-filled meadows and beaver-thick lakes are only a start of the visual delight that is Rocky Mountain. Perfect columbine-lined hiking and two visitor centers at 12,000 feet make this place almost second to none.
10	Everglades (Florida)	Uniquely situated in the space between fresh and salt water, this massive park showcases incredible diversity of species. From boat tours to backcountry kayaking to hiking on boardwalks surrounded by alligators and crocodiles, this park delights.
11	North Cascades (Washington)	Deep glacier-carved lakes, jagged alpine peaks, wildflowers, kayaking, and the remote village of Stehekin accessed only by daily ferry service or floatplane are just a few of the highlights. In Washington State on the Canadian border, the park's main access road closes for almost half the year due to snow.

12	Joshua Tree (Arizona)	Spring in this dry paradise yields a flower-carpeted desert floor punctuated by otherworldly Joshua trees with their enormous yellow flowers. Sun-kissed rocks soar in interesting formations, with climbers dotting their faces. Include a tour of the park's historic abandoned Keys Ranch and nearby Palm Springs for an unbeatable trip.
13	Sequoia (California)	Few places on earth are more spectacular than Sequoia's Giant Forest. Full of some of the largest and oldest trees in the world, this area is almost religious in its majesty. Alpine meadows, views of the high peaks of the Sierra Nevada Range, and glorious hikes are all hallmarks of this park.
14	Mount Rainier (Washington)	The iconic Pacific Northwest mountain is covered in glaciers, surrounded by miles of wildflowers, and packed with high mountain lakes. The marmot-filled Wonderland Trail runs through the park, and trails around Sunrise bring hikers to the glacier edge.
15	Denali (Alaska)	A short travel window opens to view the highest peak in the United States. Add Wonder Lake, the raging McKinley River, animal sightings, sled dog shows, and the remote backcountry and Denali will be an experience long remembered.
16	Big Bend (Texas)	This hard-to-reach park has a very special mix of the Permian Reef Chisos Mountains, historic abandoned off-the-grid ranches, stunning canyons, the Rio Grande riverbank, and the potential to have lunch in Mexico. This International Dark Sky Park delivers on its name.

17	Zion (Utah)	A jewel of Utah, Zion's unique wading hike in the Virgin River through the famous Zion Canyon Narrows is not to be missed. Add moderate hikes in the Zion oasis along the canyon walls, big-sky view hikes, and the ability to venture into vast backcountry. Zion is a treat.
18	Katmai (Alaska)	Viewing coastal brown bears up close is an experience of a lifetime. The platform at Brooks Falls brings visitors within feet of massive salmon-fishing bears. Combine with some of the world's best fly-fishing and an excursion to a remote volcano to make this trip complete.
19	Redwood (California)	This national and state park on the California/ Oregon border delivers diverse and magnificent redwood forests, ocean walks, hikes in secret verdant canyons, and the famous Elk Meadow that lives up to its name. Yurok tribal lands in the center of the park on the Klamath River make this park unique.
20	Bryce Canyon (Utah)	Images from the canyon rim down into the endless field of hoodoos at sunrise and sunset are familiar worldwide. Hiking and horseback riding in the hoodoos provides a unique and otherworldly perspective. Add the adjacent Rainbow and Yovimpa Points, with pine-rich hiking trails and sweeping views, for an unforgettable experience.
21	Crater Lake (Oregon)	The eruption and internal collapse of Oregon's Mount Mazama created the famous visible-from-space Crater Lake. Rim-side lodging, camping, and hiking make this park easy to enjoy. Views of nearby snow-covered volcanic mountains are spectacular. Boat the lake and hike the peaks for a complete perspective.

22	Haleakala (Hawaii)	A legendary Pacific Island volcano, Haleakala is home to some of the most cutting-edge atmospheric research in the world. Come for the high-elevation sunrise and otherworldly plants at the top, and enjoy the small section of the park that runs through one of the world's most beautiful rain forests to the Pacific Ocean.
23	Kings Canyon (California)	Abutting Sequoia and often seen with that park, Kings Canyon boasts some of the world's largest sequoias, a ridge hike that showcases the Sierra Nevada Range like few others, and the remote Kings Canyon itself with a lodge, campground, and near-endless hiking for all abilities.
24	Arches (Utah)	Delicate Arch, featured on Utah's license plate, showcases the perfection of Arches National Park. The many eroded sandstone protrusions and canyons are iconic and easy to see, boasting level and well-marked hiking trails. Couple the park with the fun high-desert town of Moab and Arches is hard to beat.
25	Lassen Volcanic (California)	An unsung hero of a park, this large area of northeast California has a lot to offer. Kayaking on gorgeous Manzanita Lake, hiking to Kings Creek Falls, a summit route up Mount Lassen, and boardwalks through volcanic hot pots make up the park's central section. Add beautiful Warner Valley, remote Cinder Cone, and Juniper Lake for a fantastic visit.
26	Saguaro (Arizona)	Travel deep into the Sonoran Desert to experience this fascinating park featuring the saguaro cactus. The iconic large cactus with limbs like arms is found in both of the park's noncontiguous sections to the east and west of Tucson. Hiking is fascinating, with strange desert flowers and unusual birds at many turns. See more animals at the park-abutting top-rated Desert Museum.

27	US Virgin Islands	This hard-to-reach old-school island paradise has long been a focus of preservationists, with a huge amount of national park land, immense and varied areas for snorkeling, and remnants of the sugar plantations that put this area on the Western trade route map. Add small villages and endless seafood for a very memorable vacation.
28	Death Valley (California)	This park belongs on every bucket list, but with the low point below sea level and the high summits at over 11,000 feet, few times are a good time for a complete visit. Still, enjoy the baking ancient dry lake bed, the famous Mesquite Flat Sand Dunes, canyons filmed for *Star Wars*, and two mountain ranges worth of trails. Add a stay at the gorgeous new lodging in Furnace Creek for a terrific trip.
29	Mammoth Cave (Kentucky)	The largest known cave system in the world, Mammoth Cave has many and varied cave tours coupled with abundant surface activities. Canoe the Green River, hike gorgeous southeastern forests, and ride horses in the core of United States thoroughbred country.
30	Great Basin (Nevada)	Nevada's high-elevation Great Basin Desert delivers this wonderful park, with its Lehman Caves system, 5,000-year-old bristlecone pine trees, and extensive and varied hiking throughout the park's South Snake Range. Nevada on the Utah border has plenty of snow, so visit this special park in the summer.
31	Shenandoah (Virginia)	A perfect showcase of a southeastern forest, this long and narrow park hosts the world-renowned Appalachian Trail from end to end. Easy hikes, panoramic views, historic cabin campsites, and memorable lodging makes Shenandoah a must-visit.

32	Lake Clark (Alaska)	Split into three sections, each accessed only by plane, Lake Clark is not for the faint of heart. Centered around Lake Clark's Port Alsworth, the park has some of the most incredible hiking and fishing in the world. Fly east to the park's Cook Inlet ocean coast for a lodge stay and coastal brown bear observation.
33	Congaree (South Carolina)	The last intact old-growth bottomland hardwood swamp forest in the Southeast, Congaree is teeming with life and little visited. Extensive and easy trails are filled with loud owls, fishing raccoons, and endless birds and snakes. Peacefully kayak here alone.
34	Capitol Reef (Utah)	The historic farming village of Fruita anchors this visually stunning park. Enjoy orchards and an operating bakery as well as the surrounding multilayered sandstone cliffs, long canyon hikes, views for miles, and incredible rock formations. This remote park is a hidden gem.
35	Channel Islands (California)	Getting here is half the fun, with a starting point in California's seaside city of Ventura and transportation on a ferry surrounded by leaping dolphins. The historic Scorpion Ranch triples as the ferry landing, campground, and hub for kayak trips. This life-filled island features indigenous island foxes, a plethora of cormorant colonies, and endless sea life easy to see by kayak or snorkel.

36	Kenai Fjords (Alaska)	This park is a show with three stars. Boat rides to calving tidewater glaciers and puffin colonies showcase the park's namesake fjords. The gorgeous Exit Glacier, easy to access, informs visitors about climate change in real time. And the Harding Icefield, with its quarter-waypoint Marmot Meadows, is on many an adventurer's bucket list. Stand on the shore of Resurrection Bay in Seward and watch whales cresting.
37	Carlsbad Caverns (New Mexico)	Featuring both Carlsbad Cavern and Slaughter Canyon Cave, this park has a lot to offer. Many tours, ranging from physically intense to casually educational, provide something for everyone. Home to massive migratory Brazilian free-tailed bat colonies, park rangers offer a famous sunset bat-viewing program.
38	Mesa Verde (Colorado)	Seeing the canyon-wall dwellings of Mesa Verde is believing. Tours of the Ancient Puebloan housing, both above and below the canyon rims, bring history and culture alive. Important for children and adults alike, Mesa Verde offers understanding of ancient people in a way books can almost never deliver. Hiking is easy, with classic dry pine trails and distant views of far-off mesas.
39	Glacier Bay (Alaska)	The apex of many an Alaskan cruise, Glacier Bay with its tidewater glaciers can be seen more thoroughly via a direct visit. Access the park's small hub village of Gustavus by five-hour ferry from Juneau for an even more relaxing and whale-filled experience.

40	Isle Royale (Michigan)	A clever land deal placed this island park inside the United States rather than in Canada. Ferries, seaplanes, tour boats, historic lighthouse, and a remote lodge with kayaks. Volunteer to help the wolf and moose research team as a very special treat.
41	Badlands (South Dakota)	This incredibly unique park full of bighorn sheep herds and not much else is a sight for the ages. Massive striated peaked sandstone protrusions rise from the South Dakotan plain, making for stark and windy hiking. Even though it's hard to get lost, the feeling of being a speck in a sea of sameness is profound.
42	New River Gorge (West Virginia)	Raging water slices the Appalachian Mountains, yielding superb rafting and gorge-side rock climbing. Miles of mountain biking juxtapose with historic buildings supporting some of the country's most productive coal veins.
43	Hawai'i Volcanoes (Hawaii)	A trip to the Big Island of Hawaii is not complete without venturing south to the huge volcanic Mauna Loa as it slopes into the ocean. Between the summit and the sea is the smaller Kilauea Caldera that anchors this still-active volcanic park. Otherworldly plants, ancient Polynesian petroglyphs, rain forests, raging shoreline, and a potential summit hike to Mauna Loa make this park special indeed.
44	Wrangell–St. Elias (Alaska)	Bounded by the famed Copper River, this glacier-rich park with raging rivers and historic copper mine buildings offers a vast expanse for outdoor enthusiasts. Come for the rafting and glacier hiking. Stay to learn about early Alaskan mining and to enjoy the gorgeous lodge.

45	Hot Springs (Arkansas)	Fascinating historic bathhouses anchor this small park, providing ranger-curated accessible history to visitors. Hiking is abundant, through gorgeous southeastern urban deciduous forests. Adjacent dining and fun shops make this park unique.
46	Voyageurs (Minnesota)	Come in high summer to this Minnesota water paradise on the Canadian border. Backcountry canoes for rent, a remote waterfront lodge, and plenty of ranger-narrated boat excursions complete the trip.
47	Black Canyon of the Gunnison (Colorado)	Many visitors to Colorado miss the Western Slope. This little populated area has stunning scenery, including the deep and dark Black Canyon of the Gunnison. For most, the visit includes only a short drive on the rim with limited side hikes. Expanded access to in-canyon hiking would help visitors see this park in its full glory.
48	Theodore Roosevelt (North Dakota)	There is a special beauty in the high North Dakota plains. This is a unique park with badlands, streams, and historic buildings. Wildlife is scarce, hiking is a bit monotonous, and the location is a challenge. Come ready to see the area that inspired President Theodore Roosevelt to preserve massive amounts of public land.
49	Biscayne (Florida)	Off the coast of greater Miami, Biscayne is mostly underwater. Boca Chita Key, a highlight, requires near-private boat transportation for access and is difficult to visit from mid-April through summer due to bugs. Rent kayaks close to the mainland shore, charter a boat to the park's famed distant scuba diving areas, and enjoy the historic village of Stiltsville.

50	Canyonlands (Utah)	Hiking on Island in the Sky mesa while looking out into the near nothingness of tops of canyons is beautiful in an existential way. Camp here for a true Dark Sky experience. Split into two main sections more than two hours apart, this park is challenging to navigate. Next door is Dead Horse Point State Park featuring the iconic view down to the Colorado River and its canyon.
51	Dry Tortugas (Florida)	A long day on an open-ocean catamaran ferry leads to a short visit to the fascinating historic Fort Jefferson. Ranger-led interpretive tours, a small swimming beach, jaunts around the fort perimeter, and distant views of nesting migrating birds complete the island visit. Enjoy the beaches, restaurants, and history of iconic Key West before or after the trip.
52	Guadalupe Mountains (Texas)	These fascinating Permian Reef mountains jutting up from the desert floor are visually stunning, delivering views from their summits far into Texas. The gorgeous McKittrick Canyon adds much to the mix, with the trail through this flat canyon bottom proceeding past gorgeous desert wildflowers, streams, and abandoned ranch homes.
53	Great Sand Dunes (Colorado)	This park in southern Colorado is centered around massive sand dunes. Soft and difficult to hike, the dunes reward summit hikers with an improved view of the beautiful surrounding Sangre de Cristo Mountains. The sand dunes give way to the mountainous Mosca Pass Trail in the adjacent Great Sand Dunes Preserve. From the trail, the entire sea of dunes is visible.

54	Wind Cave (South Dakota)	Combine Wind Cave with the nearby and stunning Jewel Cave National Monument for a complete cave experience. Add the adjacent and wildlife-filled Custer State Park for a trip that showcases the northern Great Plains at their best.
55	Petrified Forest (Arizona)	A geologist's dream, this park features the remains of an ancient forest covered in mud for over 200 million years. Tree became quartz, and tree-shaped fallen quartz logs are found all over this fascinating park. Short hikes abound through petrified trees and petroglyphs, and the park's northern section features panoramic views of the Painted Desert.
56	Pinnacles (California)	Mountains of rock spires protrude from the Salinas Valley in north-central California. A desert landscape dotted with small streams and interrupted by California condors flying overhead. This park's central trail provides cave access and, at the summit, sweeping 360-degree views of the north-central California.
57	Gates of the Arctic (Alaska)	The massive Brooks Range anchors this huge fly-in park. Tall peaks and pristine lakes make for perfect guided weeklong remote hiking. If time or money constrains, outfitters offer single-day flightseeing with a touchdown and potential short hike.
58	American Samoa	Called the National Park of American Samoa yet in the US national park system, this park is between worlds. One of five populated US territories, American Samoa is 3,000 miles west of Hawaii. This park is split over three distant islands and has several premier hiking trails. While here, enjoy world-class snorkeling and deep-sea fishing.

59	Cuyahoga Valley (Ohio)	Give this park a century and it will be a perfect showcase of old Ohio deciduous forests surrounding the Cuyahoga River, with trails, bike paths, and wonderful exhibits showcasing the river's historic commercial transportation modes. Currently? All of the above plus a hodgepodge of interstates, commercial and residential buildings, and limited-view driving.
60	Kobuk Valley (Alaska)	Above the Arctic Circle, this park features sand dunes, mountains, splendid tundra, and one of the largest river-crossing caribou migrations in the world. Visitors can arrange a guided outboard motor boat trip and trail-free hike from the difficult to access native village of Ambler.
61	Gateway Arch (Missouri)	For national park purists, it's hard to accept a national monument and tourist attraction as a national park. The wonderful Saint Louis Arch and the nearby historic courthouse deserve a visit, but for appreciation of history, not nature.
62	Indiana Dunes (Indiana)	Enjoy one of the most spectacular urban Great Lakes shorelines and unique hiking in the magical space between Lake Michigan and the inland forests. A park separated by the Port of Indiana on the west, three subdivisions of beach homes in the middle, and a train running through the entirety is not necessarily a recipe for respite.
63	White Sands (New Mexico)	Half of New Mexico's White Sands National Park is off limits and used for missile testing. It's tough to relax in this small park near some of the United States' most active defense research and testing facilities. Still, hiking hard gypsum sand dunes in the shadow of the San Andreas Mountains makes for a beautiful day.

THE PARKS

WASHINGTON

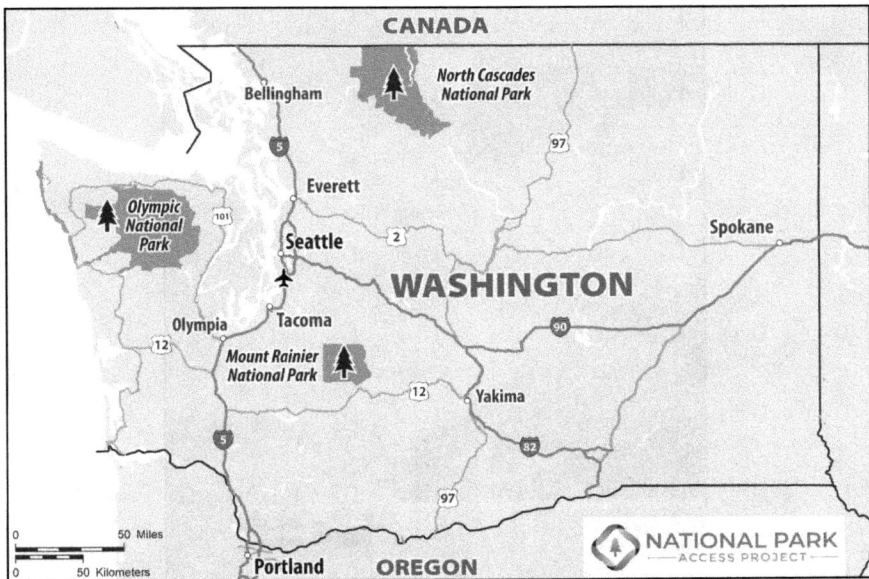

OLYMPIC NATIONAL PARK

You can count on my help in getting that national park, not only because we need it . . . but for a whole lot of young people who are going to come along in the next hundred years of America.

—President Franklin Delano Roosevelt on a 1937 visit to Port Angeles on the Olympic Peninsula near what is now Olympic National Park

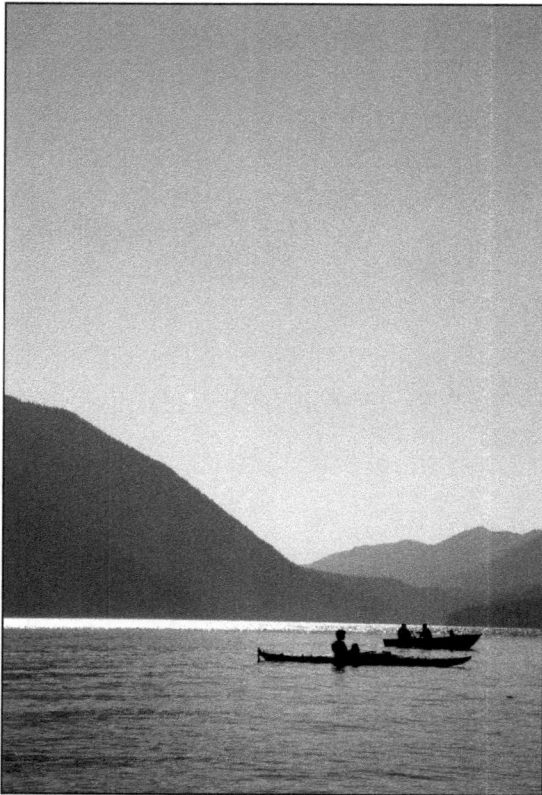

KAYAKING ON CRESCENT LAKE, OLYMPIC NATIONAL PARK
TRAVIS MANLEY/SHUTTERSTOCK

Washington State is home to two mountain ranges. The volcanic Cascade Range separates populous western Washington from its eastern agricultural region, while the smaller Olympic Range lies in the center of the Olympic Peninsula at the western edge of the state. Olympic National Park is centered on the Olympic Range but also includes a substantial portion of the coastline. The peninsula has a lot to offer—world-class peaks, low-elevation glaciers, spectacular rain forests, small villages, and pristine beaches on the its 73-mile west coast.

The illusive focal point of the nearly one-million-acre Olympic National Park is Mount Olympus at 7,979 feet. Home to the 2.6-mile-long Blue Glacier, and others like it, this is one of the most glaciated areas in the Lower 48. Mount Olympus is the center of the park, but surrounding mountains block visibility from Seattle, Tacoma, and even nearby Port Angeles. Instead, visit the park's Hurricane Ridge area for views of Mount Olympus and much of the range. Named a national monument in 1909, President Franklin Roosevelt established the area as a national park in 1938. Today most of the park (95 percent) is wilderness area, including its major peaks and most of the coastline.

In the mid-1980s, the spotted owl was used as a catalyst for preserving old-growth rain forests. Ground zero for the preservation effort was the Olympic Peninsula, where clear cutting had decimated the old trees. Today about 3 percent of the original rain forest remains. Satellite images from 1984 to 2016 show substantial regrowth due to natural regeneration and intentional planting. Areas of the national park have hiking trails through some of the original rain forest, making this park special indeed.

SCHEDULING AND LODGING

Olympic National Park is about a two-and-a-half-hour drive from Seattle-Tacoma International Airport. Western Washington, which often remains cold and rainy through June, offers the perfect climate for the park's four lush rain forests—Hoh, Quinault, Queets, and Bogachiel—as well as the many smaller rain forest areas in the park like those found in Sol Duc and Marymere Falls. Save yourself a muddy, cloudy vacation by waiting until July, August, or September to go to Olympic National Park.

Olympic National Park has five lodges and 14 campgrounds. In addition, the park offers extensive backcountry and beach camping via permit. The lodges include the **Log Cabin Resort** and **Lake Crescent Lodge**, **Sol Duc Hot Springs Lodge**, the **Kalaloch Lodge** on the Pacific Ocean, and the historic **Lake Quinault Lodge**. Associated campgrounds include **Fairholme** on Lake Crescent, **Sol Duc**, **Kalaloch**, and **South Beach** (in Kalaloch) and the **Willaby**, **Falls Creek**, and **Gatton Creek Campgrounds** on Lake Quinault. There are 10 additional campgrounds interspersed throughout the park that provide more private settings. All lodges have restaurants serving breakfast and dinner to guests and the general public. There are also markets at Lake Crescent, Kalaloch, and Quinault and grocery stores in Port Angeles and Forks.

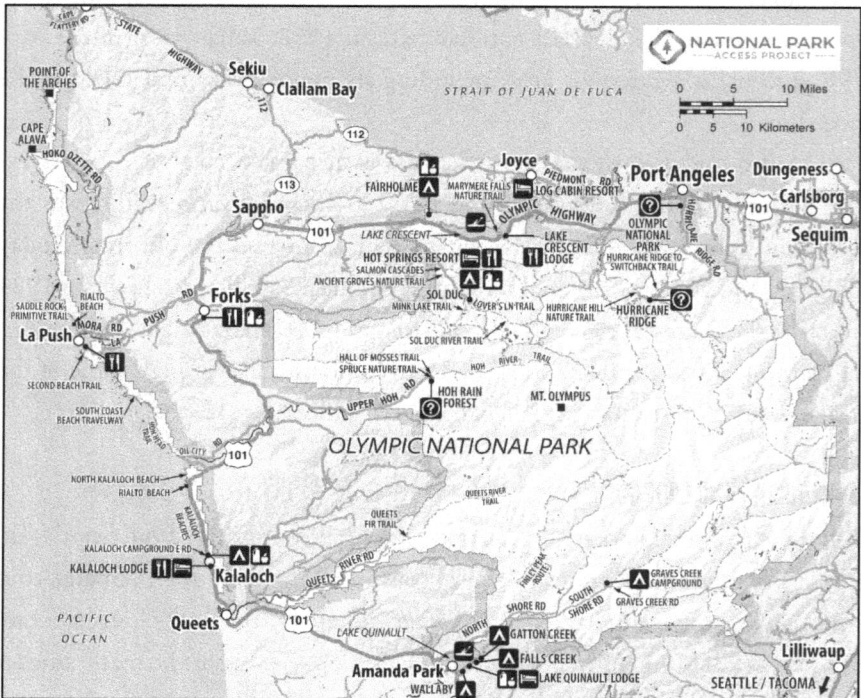

A NOTE ABOUT BEACH CAMPING

The easiest beachfront lodging/camping is in Kalaloch, with a ranger station, market, restaurant, lodge, and two campgrounds. Unfortunately, Highway 101 runs along Kalaloch Beach, making it less peaceful than it would otherwise be. The gold coast of the Olympic Peninsula is quite a bit farther north, in the car-free Olympic National Wilderness area. If time permits, divert into the backcountry and hike the Shi Shi Beach Trail to Point of the Arches or the Lake Ozette Trail to Sand Point and Cape Alava. Though Olympic National Park is open year-round, all lodges are seasonal except Quinault Lodge (open year-round) and cabins at Lake Crescent Lodge, which are open during winter weekends. Serviced campgrounds are seasonal.

THE TRIP

Day 1: Start your visit in Port Angeles at the **Olympic National Park Visitor Center**. After getting oriented, buy lunch at a nearby grocery and head to one of the hearts of the park—**Hurricane Ridge**. The stunning Hurricane Ridge can be viewed from the **Hurricane Ridge Visitor Center** viewing deck or from three trails uphill from the visitor center. The first of these is the paved **Hurricane Ridge Nature Trail** with both flat and steep sections that can be hiked together or in part. A short offshoot of this system is the **High Ridge Trail** providing sweeping almost 360-degree views at its peak. **Hurricane Hill** is the classic hike in this area, at 3 miles round trip with 800 feet of elevation gain. On a clear day the summit delivers views of the Olympic Range, Port Angeles, the Strait of Juan de Fuca, the San Juan Islands, and even Canada.

After your hike, drive an hour to **Lake Crescent**. From Lake Crescent Lodge enjoy the spectacular 1.7-mile round-trip level hike through a lush rain forest to **Marymere Falls**. Another wonderful way to explore the lake is to rent a canoe or kayak—available from both Lake Crescent Lodge and the Log Cabin Resort.

Day 2: Enjoy any remaining Lake Crescent activities before the 45-minute drive into the **Sol Duc Rain Forest** to the Sol Duc Hot Springs Resort.

Make two stops along the way—the **Salmon Cascades**, where salmon may be seen migrating up the Sol Duc River, and the half-mile **Ancient Groves Nature Trail**, where some of the most spectacular rain forest trees are found. Once at Sol Duc Hot Springs Resort, hike one of the spectacular rain forest treks in the park—**Lover's Lane Loop**. This 6-mile round trip hike with 600 feet of elevation gain leaves from the Sol Duc Resort via the **Mink Lake Trail** before it quickly cuts left to follow the Sol Duc River. Pass through old-growth hemlock, Douglas fir, and waterfalls at Canyon Creek to the apex of the loop—the beautiful Sol Duc Falls. After this relatively easy hike, veer onto the **Mink Lake Trail** for a 5-mile round-trip hike to the high mountain Mink Lake. End the day enjoying the hot-spring-fed and freshwater pools at the resort. The pools are open to the general public for a fee.

Day 3: After breakfast, pack your water shoes and drive about an hour and 15 minutes to **Rialto Beach**. Almost the entire west coastline of the Olympic Peninsula has been preserved as national park or wilderness area. Because much of the coastline is wilderness (no cars allowed), the Rialto section is somewhat unique in that it is both accessible by car and a good representation of the pristine Pacific Northwest coast. Endless sea creatures fill tidepools at low tide, and when the tide is in, visitors may glimpse sea lions, seals, and sea otters. Some beach enthusiasts prefer to veer south at the intersection with Mora Road and instead continue to **La Push** and **Second Beach**. This is a less family-friendly area, harder to reach, with rougher surf. But some consider it even more spectacular.

After a beach walk, head back to Forks and pick up lunch before traveling about an hour to the **Hoh Rain Forest Visitor Center**. From the visitor center, hike two short but lovely nature trails—**Hall of Mosses** at 1.1 miles and **Spruce Bottom** at 1.4 miles. Both are flat loops. The main hike in this area is the **Hoh River Trail** along the Hoh River and traveling to the **Blue Glacier** and **Mount Olympus** through the Hoh Rain Forest. This trek is 33 miles round trip and requires backcountry overnight permits. Hikers on the full 33-mile trek typically plan four nights in the backcountry. The start of this trail is spectacular, through the lush, dense Hoh Rain Forest and along the Hoh River. A half-day hike of three hours is enough to get a good feel of the splendor of this section of the park. When finished, drive an hour to Kalaloch Lodge or campgrounds for the evening.

Day 4: About a 10-minute drive north of Kalaloch is **Ruby Beach**. For more time on the Pacific Northwest coast, take a short detour to this pristine beach. Ruby Beach is a long, wide, fine-sand beach with a warm saltwater inlet perfect for peaceful swimming and wading. After the beach, drive about an hour southeast to the Lake Quinault area for a 5-mile hike through the **Quinault Rain Forest**. Before the hike, the Northshore Grocery in Quinault offers lunch and snacks.

Known as the Valley of the Rain Forest Giants, the **Quinault Valley** is home to some of the largest trees in the world. These include giant Sitka spruce and western red cedar as well as Douglas fir, Alaska yellow cedar, western hemlock, and mountain hemlock. The signature hike in the Quinault Rain Forest section of the Olympic National Park is the 26-mile round-trip **Enchanted Valley** hike. The hike's first section, the **Quinault River Pony Bridge Trail**, is a wonderful way to be introduced to this special area. Take the South Shore Road to the Graves Creek Campground. Not far beyond is the East Fork Quinault River Trail to Pony Bridge. At 2.7 miles each way and with about 1,000 feet of elevation gain, this rewarding trail terminates just past the bridge at a backcountry campsite on the river—a perfect place for lunch. Head back and make your way to Lake Quinault Lodge or campgrounds. Spend the rest of the day relaxing on the lake. Kayaks and canoes are available for rent from the lodge.

See the appendix for useful lodging, camping, and activity contact information.

MOUNT RAINIER NATIONAL PARK

The mountain receives our expressions and becomes part of us; we imprint our memories upon it . . . Mt. Rainier does not exist under our feet. Mt. Rainier lives in our minds."

—Bruce Barcott, *The Measure of a Mountain: Beauty and Terror on Mount Rainier*

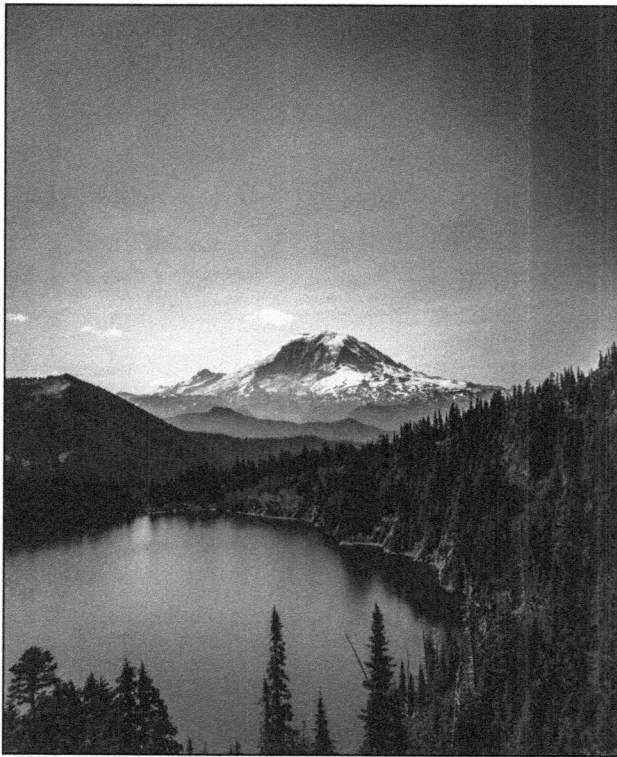

MOUNT RAINIER NATIONAL PARK
JOSHUA DRUDING/SHUTTERSTOCK

Established in 1899, Mount Rainier National Park is the fourth oldest national park, after Yellowstone, Sequoia, and Yosemite. Centered around the 14,410-foot stratovolcano Mount Rainier, with 25 named glaciers, the park is visually stunning. Though technically active, Mount Rainier has not erupted since the late 1800s. Spring runoff from abundant winter snows yields carpets of wildflowers by late June. Measuring 236,000 acres, 97 percent of the park is wilderness area.

Home to six native tribes, including the Nisqually, Puyallup, Squaxin Island, Muckleshoot, Yakama, and Cowlitz, the Mount Rainier area has a rich native history. The first non-native climber to summit Rainier was Philemon B. Van Trump in 1894. Along with John Muir and others, Van Trump promoted the area for conservation and was instrumental in Mount Rainier becoming a national park. At the same time, James Longmire was focused on recreation, promoting travel to his hot springs in what is now the Longmire historic area in the park's southeast section. Even 120 years ago, there was tension between conservation and recreation.

This beautiful park is home to abundant wildlife, including rodents like marmots, ground squirrels, and pika, as well as elk, deer, and mountain goats. The famous 93-mile Wonderland Trail runs in a circle through the park, and the Pacific Crest Trail runs along its eastern border.

SCHEDULING AND LODGING

Though Rainier National Park is open year-round, the road to the main village of Paradise is only plowed on the weekends in the winter and the road to the smaller Sunrise is only open from July through early October. For residents of the Pacific Northwest, there are plenty of ways to enjoy the park in the winter. For those traveling, come in the summer or early fall. As to spring visits, be careful. Rainier has some of the highest snowfall in the Lower 48, at an average of 640 inches annually. Spring can deliver torrential runoffs, mud, and of course the classic Pacific Northwest sunless spring weather. Seattle-Tacoma International Airport is two hours west of the park.

Rainier is home to the seasonal **Paradise Inn** (one of the original National Park Grand Lodges) and the newer **National Park Inn** as well as three serviced campgrounds—**Cougar Rock** (173 sites near the Nisqually entrance), **Ohanapecosh** (188 sites near the Stevens Canyon entrance), and **White River** (112 sites near the White River entrance). Camping reservations for the first two campgrounds can be made at Recreation.gov. All campgrounds allow walk-in campers. Groceries are available in the small town of Ashland right before the Nisqually entrance and also at Longmire, located between the two lodges. Both the National Park Inn and Paradise Inn have restaurants and small camper stores for necessities, and Paradise Inn has a casual deli for lunches.

The difference at Rainier between staying inside and outside the park is substantial. The narrow, winding park roads can become jammed with traffic in the summer. Plan your route and sleep in the park if possible, saving valuable time for park enjoyment.

BACKCOUNTRY TRAVEL AND CAMPING

Rainier National Park has five entrances. The three main entrances—Nisqually, Stevens Canyon, and White River—are how most travelers access the park. Two of the entrances, Mowich Lake and Carbon River, are in the remote northwest section of the park. These entrances are jumping-off points to access the vast Rainier National Park Wilderness, including some of the nicest sections of the Wonderland Trail and Mowich Lake, the largest in the park. Also here is the inland temperate rain forest in the Carbon River area as well the Carbon Glacier, the lowest-elevation glacier in the Lower 48. There is one campground in this section—**Mowich Lake**, with 13 sites—but most camping in this area is at one of the park's many backcountry campsites, available via permit.

CLIMBING MOUNT RAINIER

Three guide services take climbers up Mount Rainier—Alpine Ascents, International Mountain Guides, and Rainier Mountaineering. Summiting Mount Rainier is very special in that it is a technical climb that is still possible for many people. Proficient glacier climbers may obtain their own solo permit, granted after application to the park superintendent to those with an appropriate climbing résumé. Guided climbs take about four days, including training and summiting; have preset schedules; and cost thousands of dollars per climbing slot. Flying in for the summit attempt? Guide services reserve the right to cancel the climb due to poor weather and often give climbers the opportunity to come again the next year for a second attempt.

THE TRIP

Day 1: Start at the Nisqually entrance and go directly to Paradise, about 18 miles into the park. Paradise has a small parking lot that fills almost instantly, and there are not good alternatives (like parking on the side of the road). At Paradise is the **Henry M. Jackson Visitor Center**, Paradise Lodge, the **Skyline Trail**, and the shorter **Nisqually Glacier Trail**. For those not summiting Mount Rainier, the Skyline Trail is a way to get well onto the mountain face, walk on snow, and experience at least part of the thrill of the mountain. The Skyline Trail is a 5.9-mile loop, with 1,800 feet of elevation change. The hike begins through fields of wildflowers and past **Myrtle Falls**. Near the summit of the loop is **Panorama Point** with views of the small Tatoosh Range and volcanic Mount Adams as well as Oregon's Mount Saint Helens and Mount Hood. A shorter but still beautiful hike is the **Nisqually Vista Trail**, also leaving from Paradise. This 0.9-mile loop trail with 165 feet of elevation change brings you to an overlook of the Nisqually Glacier. After the hike, enjoy lunch at the Paradise Deli in the visitor center.

Head back toward the Nisqually entrance, stopping at the **Longmire Museum**, historic district, and market. From Longmire is another well-regarded hike in the park—**Rampart Ridge**. If energy remains, this 5.4-mile loop trail with 1,300 feet of elevation gain leads to Rampart Ridge and provides one of the closest and best views of the full Mount Rainier. An easier option without the view is the 1-mile **Trail of Shadows** level loop, which travels past the Longmire hot springs and by a replica of one of the park's earliest homesteads. Avoid driving on tight roads and stay the night in this section of the park.

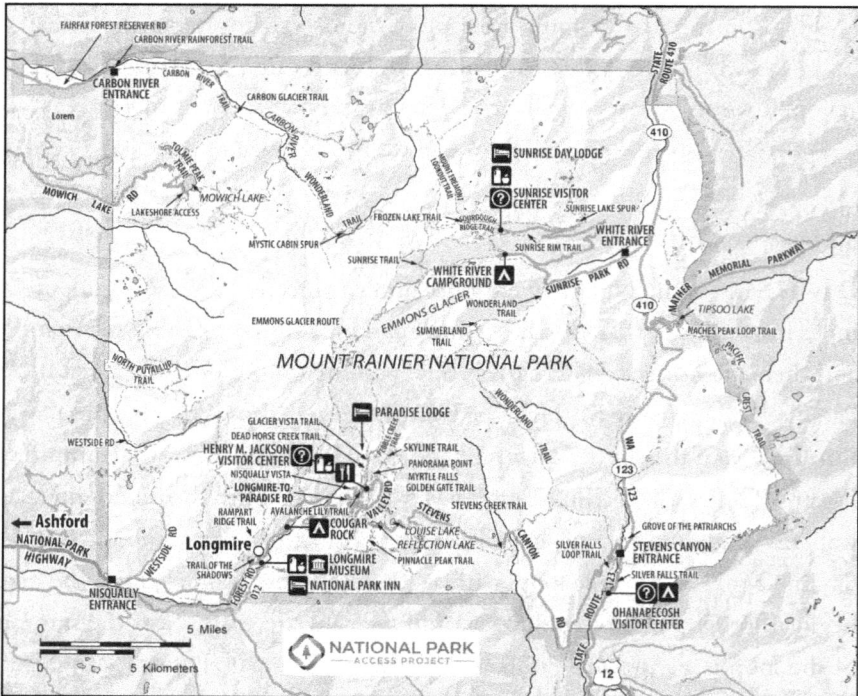

Day 2: The next area to visit extends east from Paradise to the **Ohanapecosh Visitor Center** along Stevens Canyon Road. Again, the early bird gets the worm in this park. Get up early, pack a lunch from the Longmire market,

and drive a few miles to **Reflection Lake**, where there are two small parking areas. Enjoy taking pictures of Rainier reflected in the lake, and hike on a flat section of the **Wonderland Trail** to nearby **Louise Lake**. Continue driving on Stevens Canyon Road to the **Grove of the Patriarchs** nature trail (with a tiny parking lot). This 1.3-mile level loop leads through a grove of old-growth cedars that are believed to be over 1,000 years old. From here it's a short drive to the Ohanapecosh Visitor Center and the **Silver Falls** trailhead. This trail is considered by some to be the most beautiful falls hike in the park. The Silver Falls 2.7-mile loop trail travels along the Ohanapecosh River and past the hot springs, with the falls at the midpoint. If camping, stay in Ohanapecosh. Otherwise, head back 20 miles to Paradise or 40 miles to the National Park Inn.

Day 3: The last major front-country section of the park, Sunrise, deserves a lot of time. Unfortunately, if staying in a lodge instead of camping, this will be a marathon day of driving. If camping, the White River Campground is in this part of the park.

From Paradise, pack a lunch and drive about an hour and 45 minutes past the White River entrance to the **Sunrise Visitor Center** and its small parking lot. At 6,400 feet, this is the highest point in the park reachable by car. Extending from the visitor center is some of the most pristine hiking in the national park system as well as near-direct access to a few of the park's named glaciers.

Many consider the top trail in the park to be the section of the Wonderland Trail that leads from Sunrise to the **Summerland Alpine Meadow**. This 10.5-mile round-trip hike has about 2,600 feet of elevation gain—a full day hike for most. The famous **Emmons Glacier** is on the right, where climbers may be attempting one of the classic routes up Mount Rainier. From the visitor center are somewhat easier but still stunning hikes, including **Mount Fremont Lookout** at 5.6 miles round trip with 1,200 feet of elevation gain (includes Frozen Lake), the **Sourdough Ridge Trail** to **Frozen Lake** at 2.9 miles with 600 feet of elevation gain, the **Sunrise Rim Loop Hike** at 5.5

miles with about 1,100 feet of elevation change, and the short **Sunrise Nature Trail** at 1.5 miles with 350 feet of elevation change. When finished hiking, grab a treat at the **Sunrise Day Lodge**.

Day 4: Spend the last day with a full-park view from **Naches Peak**. This loop trail on the eastern side of the park has two parking lots—one at **Tipsoo Lake** and the other at the **Pacific Crest Trail** overpass at **Chinook Pass**. The 6-mile loop hike with 1,200 feet elevation gain leads through pristine wildflower meadows to the summit of Naches Peak overlooking the east side of the park, Mount Rainier, and the alpine Dewey Lake. A portion of this hike follows the Pacific Crest Trail.

See the appendix for useful lodging, camping, and activity contact information.

NORTH CASCADES NATIONAL PARK

So shut up, live, travel, adventure, bless and don't be sorry.

—Jack Kerouac, *Desolation Angels*, inspired by his stay at the tower on Desolation Peak

DIABLO LAKE IN NORTH CASCADES NATIONAL PARK
T. SHOFIELD/SHUTTERSTOCK

Encompassing 684,000 acres of pristine, jagged, and glaciated alpine mountains, along with some of the deepest lakes in the world, North Cascades National Park is visually spectacular. The park is located in northern Washington in a nonvolcanic section of the Cascade Range and is known by some as "the American Alps." The two world-class lakes in the area are Lake Chelan and Ross Lake; both are big, glacier-carved, and very deep, with protected, almost undeveloped shoreline. Lake Chelan, at around 1,500 feet deep, is one of the deepest in the United States. Surrounding these two lakes are jagged mountain peaks, including Goode Mountain at 9,220 feet and Eldorado Peak at 8,868 feet. There is plenty of wildlife in the park, including mule and black-tailed deer, marmots, black bears, and mountain goats as well as rarely seen mountain lions and bobcats.

North Cascades National Park is split into two sections. The northern section abuts the Canadian border and is bounded on the east and south by the Ross Lake National Recreation Area. The southern section is bordered by the Lake Chelan National Recreation Area. These sections operate like a single protected area and together are considered, for travel purposes, North Cascades National Park.

Harsh winters prohibited year-round habitation by native tribes, but the Skagit peoples called the general area home and spent time here in warmer months. Explored by European trappers from the early 1800s, the North Cascades region was on the radar of environmentalists for protection as early as the naming of the first national parks. Designated a forest reserve in 1897, the area was managed by the Forest Service until those favoring greater land-use restrictions prevailed. In 1968, North Cascades became a combination of national park, wilderness area, and recreation area. President John F. Kennedy was instrumental in this effort, though President Lyndon B. Johnson signed the final authorization.

SCHEDULING AND LODGING

Intense weather on the Canadian border closes the North Cascades Highway/ State Route 20 from December through April during most years, with the shoulder months of November and May still quite cold at upper elevations. Most people visit this far-north park in the summer when Washington State has long days and spectacular wildflowers.

The two jumping-off points are distinct—the village of Chelan at the southern tip of Lake Chelan and the village of Diablo in the Ross Lake National Recreation Area. While it's possible to hike between the two areas, this is a multiday trip requiring backcountry camping. Most visitors see the north and south sections separately. This book starts with the more physically challenging north section and ends in the charming village of Stehekin on Lake Chelan.

Head toward Diablo and Ross Lake on the North Cascades Highway, passing the town of Marblemount and then Newhalem. This is the last option for motel-style lodging. Try the **Totem Trail Motel** or the **Buffalo Run Inn** (with restaurant). Lunch items or food for camping can be purchased here. Campers have a lot of options, but the three most popular front-country campgrounds are **Newhalem Creek** and, in Diablo, **Colonial Creek** and **Gorge Lake**. Reservations are available through Recreation.gov. A hybrid lodging option is the **Ross Lake Resort**, just east of Diablo. This is a collection of cabins accessible via hike-in or water taxi. Ross Lake Resort is open mid-June through mid-October, with reservations taken via a waitlist system that opens in February of the year of the trip. Plan on spending at least two nights in this section of the park. If hiking Desolation Peak is on your list, the Ross Lake Resort water taxi provides front door service to the trailhead.

To visit the southern section of the park, drive east on the North Cascades Highway and through the spectacular Methow Valley. Known for world-class backcountry skiing, wineries, and endless orchards, it's worth a side visit to any or all of the villages of Mazama, Winthrop, and Twisp. Driving straight through from Ross Lake to the village of Chelan takes about two and a half hours. The special remote village of Stehekin is not accessible by road. From Chelan, take the ferry Lady of the Lake or Lady Express, which provide year-round access to Stehekin. Note that the ferry leaves once per day at 8:30 a.m. Private floatplanes for hire are also available.

Stehekin offers lodging, boating, fishing, horseback riding, biking, extensive hiking, and winter activities, including snowshoeing and cross-country skiing. **North Cascades Lodge at Stehekin** is the primary lodging option, with standard lodge rooms and meal service (the restaurant is also open to the public). A 30-minute walk or 5-minute shuttle bus from the ferry dock brings travelers to **Silver Bay Inn** at the head of Lake Chelan. Silver Bay offers cabins and cottages with kitchens. The **Stehekin Pastry Company** restaurant near Silver Springs Inn is open during the daytime on select days and also has two cabins for rent. Finally, the **Stehekin Valley Ranch** offers six cabins, meal service, horseback riding, and kayaking tours (open to guests and the public). Near the ferry are two campgrounds—**Purple Point** and **Stehekin**. The North Cascade Lodge General Store is a good place to buy food for lunch or overnight camping.

THE TRIP

Day 1: Enter the park from the west on the North Cascades Highway, stop at the **North Cascades Visitor Center** in Newhalem, and enjoy the **Trail of Cedars Nature Walk**. This level 1.9-mile trail through old-growth cedars and Douglas firs introduces you to the Skagit River Valley and the immense hydropower this area generates. From here, spend the rest of the day orienting yourself to the area. Start with the **Diablo Lake Overlook**, which provides the best view of the small Diablo Lake just south of Ross Lake. A bit farther east is the **Ross Dam** trailhead, which leads a half mile down to Ross Dam and then joins the **Pacific Crest Trail** along **Ross Lake**. This trail extends about 12 miles along the western lakeshore and can be enjoyed in any amount. When finished, drive a bit farther east to the **Ross Lake Overlook**, which provides the iconic view of this spectacular glacier-carved area.

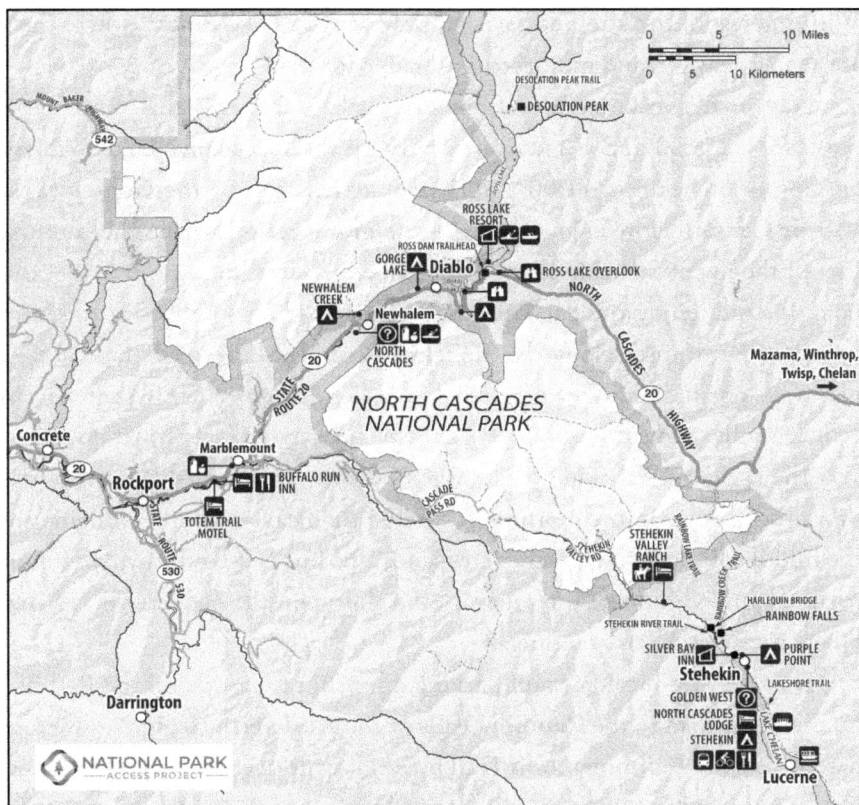

Day 2: The seminal trail in the park leads from the eastern shore of Ross Lake up to the summit of **Desolation Peak**. Getting there is half the fun, with the trailhead most easily accessed via chartered boat from the Ross Lake Resort. At about 8 miles round trip but about 4,500 feet of elevation gain, this hike is a steep grind. The first approximately 2,000 feet make the elevation less impactful by delivering near continuous views of Ross Lake.

Hikers are rewarded with panoramic views of the North Cascade Range (Skagit Peak, Hozomeen Mountain, and Jack Mountain to name a few) and will be able to see well into Canada. Because much of this trail has incredible views, it's not necessary to summit to understand the majesty of this park.

With the rest of the afternoon, spend time at Ross Lake Resort, where there are canoes, kayaks, and motorboats available for rent.

Day 3: A two-hour drive from Ross Lake, Chelan is the jumping-off point for the 8:30 a.m. *Lady Express* ferry up the spectacular **Lake Chelan**, arriving in Stehekin at 11:00 a.m. Upon arrival, stop by the **Golden West Visitor Center** before enjoying one of the most special areas in the country. Part of the joy of Stehekin is its relaxed vibe. No need to summit a big peak here. Instead, enjoy the flat **Lakeshore Trail** heading south from the ferry dock. Or head north along the **Stehekin River Trail**. To really take it easy, just walk north along the dirt Stehekin Valley Road, which has almost no vehicle traffic, and stop for a pastry at Stehekin Pastry Company if open.

The Lodge at Stehekin operates the **Red Bus**, which provides transportation up the valley in the morning, accessing trailheads and other lodging. In the middle of the day when the ferry lands, the bus is used for two one-hour narrated guided tours of the valley. In the afternoon the bus returns to bring hikers back to the ferry landing.

Day 4: After breakfast and packing a lunch, take a ride on the Red Bus up the valley road to the **Rainbow Falls** or the **Harlequin Bridge** stop. From here, access the **Rainbow Loop Trail** by heading up the road to the trailhead. This 5-mile trail is not in fact a loop. It climbs about 1,200 feet up from the road, where it meets the **Rainbow Creek Trail.** For an extra 2 miles of hiking, take this trail to a bluff with 180-degree views of the lake and surrounding mountains. Continue on the Rainbow Loop Trail to the **Rainbow Bridge** backcountry campground. From the bridge the trail opens up with views of Lake Chelan and surrounding mountains, gradually descending back to the road, but now only an easy flat 1-mile walk to the village.

Day 5: There are two ferries back to Chelan—at noon (arriving at 2:45 p.m.) and at 2:00 p.m. (arriving at 6:00 p.m.). With the extra time, consider kayaking around the top of the lake and the mouth of the river or biking parts of the valley floor not yet visited. Guests of the Lodge at Stehekin may rent a kayak on an hourly basis, and the Stehekin Valley Ranch offers guided kayak tours. The lodge also rents bicycles. End the day enjoying a ferry ride down the spectacular Lake Chelan.

**See the appendix for useful lodging, camping,
and activity contact information.**

NORTHERN CALIFORNIA AND SOUTHERN OREGON

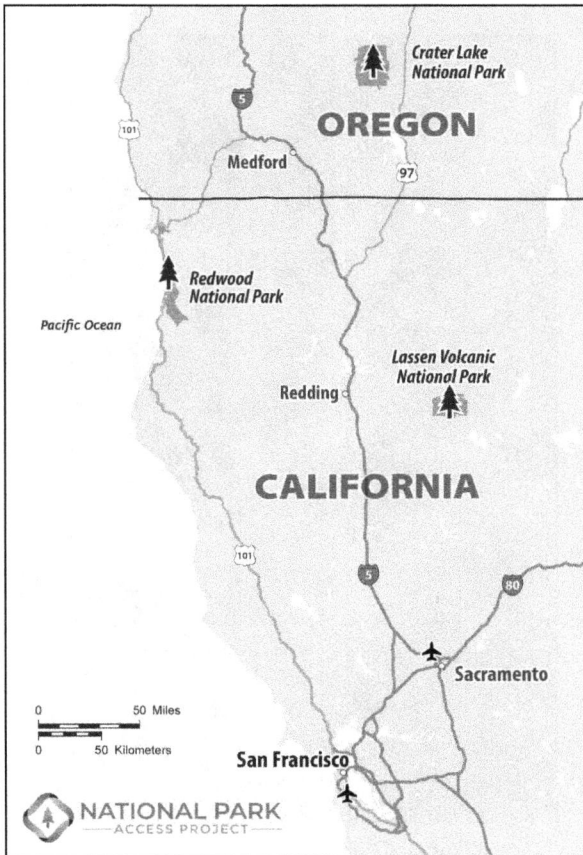

REDWOOD NATIONAL AND STATE PARKS

The redwood is the glory of the Coast Range. It extends along the western slope, in a nearly continuous belt about ten miles wide, from beyond the Oregon boundary to the south of Santa Cruz, a distance of nearly four hundred miles, and in massive, sustained grandeur and closeness of growth surpasses all the other timber woods of the world.

—John Muir, from his 1897 essay "The American Forests"

REDWOOD NATIONAL AND STATE PARKS
R. ALAN MEYER/SHUTTERSTOCK

The combined Redwood National and State Parks preserve much of the 37-mile northwest coastal region of California from just north of Eureka to the Crescent City area. The park is home to almost 40,000 acres of old-growth coast redwood forest and encompasses 139,000 total acres, of which about half is federal and half is state land. Coast redwood trees are close cousins to the giant sequoia trees found in Yosemite, Kings Canyon, and Sequoia National Parks. The area including Redwood National and State Parks is the far northern end of their range.

Redwood National and State Parks consists of four parks. Two of these, Redwood National Park and Prairie Creek Redwoods State Park, are on the south side of the Klamath River. The other two, Del Norte Coast Redwoods State Park and Jedediah Smith Redwoods State Park, are on the north side. The Klamath River and its extended shoreline is Yurok Tribe territory and marks the western edge of the Yurok Reservation. The Yurok is the largest tribe in California and hosts multiple businesses within its western boundary, including a casino, hotel, campgrounds, and restaurants.

Though native peoples have lived in the area for thousands of years, Western explorers first reached northern California and noted the "noblest tree," or coast redwood, in the late 1820s during a trapping trip led by Jedediah Smith. The trees were put on the proverbial map, and loggers followed. The area at one time had about two million acres of old-growth redwoods. By the early twentieth century there was little left, and preservation of the remainder began through creation of 26 small state parks. Three of those, named above, were encompassed by the creation of the national (and state) park in 1968 by President Lyndon B. Johnson. Restoration efforts since the late 1990s have mostly eliminated logging roads, and small redwood trees have been replanted. In about 250 years, these trees will be in their early majesty.

SCHEDULING AND LODGING

This temperate part of the country can be visited anytime. In December and January, highs are in the mid-fifties, while in July and August, highs are in the low eighties. If interested in staying dry, the park has two dry months, July and August, with June and September also offering mostly dry weather. In peak winter, Redwood National Park gets up to 16 inches of rain per month, with significant rain falling more than half the days.

Redwood National Park is about 5 hours and 45 minutes from Portland, San Francisco, and Sacramento. Lodging options outside the park are abundant, with the small towns of Eureka and Trinidad to the south and Crescent City to the north. There is no hard-walled lodging inside the park, though the privately owned **Elk Meadow Cabins** in Orick are nearly on the park boundary. The Yurok Reservation offers a **Holiday Inn Express** in Klamath, which is about the center of the combined national and state park, and the **Historic Requa Inn** is a boutique option (with dining), also in Klamath, but near the Klamath River edge. At the north end of the combined park, in the small village of Hiouchi, is the **Hiouchi Motel** abutting Jedidiah Smith State Park.

There is no front-country camping in the national park, though in the abutting state parks there are four campgrounds. These include **Jedidiah Smith**, **Elk Prairie**, and **Mill Creek**, with a combined 300-plus sites, RV capacity, and hot showers. Jedidiah Smith and Elk Prairie each have four camping cabins (no kitchens) that may be reserved up to six months in advance. **Gold Bluffs Beach** is a small campground near the ocean accessed by a long, winding dirt road.

Orick offers a small grocery store, while the Yurok Tribe property has a mini-mart and two restaurants (Country Club and Abalone Grill). Hiouchi offers the small Hiouchi Hamlet grocery store and the Hiouchi Café serving breakfast, lunch, and dinner.

TALL TREES GROVE TRAIL PERMIT

The national park section of the park has two signature trails—the short Lady Bird Johnson Grove and the longer Tall Trees Trail. This second trail descends through a redwood forest to Redwood Creek and a grove of what are believed to be the tallest coast redwoods. The road to the trailhead is blocked by a padlocked metal gate opened by a code. The park allows 25 groups to hike the trail each day, with email reservations possible seven days to 48 hours before the hike. The permit and gate code are then issued via return email. If the permits have not all been taken, extras may be available at the Kuchel Visitor Center. This hike is not to be missed.

BOATING ON THE KLAMATH

Though not part of national or state park property, outfitters in the Klamath area have access to the river for rafting, paddleboarding, and kayaking excursions. Rogue Outdoor Sports in Klamath provides single or double kayaks and life jackets and delivers patrons about 6 miles up the Klamath River for a several-hour paddle of this special area. Consider adding this additional half-day excursion.

THE TRIP

Day 1: Heading north on Highway 101, the **Kuchel Visitor Center** at the park's south entrance is the place to start. After getting oriented, pick up a picnic lunch at the Orick Market. Highway 101 leads from the visitor center, past the market, and to the entrance of Redwood National Park proper. Here the two marquee hikes, **Lady Bird Johnson Grove** and **Tall Trees Grove,** can be enjoyed in either order. The Lady Bird trail is a level 1.4 miles through giant redwoods. The Tall Trees Grove hike in contrast is 3.5 miles round trip with 750 feet of elevation gain. Far from cars and people, this trail is silent, leading down to Redwood Creek and a famous grove of old-growth redwoods including the **Libbey Tree**, at one time the world's tallest known living thing.

After these hikes, head up Highway 101. Very shortly there is a cutoff to the left onto Davison Road. Take this road, which becomes dirt and leads steeply down to the Pacific Coast and the Gold Bluffs Beach Campground. Just past the campground is the **Fern Canyon** trailhead. This 1.1-mile level

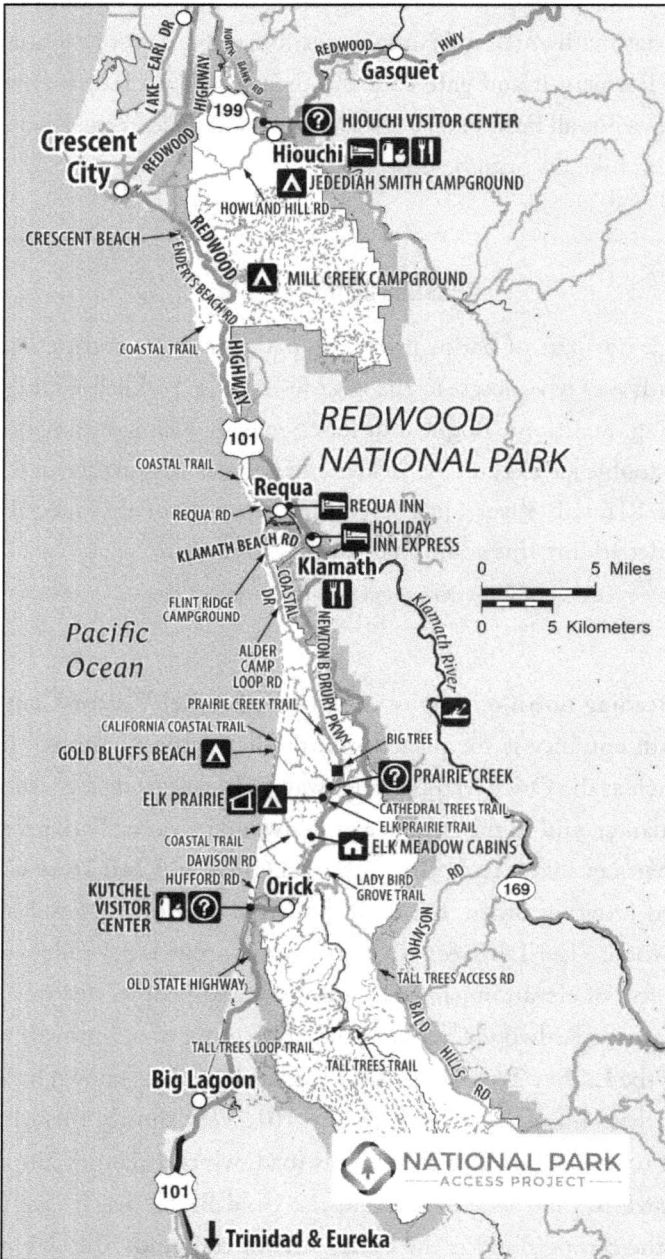

loop trail leads through Home Creek and its canyon walls filled with varied species of ferns. The loop includes a walk through the creek bed and then up the short canyon wall to return along the canyon rim. Fern Canyon is considered one of the top attractions in the park. Returning up the dirt road, the **Trillium Falls Trail** is on the right, before the highway. This beautiful trail has 18 groves of redwoods named for instrumental boosters of the park. In the spring, trillium flowers surround the small waterfall at the center of the hike.

Head left on Highway 101 to an almost immediate second left on the **Newton B. Drury Scenic Parkway**, which runs 10 miles through the center of Prairie Creek Redwoods State Park. Shortly after entering the parkway, stop at the **Prairie Creek Visitor Center**. If camping or staying at one of the four camper cabins, the Elk Prairie Campground is here. This is also where much of the park's level hiking is located. Three trails extend from the parking lot. The famous **Big Tree Loop Trail** at 3.2 miles includes the **Cathedral Tree Trail** and the **Prairie Creek Trail**. This is considered one of the best places in the world to see a large grove of coast redwoods. The **Elk Prairie Loop Trail** runs on either side of the Scenic Parkway and behind the campground. Here, at sunrise and sunset, the herd of elk that makes this area home comes out in force.

Day 2: After breakfast, spend some time at the mouth of the Klamath River, a signature feature of Redwood National Park. The famous **California Coastal Trail** runs the length of the park, with trail access points from both the north and south sides of the Klamath River. On the south side of the river is the short **Coastal Drive** and on the north side is the **Klamath River Overlook**, considered one of the best areas in California for late-fall shore-based whale sightings in California. After a shoreline visit, head up Highway 101. The Woodland Villa Market is a lunch option.

Travel north past Del Norte State Park. Del Norte is home to Mill Creek Campground and the difficult and long Mill Creek Horse Trail (over 10 miles). Instead of this trail, continue north toward Crescent City and the coastal section of Del Norte State Park. Near the southern boundary of Crescent City is **Crescent Beach**. The beach is accessed via **Enderts Beach Road**, which provides various pullouts and opportunities to walk along the beach, explore tide pools, and hike the Last Chance section of the **California Coastal Trail**. After a beach walk, visit the National Park Service **Crescent City Information Center** and the famous **Battery Point Lighthouse**.

Just east of Crescent City is Humboldt Road and the **Howland Hill Scenic Road**. This winding 10-mile dirt road through Jedidiah Smith State Park is considered to have some of the most spectacular examples of large old-growth redwoods. About halfway along the road is the well-marked **Boy Scout Tree Trail**, at 4.8 miles round trip with 875 feet of elevation gain. This is a signature hike in the park, showcasing one of the most pristine collections of old-growth redwoods in existence. Following the hike, continue along the Howland Hill Scenic Road. Near its end is **Stout Grove**, one of the park's most famous groves of redwoods. After viewing the grove, continue to Highway 199 and make a left to Jedidiah Smith Campground and the half-mile walk through the **Simpson-Reed Grove** of large redwoods. Here is the **Hiouchi Visitor Center** as well as the Hiouchi Motel, café, and market.

**See the appendix for useful lodging, camping,
and activity contact information.**

CRATER LAKE NATIONAL PARK

I thought I had gazed upon everything beautiful in nature as I have spent my years traveling thousands of miles to visit the beauty spots of the earth, but I have reached the climax. Never again can I gaze upon the beauty spots of the earth and enjoy them as being the finest thing I have ever seen. Crater Lake is above them all.

—author Jack London, 1911

PHANTOM SHIP AND CRATER LAKE AT CRATER LAKE NATIONAL PARK
NAGEL PHOTOGRAPHY/SHUTTERSTOCK

Located in southern Oregon, Crater Lake is the deepest lake in the United States at 1,943 feet and the seventh deepest lake in the world. Created 7,700 years ago by the eruption of Mount Mazama, Crater Lake was formed after the mountaintop collapsed and slowly filled with water. Crater Lake and Mount Mazama comprise part of the Cascade Range, which extends from northern California to southern British Columbia. The park was established in 1902, in part through the 17-year effort of journalist William Gladstone Steel. In addition to being instrumental in the park's designation, Steel constructed the historic Crater Lake Lodge in 1915. Renovated over the years, Crater Lake Lodge was rebuilt in 1995.

Other highlights in the park include Wizard Island (a cinder cone within the lake, 763 feet above the waterline), concentrations of volcanic vents accessed via hiking trails, and views of surrounding mountains like Mount Scott and Mount McLaughlin. This is a small park, measuring 183,000 acres, that packs a big visual punch.

SCHEDULING AND LODGING

Though the park is open year-round, like many national parks at higher elevations, the season of unimpeded access is short. The crater is circled by the 33-mile Rim Road, divided into the access road to Rim Village, the East Rim Drive, and the West Rim Drive. The access road to Rim Village is open year-round. West Rim Drive opens for the season between mid-May and mid-June, while the east section opens between mid-June and mid-July. The Rim Drive roads close for the year upon the first snow or November 1, whichever comes first, and the area gets an average of 44 feet of snow a year. The best time to visit is from mid-July through Labor Day, which is the short window when the boat to Wizard Island operates.

Crater Lake is remote, so it's worth staying either at the expensive **Crater Lake Lodge** in Rim Village with views of Crater Lake or in the village of Mazama 7 miles down the mountain from the rim. Mazama has **Mazama Village** with 40 cabins and **Mazama Campground** with 214 sites. Dining

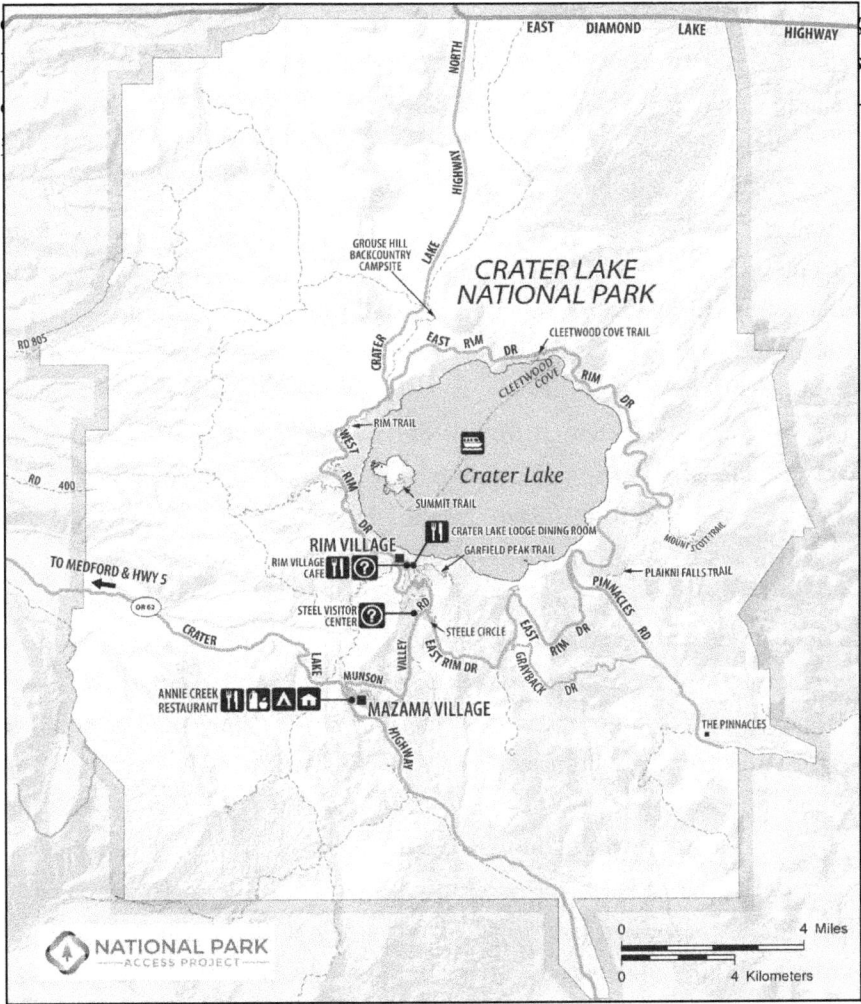

THE TRIP

Day 1: Get the lay of the land by stopping by the **Steel Visitor Center** just before **Rim Village**. After the visit, park in Rim Village and enjoy the **Rim Trail**. This hike leads left/west from the parking lot around a portion of the crater rim, up the small **Watchman Peak**, and ends at **Merriam Point**. To enjoy and understand Crater Lake, even hiking a small part of the 6-mile (each way) hike is sufficient. Though the perspective of the rim and surrounding mountains changes, the majesty of Crater Lake is visible from anywhere, including from Rim Village.

After exploring the rim, to the right/east of Rim Village is the **Garfield Peak** hike. This 3.4-mile round-trip hike with just over 1,000 feet of elevation gain delivers panoramic views of Rim Village, Crater Lake, Wizard Island, and the surrounding Cascade Range. A more distant perspective can be had from the **Mount Scott Trail** accessed from East Rim Road. This 4.2-mile round-trip hike has slightly more elevation gain but leads to the highest point in the park.

Day 2: If lucky enough to visit during the six-week boat tour season, make sure to enjoy a trip to **Wizard Island**. The dock is on the opposite side of Crater Lake from Rim Village. Take the East Rim Drive to the **Cleetwood Cove Trail**, a 1.1-mile hike down from the rim to Cleetwood Cove. From here, there are two morning departures and three return trips in the afternoon. The Wizard Island summit hike takes about 30 minutes and provides a different perspective of this beautiful place.

From the Wizard Island boat dock trailhead, double back on East Rim Drive and turn onto Pinnacles Road to the **Plaikni Falls** trailhead. This 2-mile round-trip level hike travels through old-growth fir and hemlock forests to a lush base of wildflowers around Plaikni Falls. When finished, continue on Pinnacles Road to its terminus where **The Pinnacles** are located. This 1-mile round-trip level hike extends along Wheeler Creek, which was submerged during the volcano eruption thousands of years ago. As the creek regained something like its old appearance, portions of the volcano vents did not erode. These unique geological features, known as pinnacles, define this area as both a mountainous wilderness and the site of a major volcanic eruption.

**See the appendix for useful lodging, camping,
and activity contact information.**

LASSEN VOLCANIC NATIONAL PARK

Many volcanic cones rise, sharp and steep, some with craters in their tops, into which we can see—circular hollows, like great nests of fabulous birds.

—William H. Brewer of the California Geological Survey, written while on the summit of Lassen Peak in 1863

HYDROTHERMAL VENT IN LASSEN VOLCANIC NATIONAL PARK
LINDSAY SNOW/SHUTTERSTOCK

Lassen Volcanic National Park is located at the southern end of the Cascade mountain range. Its subregion is known as the Shasta Cascade Range, in recognition of nearby 14,179-foot Mount Shasta. The park is one of the few areas in the world showcasing all four types of volcano. A park centerpiece, Lassen Peak at 10,463 feet, is the largest plug dome volcano in the world. Cinder Cone, in the park's remote northeast corner, is one of five cinder cone volcanoes in the park. Mount Harkness is one of the park's two shield volcanoes. And Brokeoff Mountain, also known as Mount Tehama, is a composite volcano or stratovolcano.

On May 22, 1915, Lassen Peak erupted, with ash extending as far as 200 miles to the east. This was the last major eruption in the volcanic Cascade Range until Mount Saint Helens erupted in 1980. The volcanic activity and increasing recognition of the unique geological nature of the area resulted in the designation of Lassen Volcanic National Park in 1916, making it the fifteenth United States national park. The park was in part a merger of two national monuments, Cinder Cone and Lassen Peak, both of which had been designated in 1907 by President Theodore Roosevelt.

SCHEDULING AND LODGING

Lassen Volcanic National Park is a three-hour drive north of Sacramento. This high-elevation park has a short season, from mid-June to early October. The park's main access road, Volcanic Legacy Scenic Byway, extends in a semicircle from the Kohm Ya-mah-nee Visitor Center at the park's southwest to Manzanita Lake at the park's northwest. There are eight campgrounds, seven of which allow reservations. Major campgrounds include **Southwest Campground** near the visitor center (walk-in), **Summit Lake (North and South)**, **Warner Valley**, and **Manzanita Lake**. Manzanita offers showers, a camp store, and 20 camping cabins. The cabins provide beds but not bedding.

The park has two main areas: the Volcanic Legacy Scenic Byway with associated attractions, and the more remote Warner Valley. Road access to the Warner Valley entails a several-hour drive, including exiting and reentering the park. Here are the **Warner Valley Campground** and the **Drakesbad Guest Ranch** with a two-night minimum stay required. If a stay at Drakesbad is not in the cards, the ranch allows visits for a meal, horseback ride, or guided hiking/fishing trip. Reservations for all activities and meals are required.

Outside the park to the south on Highway 36 between the Kohm Yamah-nee entrance and the Warner Valley entrance is the **Highlands Ranch Resort** (upscale) and co-owned **Village at Childs Meadow Motel** (modest) as well as RV and camping sites. To the north of the park near the town of Old Station is the **Hat Creek Resort and RV Park**.

REMOTE AREAS - JUNIPER LAKE AND CINDER CONE

With extra time, consider two other beautiful areas worth visiting. Juniper Lake is about an hour east of Warner Valley and is the largest lake in the park. There are no services here, though there is a campground, ranger station, and plenty of remote hiking. Two hours north of Juniper Lake and one hour east of Manzanita Lake is the Cinder Cone area. Here is the Cinder Cone Nature Trail, a 4-mile round-trip hike including climbing to the rim of Cinder Cone—not easy given the shifting soil but an opportunity to see very unique volcanic terrain. The complete hike takes about three hours.

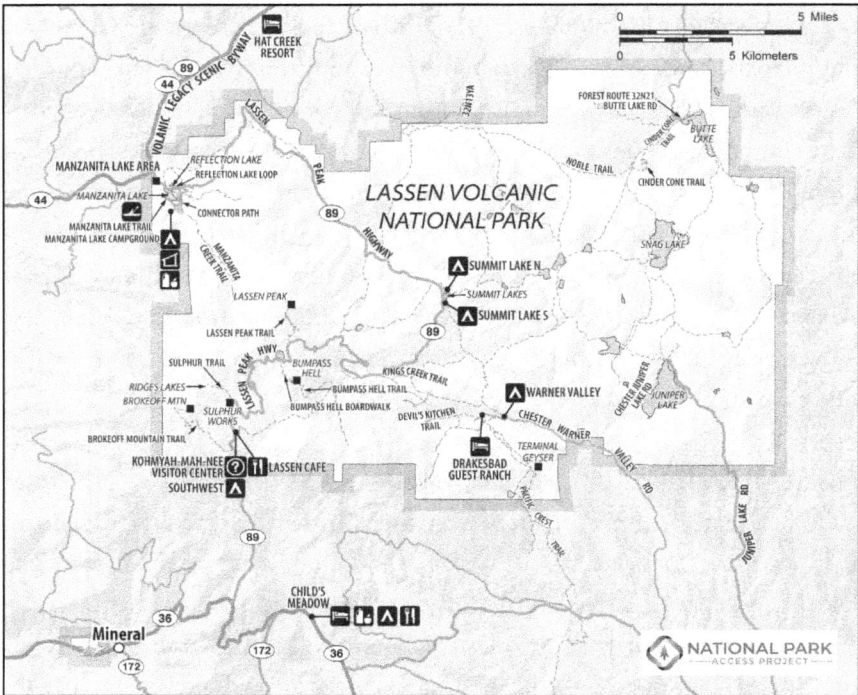

THE TRIP

Day 1: Begin the visit at either the **Kohm Ya-mah-nee Visitor Center** at the southwest entrance or at the **Manzanita Lake** entrance. Both options have areas to buy lunch, with Kohm Ya-mah-nee offering the **Lassen Café** and Manzanita a camper store. Along the 30-mile **Volcanic Legacy Scenic Byway**, stop at **Sulphur Works** with its hot pots and steam vents close to the road. There is a nice hike here (**Ridge Lake**) at 2.3 miles round trip that features hot pots.

Near here is the **Bumpass Hell Trail**, a signature hike in the park. This easy 2.7-mile round-trip stroll, largely on boardwalks, goes through the park's largest (16 acres) hydrothermal area. This is the main section of steam and discharge from the Lassen hydrothermal system, with **Big Boiler** one of the hottest fumaroles in the world at 322 degrees Fahrenheit.

Also off the byway is the gorgeous **Kings Creek Falls Trail**, a mostly flat 2.7-mile round-trip hike along Kings Creek. Make sure not to miss the Manzanita Lake and smaller **Reflection Lake** level loop hikes, with views of Mount Lassen from much of the shoreline. Kayaks and paddleboards are often for rent at the lake near the Manzanita campground.

Day 2: If interested in taking a day for a long, hard hike with incredible views, there are two choices. **Brokeoff Mountain** is at the southwest corner of the park. The 7.6-mile round trip hike climbs 2,582 feet to the 9,236-foot summit. Pass through varying terrain from lush meadows to the barren summit. Views are panoramic of Lassen Peak, surrounding mountains and alpine lakes, and the volcanic area of the national park. The other high-mountain choice is **Lassen Peak**, a 5.1-mile round trip hike with 2,000 feet of elevation gain, and a summit of around 10,500 feet. This is the signature high-peak hike in the park, with sweeping views of the volcanic park and Mount Shasta. These hikes can take at least five hours.

Day 3: Hit the road early and head west to **Warner Valley** and the historic Drakesbad Guest Ranch. If not staying here, consider calling ahead to reserve a spot for lunch, which is served at 12:30 p.m. Hiking in the Warner Valley is divided into two sections. The 3.6-mile **Devil's Kitchen** hike leads through beautiful meadows and forests, terminating at volcanic vents and **Hot Springs Creek**. After a picnic or lunch at the ranch, take the second main hike in the valley to **Terminal Geyser**. This 5-mile round-trip hike along the **Pacific Crest Trail** leads past a thermal pond to a small area of thermal vents.

See the appendix for useful lodging, camping, and activity contact information.

CENTRAL CALIFORNIA

PINNACLES NATIONAL PARK

The doorway to the Garden of the Gods, but on a grander scale. Here the cliffs of many-colored rock rise hundreds of feet in sharply defined terraces, or great domes or pinnacles. Beyond, and scattered over an area of some six square miles is a mass of conglomerate rocks wonderful in extent and in fantastic variety of form and coloring.

—Schuyler Hain, homesteader and advocate for the Pinnacles area

PINNACLES NATIONAL PARK
35KAIROS/SHUTTERSTOCK

The 26,000-acre Pinnacles National Park is located east of California's Salinas Valley and is named for the fascinating vertical protrusions or pinnacles remaining after erosion of an ancient volcano. Enjoy 360-degree views, gorgeous desert wildflowers, side trips into caves, and possibly a glimpse of one of the nearly 100 high-flying California condors that call the area home.

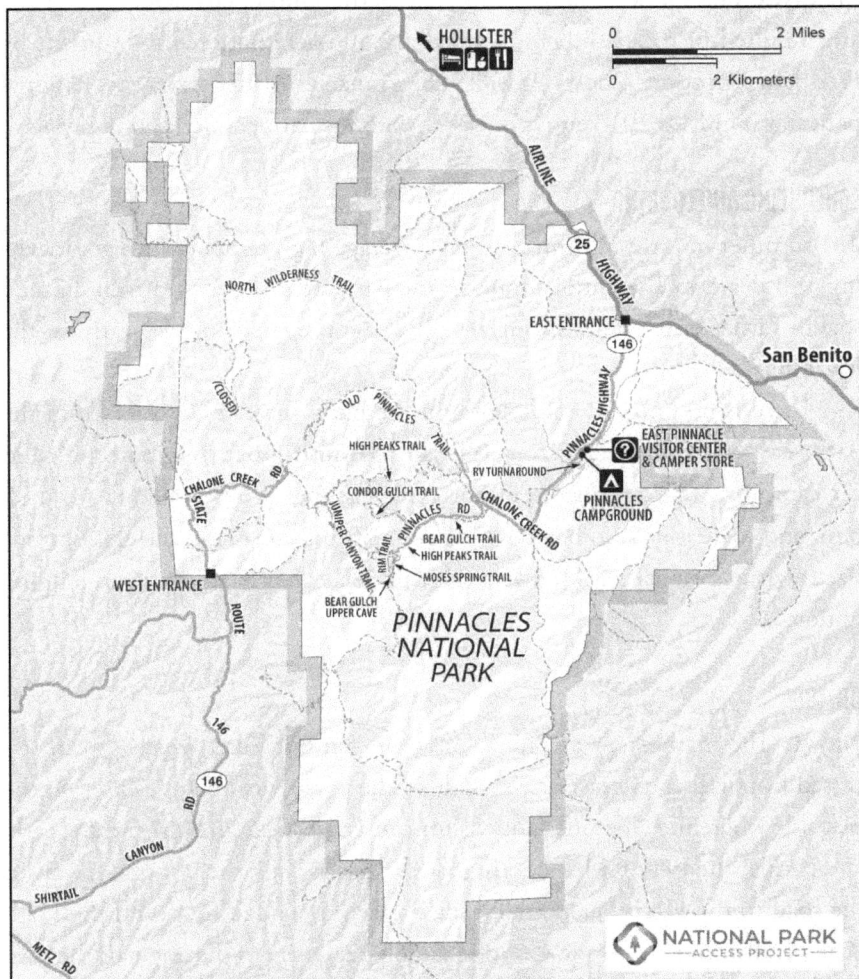

The park has a rich Native American history, with evidence that native peoples were in the area as long as 2,000 years ago. Early European settlers making their way to California's coast also visited Pinnacles, and it became a popular vacation spot beginning in the late 1800s. The greatest advocate for what would become the park was Schuyler Hain, a homesteader from Michigan who lived in the area and led tours through Bear Valley and into the caves. His speaking and writing about the unique characteristics of the area resulted in the park being named a 2,500-acre national monument by President Theodore Roosevelt in 1908. Pinnacles made its way to national park status only in 2013 and is one of the newest national parks in the system.

SCHEDULING AND LODGING

The summer months at Pinnacles have average high temperatures approaching 100 degrees. The famous trails in the park are exposed with very limited shade. Either visit in the spring or fall or be prepared to hike early in the morning in the summer.

There is no hotel/motel lodging in the park. Instead, accessed from the park's east entrance is the **Pinnacles Campground** supporting both RVs and car camping. The camp store/visitor center is open from 9:30 a.m. to 4:30 p.m. and there is an outdoor pool. About a 30-minute drive, the closest mid-size town to Pinnacles is Hollister, which offers extensive dining and lodging options.

THE TRIP

Day 1: The main event at Pinnacles is the summit hike, which can be accessed from either the east or west side of the park. Most people enter on the east side where the amenities and visitor center are located. Start the day early and park at the **Bear Gulch** parking lot trailhead. Walk the rest of the way up the road to the **High Peaks** trailhead. It's recommended to ascend the High Peaks Trail and descend the **Condor Gulch Trail** due to the angle of the sun. The hike is 5.5 miles round trip with about 1,500 feet of elevation gain. Add about a mile at the beginning by diverting to the **Moses Spring Trail**, the **Bear Gulch Cave Trail**, and the **Rim Trail**. This triangle offshoot connects with the High Peaks Trail and provides an opportunity to see one of the caves for which Pinnacles is so well known. The trickiest part of the full hike is the summit section, where hikers navigate a few ladders and steep stair-like sections. Other than this small area, the hike is gradual with panoramic views of the **Salinas Valley** to the west. At the summit the path connects with the **Juniper Canyon Trail**, which leads to the west parking lot. The full trail system at Pinnacles is concentrated in a relatively small area, and this national park is easily seen as a day trip.

See the appendix for useful lodging, camping, and activity contact information.

YOSEMITE NATIONAL PARK

[California] shall accept this grant upon the express conditions that the premises shall be held for public use, resort, and recreation; shall be inalienable for all time.

—from the *Yosemite Valley Grant Act* signed by
President Abraham Lincoln, June 30, 1864

YOSEMITE FALLS, YOSEMITE NATIONAL PARK
PAUL B. MOORE/SHUTTERSTOCK

Yosemite is one of the most spectacular and important parks in the national park system. The park offers lush valleys, alpine meadows, sharp peaks, slow climbs, torrential waterfalls, and many overlooks. It has arguably the nicest lodge in the national park system—the Ahwahnee Hotel—and the most extensive backcountry hut-to-hut trail system where breakfast and dinner are served and guests sleep in canvas-walled platform tents. With the Badger Pass ski area, abundant cross-country skiing and snowshoeing, and spectacular fall foliage, Yosemite is a must-visit jewel in the national park crown.

Though Yellowstone was the first national park, and Hot Springs National Park in Arkansas has a claim as the first preserved federal recreation land, the idea of the national park system as we know it today started in Yosemite. Early preservationists in the Sierra Nevada area were alarmed by extensive logging and convinced President Abraham Lincoln in 1864 to enact the Yosemite Valley Grant Act preserving Yosemite Valley and the Mariposa Grove of Giant Sequoias for the state of California. Enter John Muir, the outdoor enthusiast, writer, conservationist, and activist, who successfully advocated for the conversion of a large swath of the Sierra Nevada Range to national park status. In 1890, President Benjamin Harrison converted 1,500 square miles of land, including many known groves of giant sequoias, into the first national park. Only in 1906, though, did Yosemite Valley and the Mariposa Grove of Giant Sequoias transfer from state to federal ownership. The most recent addition to Yosemite was in 2016 when the 400-acre Ackerson Meadows was added on the park's west side, bringing the total size to around 750,000 acres.

The average visitor to this classic park spends between four and nine hours there, based upon a 2005 park visit study. The park warrants more time, offering unique ecosystems including the Mariposa Grove in the southern section of the park, Yosemite Valley with its famous waterfalls, and Tuolumne Meadows in the park's northeast section. Some of the park's great peaks loom over the valley floor, including El Capitan and Half Dome. Extensive lodging, camping, and High Sierra backcountry serviced platform tents make coming here and staying here a breeze.

SCHEDULING AND LODGING

Yosemite is about four hours from San Francisco, three hours from Sacramento, and two hours from Fresno, which has the Fresno Yosemite International Airport. While in the area, consider driving three hours south to Kings Canyon National Park and the abutting Sequoia National Park. These three parks showcase the majesty of giant sequoias in a very special way.

Yosemite is a year-round park, though most people visit in the summer months. Fall is stunning; spring can be a slow thaw. The road to Glacier Point, which provides a sweeping view of the park, is closed in the winter, typically from mid-November to mid-June. Tioga Road, the access point for higher-elevation hikes and Tuolumne Meadows, is also closed in the winter.

There are ample hard-walled lodges in the park, including, as mentioned above, the expensive and stunning **Ahwahnee Hotel** in Yosemite Valley. An alternative to staying here is having a beverage in the grass courtyard or dining in the historic dining room. A more modest option in Yosemite Valley is the **Yosemite Valley Lodge**, with the other two hotels in the park including the **Wawona Hotel** at the south entrance near Mariposa Grove and **White Wolf Lodge** off Tioga Road near the park's northwest entrance.

Yosemite offers "glamping" options in the form of platform tents with canvas sides and metal beds with mattresses. Bring your own sleeping bag and be prepared to share a bathroom. Two options are in Yosemite Valley—**Curry Village** and **Housekeeping Camp**—while another, **Tuolumne Meadows Lodge**, is near Tuolumne Meadows. The ultimate in glamping, though, is the **High Sierra Camps**—five backcountry locations that offer a platform tent, breakfast, dinner, and a packed lunch for the road. Hard to reserve? You bet. Reservations are by lottery, submitted the year before your trip.

If all this sounds expensive and difficult, try camping in one of the nearly 1,500 campsites located throughout the park. About half the campgrounds take reservations and half are first come, first served. Camping in Yosemite Valley at **Upper Pines**, **Lower Pines**, and **North Pines** can be loud and a bit raucous. Other campgrounds like **Wawona**, **Bridalveil Creek**, and

Porcupine Flat are more subdued. There is something for everyone.

All the hotels mentioned above have restaurants, and markets are located at Wawona, Yosemite Valley, and Tuolumne Meadows.

THE TRIP

Day 1: The south gate of Yosemite is the access point for the **Mariposa Grove.** Parking at the grove is limited; shuttle service is available from Wawona. The Mariposa Grove hike is a 4-mile moderate loop taking you through groves of giant sequoias with signage at many of the oldest, tallest, and most interesting trees. The apex of the hike is **Galen Clark's Cabin**, which serves as the small **Mariposa Grove Museum**. After the grove, grab a snack at Wawona's Pioneer Gift and Grocery and drive one hour northwest to **Glacier Point**. This famous viewpoint offers a short 10-minute walk to the vista as well as interpretive signage and a small store. Stay here for the loop hike of **Sentinel Dome** and **Taft Point**. At 4.9 miles with 1,000-foot elevation gain, this terrific hike takes about three hours and provides sweeping views of the Yosemite Valley, waterfalls, and surrounding mountains.

Day 2: Begin the visit at the very nice **Yosemite Valley Visitor Center**. To get a good sense of the valley, walk 15 minutes west to the Yosemite Valley Lodge, where bicycles are available for rent, and enjoy biking the 12-mile **Yosemite Valley Loop Trail**. See **Yosemite Falls**, the Merced River that forms the base of Yosemite Valley, and different views of Half Dome and El Capitan. Buy lunch at the Yosemite Lodge Gift Shop and then take the free **Valley Shuttle** (or a 45-minute walk) from Yosemite Lodge to the **Mirror Lake** trailhead. A mile walk with 100 feet of elevation gain brings hikers to the storied Mirror Lake and the famous reflected view of **Mount Watkins** on the lake surface. Enjoy a snack at the lake before heading back to Yosemite Village either via shuttle or a 30-minute walk. Treat yourself to dinner at the Mountain Room Restaurant and Lounge at the Yosemite Valley Lodge.

Day 3: One of the most popular hikes in the park, the **Vernal/Nevada Falls** trail leads from the valley floor along a waterfall to a panoramic viewpoint where hikers can bask in the sun and have lunch. The shuttle provides service to the trailhead, or it's about a 30-minute walk from the center of Yosemite Valley. The entire four- to five-hour hike climbs about 2,000 vertical feet on this 5.7-mile round trip to the summit at Nevada Falls, with an easier option of stopping at the lower Vernal Falls. The summit provides a close-up view of **Half Dome** and its climbers.

SHOULD YOU HIKE HALF DOME?

The iconic peak overlooking Yosemite Valley, Half Dome is home to rock climbers and a few lucky hikers. Fifty permits per day can be reserved in advance, with an additional 25 available the day of your hike. Depending upon route and hiking speed, Half Dome can take 10 to 15 hours round trip and cover an elevation gain of nearly 5,000 feet, or 3,000 feet above Nevada Falls.

Day 4: Grab lunch at the Village Store and head out of the valley and onto the famous Tioga Road toward **Tuolumne Meadows.** The drive is about one and a half hours, leading from the south to the north side of Half Dome and surrounding peaks. This high alpine meadow offers several great and easy hikes. Past the **Tuolumne Meadows Visitor Center**, drive another mile and a half and park at the **Lembert Dome** trailhead parking lot. This can serve as a base for one or two easy hikes. Start with a flat 1.5-mile round-trip loop hike through **Tuolumne Meadows** including **Soda Springs**, the **Parsons Memorial Lodge**, and the Tuolumne Meadows Visitors Center. Once back at the trailhead and parking lot, begin either the **Young Lakes Trail** or walk or drive 1 mile east to the **Dog Lake** trailhead. This 3-mile level triangle hike leads to the beautiful Dog Lake, suitable for swimming and a picnic lunch, and also to the short Lembert Dome offshoot hike for a panoramic view of Tuolumne Meadows. Spend the night in this section of the park and enjoy sunset walks and abundant wildlife.

Day 5: The May Lake High Sierra Camp is the easiest and most accessible backcountry glamping hike. For those lucky enough to get advanced or last-minute reservations, enjoy. If not, this area is still not to be missed. The **May Lake/Mount Hoffman** hike offers a full day of activity with lots of distinct rewards. Begin with a 1.2-mile hike to May Lake, with an elevation gain of just over 500 feet. There are paths around the lake in both directions, but heading east leads to the steep **Mount Hoffman Trail**. The 2.2-mile one-way marmot-filled hike to the summit gains 2,000 feet of elevation. The reward is a 360-degree view of the High Sierra Range and what John Muir believed was the best view in the park.

**See the appendix for useful lodging, camping,
and activity contact information.**

KINGS CANYON NATIONAL PARK

All the meadows are well covered with oak, alder, cottonwood and willow. The river abounds with beaver and fish. It is a location suitable for a mission, although there would also have to be a presidio.

—Father Pedro Muñoz, member of the 1806 Spanish expedition that came upon the area

GRIZZLY FALLS IN KINGS CANYON NATIONAL PARK
JUAN CAMILO BERNAL/SHUTTERSTOCK

With two distinct sections, Kings Canyon National Park offers an opportunity for two unique experiences. The first is the giant sequoias. These trees are native only to the western slope of the Sierra Nevada Range and also only to a certain latitude and elevation. Both Kings Canyon National Park and Sequoia National Park (abutting to the south) have large groves of these majestic trees. The giant sequoias in Kings Canyon are centered around the Grant Grove area, with miles of bucolic hiking as well as a village center. This is a wonderful place to start the trip. The second feature of the park is the Kings River and Kings Canyon, which require a nearly 30-mile drive on the narrow, winding Kings Canyon Scenic Byway. This second section has lush meadows and two of the park's signature hikes. The two sections are quite different, and a visit to the park should include both areas.

Though inhabited by Native Americans for thousands of years, the Kings River was put on the map by a party of Spanish explorers who, according to diary records, are believed to have reached the area in early January 1806. The river was referred to as Rio de los Santos Reyes (River of the Holy Kings), with this name appearing on maps a few years later. Following land transfers and California statehood in 1850, the area became part of Mariposa County. In 1890, Grant Grove was named General Grant National Park along with Sequoia National Park to the immediate south. Though advocates had hoped to include Kings Canyon, the larger park as seen today was only combined, expanded, and renamed Kings Canyon National Park in 1940, designated by President Franklin Roosevelt. Surrounding the park is the Sierra National Forest, the Sequoia National Forest, the Inyo National Forest, and the Jennie Lakes Wilderness. A pristine area indeed.

SCHEDULING AND LODGING

Kings Canyon is about four hours from San Jose and San Francisco International Airports and is not far south of the south entrance to Yosemite National-al Park. The park is open year-round, with robust winter activities including cross country skiing and snowshoeing. The road to Kings Canyon, as well as the road connecting Kings Canyon and Sequoia, closes for long stretches in the winter. Summer is the low-risk time to see the full park.

There are two in-park lodging options—the **John Muir Lodge/Grant Grove Cabins** in Grant Village and **Cedar Grove Lodge** in Kings Canyon. These two distinct areas of the park also offer many campsites, with **Sunset**, **Azalea**, and **Crystal Springs** campgrounds near Grant Grove and **Canyon View**, **Sheep Creek**, **Sentinel**, and **Moraine** campgrounds in Cedar Grove. Both Grant Grove Village and Cedar Grove Village have a restaurant and camp store. If these lodging options are full, try the **Montecito Sequoia Lodge** on state forest land between the Kings Canyon and Sequoia parks. Set up like a family camp, the lodge offers a small pond with kayaking, a restaurant, and modest motel-style rooms.

SEQUOIA PARKS CONSERVANCY MAPS

A high-resolution topographical map of Grant Grove is for sale at the visitor center. This worthwhile map includes hiking trails and the location of some important trees.

THE TRIP

Day 1: There's easily a full day of hiking in the Grant Grove Village area. Start with the **Kings Canyon Visitor Center** and the Grant Grove Village Store for lunch or snacks. From here, it's about a mile walk or drive to the **General Grant Tree**. There's a small parking lot and a nicely maintained half-mile trail around the General Grant Tree, the largest tree in Kings Canyon. This whole area is full of giant sequoias, with other great trails including the **North Grove Loop Trail** at 1.3 miles and the **Day Ride Trail** at 2.3 miles. Both are accessed from the General Grant Tree parking lot. A third option accessed from the service road just off the parking lot is the 7-mile round-trip **Sunset Trail** past **Ella Falls Trail** down to Sequoia Lake. This trail doesn't have many giant sequoias but provides a sense of the majesty of the forest overall. Sequoia Lake is owned by a YMCA, and only partial access is possible.

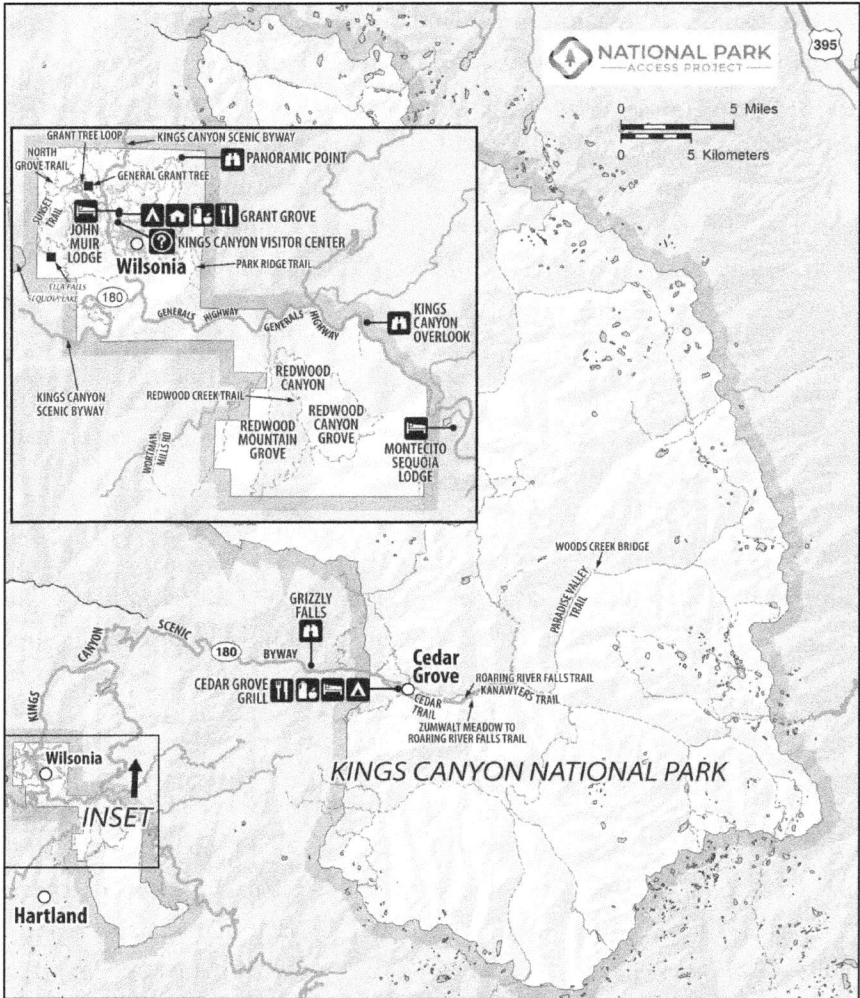

The other major focal point of Grant Village is **Panoramic Point** and the **Park Ridge Trail**. The access road to the small Panoramic Point parking lot is behind John Muir Lodge, with about a 0.3-mile hike to get to the point itself. This point offers arguably the best view in Kings Canyon, looking down at **Hume Lake** and east to the peaks of the Sierra Nevada Range. You'll see **Mount Stewart**, whose namesake George W. Stewart, along with John Muir, did so much to preserve this land. From here is the 5-mile round trip hike to the **Park Ridge Fire Station**, which leads along the ridge and provides views of the Sierra Nevada peaks for about the first half of the hike. The second half of the hike parallels the service road to the fire tower, which offers spectacular views. Hiking even part of this trail provides a good sense of the majesty of the Sierra Nevada Range.

Day 2: Highway 180 is the **Kings Canyon Scenic Byway** from Grant Grove Village to **Cedar Grove**. Take this one-hour scenic drive and extend it by stopping at panoramic overlooks. Near the end is **Cedar Grove Village** and its campgrounds, hotel, café, and camper store. Just past Cedar Grove Village is the **Roaring River Falls** trailhead, the **Zumwalt Meadow** trailhead, and the Roads End parking lot. These attractions are connected via hiking trails or can be seen by individual stops. The latter option saves time and energy for the **Mist Falls Trail**, which starts at Roads End. Roaring River Falls is accessed just off the road, and the beautiful Zumwalt Meadow hike is a 1-mile loop. Once at Roads End, there are a number of trailheads accessing some very long hikes. The most famous of these is **Mist Falls/Paradise Valley**, a 17.5-mile round-trip hike up Kings Canyon and through some majestic terrain. Strong hikers can make a day of the Paradise Valley hike, but many only go to Mist Falls. This is about 8 miles round trip, much of the hike level along the side of Kings River, gaining under 1,000 feet toward the end near the falls. End the day in Cedar Grove Village. The lodge puts out lawn and balcony chairs with views of the river.

Day 3: Immediately on the right when returning to Grant Village is a small parking area leading to a short walk to **Grizzly Falls**. This raging waterfall is a signature sight in Kings Canyon and well worth a stop. After the hour drive back to the park entrance, grab lunch in Grant Village before heading south on Generals Highway toward Sequoia National Park. A few miles down the road is a small parking lot on the right. This turnout accesses a seasonal dirt road leading to the **Redwood Mountain Grove**. Access is tricky, as the dirt road is only wide enough for one car with any oncoming cars having to pull off to the side. The destination is worth it, though, as the Redwood Mountain Grove is a very large grove of giant sequoias with a 10-mile outer loop trail along with a center trail (**Redwood Canyon Trail**) that can make either loop into about a 6-mile hike. This is a wonderful shady valley hike that is fairly level and incredibly peaceful.

See the appendix for useful lodging, camping, and activity contact information.

SEQUOIA NATIONAL PARK

We are now in the mountains and they are in us, kindling enthusiasm, making every nerve quiver, filling every pore and cell of us.
—John Muir, *My First Summer in the Sierra*

Two giant sequoia trees in Sequoia National Park
Filip Fuxa/Shutterstock

Sequoia National Park was among the very first national parks designated. Yosemite to the north was named a state park in 1864. Yellowstone became the first national park in 1872, and then in 1890, Yosemite, Sequoia, and Grant Grove (General Grant National Park) were named national parks under the same legislation. This famous effort by John Muir, George Stewart, and many others laid the foundation for the enviable national park system we have today.

Though Yosemite, Kings Canyon, and Sequoia all have groves of giant sequoia trees, John Muir and others sensed that the largest trees in the densest grove were in what would become Sequoia National Park. Though at the time this was only instinct, it turned out to be true. With over 8,000 giant sequoia trees and the largest giant sequoias in the world, Sequoia National Park's Giant Forest is nothing short of a miracle of nature. These spectacular trees are important for a number of reasons. The species is the largest tree and the largest living organism on the planet by volume. They are about the oldest living things on earth, with the oldest giant sequoia around 3,300 years old. The trees, due to their thick bark, survive fire. The tannins in their trunk resist insect infestation. And they don't blow over in the wind due to their dispersed root system.

The 9 square miles that make up the Giant Forest also encompass gorgeous meadows, including the famous Crescent Meadow. On the edge of the Giant Forest is the Moro Rock promontory providing a spectacular view of the highest part of the Sierra Nevada Range, including the tallest mountain in the continental United States—Mount Whitney at 14,505 feet. In the park's southwest corner is the interesting Crystal Cave system, one of five major caves in the national park system.

SCHEDULING AND LODGING

Like Kings Canyon, Sequoia National Park is open year-round, though there are seasonal road closures due to snow. The Giant Forest and Crescent Meadow are spectacular in the summer, and this is a great season for a first visit to the park.

Wuksachi Lodge (and Peaks Restaurant) is the premier place to stay in the Kings Canyon/Sequoia system. **Montecito Sequoia Lodge** is in the Sequoia National Forest between Kings Canyon and Sequoia and represents a well-located, more affordable option. The center of Sequoia National Park is **Lodgepole Village**, and here there's a large campground served by the Lodgepole Market and Grill. If Lodgepole is full or if a less crowded campground is desired, Sequoia has ample camping at five campgrounds.

For many, a visit to the High Sierras is not complete without a backcountry trip. Yosemite National Park has a series of High Sierra Camps connected by hiking trails. Sequoia has just one—the **Bearpaw High Sierra Camp**. Accessed from the Giant Forest via the 11.5-mile High Sierra Trail, this option provides rustic backcountry lodging and meal service in a spectacular setting. Reservations sell out quickly and typically open for the summer starting January 2. Finally, located in the remote south section of the park is the **Atwell Mill** campground and privately owned **Silver City Resort** with restaurant and store.

SEQUOIA PARKS CONSERVANCY MAP

The Sequoia Parks Conservancy sells a detailed topographic map of the Giant Forest, including shuttle stops, hiking trails with distance and elevation, and restroom locations.

GIANT FOREST TRANSPORTATION

Sequoia National Park operates a shuttle system serving the Giant Forest. Stops include the **Lodgepole Village Visitor Center**, Wolverton, General Sherman Tree, the Giant Forest Museum, Moro Rock, and Crescent Meadow. The major transit hubs are Lodgepole, Sherman Tree, and the Giant Forest Museum. For drivers to the Giant Forest, there's only one good parking option, General Sherman Tree, where there's a medium-size parking lot with direct access to the Giant Forest. Arrive early to get a space.

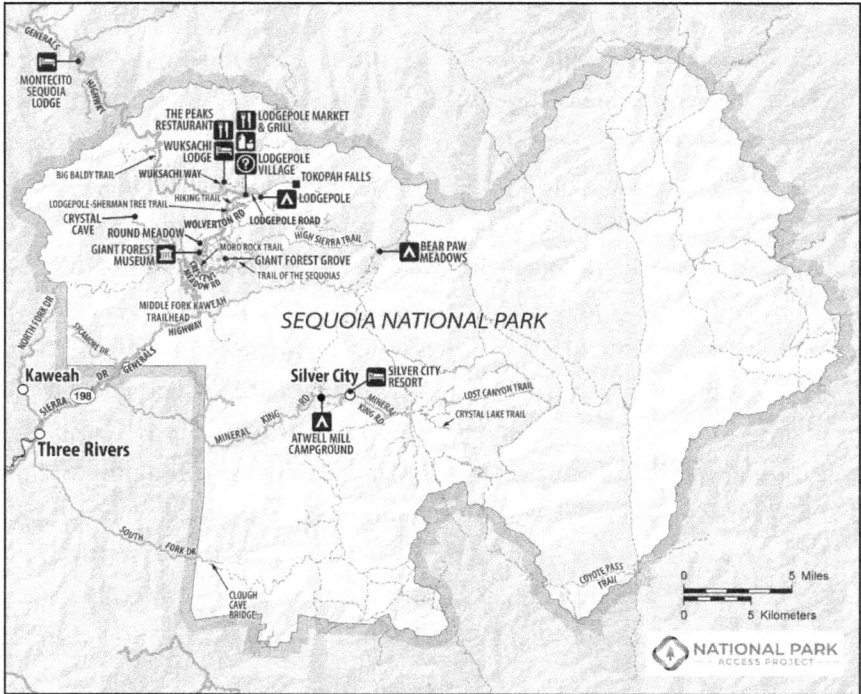

THE TRIP

Day 1: Pack a lunch, as there is no food service in the **Giant Forest**. The natural sequence of the day is to start at **General Sherman Tree**, hiking through the Giant Forest to **Crescent Meadow** (and Log Meadow), then **Tunnel Log** and **Moro Rock**, finally ending at the **Giant Forest Museum**, where there is frequent shuttle service. The full loop is about 12 miles, including **Round Meadow** near the Giant Forest Museum.

This 9-square-mile area is not only one of the most beautiful in the national park system, with immense sequoias, lush meadows, and spectacular views, it's also one of the more accessible hiking systems, as there is very little overall elevation gain. The only difficult section is the Moro Rock climb, which has hundreds of stairs but with a reward of panoramic views.

Day 2: Open from late May through late September, the marble **Crystal Cave** with a river running through the bottom is about a 45-minute drive from Lodgepole Village. There are two tour options—a 50-minute Family Tour happening about every hour and a one-and-a-half-hour Discovery Tour at the end of the day. Reservations are required two days in advance, with remaining tickets sold at the Lodgepole Visitor Center. Tickets are not available at the cave.

With extra time, a signature hike in the park is **Big Baldy**, a 5.5-mile loop hike with about 1,300 feet of elevation gain accessed off Generals Highway near the north end of the park. This hike delivers 360-degree views, including the peaks of the Sierra Nevada Range to the east and the foothills to the west.

Day 3: The park's remote southeast section is little visited and requires exiting the park at the **Foothills Visitor Center** and entering again via the winding Mineral King Road. This hour-and-a-half drive leads deeper into the Sierra Nevada mountains, delivering pristine alpine vistas and lush valleys. Silver City itself is an inholding of privately owned land entirely surrounded by the park. A lodge, restaurant, and store are here, along with a nearby national park campground. The **Kaweah River** runs along the valley floor, with the easy **Cold Springs Nature Trail** extending 2.3 miles round trip along the riverbank and the steep 6.2-mile round-trip **Paradise Ridge Trail** leading 2,000 feet up from the valley floor to provide a panoramic view of the Sierra Nevada Range.

See the appendix for useful lodging, camping, and activity contact information.

CHANNEL ISLANDS NATIONAL PARK

Finding these sites and the definitive evidence for early occupation is crucial and tells us that people were there, occupying the landscape at the end of the Pleistocene.

–Dr. Torben Rick of the Smithsonian Institution, leader of the survey that uncovered nearly 20 prehistoric sites of human activity on Santa Rosa Island

CHANNEL ISLANDS NATIONAL PARK
TRAVEL STOCK/SHUTTERSTOCK

Located off the coast of greater Los Angeles, the Channel Islands are easy to visit and well worth the trip. The eight islands include three outside the national park, the largest of which are Catalina and San Clemente. Catalina Island is accessed from downtown Los Angeles via ferry. The national park islands to the north are accessed via ferry from Ventura and include three larger islands—Santa Cruz, Santa Rosa, and San Miguel. Due to a land dispute, Santa Cruz is largely owned by the Nature Conservancy, with use of this part of the island more restricted.

The islands have been occupied by humans for thousands of years, and archaeologists are still actively researching early human activity there. The Chumash people of what are now called the Channel Islands are believed to be some of the earliest human inhabitants of North America's west coast. The California land rush of the 1800s spilled onto the Channel Islands, with ranchers settling the area for grazing. By the early 1900s, the US Navy gained control of San Miguel Island. Continuing consolidation and activity by the US government brought the northern Channel Islands mostly into government ownership. By 1938, the northern Channel Islands were named a national monument and by 1980 had become a national park.

Removal of invasive species associated with years of ranching has been a big project at the park over the past 50 years. The islands were overrun by goats, feral pigs, and rats. Removing these and other nonnative animals has allowed for reintroduction of bald eagles, peregrine falcons, and the famous and ubiquitous island fox.

The main activities on the Channel Islands are hiking and kayaking. Miles of coastal and inland trails provide incredible views, while kayaking allows access to caves full of shorebirds as well as hidden beaches. For those who can accept summer water temperatures between 60 and 65 degrees, the Channel Islands are a world-recognized location for snorkeling and scuba diving.

SCHEDULING AND LODGING

The Channel Islands are open year-round with the Island Packers Cruises ferry out of Ventura serving Santa Cruz Island every day. For a longer trip to the islands, though, it makes sense to travel in the summer. This is the season to watch blue whales migrate through the Santa Barbara Channel and is the most comfortable time to camp on the island. Also, Island Packers offers service to other islands in the national park, but only during summer or near-summer months. Service to Anacapa and Santa Rosa Islands occurs several times per week, while service to San Miguel and Santa Barbara is several times per month. Unfortunately, the ferry does not travel island to island. Instead each visit is from Ventura, to the island, and then back to Ventura. The trip suggested here only visits Santa Cruz Island, as this trip can be taken anytime and because Santa Cruz has on-island kayak rentals. Check the Island Packers website for multi-island travel options.

The ferry to Santa Cruz Island is available in the morning or late afternoon. To enjoy both hiking and kayaking, spend at least 24 hours, ideally with a morning departure the first day and an afternoon return on the second. To accomplish this, consider staying in Ventura the night before the island camping trip. There are two hotels abutting the **Ventura Harbor Marina**— the **Holiday Inn Express** and **Four Points by Sheraton**. Camping is available at **McGrath State Beach and Campground** 2 miles south of the marina. On Santa Cruz Island there is the 31-site **Scorpion Ranch Campground**, with reservations opening six months in advance. To make an overnight ferry reservation, verification of camping reservations with campsite number is required. The Santa Cruz ferry also stops at **Prisoners Harbor** for backcountry camping. Prisoners Harbor is about 13 miles walking from Scorpion Ranch, so these are two distinct options.

There is no food service on any of the islands and no grocery or convenience store near the marina, though Ventura has many grocery stores within a short drive.

KAYAKING AND SNORKELING

Other than bringing your own kayak, there are two ways to arrange Channel Island kayaks. The inexpensive option is to prearrange rented kayaks from Channel Islands Kayak Center and reserve berth space from Island Packers ferry. Rented kayaks will be brought to the ferry. This option provides the ability to kayak as long as desired and to kayak multiple times during the island visit. For novices, the Channel Island caves and their heavy surf can be deep, dark, and quite disorienting.

The second option is a guided kayak tour by Channel Islands Adventure Company. This three-hour reserved tour meets at the Scorpion Ranch ferry stop. The company provides gear including kayaks, paddles, life jackets, and wetsuits as well as space to store belongings during the trip. The tour explores a number of the island's caves as well as the tidal areas. Channel Islands Adventure Company also rents snorkeling gear. There is abundant shallow water full of vibrant fish near the ferry dock.

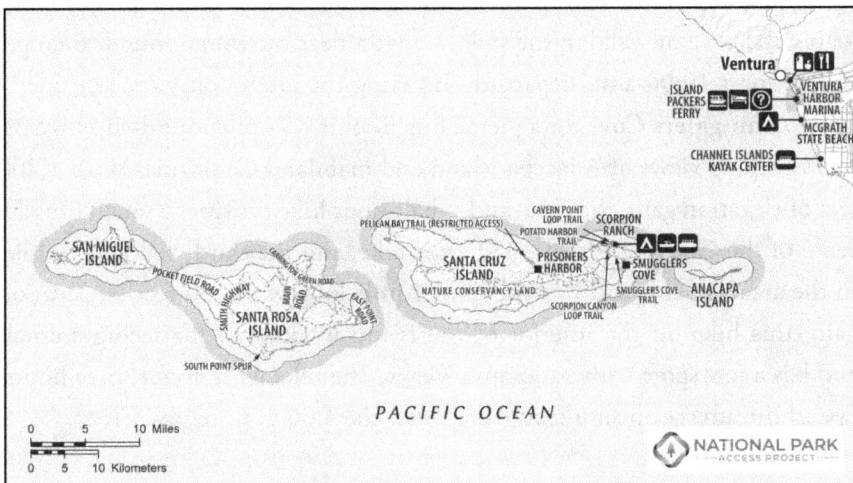

THE TRIP

Day 1: The ferry ride is a treat and a wonderful stand-alone activity. Marine wildlife is abundant at the Ventura marina, in the harbor, in the sky, and of course along the one-hour journey to **Santa Cruz Island**. Passengers have a good chance to see dolphins, several kinds of whales, sea lions, seals, otters, and more. Arrive at **Scorpion Ranch**, get settled, and begin kayaking, either on your own or with a guide. Marine mammals swim to the kayaks while shore birds soar overhead and nesting birds fly in and out of the caves. In the shallow areas, vibrant fish as well as other marine plant and animal life are easy to see.

After the kayak trip, set up camp and spend the afternoon at the small **Scorpion Ranch Visitor Center** and hiking the 1.6-mile **Cavern Point Trail** that leads up to the bluff overlooking the harbor and across the Santa Barbara Channel looking northeast. The loop trail arrives back at the campground. Extend the hike by continuing on the Cavern Point Trail to the **Potato Harbor Trail**. The loop, including both trails, is 4.9 miles.

Day 2: For those taking the morning ferry back to Ventura, enjoy snorkeling the cove or walking the valley/canyon near the campground, then get in line for a 10:00 a.m. departure. If taking the afternoon ferry, consider a trek to **Smugglers Cove** for a picnic lunch. This 7.7-mile round-trip hike offers sweeping views of Anacapa Island and mainland California. With 1,200 feet of elevation gain, this four-and-a-half-hour hike provides a much broader sense of the Channel Islands. A shorter hike, and the third well-known hike in the area, is **Scorpion Canyon**. A 4.5-mile loop with 750 feet of elevation gain, this hike on the interior of the island works well for seeing animals and has a few spots with panoramic views. The hike takes about three hours. Spend the afternoon snorkeling and catch the 4:00 p.m. return ferry.

See the appendix for useful lodging, camping, and activity contact information.

CALIFORNIA AND
NEVADA DESERTS

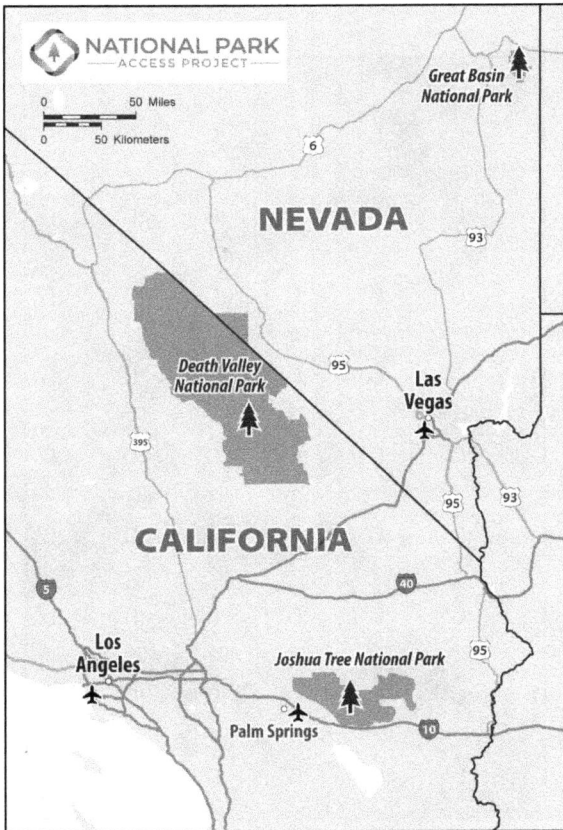

JOSHUA TREE NATIONAL PARK

One time I saw a tiny Joshua tree sapling growing not too far from the old tree. I wanted to dig it up and replant it near our house. I told Mom that I would protect it from the wind and water it every day so that it could grow nice and tall and straight. Mom frowned at me. "You'd be destroying what makes it special," she said. "It's the Joshua tree's struggle that gives it its beauty."

—Jeannette Walls, from her 2006 book *The Glass Castle*

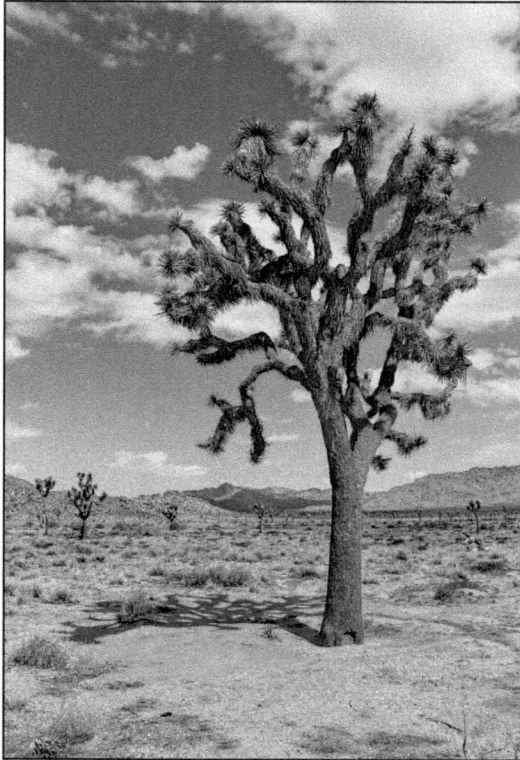

JOSHUA TREE NATIONAL PARK
MICHAEL MANTKE/SHUTTERSTOCK

Known for its rock climbing, stargazing, and day hiking, Joshua Tree is an easy park to visit. Located in southeast California, the park can be accessed from Las Vegas, Los Angeles, or nearby Palm Springs. The park straddles two deserts—the Sonoran and the Mojave. Joshua trees only grow in the Mojave Desert, so this section (the northwest part of the park) is where most visitors spend their time. The southeast Sonoran Desert portion of the park has many types of cacti and light hiking and contains most of the park's designated wilderness area. The oldest Joshua trees are 500 to 1,000 years old and at peak maturity can be up to 60 feet tall. Under the right conditions, these otherworldly plants flower in springtime. The 800,000-acre Joshua Tree National Park began as a national monument in 1936 and became a national park in 1994.

Lack of water and harsh conditions made this part of the country inhospitable to all but the heartiest. Native tribes traversed the area seasonally, and the first western travelers arrived around 1850. Bill Keys, a miner and jack-of-all-trades settled in the park in the early 1900s with his wife, Frances. They would go on to have seven children and eke out an existence in this harsh landscape for the next 50 years. Ranger-led tours of the historic Keys Ranch are a must.

The geologic history of the park is also fascinating, with some rock formations as old as 1,600 million years. The rock extrusions in Joshua Tree began through a combination of lava pushing in small bursts through the earth's crust and then torrential rain eroding looser soil and rock. The result is a fascinating desert vista peppered with collections of eroded rock formations that help define the landscape.

SCHEDULING AND LODGING

The Joshua tree's spectacular springtime bloom does not happen every year and can occur anytime from February through June. For those able to be a bit spontaneous, the ideal time to visit is when the trees and surrounding desert floor are in bloom.

Camping here is easy and pleasant. With eight campgrounds and 500 campsites, there's something for almost everyone. Of the campgrounds, four (**Black Rock**, **Cottonwood**, **Indian Cove**, and **Jumbo Rocks**) take advance reservations, with the campsites selling out many weekends during peak season in April and May.

For noncampers, other lodging options abound. Though the small town of Joshua Tree on the northern border of the park has a few inns, the bulk of the lodging is in Twentynine Palms. This small desert town is home to the park's Oasis Visitor Center, the North Entrance Station, hundreds of hotel rooms, many restaurants, and also guide services that support both novice and experienced rock climbers. Two hotel options are the newer **Fairfield Inn and Suites by Marriott Twentynine Palms** and the kitschy **29 Palms Inn**.

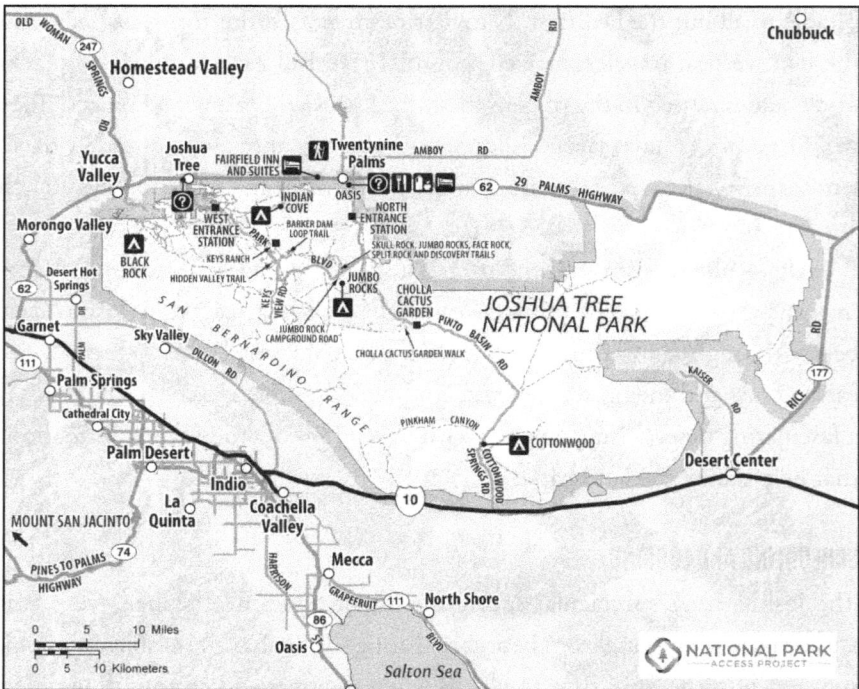

Joshua Tree National Park is about 40 minutes east of Palm Springs, two and a half hours east of Los Angeles, and three hours southwest of Las Vegas.

HIKING IN THE PARK

Desert parks are not the right place for long hikes. A lot of water is required to hike safely, and the ability to refill and purify water is zero or near zero. There are a few long hikes in Joshua Tree National Park, including the California Riding and Hiking Trail (37.6 miles one way), Lost Horse Mine Trail (7-mile loop), and Boy Scout Trail (8 miles one way). They are not included in the suggested itinerary. The heart of the park is designed for a nice amount of total hiking mileage in shorter 1 to 3-mile jaunts. These short hikes allow plenty of opportunities to refresh water using self-provided supplies in your car. There are no services inside the park boundaries. Stock your car with food and more water than you think you'll need before entering the park.

THE TRIP

Day 1: Begin at the **Joshua Tree Visitor Center** and the west entrance and when finished, head about 10 minutes east to **Twentynine Palms**, the hotels, grocery stores, and the **Oasis Visitor Center**, which is the park's main visitor center.

A unique offering in the park is **Keys Ranch**, home of early Joshua Tree settler Bill Keys. This historic property is a few miles beyond a locked gate and is accessed only via a ranger-guided morning visit. Advanced reservations and a small fee are required. The tour showcases the historic buildings and classic examples of the park's Joshua trees and features some of the park's famous rock formations. The walk is about 0.6 miles. A nice hike near the ranch is the 1.8-mile **Barker Dam** loop trail that leads to the often-dry Barker Dam, the bottom of which is visible from Keys Ranch. Signs to the trailhead are posted when exiting Keys Ranch Road.

After Barker Dam, head to **Hidden Valley**. This is an easy 1.2-mile loop trail and one of the prettiest in the park. Surrounded by rock walls and rock climbers, the trail offers diverse desert flora from Joshua trees to cacti. After the hike, drive to **Keys View**, a high point of the **San Bernardino Range**. From here, look back on Palm Springs, the Coachella Valley, and Mount San Jacinto. To the south is the **Salton Sea**, an inland water body created by accident in 1905. Though it is slowly evaporating, this more than one-million-acre water body is an interesting part of the Southwest landscape. This is a great spot for lunch, though windy and chilly compared to the park floor.

Head back to the main park road (Park Boulevard) and turn right. After about 10 minutes the **House of Horrors** is on the left. This field of cacti and Joshua trees is accessed by a 0.6-mile walk between three huge rocks—again, look for climbers.

After the walk, keep driving northeast on Park Boulevard, leaving the main concentration of Joshua trees and heading toward a collection of some of the park's great rock formations. Park near **Skull Rock**, where four trails intersect. From Skull Rock (visible from the road), head first to the **Discovery Trail** (0.7-mile loop) that connects to the 0.2-mile **Face Rock Trail**, which then connects to the 1.9-mile loop **Split Rock Trail**.

Continue northwest on Park Boulevard and almost immediately turn right to **Cholla Cactus Garden**. This road leaves the Mojave Desert and enters the Colorado Desert portion of the Sonoran Desert. The terrain is different, as are the plants. The Cholla Cactus Garden is a smallish collection of cacti and other desert flowers and plants. If the desert flowers are in bloom, this is a wonderful drive.

As you settle in for the night, take time to stargaze. The park is known for clear night skies and limited light pollution.

Day 2: Joshua Tree National Park is a hub for rock climbers. Take advantage of the resources in the area and hire a guide for the day. There are many guide services offering an array of options from hourly to full day to overnight tours. A guided rock-climbing excursion displays the park in a different way.

**See the appendix for useful lodging, camping,
and activity contact information.**

DEATH VALLEY NATIONAL PARK

The Mojave is a big desert and a frightening one. It's as though nature tested a man for endurance and constancy to prove whether he was good enough to get to California.

—John Steinbeck, from his 1962 book *Travels with Charley: In Search of America*

Mesquite Flat Dunes at Stovepipe Wells, Death Valley National Park
Kit Leong/Shutterstock

This very unique part of the country is the result of being one mountain range too far east to get any appreciable water. As weather comes to the western United States from the Pacific Ocean, it first hits the Sierra Nevada Range, where 30 to 40 inches of annual moisture is dropped. Moving east, the Inyo and White Mountains get 10 to 12 inches. Moving east again, the Panamint Range on the western boundary of Death Valley National Park gets under 10 inches. Death Valley itself typically sees around 2 inches of rain each year. And the Amargosa Range on the east side of the valley gets almost no precipitation. Couple this almost zero moisture with the extreme elevation changes and this is a place unlike any on earth. The top of the Panamint Range, Telescope Peak, is over 11,000 feet. The floor of Death Valley, called Badwater Basin, is nearly 300 feet below sea level. The result is not only a bone-dry landscape but one of visual extremes.

Death Valley National Park measures 3.3 million acres and is the largest national park outside Alaska. The park is part of the Great Basin, a desert area extending from California through Nevada and into Utah. The Great Basin is sufficiently dry that precipitation drains into the basin and is fully used by flora and fauna. There is no further drainage into the Pacific Ocean or the Gulf of Mexico. Within the Great Basin there are numerous dry lake beds. Death Valley, the park's namesake, is the dry lake bed of Lake Manly. This lake was full about 175,000 years ago and again about 25,000 years ago. Current weather patterns flush salts and other minerals into the lake bed. Any water quickly evaporates, leaving a thick white mineral crust on Badwater Basin, a highlight of the park. Other key areas to see include canyons, sand dunes, a volcanic crater, mountain peaks, oases with waterfalls, and streams with prehistoric fish.

Death Valley is home to 314 acres of tribal land transferred by President Bill Clinton in 2000 to the Timbisha Shoshone Tribe. This tribal area, entirely surrounded by national park land, is unique in the national park system. About 20 Timbisha Shoshone live on the land, located near Furnace Creek, and visitors can often purchase food or souvenirs at the small village.

Death Valley got its name from a gold rush traverse gone bad. A group of European travelers called the Bennett-Arcane party got stuck in the valley over the winter from 1849 to 1850. Though they did survive, they exited the area saying, "Goodbye, Death Valley."

SCHEDULING AND LODGING

Nearly every year sees a death in Death Valley. From May through September, average temperatures exceed 100 degrees and in peak summer approach 120 degrees. These averages do not include certain days when temperatures spike. The park routinely has a few days above 130 degrees. Even with enough water, the human body cannot adapt to such extreme heat. Surprisingly, the busiest month to visit Death Valley is August. Beat the crowd and visit in April when the desert wildflowers bloom and the average desert-floor temperature is about 90 degrees.

Despite the heat, camping in Death Valley is normally pleasant. Spring nights are in the mid-sixties and stargazing is spectacular. There are two main campgrounds, **Stovepipe Wells** and **Furnace Creek**, but only one is open at a time. Check the reservation site for their exact date ranges, which vary each year. Both campgrounds are serviced and located near lodging with restaurants, a grocery store, gas station, and ranger station.

The park also provides four lodging options. The most prominent is the **Oasis at Death Valley** and its sister property, the **Ranch at Death Valley**. Both of these are located in Furnace Creek at the top of Badwater Basin. These properties are expensive (the Oasis more so) but offer amenities like shopping, groceries, restaurants, pools, horseback riding, and the like. The Inn Dining Room at the Oasis at Death Valley provides fine dining in a restored 1920s luxury setting overlooking the salt flats and mountain ranges. Reservations are required. The other two lodging options include the **Stovepipe Wells Village Hotel** and **Panamint Springs Resort**. Both of these are modest motels, with Stovepipe being a bit more typical of national park lodging and Panamint more of a rustic experience.

McCarran International Airport in Las Vegas is the closest airport to Death Valley, about two hours to the east. Death Valley can also be tied in with Joshua Tree National Park (fly in to Palm Springs and out of Las Vegas or vice versa), and connecting the two allows travel through the Mojave Desert National Preserve.

HIKING IN THE PARK

Death Valley has some surprisingly long hikes for being one of the hottest places on the planet. Plan your trip carefully. Rangers suggest hiking early in the morning or later in the evening and consuming one to two gallons of water per person per day.

THE TRIP

This suggested itinerary assumes travel from Las Vegas. If coming from the south (Los Angeles/Palm Springs), the order would be reversed.

Day 1: A great place to start a visit to Death Valley is Stovepipe Wells, with services described above. Begin with one of the three canyon hikes in the park—**Mosaic Canyon**, just west of Stovepipe Wells. Though 4 miles round trip, the shade in the canyon helps control the temperature. Like many things in Death Valley, the canyon has an otherworldly feel. On the other (southeast) side of Stovepipe Wells is a small side trip—the **Salt Creek Interpretive Trail**. If not in a desert, this would be underwhelming. But the water, ancient fish, and interpretive signage makes Salt Creek worth a visit.

Stay the night in the Stovepipe Wells area, and once the sun has set, head out to **Mesquite Flat Dunes**. There's a large parking lot providing access and no marked trail. Bring a headlamp and walk toward the highest dune. To the top of the dune and back is around 3 miles, but walking only a part of the way provides a near complete experience. There will be plenty of people here, all enjoying the dunes and the sparkling night sky. Take advantage of the location and repeat the next morning. At 5:30 a.m., there will again be plenty of other visitors.

Deep Springs Gold Point NATIONAL PARK ACCESS PROJECT

DEATH VALLEY NATIONAL PARK

Beatty

Owenyo Lone Pine Keeler Bartlett Cartago Olancha Darwin Haiwee Little Lake Inyokern Ridgecrest Westend Trona Valley Wells

Stovepipe Wells Mesquite Flat Sand Dunes Salt Creek Interpretive Trail Mosaic Canyon Rd Mosaic Canyon Trail Panamint Springs Resort Darwin Falls Darwin Falls Hike Wildrose Peak Charcoal Kilns Telescope Peak Panamint Range Badwater Basin Dante's View

Furnace Creek Borax Works The Ranch The Oasis Zabriskie Point Artist's Palette Hike Natural Bridge Hike Badwater Lake Manly Coffin Peak

Ubehebe Crater Rim Hike Scotty's Castle Steel Pass

Amargosa Valley Las Vegas Shoshone Tecopa

0 5 10 Miles
0 5 10 Kilometers

Mojave Desert Preserve

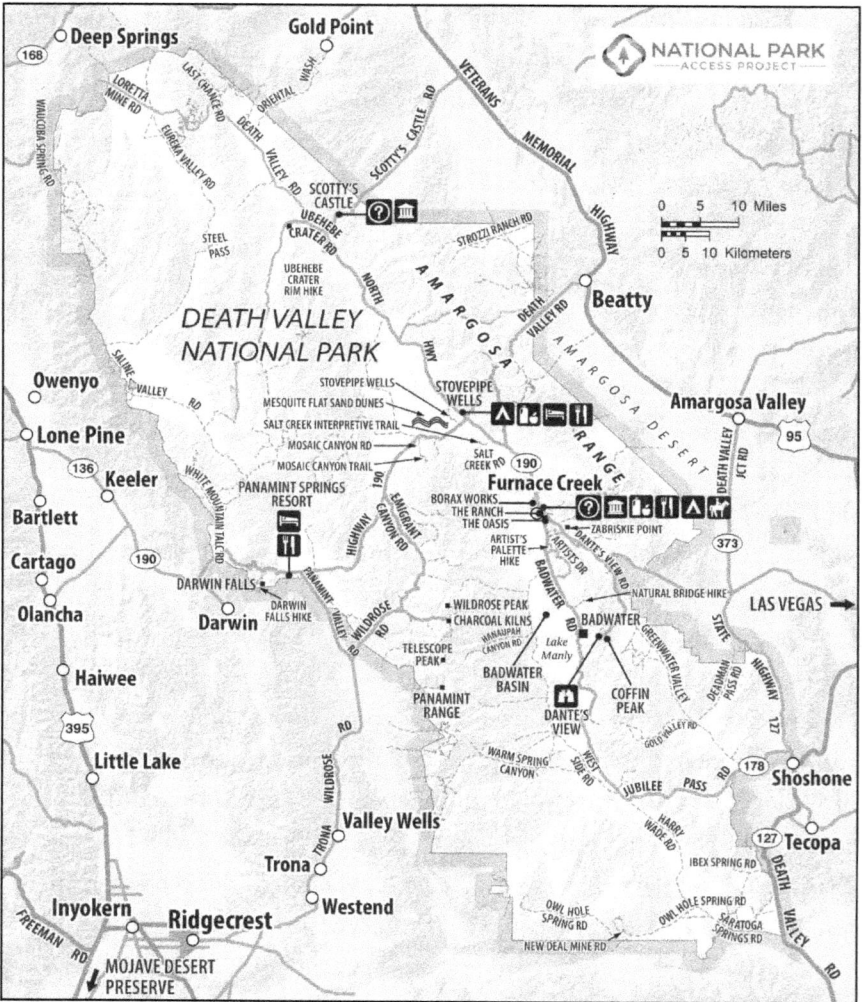

Day 2: The **Ubehebe Crater** (and Little Hebe Crater) is one hour north of Stovepipe. This dormant volcanic crater was active as recently as 300 years ago and provides views of the raw and barren northern Death Valley landscape. There's a parking lot at the crater that provides access to a 2.2-mile loop trail around the rim. The crater in spring is covered with tiny wildflowers.

Also in this part of the park is **Scotty's Castle**, which has been closed since 2015 due to flooding and does not yet have a firm reopening date. In the late 1800s when Death Valley was being prospected for gold and minerals, Walter E. Scott was both a huckster to potential mining investors and an ambassador for the Death Valley area. He was befriended by one of his investors, Chicagoan Albert Johnson, who lost his investment with Scotty but enjoyed the friendship so much that he built Scotty's Castle in the early 1920s. Historically a major attraction in the park, with rangers in period clothes providing tours, Scotty's Castle should be part of a visit if open. In the meantime, the park offers ranger-led **Flood Recovery Tours** for a fee on Sundays from December through mid-April.

Head back to Stovepipe Wells and to a shorter afternoon hike—**Darwin Falls**, near the park's west edge. This is a pretty hike through a dry streambed with short canyon-like walls on each side. The trek is 1 mile each way, with the last third of a mile a small oasis terminating in a waterfall (Darwin Falls). More ambitious hike alternatives include two high-peak hikes—**Telescope** (11,000 feet) and **Wildrose** (9,000 feet). These hikes are 8 and 12 miles round trip respectively and lead to summits that provide views of Badwater Basin and surrounding ranges. Near the trailheads are the charcoal kilns, 10 beehive kilns completed in 1877 to provide a source of fuel for mining. These are believed to be some of the best-preserved kilns in the country.

After the short or long hike, stay the night at the Panamint Springs Resort. This nonresort collection of motel/cabins is a fun spot with a decent restaurant and great views of the Panamint Range.

Day 3: Leave the Panamint Range and head to the **Furnace Creek** area. Just before Furnace Creek is a small outdoor exhibit—the **Borax Works**. The raw and ravaged sections interspersed throughout the park are evidence of prior mining. Despite efforts to find gold, Death Valley ended up being rich in the cleaner borax, found in the salt beds and elsewhere. Borax Works is the remnants of a portion of this mining operation. After the Borax Works, head to the **Furnace Creek Visitor Center** and then visit **Furnace Creek** and/or the **Timbisha Shoshone** villages.

From here, head south along the dry bed of Lake Manley to **Badwater Basin**, the lowest point in the United States. There's parking at Badwater and a trail in the form of compressed salt/minerals that can be walked for minutes or hours. After Badwater, turn around and head a short distance north to the **Natural Bridge** canyon hike. Though getting to the trailhead requires driving on a steep dirt road, once at the trailhead there are incredible views back to Telescope Peak. The hike itself is easy, at 2 miles round trip. The natural bridge is even closer to the trailhead so if hot or tired, just turn around here.

On the way back to Furnace Creek is the one-way **Artists Palette** drive that leads into the Amargosa Range. There are two places to take short hikes (about a quarter mile each) featuring the myriad of colors in the stone and sand caused by varying mineral deposits. Upon exiting Artists Palette, keep heading north to the trailhead for **Golden Canyon**. This is a loop hike, the longest canyon hike in the park at about 6 miles. If traveling with a group (at least two vehicles), this hike can become a one-way trip to or from the spectacular **Zabriskie Point**, which is the summit of this hike and also accessible by car. Not only will this plan cut the hike in half to about 3 miles but allows for hiking mostly downhill.

From Zabriskie Point, drive about half an hour to **Dante's View** near the summit of **Coffin Peak** in the Amargosa Range. There are two hikes from the parking lot—to the left a shorter hike to lookout points over Badwater Basin to Telescope Peak and to the right a longer ridgeline hike with the same views. The views here are spectacular and really show the juxtaposition of the mountain range and lake bed. Consider staying the night in Furnace Creek.

**See the appendix for useful lodging, camping,
and activity contact information.**

GREAT BASIN NATIONAL PARK

The valleys are bigger than you ever remember, and so are the mountains that bound them, each one popping up sequentially from below the horizon—a landmark. The basins feel more like oceanic fjords (temporarily dry) than valleys. There appears to be nothing in them, just a low growth of black sage and grass, with less conspicuous plants next to the playas.

—Stephen Trimble, *The Sagebrush Ocean: A Natural History of the Great Basin*

BRISTLECONE PINE, GREAT BASIN NATIONAL PARK
JOHNNY ADOLPHSON/SHUTTERSTOCK

Of the four United States deserts, Great Basin is the largest at 190,000 square miles. It's also the only desert that is not hot for most or all of the year. Covering virtually all of Nevada and extending into Utah, Idaho, and California, the desert's elevation ranges from valleys at near sea level to peaks over 13,000 feet. The high peaks are home to the bristlecone pine tree, the oldest known living organism in the world. Some of these trees are estimated to be over 5,000 years old.

The Dark Sky movement, which tracks areas in the United States and internationally that are particularly unpolluted by light, names Great Basin National Park as one of the places in the United States with the least light pollution. Not only is the park far from major population centers, the basin and range topography shields the park from even quite distant light sources. Experiencing night sky activities here is a must.

Great Basin National Park began as the 150,000-acre Lehman Caves National Monument, named by President Warren Harding in 1922. Lehman Caves served as the anchor for what became Great Basin National Park in 1986. The national park and the adjacent Highland Range Wilderness now each have about half the original land. Great Basin National Park kept the Snake Range, considered one of the most beautiful mountain ranges in the basin and range area. The Snake Range is also home to the highest mountain in Nevada—Wheeler Peak. Limestone and marble caves are a feature of the basin and range region, with eight major cave systems in Nevada alone. (Five United States national parks have major cave systems—Mammoth Cave, Carlsbad Caverns, Sequoia, Wind Cave, and Great Basin.) At about a quarter mile in length, Lehman Caves is the smallest of the major cave systems. Still, Lehman Caves has great diversity of formations, making it a unique and special place to visit.

SCHEDULING AND LODGING

Though Great Basin National Park is within a desert, the park proper is in the mountains. The lowest elevation within the park is about 7,000 feet, while the mountain peaks are over 11,000 feet. The park is open year-round, but camping, the café, regular cave tours, and most roads are only open from early May through late October. Because the bristlecone pines are at 11,700 feet, it makes sense to save this park for the summer months when the snow melt is gone.

It's not easy to get here from any major city, but Salt Lake City is about three and a half hours northeast, while Las Vegas is about four and a half hours southwest. Traveling from Las Vegas leads through the small town of Ely, Nevada. On a few Friday evenings in the summer, the Nevada Northern Railway operates the Great Basin Star Train that takes people to and from the park via train and then on a ranger-led tour of Great Basin National Park at night. The trip is from 7:30 to 10:30 p.m. and is a terrific way to start a visit. Seats sell out well in advance. Another option is to visit the park on a Saturday night in April through October. Rangers lead night sky programs at 7:30 and 8:00 p.m. During peak season, additional programs are offered on Tuesday, Thursday, and Sunday nights.

Within the national park there is no hard-walled lodging, though there are five campgrounds (**Upper** and **Lower Lehman, Wheeler Peak, Baker Creek,** and **Grey Cliffs**) as well as additional backcountry camping. Just outside the park in the tiny town of Baker, Nevada, lodging options include the **Stargazer Inn,** the **Whispering Elms Motel and RV Park,** the 29-room **Border Inn (and Casino),** and the new four-room **Hidden Canyon Retreat.** With 170,000 visitors concentrated over three or four months, peak travel days can see well over 1,000 visitors. Lodging reservations are important.

Kerouac's at the Stargazer Inn serves breakfast and dinner, while the Great Basin Café at the Lehman Caves Visitor Center serves lunch. The Border Inn has a small grocery store and also serves meals continuously from 6:00 a.m. to 10:00 p.m.

Reservations for Lehman Caves tours are online, with two long and two short tours typically offered each day. The tours take a maximum of 20 people and are offered from March through October.

THE TRIP

Day 1: Begin the trip at **Great Basin Visitor Center**, which has terrific videos of park highlights, especially the night sky. Enter the park and veer right onto the 24-mile round-trip **Wheeler Peak Scenic Drive.** This winding drive should take about half an hour each way. Park at the top lot (Bristlecone Pine Lot), which provides the best trail access.

Two of the park highlights are here—the **Bristlecone Trail** and the **Alpine Lakes Loop Trail**. Start to the right with the 2.7-mile loop trail, which leads to Stella Lake and then Teresa Lake and has under 500 feet of elevation gain. **Wheeler Peak** rises 3,000 feet above the trail and summer wildflowers abound. Past Teresa Lake, turn right onto **Bristlecone and Glacier Trail**. After about a mile is **Bristlecone Grove**, which has its own mini pathway among the famous trees. Heading back to the parking lot, the **Sky Islands Forest Trail** is on the right. This 0.3-mile wheelchair-accessible interpretive trail is the perfect icing on the cake. The combination of the Alpine Lake loop hike and offshoots is about 4.5 miles. Nevada has one small glacier, the **Rock Glacier**, at the end of the Bristlecone and Glacier Trail. Extending the hike to include the glacier adds about 3 miles and about 1,000 feet of elevation. Enjoy a well-earned evening in Baker.

Day 2: Bring a coat and head to the **Lehman Caves Visitor Center** and a morning **Grand Palace Tour** of Lehman Caves, which extends through the entire cave system. This highly informative ranger-led tour of otherworldly formations is a real treat. After the caves, enjoy the visitor center and a second interpretive trail around the rear and side of the center. Here is the **Rhodes Cabin**, home to early cave explorers and tour guides. The Great Basin Café at the visitor center offers lunch.

A terrific afternoon hike is the **Pole Canyon Trail.** Accessed down the hill from the Grey Cliffs camping area, this 7.4-mile hike along Baker Creek can be shortened, and even an hour or so walk on this gentle trail provides a wonderful sense of the park's rivers, streams, flowers, and views.

Consider an early dinner (restaurants close early here) and spend the evening at a ranger-led astronomy presentation. Once a month the full moon obscures the astronomy presentation and a separate full moon presentation is provided by the rangers. The full moon ranger-guided walk requires advance reservations.

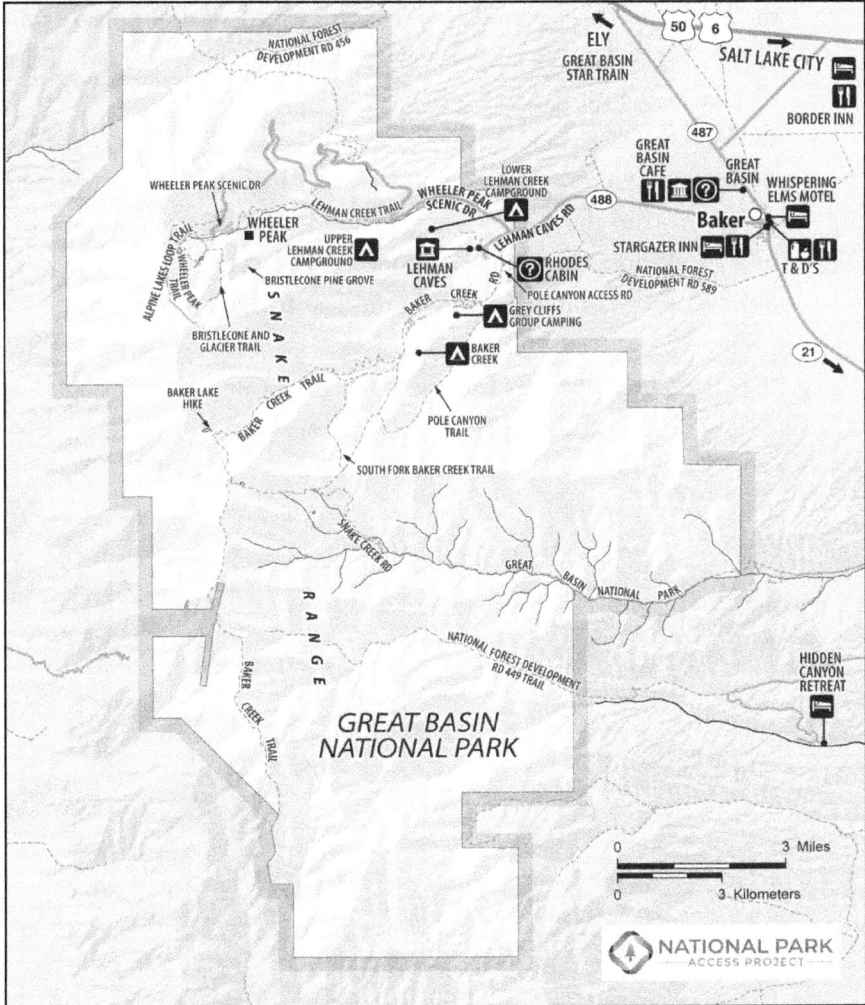

Day 3: Some of the best trails at Great Basin are long. Here are a two of the marquee hikes in the park:

- **Wheeler Peak:** From the Wheeler Peak Scenic Drive, park in the lower lot (before the Bristlecone parking lot). From here, hike 8.2 miles round trip with an elevation gain of nearly 3,000 feet to the 13,063-foot summit of Wheeler Peak. This is the high point in the park and the highest peak in Nevada, with the expected stunning panoramic views. Proper clothing and enough food and water is necessary for this high-elevation hike.
- **Baker Lake:** Right before the Lehman Caves Visitor Center is a left turn toward Grey Cliffs and Baker Creek camping. Drive to the end of this road to the Baker Creek trailhead to Baker Lake. This 10.4-mile round-trip hike climbs 2,600 feet along a creek bed full of wildflowers before climbing steeply to the lake at about 11,000 feet.

See the appendix for useful lodging, camping, and activity contact information.

ARIZONA

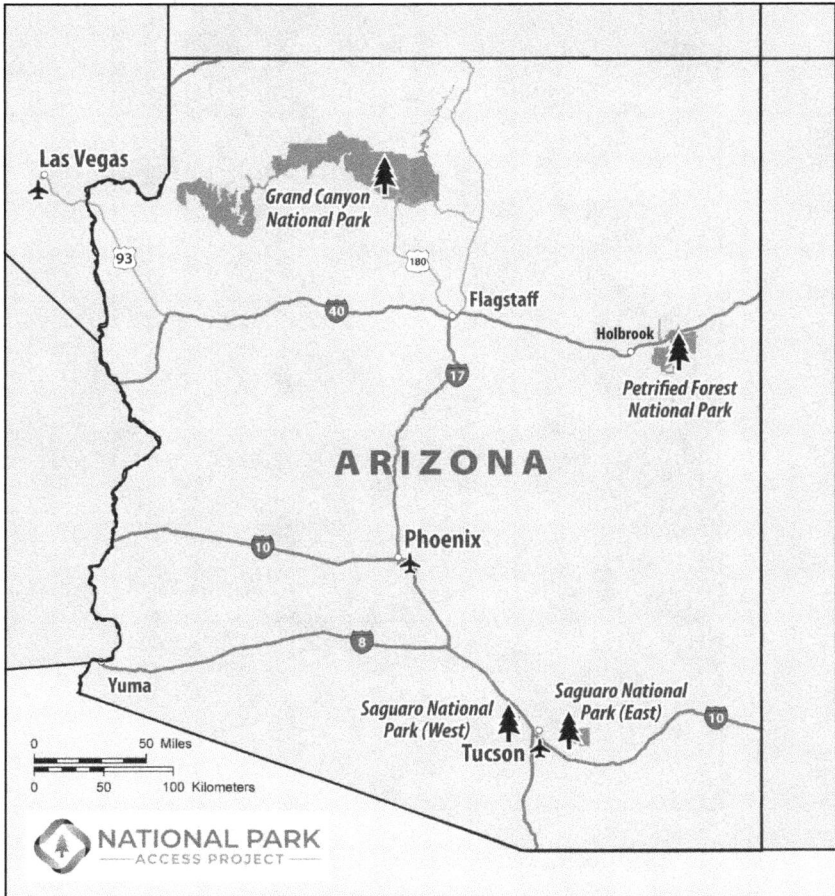

Las Vegas

Grand Canyon
National Park

93

180

40

Flagstaff

Holbrook

Petrified Forest
National Park

17

ARIZONA

10

Phoenix

8

Yuma

Saguaro National
Park (West)

Saguaro National
Park (East)

10

Tucson

| 0 | 50 Miles | |
| 0 | 50 | 100 Kilometers |

NATIONAL PARK
ACCESS PROJECT

GRAND CANYON NATIONAL PARK

Politicians wanted to mine the Grand Canyon for zinc and copper, and Theodore Roosevelt said, "No."

—Douglas Brinkley, *Wilderness Warrior: Theodore Roosevelt and the Crusade for America*

GRAND CANYON NATIONAL PARK SOUTH RIM
RALUCA MARIN/SHUTTERSTOCK

A stunning chasm in the earth visible from space, the Grand Canyon is one of the largest canyons in the world. At 277 miles long, 18 miles wide, and 6,093 feet deep, the Grand Canyon sits at the southwest corner of the Colorado Plateau, which itself encompasses 140,000 square miles covering parts of Arizona, Colorado, New Mexico, and Utah. The Colorado River carved the Grand Canyon between five and six million years ago, revealing a cross section of earth dating back nearly two billion years.

Archaeological finds indicate that humans have been in the area for at least 12,000 years. Known as Ancestral Puebloans, these first occupiers were followed by the Paiute, Navajo, Zuni, and Hopi tribes. For the past 800 years, the Havasupai people have called the area home and are today involved in commercial tourism throughout the region.

Though Spanish exploders visited in the 1500s, Western influence took off in the mid-1880s when miners, surveyors, and others determined that the Grand Canyon would be more profitable as a tourist destination. President Benjamin Harrison granted federal protection to the area as a forest reserve in 1893, the railroad made its way from Flagstaff to the south rim in 1901, and President Theodore Roosevelt named the Grand Canyon a federal game reserve and later a national monument in 1908. In 1919 Grand Canyon achieved national park status.

Grand Canyon National Park is one of the largest parks in the Lower 48 at 1.2 million acres. In 1975 the park ceded 185,000 acres to the Havasupai people after they successfully convinced the United States Congress to grant this once-ancestral land back to the tribe. Grand Canyon sees about six million visitors each year. Of those, only about 150,000 visit the North Rim.

SCHEDULING AND LODGING

Grand Canyon South Rim is easy to reach, with Flagstaff Pulliam Airport an hour and a half to the south and Phoenix Sky Harbor International Airport three and a half hours to the south. McCarren International Airport in Las Vegas is about four and a half hours west of both the South and North Rims.

For a memorable experience, start the trip in Williams, Arizona (near Flagstaff), and take the Grand Canyon Railway to Grand Canyon Village on the South Rim.

The best time of year to visit is late spring (May/June) and early fall (late September/October). Snow covers the canyon rim from November through mid-April, and summer can be intolerably hot and dry. North Rim winters last somewhat longer, making the window to visit both rims at the same time even smaller—approximately mid-May through mid-June and mid-September through mid-October.

Grand Canyon has some of the best lodging in the national park system. On the South Rim, **El Tovar** is a jewel in the crown of the national park lodges. Perched on the rim of the canyon, the hotel has rooms with sweeping views and inside and outside rim-view dining. Next door are three modest motel-style options—**Thunderbird**, **Kachina**, and **Bright Angel**. Any room on the second floor of either Thunderbird or Kachina provides a canyon view. Bright Angel Lodge is larger, with some canyon-view rooms and others facing the parking lot and train station. This lodge offers select rooms with shared bathrooms at a reduced price. If traveling with three or fewer people, consider the Bright Angel free-standing cabins. Away from the rim are two additional in-park options—the **Maswik Lodge** and the **Yavapai Lodge and RV Park**. In addition to the dining room at El Tovar, Bright Angel has two restaurants and a coffee shop, and Yavapai has a casual dining hall as well as a tavern. There is one hotel on the North Rim—**Grand Canyon Lodge** and dining room.

Ample camping is available both in Grand Canyon Village and on the North Rim. **Mather Campground** in the South Rim village offers 319 sites, while the **North Rim Campground** offers 90 campsites. Both have nearby general stores.

Though the rims are spectacular, prime time for many is in the canyon. At the bottom of the canyon is the historic **Phantom Ranch** with 30 backcountry camping sites, 11 cabins, bunkhouses with a limited number of beds, and a restaurant (reservations only). Beds and cabins are available via a lottery system, though a campsite is relatively easy to reserve and campers may eat breakfast and dinner at the Phantom Ranch Canteen. If the campsites are scarce at Phantom Ranch, consider camping at the fascinating **Indian Gardens Campground**, a wooded area on the canyon wall between the South Rim and the Colorado River. This grass- and tree-filled section is full of deer and woodland animals, making it a unique place to spend the night.

MULES FOR HIRE

From the South Rim, visitors can hire a mule for a ride to and from Indian Gardens or Phantom Ranch. Overnight backpackers can also use mule service to carry gear to and from either location. Mule rides require reservations significantly in advance, but gear service can be arranged with less notice. Short one-hour canyon rides are offered from the North Rim stables.

RIM TO RIM CHALLENGE

The rim-to-rim challenge—hiking the 24 miles between the South and North Rim—is on many a bucket list. The classic route starts at the North Rim and hikes down about 3,700 feet over 7 miles to the **Cottonwood Campground**. Some hikers stop here for the night, and others hike the remaining 7 miles and about 2,300 feet to Phantom Ranch to spend one or two nights. The uphill hike to Bright Angel on the South Rim is another 10 miles and 6,000 feet of elevation gain. This challenge is also logistical in that hikers either need to hike back or get a (long) ride to their starting point.

RAFTING THE GRAND CANYON

Rafting the Colorado River is a wonderful addition to visiting one or both of the Grand Canyon rims. The launch area is typically Lee's Ferry, located about four hours northeast of the South Rim and two hours northeast of the North Rim, and the pullout is Lake Mead or a midpoint like Phantom Ranch for those with a guide service that can accommodate midpoint departures. Once you begin, there is a decent time commitment, with the float trip to Phantom Ranch taking around five days and the trip to Lake Mead about another seven days.

Another option is to raft the Glen Canyon section of the Colorado River before the difficult-to-exit Grand Canyon. A half-day motorized raft trip is operated out of Page, Arizona (about four hours from the South Rim), by Wilderness River Adventures. This option puts in below Glen Canyon Dam and exits at Lee's Ferry, thus missing the Grand Canyon proper. This narrated trip provides spectacular views of low canyon walls and associated petroglyphs. The time commitment is approximately 10:00 a.m. to 3:30 p.m. plus driving.

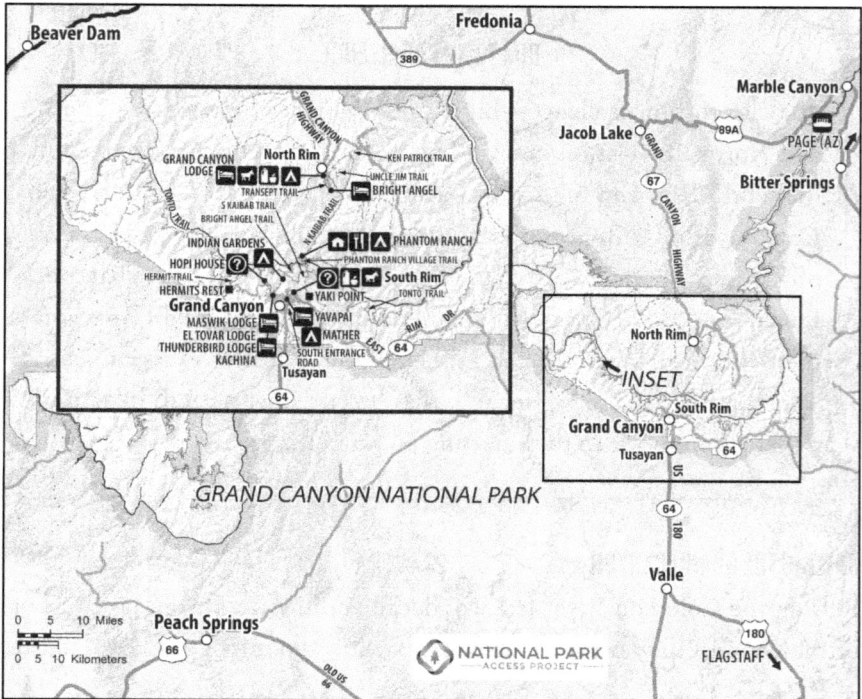

THE TRIP

Day 1: The hub of the park is **Grand Canyon Village** and the paved **South Rim** walk extending 2 miles from **Bright Angel** to the **Grand Canyon Visitor Center**. In the middle is the **Hopi House** with historical exhibits and sweeping views. From both the visitor center and the Bright Angel area there are various ranger talks and walks throughout the day. The visitor center is new and has wonderful films and other exhibits as well as a large bookstore and café.

This well-organized park has a shuttle serving the South Rim, which extends well beyond the paved walking area. The shuttle reaches **Hermits Rest** about 7 miles to the west and **Yaki Point** 5 miles to the east. For additional and much less crowded yet level hiking, take the shuttle to one of these points and walk back to the village center. Alternatively, rent bicycles at the visitor center complex and see both areas. Most roads are paved and lightly traveled.

Day 2 (and Day 3 if camping in the canyon): The classic full Grand Canyon hike is 17.5 miles, starting at the **South Kaibab Trail**, heading down into the Grand Canyon to the Colorado River (or a bit beyond to Phantom Ranch), staying the night, and hiking back up the **Bright Angel Trail** through Indian Gardens. This circuit has the advantage of the hike down being somewhat exposed so the views are spectacular, while the hike up goes through the shaded Indian Gardens where hikers can rest and rehydrate.

For a serious hike into the canyon without staying at Phantom Ranch, there is a cutoff partway down the South Kaibab trail called **The Tipoff** that connects with the **Tonto Trail** to Indian Gardens and the leads up the Bright Angel Trail to the South Rim. This is a 12.5-mile loop and can be done in one long day.

Beyond these two long hikes, there are infinite options to hike partway into the Grand Canyon. From Bright Angel to Indian Gardens is 9 miles round trip and has options along the way to stop and turn around. The **Mile and a Half Resthouse** and the **Three Mile Resthouse** are both terrific places to have a snack in an open-walled stone shelter while enjoying the shade and the view.

Day 4: Prepare for a single-day **raft trip** of the Colorado River by either staying the prior night in Page, Arizona, or getting up early to make the drive. In the shoulder season, check in is at 10:00 a.m. with departure at 11:00 a.m., while high season also has a 12:00 p.m. departure option. The trip finishes between 3:00 p.m. and 5:00 p.m., providing enough time to get to the North Rim if desired.

Day 5: The drive to the **North Rim** culminates at **Bright Angel Point**. Here is the Grand Canyon Lodge as well as dining, a campground, general store, gas station, and mule stables. There is plenty of hiking, including the rim-view 1.6-mile **Transept Trail** and a 3-mile loop (**Ken Patrick Trail** and **Uncle Jim Trail**) with a stunning canyon overlook point. The **North Kaibab Trail** heads down from the North Rim into the canyon and to Phantom Ranch, with lots of stops along the way.

See the appendix for useful lodging, camping, and activity contact information.

PETRIFIED FOREST NATIONAL PARK

Here, one sees the Painted Desert with its fantastic coloring, the petrified forests . . . There is no place in the world at present so accessible, and at the same time so full of the most romantic interest, as are the territories of Arizona.

—John G. Bourke, from his 1874 book *On the Border with Crook*

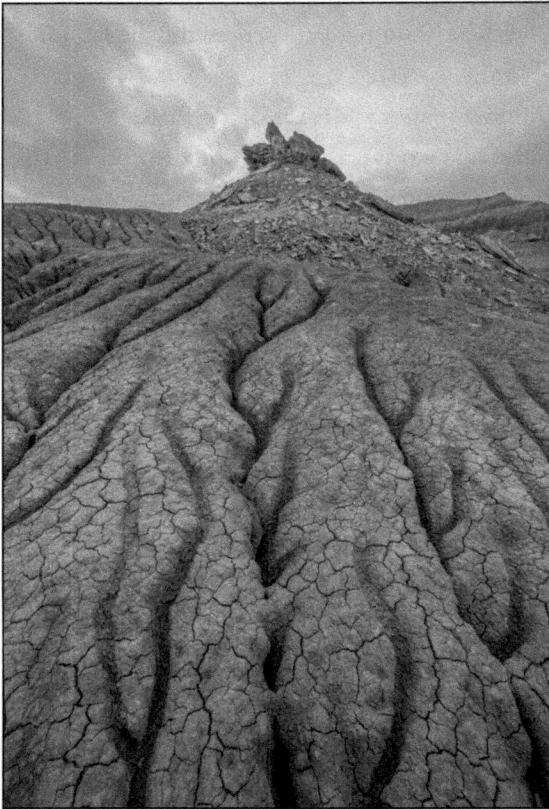

TEPEES FORMATION IN PETRIFIED FOREST NATIONAL PARK
STEVEN GUO/SHUTTERSTOCK

Petrified Forest National Park is named for the petrified logs found in great numbers in the middle of the desert in northern Arizona. In addition to ubiquitous petrified wood, the park's northern section encompasses the incredibly beautiful Painted Desert. Unless camping under the stars and slowly visiting this fascinating area, it's easy to see the park in a single day.

Petrified Forest traces its origin to the Late Triassic Period about 225 million years ago. Pangea, earth's connected single land mass, was breaking up at this time. Weather patterns buried these trees under silt, ash, and dirt, with the forest then separating around the world as the tectonic plates shifted. Similar petrified trees have been found in numerous places around the world, though Petrified Forest National Park represents the largest concentration of fossilized wood in the world.

About 60 million years ago the Colorado Plateau, on which the park sits, began to rise and create erosion and other soil disruption. The "trees" became visible and were later understood to have been transformed via the process of permineralization, which means that the organic tree materials had been replaced with minerals, mostly silicate such as quartz. Because quartz presents in various ways—micro gemlike, blue agate, pink, and so forth—the quartz trees are varied in appearance and truly spectacular. These fallen majestic soldiers, when broken, appear perfectly sliced in half because quartz breaks in a clean line.

Petrified Forest National Monument was created by President Theodore Roosevelt in 1906 and was converted into a national park by Congress with the signature of President John F. Kennedy in 1962. The park sees around 650,000 visitors each year, about a tenth of the nearby Grand Canyon.

SCHEDULING AND LODGING

Located in northwest Arizona, Petrified Forest is one and a half hours east of Flagstaff, three and a half hours northeast of Phoenix, and three hours southeast of Grand Canyon Village. Though there is no lodging in the park, the small town of Holbrook 20 minutes west has a number of midpriced hotels. While there isn't a formal campground in the park, it's easy to get a backcountry camping permit from the ranger. Some of the backcountry sites are close enough to parking to make them similar to car camping. In the northern Painted Desert section of the park is a secondary visitor center with an attached gift shop and restaurant—the Painted Desert Diner. This is a nice place to get snacks or lunch.

Petrified Forest can be visited anytime. Like any high desert, summers are blistering and winters are bracing, but the park is open year-round. The best times to visit are spring and fall.

THE TRIP

Day 1: To best access the Petrified Forest interpretive exhibits, start the trip on the south side, entering via Highway 180, and stop at the **Rainbow Forest Museum and Visitor Center**. This is a relatively small building with some terrific exhibits and the ability to walk through the **Giant Logs** immediately behind the building and the **Long Logs** across the road in front.

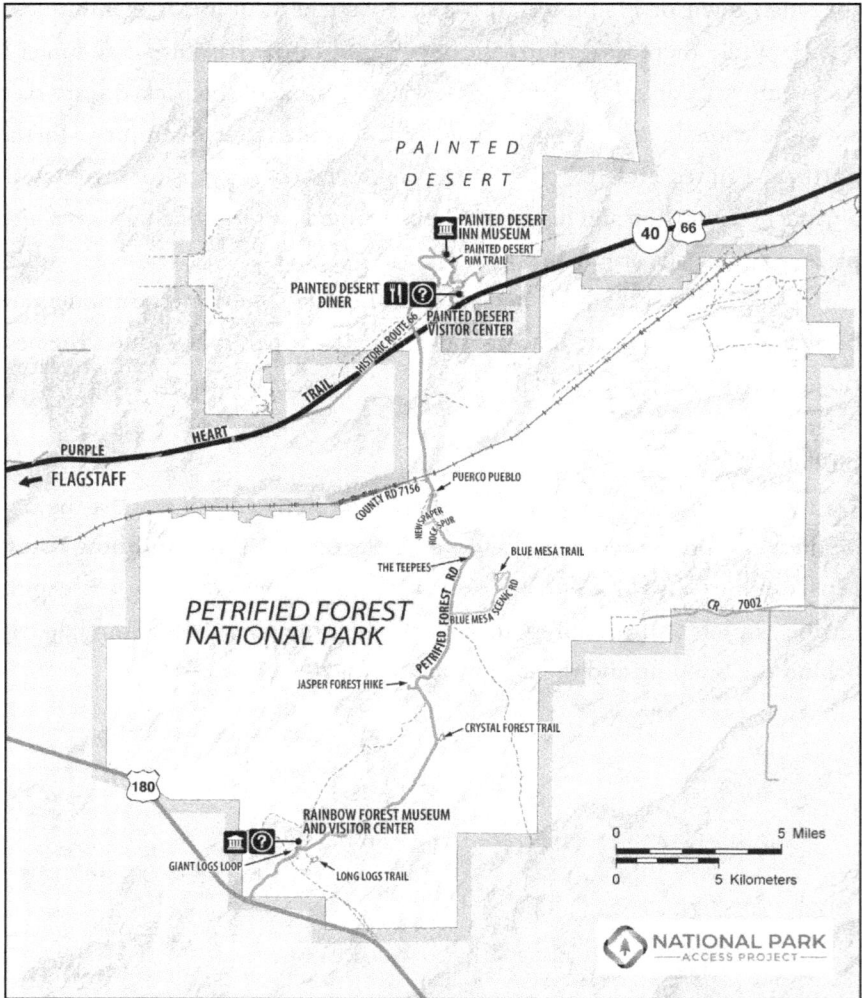

The park is designed such that after the visitor center, travelers may drive limited distances and enjoy short, level hikes exploring the park's various features. Start by driving about 10 miles north to the 0.75-mile **Crystal Forest** walking loop. The sheer volume of fallen quartz trees is fascinating, as is the potential to get close to these amazing specimens. Drive north another approximately 5 miles to the second hike—**Jasper Forest**. This hike extends 2.5

miles round trip through a dense section of fallen petrified wood and around Eagle Nest Rock. After the Jasper Forest hike, leave the main concentration of petrified wood and head north to the **Blue Mesa** turnoff on your right. This area offers a 3.5-mile loop drive and a 1-mile round-trip hiking trail. Blue Mesa extends through hills of unique bluish bentonite clay as well as some petrified wood.

Continue north and stop at **Newspaper Rock**, where there are more than 650 petroglyphs. This rock art dates from 650 to 2,000 years ago and is accessible from a viewing platform. The final stop in this section is **Puerco Pueblo**, a paved 0.3-mile walk through the remains of a hundred-room pueblo. This area also has petroglyphs and provides closer viewing.

From here, head north into the **Painted Desert**. Stop for lunch at the Painted Desert Diner and adjacent **Painted Desert Visitor Center** and then continue to the **Painted Desert Inn Museum**, which closes at 4:30 p.m. This lovely adobe building has an incredible view of the Painted Desert and plenty of descriptive signage. Tours are self-guided. Once finished viewing the museum, the 1-mile round-trip **Painted Desert Rim Trail** is right outside. This is one of the most beautiful trails in the park and is not to be missed.

See the appendix for useful lodging, camping, and activity contact information.

SAGUARO NATIONAL PARK

[A] great natural area for maintaining the botanical and zoological forms of the Southwest under natural conditions.

—Homer L. Shantz, president of the University of Arizona, describing his vision for Saguaro National Monument

CACTUS IN SAGUARO NATIONAL PARK
MANUELA DURSON/SHUTTERSTOCK

Pronounced "sahwahrow," the saguaro cactus is the star of the park. These distinctive tall cacti grow only in the Sonoran Desert from southern Arizona into Mexico. Living as long as 150 years, saguaro cacti grow slowly, only adding side arms midway through their life. They are protected in Arizona and cannot be cut down.

Such large cacti, often 40 feet high or taller, need an incredible reservoir of water to make it through the long, dry months common in the desert. Because Tucson has a rainy season, even called a monsoon season, from mid-June to mid-September, there is ample time for the plants to fill themselves with water, some reaching peak weight of 3,200 to 4,800 pounds when saturated. Saguaro cacti are home to many animals, but the most noticeable are the gilded flicker and Gila woodpecker that create holes in the cacti. Hikers will see birds flying in and out of these cavernous nests all day.

Saguaro National Park is relatively new, only designated in 1994. The park is separated into east and west sections, around 35 miles apart and requiring a 45-minute to an hour drive between sections. The city of Tucson lies in the middle, with four small mountain ranges surrounding the city—the Tucson Mountains (Saguaro West), the Rincon Mountains (Saguaro East), the Santa Rita Mountains to the south, and the Santa Catalina Mountains to the north. Saguaro National Park is a juxtaposition of desert, mountains, and the central city of Tucson. There is something for everyone.

SCHEDULING AND LODGING

Tucson International Airport makes this park easy to reach. And the city of Tucson, with lodging ranging from budget motels to world-class spas, makes staying here a breeze. The best time to visit is mid-October to mid-April, with March showcasing the famous desert wildflowers, including the flowering saguaro—the state flower of Arizona. Saguaro National Park does not have front-country camping. Instead, there are various small, somewhat difficult-to-reach backcountry campgrounds. Reservations are available on Recreation.gov.

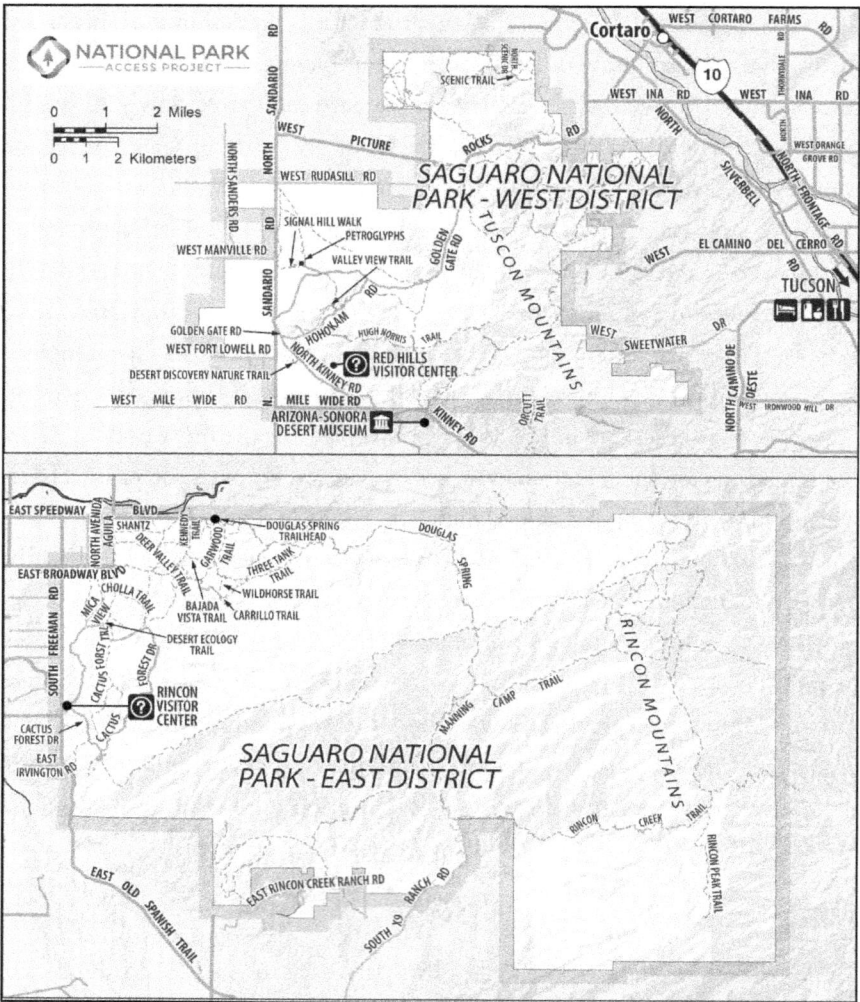

THE TRIP

Day 1: Starting a trip outside the park seems a bit odd, but in the case of Saguaro National Park, one of the most terrific activities is actually just outside the park boundary. The **Arizona Sonora Desert Museum** is immediately to the south of Saguaro West and provides a wonderful introduction to the natural activity happening all around you—activity that in a desert is hard to see. Enjoy the javelinas (miniature wild pigs), flowering cacti gardens, desert birds, caves with bats, and much more. This indoor and extensive outdoor complex with café can take up to four hours to tour. Some rank it among the top museums in the United States.

There are no services in Saguaro West, so pack water and a lunch or snacks. From the museum, head north into Saguaro West and stop at the **Red Hills Visitor Center**. After the visit, embark on walks and hikes through the fascinating saguaro. A first stop can be the 0.4-mile **Desert Discovery Loop Trail** just north of the visitor center. Continue north and turn right on Hohokam Road (**Scenic Bajada Loop Drive**), which accesses many of the trails on this side of the park, including the 8-mile round-trip **Hugh Norris Trail** on the right. Walk as much of this trail as comfortable, or try the 0.8-mile **Valley View Trail** on the left. Continue on Hohokam Road until its terminus and turn left onto **Golden Gate Road** to complete the scenic loop drive. Panoramic views showcase the vast undeveloped countryside and the amazing cacti. Stop on your right at **Signal Hill** and take a short walk through the **petroglyphs**.

Day 2: Most of Saguaro East is not dense with the famous saguaro cacti, though the **Douglas Spring** trailhead serves a number of hiking trails that are relatively flat and travel through thousands of the famous plants. The park is thought to be home to 1.6 million saguaro cacti overall, and that statistic is believable when hiking in this section. It's about 7 miles from the trailhead to the **Rincon Visitor Center**, which offers limited exhibits and birds in their cacti nests right outside the window. This hike can be hot and dry, so bring lots of water and start as early as possible. Taxi or ride-share back to your car at the Douglas Springs trailhead. The 8-mile **Cactus Forest Drive**, which begins and ends at the Rincon Visitor Center and travels through similar terrain, is also a must-see. The loop drive accesses a small paved walk through the cacti. Saguaro East is in the shadow of the beautiful Rincon Mountain Range where most of the backcountry camping is located.

See the appendix for useful lodging, camping, and activity contact information.

UTAH

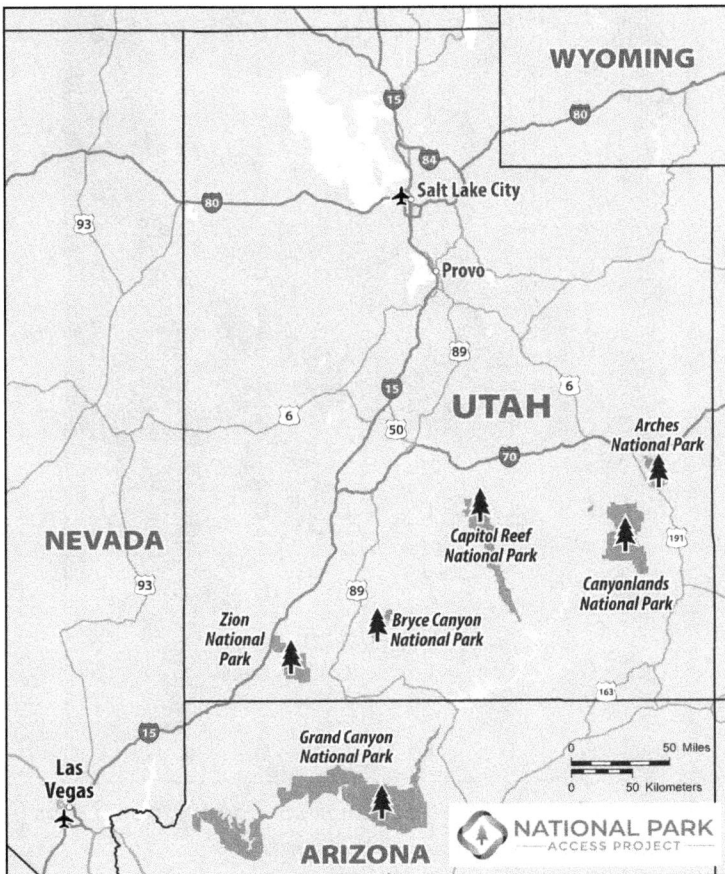

ZION NATIONAL PARK

*These are the Temples of God, built without the use of human hands.
A man can worship God among these great cathedrals as well as in any
man-made church—this is Zion.*

—Mormon pioneer Isaac Behunin in 1862 when
he saw what is now Zion National Park

THE NARROWS AND SENTINEL MOUNTAIN, ZION NATIONAL PARK
JKO PHOTOS/SHUTTERSTOCK

Located in southwest Utah, Zion National Park encompasses 146,000 acres of high desert on the Markagunt Plateau section of the larger Colorado Plateau. Though the park has three canyon systems—Kolob, Wildcat, and Zion—the vast majority of travelers focus their visit on Zion Canyon. Considered by many to be one of the most beautiful oasis-like areas in the country, Zion Canyon was carved by what is now named the Virgin River. This magical place begins in the busy town of Springdale, then past the visitor center into the lush mouth of the canyon. The canyon road (Zion Canyon Scenic Drive) extends for 8 miles, with canyon walls progressively narrowing until canyon access is only on foot. Beautiful base-canyon hikes, as well as the famous and precarious Angels Landing canyon wall hike, deliver a breathtaking outdoor experience.

The native people most closely associated with the area are the Southern Paiutes, known to have been present here for at least the last 1,000 years and still living today in parts of the region. Western influence was propelled by Mormon pioneers in the 1850s, and by 1858 Mormon settlers were living in and near Zion Canyon. In the decade to follow, Mormon families farmed the canyon floor and Mormon settler Isaac Behunin named it Zion Canyon. This important religious term is translated as "the promised land." By the 1870s the Zion region was broadly explored and was federally protected by President Howard Taft in 1909, but under the native name Mukuntuweap National Monument. The Mormon uproar was swift and sustained, and by 1919 the park's name was changed to Zion National Monument. By the end of 1919, Zion had been enlarged and become a national park. In 1956 the park was enlarged again when the Kolob Canyon section was added.

SCHEDULING AND LODGING

About two and a half hours east of Las Vegas, Zion is relatively easy to reach. The park is open year-round, though the best time to visit is in the spring and fall. Cars are not allowed inside Zion Canyon from March through November except for those staying at the park's only lodge—**Zion Lodge**. This beautiful lodge on the Virgin River overlooking the canyon wall is worth the splurge. Ample additional lodging at many price points is located at the park entrance in the town of Springdale.

This is an easy place to camp, both due to the generally nice weather, but also because the two reservable campgrounds, **Watchman** and **South**, are close to the main entrance on either side of the visitor center, both fronting the Virgin River. The visitor center operates ticketed shuttles into the park. It is very important to buy your tickets in advance, as they sell out.

Zion Lodge has a nice dining room open for breakfast, lunch, and dinner as well as the seasonal Castle Dome Café open from approximately March through November. The lodge gift shop and visitor center sell snacks. Springdale has multiple grocery stores.

Though Springdale is the hub, the park actually has three entrances. The other two are the northwest Kolob Canyon, which has a short viewpoint road as well as backcountry trail access leading 40 miles into Zion Canyon, and Zion Mount Caramel Highway, which enters from the east. The trip below assumes both these secondary entrances are seen on the last day.

RIVERSIDE TRAIL, THE NARROWS

A walking trip into the Narrows is a signature activity in this park. At the end of Zion Canyon Scenic Drive begins the **Riverside Trail** at 1.9 miles round trip along the banks of the Virgin River. At the midpoint of this walk, hikers can continue hiking in the river itself, known as a hike through **The Narrows of Zion Canyon**. The walk can be quite short or extend miles into the canyon and its offshoots. To best enjoy yourself, water shoes, waders, and a walking stick are a must. These can all be rented in Springdale but in peak season need to be reserved in advance.

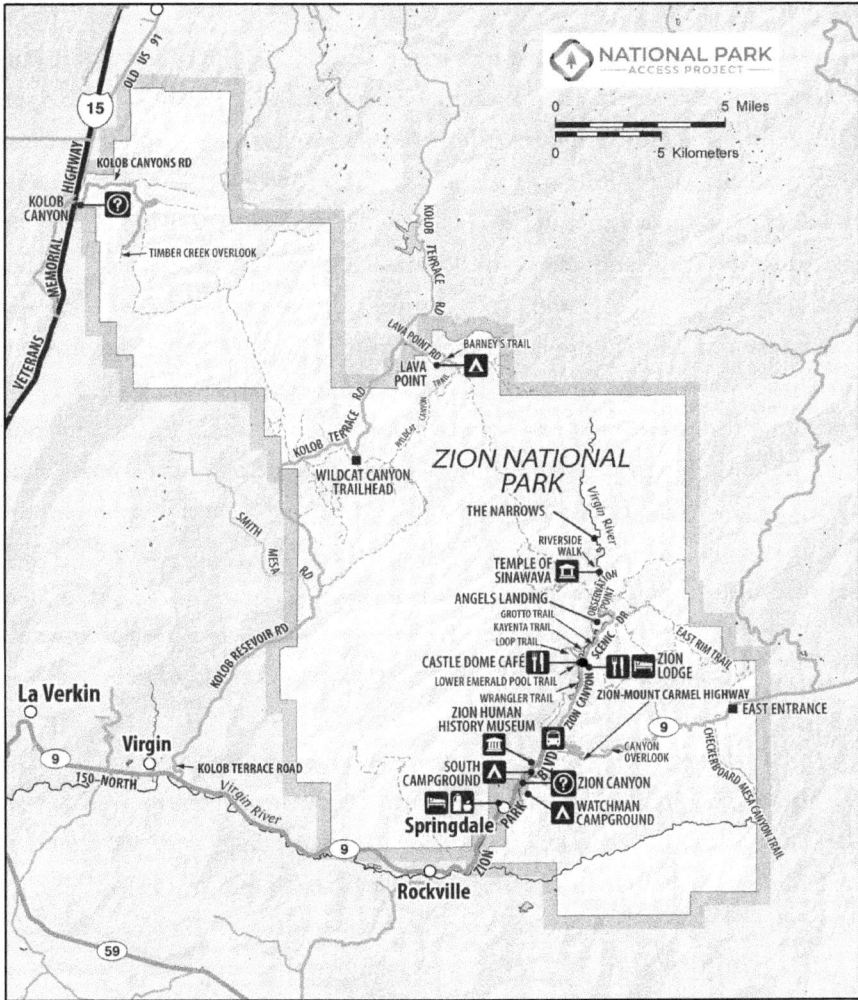

Though rare, the Virgin River and its tributaries can flash flood—not only during spring runoff but also in times of heavy rain. There have been at least three multiple-fatality events since the 1960s, including of groups with significant outdoor experience. If planning to walk the Narrows, consult the hourly weather forecast and be aware that this hike is considered dangerous.

THE TRIP

Day 1: Start at the **Zion Canyon Visitor Center** and the nearby **Zion Human History Museum**. Then, either take the shuttle or drive to Zion Canyon Lodge. This is a hub for hiking and here there are two great options—short and moderate versus long and steep. The short loop hike is from the lodge to lower then upper **Emerald Pools** (0.8 miles, 650 feet elevation), down on the **Kayenta Trail**, and across the Virgin River to **The Grotto** and back to the lodge. This is an easy and lovely 3 miles. The longer connected hike, and one not suitable for children, is **Angels Landing.** On many a bucket list, this 5-mile round-trip hike starts from the Kayenta trailhead and climbs 1,600 feet along the canyon wall. The final half mile requires holding a chain "railing" while walking along a precipice. Hands must be free for this nail biter, and young, or even not-so-young, children and anyone afraid of heights are highly discouraged. Angels Landing provides sweeping views of the plateau, canyon, and Virgin River.

Day 2: From the lodge or the visitor center, bring your river hiking gear and take the shuttle to the **Temple of Sinawava** at the end of Zion Canyon Scenic Drive. Here is the trailhead for the level Riverwalk Trail, a 1-mile pathway that takes you into the Narrows, also known as the **North Fork of the Virgin River**. A typical hike is about 3 miles into the canyon to **Wall Street**. This area connects with **Orderville Canyon** on the right and, after another half mile, with **Veiled Falls**. This hike is at least six hours, or a full day of somewhat tough walking on the river bottom.

Day 3: The **Zion Mount Carmel Highway** turns immediately east upon entering the park, bypassing the shuttle-only Zion Canyon and leading through a tunnel to the top of the canyon's east rim. There are several parking areas here, accessing short (**Canyon Overlook**) and long (**East Rim Trail**) hikes that deliver spectacular postcard views of the full Zion Canyon. After exploring this area, and upon leaving Zion Canyon via Highway 9 in Springdale, the dirt 21-mile each way **Kolob Terrace Road** is on the right at the town of Virgin and leads to the picnic-perfect **Lava Point** with views of

Wildcat Canyon. After enjoying this area, continue west on Highway 9 and north on Highway 17 and Interstate 15 to reach the **Kolob Canyons Visitor Center** and the **Kolob Canyons Road**, which provides views of the smaller Kolob Canyon and the 1-mile round trip **Timber Creek Overlook Trail**.

See the appendix for useful lodging, camping, and activity contact information.

BRYCE CANYON NATIONAL PARK

It's a hell of a place to lose a cow!
—attributed to Ebenezer Bryce regarding the canyon

BRYCE CANYON NATIONAL PARK
KEIKI/SHUTTERSTOCK

Bryce Canyon National Park is situated on the edge of the Paunsaugunt Plateau, created approximately 10 to 20 million years ago by an uplift from the larger Colorado Plateau. Though the park measures 60 square miles, the heart of the park, the famous and oft-photographed hoodoos in the Bryce Amphitheater, comprise less than 6 square miles. While the pine forests of the plateau are lovely, a primary reason to go to Bryce is to see and hike through the bizarre, spectacular, strange, stunning, and unbelievable hoodoos. Formed from silt and soil deposits starting 97 million years ago, the hoodoos have been selectively eroded through freeze and thaw cycles that occur around 200 days each year.

Home to native peoples as long as 15,000 years ago, the first believed inhabitants in the Bryce Canyon area were the Paleo-Indians, followed by the Anasazi, Ancestral Puebloans, and Fremont peoples around 700 and then the Paiutes from 1200. Western exploration began in the 1700s but took off around 1875, led in part by surveyor Major John Wesley Powell. Settlement also began around this time, with Mormon Ebenezer Bryce working to irrigate the broader area and render it suitable for farming and ranching. The plateau and canyon became known as Bryce's Canyon and, through railroad exploration and other travel, caught the eye of preservationists. President Harding established Bryce Canyon as a national monument in 1923, and it gained national park status by 1928. Bryce Canyon sees just under three million visitors each year.

SCHEDULING AND LODGING

Located about four hours northeast of Las Vegas, the road to Bryce Canyon passes by Zion National Park. Many people combine the two parks, and also perhaps Utah's Capitol Reef National Park, located about two hours northeast of Bryce Canyon. If traveling south, Grand Canyon's North Rim is about three hours from Bryce.

The highest national park in Utah, at 8,000 to 9,000 feet elevation, Bryce can remain cold and snowy well into spring. While the park is open year-round, the Park Road is closed in winter, and the historic freestanding cabins comprising the **Lodge at Bryce Canyon** are open seasonally from around the beginning of April to the end of October. Outside the park, lodging options in nearby Old Bryce Town include **Best Western Plus Ruby's Inn**, **Best Western Plus Bryce Canyon**, and **Bryce View Lodge**. The in-park campground is the **Sunset Campground** near the Bryce Amphitheater. **Ruby's Inn RV Park and Campground** is immediately outside the park boundary. In-park dining options include the Lodge at Bryce Canyon Restaurant, Valhalla Pizzeria and Coffee Shop, and the General Store. Old Bryce Town also has ample dining choices and a market.

An inspiring activity is a full (or near-full) moon hike through the hoodoos. Check the moon cycle before you go. Bryce is also an International Dark Sky Park.

SHUTTLE SERVICE AND RAINBOW POINT SHUTTLE TOUR

Guests of the Lodge at Bryce Canyon may park their car at the amphitheater-fronting lodge during their stay. For others, the park offers free shuttle service to the Bryce Amphitheater rim and also Old Bryce Town. From April through November, the park also offers the free, narrated Rainbow Point Shuttle Tour twice daily. This tour covers park history and extends to the farthest points on the 18-mile Park Road—**Rainbow Point** and **Yovimpa Point**. Cars are permitted on this road.

THE TRIP

Day 1: Start at the **Bryce Canyon Visitor Center** and, after getting oriented, first drive the Park Road even if later planning to take the Rainbow Point bus tour. The road has various viewpoint pullouts that are worthwhile as well as the Rainbow Point/Yovimpa Point terminus. Here there is a parking lot and a short 1-mile hike—the **Bristlecone Loop Trail**. Extending through pine trees with wonderful views, this is a great place to get oriented to the larger area. The distinctive and long-lived bristlecone pine can be found here.

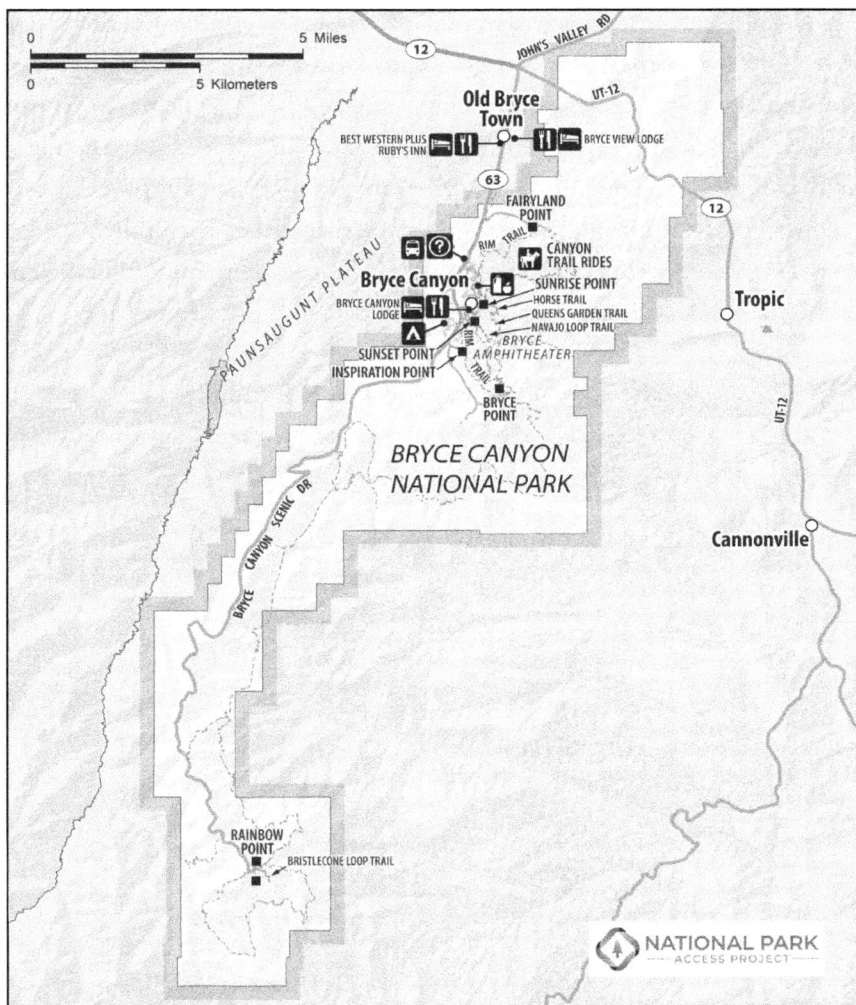

Continue to the **Bryce Amphitheater** and the **Rim Trail.** This trail runs the 11-mile western length of the Amphitheater from **Inspiration Point** on the south to **Fairyland Point** at the north. Shuttle buses from the lodge serve both locations, enabling the hiking distance to be cut roughly in half. The Rim Trail looks down on the hoodoos and provides a broad perspective of the massive expanse of beautiful, otherworldly hoodoo spires.

Day 2: The must-do activity in the park is a hike into the hoodoos. Two trails, **Queens Garden** and **Navajo Loop**, form a loop of about 3.5 miles. The hike is fairly steep at times, though wide and well planned. As with any high-desert hike, be sure to bring enough food and water. Ranger-guided hikes happen often and help bring these formations to life. Split the day into two parts, with a morning or afternoon horseback ride. The bridle path has a winder circumference than the hoodoo hike, providing more time in surrounding forests. Canyon Trail Rides offers two- and three-hour trips.

See the appendix for useful lodging, camping, and activity contact information.

CAPITOL REEF NATIONAL PARK

The present Superintendent recognizes the conflict of private land but can see no reason why [a] majority of present owners cannot continue to reside and operate their ranches within the monument. With encouragement from the Service these owners can be persuaded to develop and maintain their property in conformity with standards to be established.

—park superintendent Paul R. Franke in 1943 regarding the Fruita settlements, as quoted by Cathy A. Gilbert and Kathleen L. McKoy in their *Cultural Landscape Report: Fruita Rural Historic District, Capitol Reef National Park*

HICKMAN BRIDGE, CAPITOL REEF NATIONAL PARK
MACIEJ BLEDOWSKI/SHUTTERSTOCK

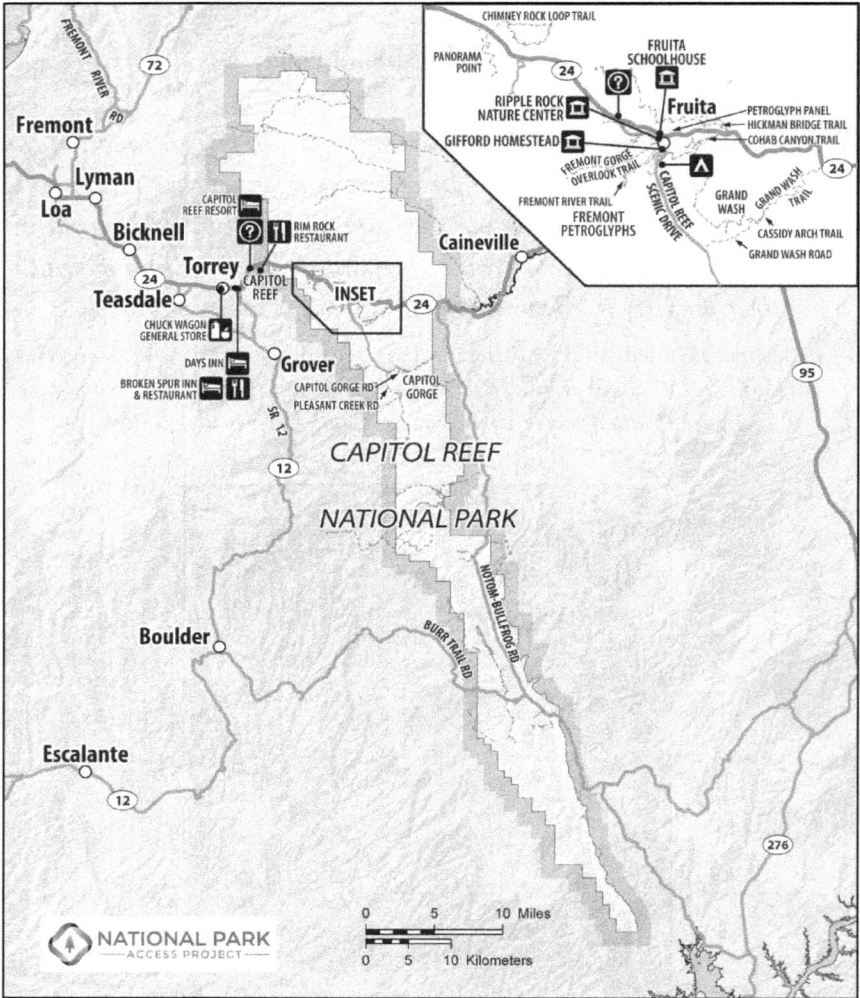

Located in central Utah, Capitol Reef National Park preserves about 250,000 acres of high-desert sandstone and limestone cliffs as well as a desert river valley and historic farming area. With elevations between 6,000 and 9,000 feet, this Colorado Plateau park has a high-desert climate. Home to the Fremont peoples from about 600 to 1800, a must-see feature of the park is the Fremont Petroglyphs found carved throughout the park. Mormon settlers arrived around 1870, making a home of the same Fremont River Valley previously occupied by the Fremont people. Naming their settlement "the Junction" and later Fruita, this exceptional area for agriculture became a subject of dispute as the National Park Service sought to preserve Capitol Reef in the late 1930s when the park was named a national monument by President Franklin Roosevelt. Land disputes continued into the 1940s, but ultimately the inholdings were acquired by the United States government and the area was made a national park in 1971. Now known as the Fruita Rural Historic District and home to the Capitol Reef Visitor Center, Fruita offers preserved Mormon settler–era buildings, a working farm, and even pie and treats for sale at the Gifford House open each year from mid-March through October.

As with many of Utah's spectacular parks, the highlight is the stark sandstone landscape. A crown jewel of the park is the 100-mile Waterpocket Fold, a giant wrinkle or buckle in the earth's crust extending from Thousand Lake Mountain down to Lake Powell. The park is named for the white sandstone domes in areas of the Waterpocket Fold that to some appear similar to domes placed on capitol buildings. The park is long (north to south) and narrow (east to west). There is only one major road in the park, Highway 24, extending across Waterpocket Fold from west to east. Waterpocket Fold is a backdrop for smaller wonders, including Chimney Rock, Hickman Arch, Cassidy Arch, Capitol Gorge, and Cohab Canyon. The north and south areas of the park have limited access and are available for backcountry hiking and camping.

SCHEDULING AND LODGING

Capitol Reef is about three and a half hours south of Salt Lake City and two and a half hours west of Canyonlands and Arches National Parks. Though the park is open year-round, peak visitation is in the summer, while optimal weather is in May, June, and September. As noted above, Gifford House is open from mid-March through the end of October, a proxy for the park's high season.

Though there are no lodges inside the park, the village of Torrey just to the east has ample lodging, including the budget **Broken Spur Inn** and **Days Inn** as well the more upscale **Capitol Reef Resort**. The first two options are in Torrey proper, while Capitol Reef Resort is located just far enough west to be surrounded by red stone cliffs rather than farmland. Stay in this area if possible. Both areas offer dining while, the Chuck Wagon General Store is in Torrey. The place to camp is the **Fruita Campground** on the Fremont River. Capitol Reef National Park is a Dark Sky Park with virtually no light pollution and offers spectacular stargazing.

THE TRIP

Day 1: Upon entering the park from Torrey, make sure to stop at **Panorama Point**, located about 5 miles west of **Fruita**. This is one of the best areas to see the major sections of the park's sandstone and limestone cliffs, made even more stunning at sunrise and sunset.

Continue to Fruita and the **Capitol Reef Visitor Center**. Also in Fruita are historic buildings, including the **Gifford House** (with pie and treats for sale), orchards (fruit picking allowed in season), and the old schoolhouse built in 1898. The **Ripple Rock Nature Center** runs youth-oriented nature programs periodically throughout the day, and there are twice-daily ranger-led programs at the amphitheater at the Fruita Campground. Walking around Fruita (or driving between historic buildings) can take several hours.

From Fruita, take the 10-mile **Scenic Drive Road** and then turn left on the short dirt Capitol Gorge Road. These marquee roads lead through magnificent scenery to the **Capitol Gorge** trailhead. This level 4.5-mile round-trip hike is a highlight of the park and can easily be hiked in part—even as a short walk in and out of the gorge.

Heading back to Fruita, take the Grand Wash Road to the **Grand Wash Trail**. This trail provides access to the 4-mile round-trip **Cassidy Arch Trail** with about 800 feet of elevation gain. The Cassidy Arch hike is considered one of the best in the park, leading through not only the flat canyon-like trail

(Grand Wash) but up the sandstone and limestone cliffs. Constantly changing views of the surrounding desert, cliff walls, and ultimately the reward of the Cassidy Arch makes this one of the most photographed places in the park.

Pass back through Fruita and exit Scenic Drive, turning right (east) on Highway 24. Almost immediately on your left are the **Fremont Petroglyphs**, accessible via a short boardwalk. Drive a few miles farther east to the Hickman Bridge trailhead parking lot and end the day on the 1.7-mile **Hickman Bridge** hike. This natural bridge (Hickman Arch) is a Utah classic, providing panoramic views of the park and iconic photo opportunities.

**See the appendix for useful lodging, camping,
and activity contact information.**

CANYONLANDS NATIONAL PARK

[S]trange, weird, grand region of naked rock with cathedral-shaped buttes, towering hundreds or thousands of feet, cliffs that cannot be scaled and canyon walls that shrink the river into insignificance.

—Major John Wesley Powell in 1869,
describing the future Canyonlands National Park

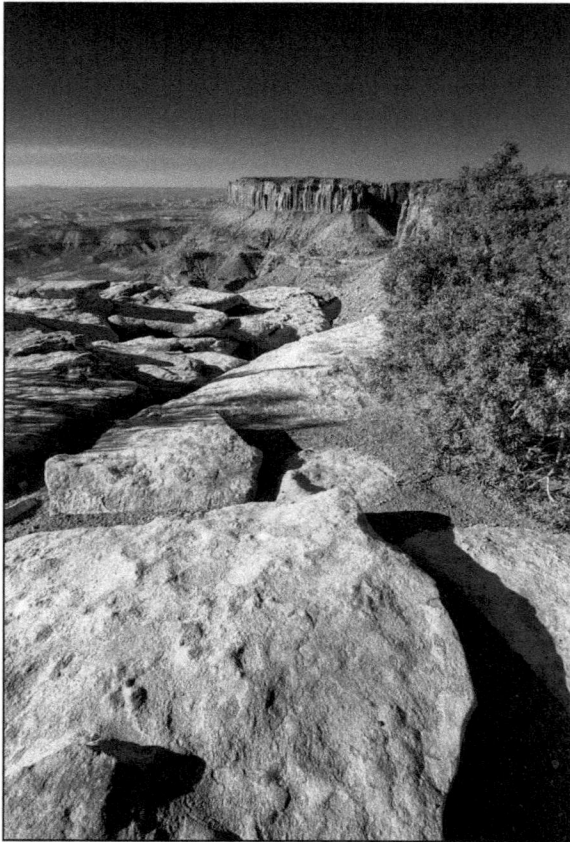

GRANDVIEW POINT, CANYONLANDS NATIONAL PARK
DEAN FIKAR/SHUTTERSTOCK

Located in southeast Utah about four hours southeast of Salt Lake City, Canyonlands is half an hour west of the more-visited Arches National Park, each situated near the popular vacation destination town of Moab. Canyonlands National Park is on the Colorado Plateau and home to the confluence of the Green and Colorado Rivers. Once converged, the two rivers become the Colorado River, raging through Cataract Canyon and into Lake Powell. These major waterways carved canyons and rock formations in the landscape, making it otherworldly yet classic Utah. Layers of eroded rock tell the story of ancient sea creatures, the uplift of the massive plateau from sea level, mountain ranges ground down, and now wonderful sandstone rock formations resulting from the uneven erosion. A one-time home of the Ancestral Puebloan peoples, who inhabited Canyonlands until around 1200, the park still has petroglyphs, stone and mud dwellings, and granaries from this culture that was one of the first farming groups in the American Southwest.

Encompassing just under 350,000 acres, the Green and Colorado Rivers divide Canyonlands into three or four sections. These include the most-visited Island in the Sky mesa north of the confluence of the two rivers, The Maze west of Cataract Canyon, and the Needles to the east. The Maze consists of backcountry hiking and camping and is not covered in this book. The fourth section is Horseshoe Canyon, with remote access off Highway 24 in the northwest section of the park. This three- to five-hour drive and 8-mile hike leads to the Grand Gallery, one of the greatest collections of ancient rock art anywhere in the world. Also in this area is 200 acres of grassland that has never been grazed by cattle. This ancient grassland area is not open to the public and has been the subject of research for over 50 years. Because of the location and access, this book does not discuss a trip to Horseshoe Canyon. The focus is on Island in the Sky mesa and the Needles.

SCHEDULING AND LODGING

At about 6,000 feet, Canyonlands has a high-desert climate that can be uncomfortably cold in the winter and too hot in the summer. Try to visit in the spring or fall. The distance between the two sections is about two hours. Both sections can be seen in one day for fast-hiking early risers, but for mere mortals, two days are needed to enjoy this park.

Though there is no lodging inside the park, nearby Moab has ample hotel rooms, house shares, hostels, RV parks, and campgrounds. Inside the park there are two campgrounds—**Willow Flat/Island in the Sky** with 12 first-come, first-served campsites and **Squaw Flat/The Needles** with 26 campsites. The Needles sites may be reserved in the spring and fall. In the summer they are first come, first served.

This is a great place for fair-weather campers. Not only is Canyonlands an International Dark Sky Park, but temperatures are comfortable in the spring and fall, and groceries can easily be purchased in Moab.

A NOTE ABOUT BIKING AND FOUR-WHEEL DRIVE OPTIONS

The White Rim sits below the Island in the Sky mesa perimeter and above the Green and Colorado Rivers. On the White Rim is a 100-mile dirt road where four-wheel-drive vehicles and mountain bikes are allowed with a day-use permit, available online up to 24 hours before your trip. Backcountry camping in this area is also permitted, using a separate permit. Bikes are not available for rent within Canyonlands National Park. However, in Moab, Rim Cyclery, Chile Pepper, Poison Spider, and Bike Fiend rent both bikes and bike racks.

The Needles section provides a good option if you're looking for four-wheel-drive adventures. The road to the Confluence Overlook is accessible by four-wheel-drive vehicle, making an 11-mile round-trip hike into a 2-mile round-trip walk. A permit is not required for this road.

THE TRIP

Day 1: Utah has so much preserved land that it's sometimes hard to prioritize between a spectacular state park and national parkland. Here you don't have to, as the entrance to **Dead Horse Point State Park** is immediately to the east of the northern entrance to Canyonlands. Stop here first and stand 2,000 feet above the Colorado River and its carved canyons, enjoying an incredible view of the sandstone landscape and getting oriented to the area.

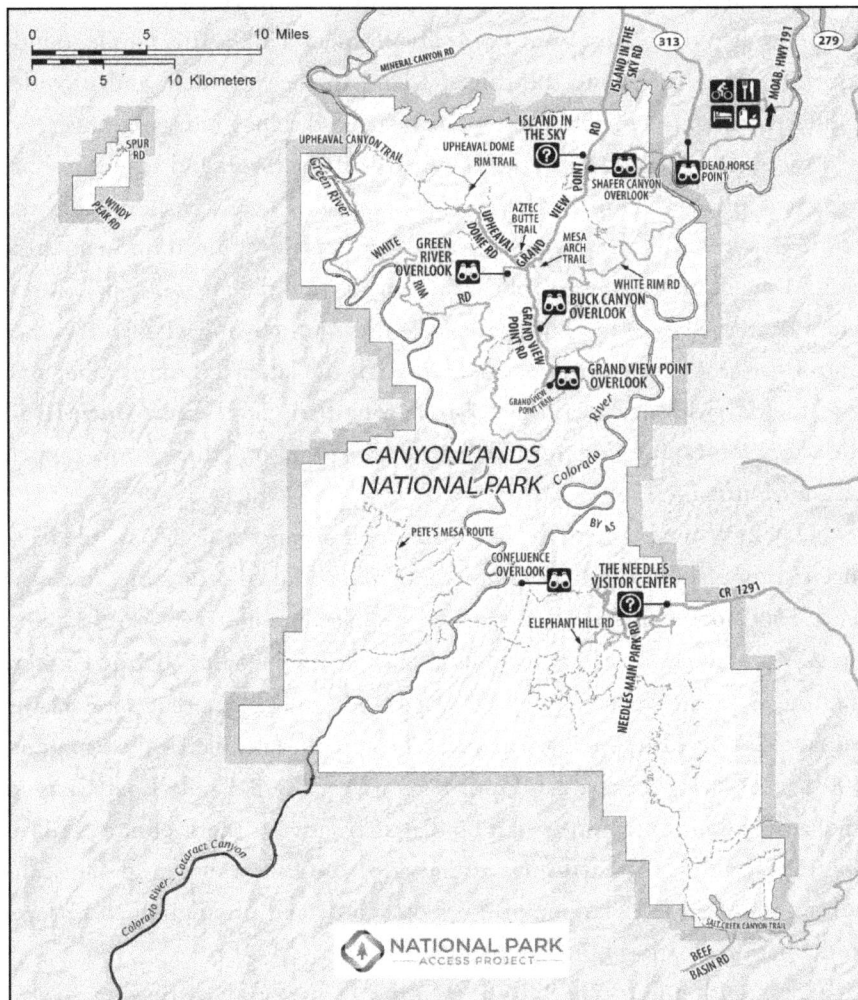

Enter the park and stop at the **Island in the Sky Visitor Center**. Then spend some time on the Island in the Sky mesa by driving to various overlooks, some with short associated hikes. Start at **Shafer Canyon Overlook** near the visitor center and then **Mesa Arch** for a half-mile round-trip walk to the most photographed vista in the park. Move on to **Buck Canyon Overlook** and then the **Grand View Point Overlook** and hike. This 1-mile round-trip hike takes you along the rim of Island in the Sky mesa and provides endless views of the myriad carved canyons and distant mountain ranges.

When returning, stop at the **Green River Overlook** and take the short hike to **Upheaval Dome**. There are two options here—a short half-mile round-trip hike to the crater rim and a longer 2.4-mile round-trip hike around the dome's exterior. Upheaval Dome has a different soil/rock composition from the rest of the park, with geologists not knowing whether it comes from a salt dome or an impact crater, though the latter has more adherents. End the day with a stop at the 1.7-mile round-trip level **Aztec Butte Trail** for a view of **Taylor Canyon** looking north to the sometimes snow-capped La Sal Mountains.

Day 2: While Island in the Sky is about 30 minutes from Moab, the Needles section is about two hours southwest. Named for colorful spires of Cedar Mesa Sandstone that dominate the area, the Needles offers views of Island in the Sky and a variety of canyon hikes. Start at the **Needles Visitor Center**, then head to the Squaw Creek Campground parking lot that accesses the **Squaw Flat and Big Spring Canyon** hike, a level 6.6-mile loop with about 500 feet of elevation change. From here, access the 3.3-mile **Lost Canyon** hike as a second but connected loop. An alternative is the **Elephant Hill** to **Druid Arch** hike. This 10-mile, round-trip, 1,400-foot elevation gain canyon-to-arch trail leads to one of the most iconic and photographed features in the national park—Druid Arch.

Later, with a four-wheel drive, take the 11-mile round-trip dirt road to the short **Confluence Overlook** hike and enjoy the raging Colorado and Green Rivers as they converge and become the Colorado River. Canyonlands is in about the midpoint of the national parks in terms of annual visits, but the Needles section receives only about 20 percent of Canyonlands' visitors. These beautiful hikes offer a nice level of solitude.

See the appendix for useful lodging, camping, and activity contact information.

ARCHES NATIONAL PARK

Standing there, gaping at this monstrous and inhumane spectacle of rock and cloud and sky and space, I feel a ridiculous greed and possessiveness come over me. I want to know it all, possess it all, embrace the entire scene intimately, deeply, totally . . .

—Edward Abbey, from *Desert Solitaire* (1968)

DOUBLE ARCH, ARCHES NATIONAL PARK
TUPUNGATO/SHUTTERSTOCK

One of the iconic national parks in the United States, Arches has the densest concentration of natural stone arches in the world. Over 2,000 natural sandstone arches dot the park along with other special geologic features like pinnacles, red rock canyons, and giant stone bluffs. At sunrise and sunset, Arches has some of the most spectacular vistas in the country.

On the Colorado Plateau, the park sits on a great salt bed called the Paradox Formation, deposited over 300 million years ago when seas flowed into the region. Debris and soil filled the area over the unstable salt bed, with a layer of Entrada Sandstone at the top. Geological upheaval created the park's major fins and towers, while gradual erosion from the park's 8 to 10 inches of rain each year created the arches.

Humans have made the general area home for at least 10,000 years, and native peoples were active until the mid-1800s. Tourism associated with the westward railroad expansion put Arches on the map, with President Herbert Hoover naming the park a national monument in 1929 and Congress converting it to national park in 1971.

SCHEDULING AND LODGING

At about 5,500 feet above sea level, Arches has a classic desert climate, with highs in July and August of near 100 degrees and lows in December and January near 20 degrees. Visit this spectacular park in the spring or fall. The trip below suggests two days to visit Arches, which allows time for the full Devils Garden hike and also the Fiery Furnace hike. If not intending to see the Fiery Furnace or the rear section of the Devils Garden, Arches can be visited in one day.

Moab is about 15 minutes south of the Arches entrance. Full of lodging, restaurants, tour operators, and plenty of young people, this is a great place to stay. On the other hand, nine of the major arches in Arches National Park are near the famous **Devils Garden Campground**. This 51-site campground accepts reservations from March through October. Stay here and on a clear night enjoy this International Dark Sky Park. Groceries and other camping essentials are available in Moab.

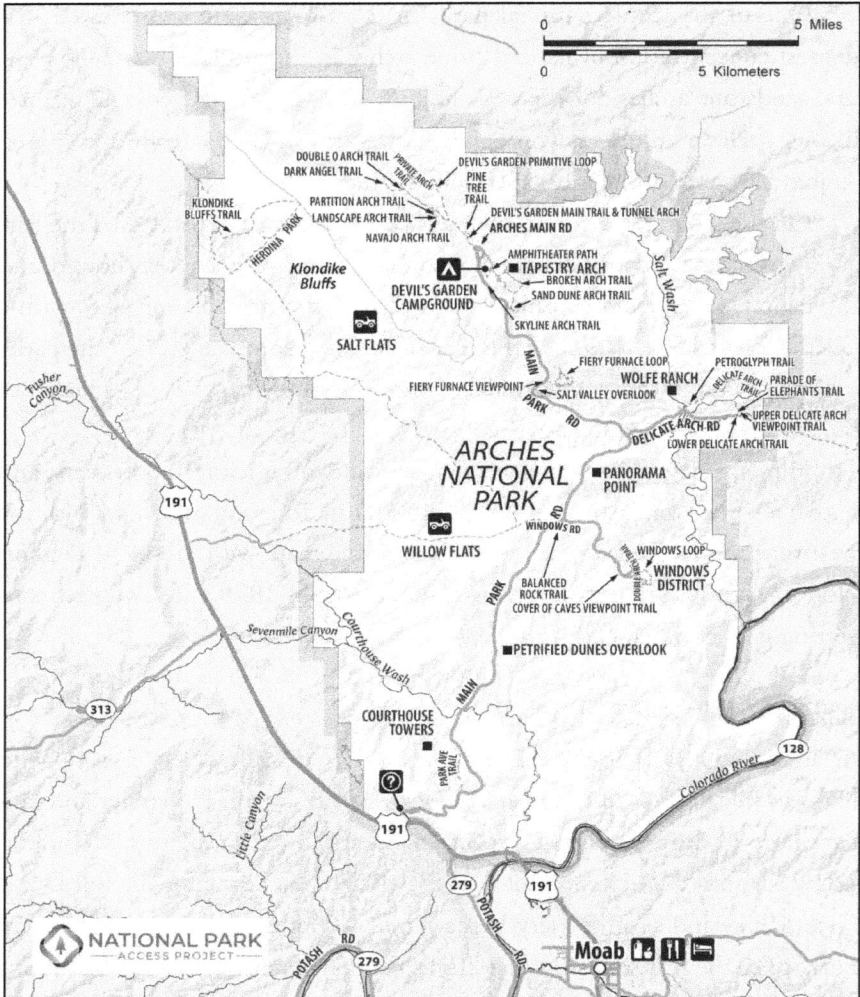

A NOTE ABOUT FOUR-WHEEL-DRIVE VEHICLES AND MOUNTAIN BIKING

Arches National Park used to have its entrance a bit farther north on High-way 191. Willow Flats and Salt Flats Roads can still be used to enter the park with a four-wheel drive. Though mountain biking is a signature activity in the sandstone hills around Moab, off-road biking is not allowed inside of Arches.

If mountain biking is an objective, set aside some extra time before or after your Arches visit.

FIERY FURNACE HIKE

Visible from an overlook, the famous Fiery Furnace is a labyrinthine area of small desert canyons, wildflowers, and sandstone features. There are often ranger-led hikes in this area, but for private hikes, a special permit is required to access the area since its canyons and dead ends often lead to people getting disoriented or lost. The permit (available while supplies last, so go early) may be obtained at the visitor center the day of your visit.

THE TRIP

Day 1: Begin at the **Arches Visitor Center**. From here, start on the 36-mile round-trip **Main Park Road**, covering most of it on Day 1 but saving the major collection of arches in Devils Garden for Day 2. Shortly past the visitor center on the left is the **Park Avenue Trail** leading down a few stairs to a level 1.8-mile round-trip walk through red rock fins and towers. After the walk, keep driving and enjoy pullout views of **Courthouse Towers** and **Petrified Dunes**. These dunes are the former home of an ancient salt lake, similar to those found in the Mojave Desert and Death Valley.

Continue to the **Balanced Rock** parking lot and short quarter-mile Balanced Rock **Trail**. When finished, turn right toward the **Windows District**. At the end of this road are two parking areas accessing two short walks. The 0.6-mile **Parade of Elephants Trail** leads to **Double Arch**, while the 1-mile **Windows Loop Trail** provides views of **Turret Arch**, **North Window**, and **South Window**. This is the first major concentration of arches, with wonderful views and photo opportunities. Head back to Main Park Road and turn right. Stop at the **Panorama Point** turnout on your right.

Continue again on the main road and turn right on **Delicate Arch Road**. At its terminus there are two hiking choices to see the spectacular sandstone **Delicate Arch**. The signature hike to Delicate Arch is 3.1 miles round trip with about 600 feet of elevation change. Alternatively, a lower parking lot provides 1.2-mile round-trip access to a viewing area. The longer hike passes the small historic **Wolfe Ranch** building and the **Ute petroglyphs**. The beautiful Delicate Arch image is used on Utah license plates and has been used on a United States postage stamp.

Day 2: Enter the park again and stop at the visitor center to get a permit if intending to hike the 2-mile Fiery Furnace maze. Head into the park and stop at **Fiery Furnace** on the right. Either enjoy the overlook or the hike, and then continue toward Devils Garden. There are two sections of hiking here. Stop at the first section—the parking lot leading to **Sand Dune Arch**. From here, enjoy a loop hike along the desert floor, with wonderful surrounding rock formations, red rock canyons, and remote plateaus. The hike leads from Sand Dune Arch in a loop to and through **Broken Arch** to **Tapestry Arch** and then to the Devils Garden Campground before looping through red rock canyons back to the parking lot.

The two final hiking areas are accessed from the main parking lot at Devils Garden. The paved and crowded 2-mile round-trip main trail leads to **Tunnel Arch**, **Pine Tree Arch**, and **Landscape Arch**. From Landscape Arch the trail leads farther into Devils Garden, to **Navajo Arch**, **Partition Arch**, **Double O Arch**, **Dark Angel**, and **Private Arch**. The full loop is an additional 6.5 miles round trip with 1,000 feet of elevation change. Some of the arches are massive. Landscape Arch is the second largest arch span in the world at over 300 feet.

**See the appendix for useful lodging, camping,
and activity contact information.**

COLORADO

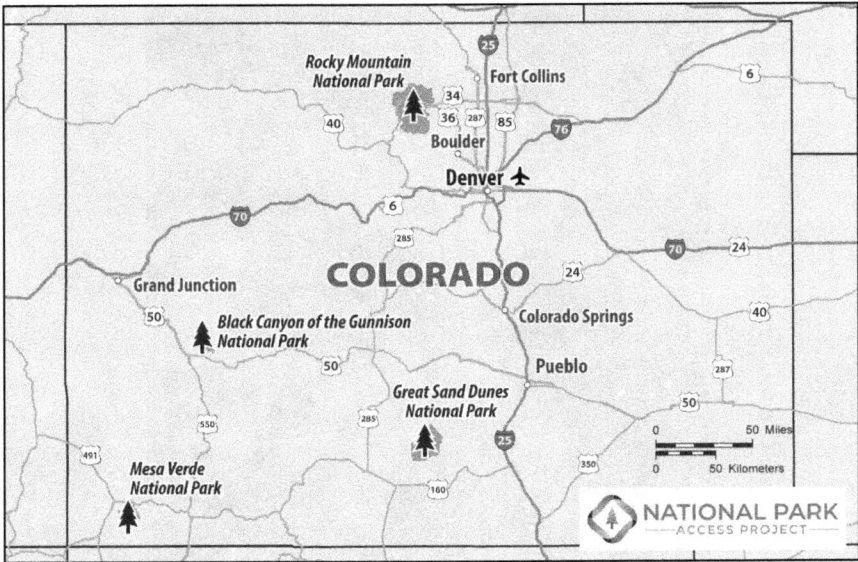

ROCKY MOUNTAIN NATIONAL PARK

The Rocky Mountains realize—nay, exceed—the dream of my childhood.
It is magnificent, and the air is life-giving.

—from *A Lady's Life in the Rocky Mountains* by Isabella Bird, nineteenth-century
English explorer, writer, photographer, and naturalist and the first woman to be
elected Fellow of the Royal Geographical Society

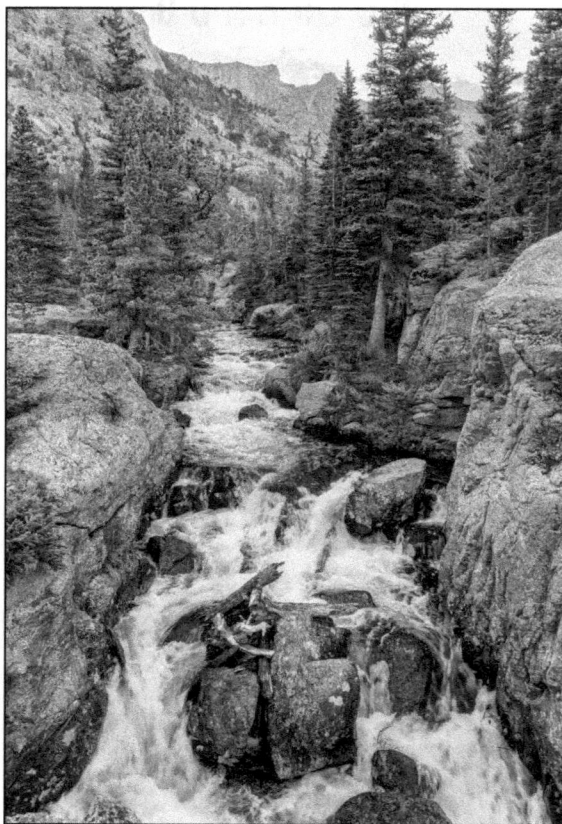

GLACIER CREEK AT THE TOP OF GLACIER FALLS IN
ROCKY MOUNTAIN NATIONAL PARK
COLIN D. YOUNG/SHUTTERSTOCK

The vast Rocky Mountain Range has some spectacular areas, and Rocky Mountain National Park is one of them. Located about an hour and a half northwest of Denver, the park's visual apex is the 14,250-foot Longs Peak, which presides over Colorado's Front Range. The historic town of Estes Park is the customary gateway to the park. From here the famed Trail Ridge Road leads to the Alpine Visitor Center and the Continental Divide while providing some of the best views the country has to offer. The "other side" of the Continental Divide is the much less visited Western Slope. Here is the Kawuneeche Visitor Center and the three-lake system including Grand Lake, Shadow Mountain Lake, and Lake Granby, along with gentler hiking.

Though currently a playground for outdoor enthusiasts, Rocky Mountain National Park was first inhabited by humans about 11,000 years ago when nomadic native hunters came through the area, culminating with the Ute Tribe that traveled and hunted here until the late 1700s. By the early 1820s, trappers, gold miners, and explorers were active, including explorer Major Stephen H. Long, for whom Longs Peak is named. The early 1900s saw the area identified for preservation, with naturalist Enos Mills a lead champion of the park both in Colorado and in the US Congress. In 1915, President Woodrow Wilson signed the Rocky Mountain National Park Act. Major infrastructure, including Trail Ridge Road, was constructed during the Great Depression. There are now over 265,000 acres within the park boundaries.

Rocky Mountain National Park is loosely divided into seven sections—the Wild Basin hiking system about 30 minutes south of Estes Park; Longs Peak with its access trails and summit hike; the Bear Lake hiking system with direct shuttle service from Estes Park; the Fern Lake hiking area, also with shuttle service; the northern and less visited Fall River area north of Estes Park village; the Alpine Visitor Center and Continental Divide; and the Western Slope. This suggested trip includes each of these sections except the difficult hike up Longs Peak. The park is an easy place to see big game, including deer, elk, moose, bighorn sheep, bear, coyote, and mountain lions. Charming smaller animals also abound, including marmot, beaver, otter, and several hundred species of birds.

SCHEDULING AND LODGING

Because the park's low elevation is around 8,000 feet and extends to over 12,000 feet at the Alpine Visitor Center, the season is short for much of the park. Trail Ridge Road typically opens in late May and closes in mid-October. This peak season is the period during which the shuttle operates. Due to the snow melt, which at times results in rushing water, visiting in the spring is difficult. Fall visitors should make sure to come in time to see the famous turning of the aspen trees in September and the bugling elks from mid-September to mid-October. Winter visitors are treated to a park open to cross-country skiing and snowshoeing, with many hotels in Estes Park open year-round.

Though the park does not have any hard-walled lodging within its boundaries, Estes Park has hundreds of hotel rooms at many price points. The expensive **Stanley Hotel** (on the National Historic Register) offers dining (open to the public) as well as historic tours. In addition to the many midpriced hotels, the park-abutting **YMCA of the Rockies** provides freestanding cabins and meal service, while the **Wildwood Inn** is located in the more remote Fall River Road area near the park's north entrance. On the Grand Lake/Western Slope side of the park, consider **Western Riviera Lakeside Lodge**.

Rocky Mountain National Park has five campgrounds—**Longs Peak** with 26 sites, **Glacier Basin** with 150 sites, **Moraine Park** with 225 sites, **Aspenglen** with 52 sites, and **Timber Creek** on the Western Slope with 98 sites. This sounds like a lot of camping capacity, but in peak summer it is often sold out. If camping is full, consider the **Estes Park KOA**.

SHUTTLE SERVICE–ESTES PARK VISITOR CENTER

The **Estes Park Visitor Center** is the shuttle service hub for visits to the **Sprague Lake/Bear Lake** and **Moraine Park/Fern Lake/Cub Lake** hiking systems. The building offers four levels of structured parking.

DRIVING AND PARKING

Trail Ridge Road and the Alpine Visitor Center are not served by the shuttle. The Alpine Visitor Center has very limited parking. Leave early and be prepared to wait in line to get a parking space. Parking at the various trailheads on the way to and including Bear Lake and Fern Lake is limited. Either take the shuttle or leave very early via car to secure a parking space. When lots are full, rangers at the entrance gates to the park will not let cars enter and will instead direct travelers back to the shuttle at the Estes Park Visitor Center.

HIKING LONGS PEAK

Colorado "fourteeners" are the 58 mountains in Colorado's Rocky Mountain Range that exceed 14,000 feet. One of these is in Rocky Mountain National Park—Longs Peak. This 14.5-mile round-trip hike with 4,000 feet of elevation gain is the most dangerous of all the fourteeners, in part due to the sheer drop-offs near the top. On average, two people die each year attempting the summit, whether by falls, hypothermia, dehydration, or cardiac arrest.

THE TRIP

Day 1: Once settled in Estes Park, drive to the **Estes Park Visitor Center** and obtain hiking maps for the **Wild Basin** area, the **Bear Lake Trail System**, and the map/schedule for the shuttle. When finished, drive about 3 miles inside the park boundary to the in-park **Beaver Meadow Visitor Center** and then to the **Deer Mountain** trailhead. This 6-mile round-trip hike with 1,200 feet of elevation gain provides a panoramic view of the lower regions of the park and the town of Estes Park. When finished, exit the park via **Fall River Road** and stop at the **Fall River Visitor Center**. End the day enjoying the sculpture-lined **Riverwalk** in Estes Park.

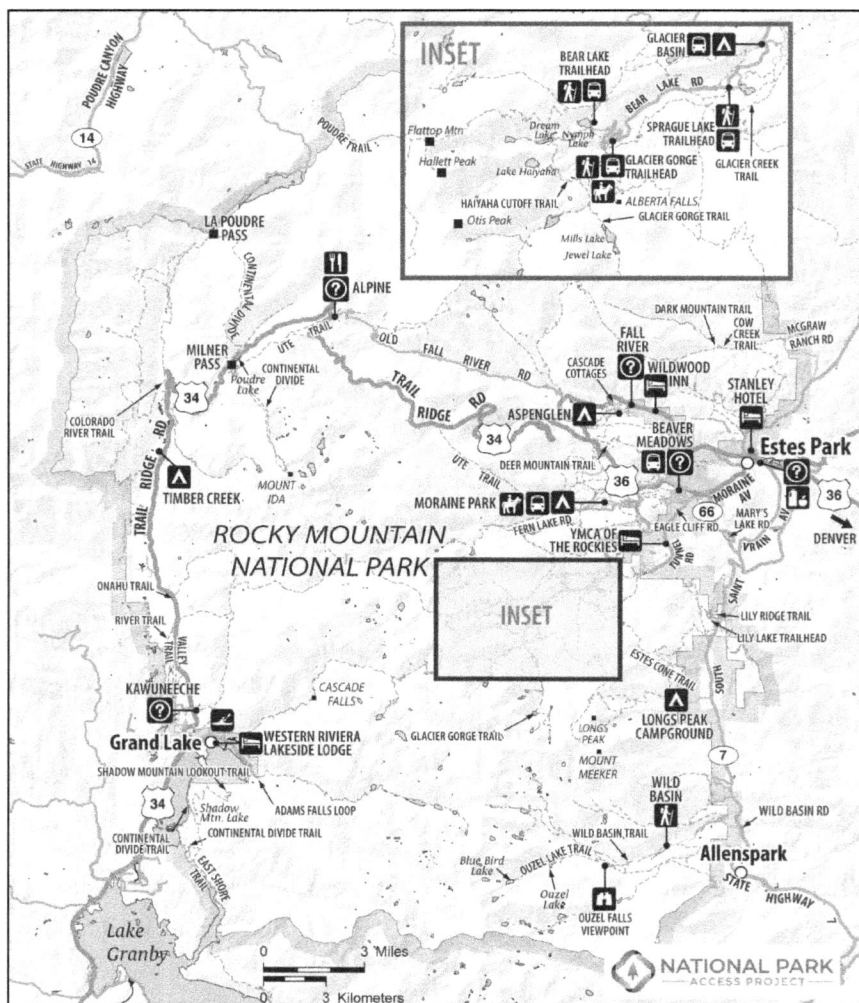

Day 2: The picturesque **Wild Basin** area in the southeast section of the park contains some of the park's signature trails. On the 30-minute drive south from Estes Park, Longs Peak will be on the right. In the Wild Basin section of the park is the **Bluebird Lake** hike, which showcases the area and offers short, medium, and long hiking options. The short version is a round-trip 5.4-mile hike to **Ouzel Falls**, with the medium version extending to a

10.2-mile hike to **Ouzel Lake** and the long option at 12.6 miles round trip reaching Bluebird Lake. In addition to lovely rivers, falls, and lakes, this hike offers terrific views of Mount Meeker and Longs Peak. When returning to Estes Park, the 0.8-mile flat Lily Lake loop hike is on the left. This is a great place to see beaver, otter, and aspen trees.

Day 3: Spend the day riding in the beautiful Rocky Mountain high country. The two hiking areas served by shuttle, Bear Lake and Fern Lake, also have associated stables. **Glacier Creek Stables** serves the Bear Lake/Sprague Lake area and **Moraine Park Stables** serves the Fern Lake area. Though both sections have spectacular hiking, Bear Lake is perhaps considered the superior hiking choice, making Moraine Park a good option for riding. Moraine Park Stables offers a four- and six-hour ride through the Fern Lake area, including Beaver Meadows.

Day 4: The **Bear Lake** area has some of the most beautiful hiking in the world. Start at the **Glacier Gorge** trailhead parking lot and shuttle stop. From here, interconnected hiking trails extend to numerous lakes. An example of a manageable and gorgeous trip is the 9-mile loop hike that travels first to **Alberta Falls** and then along **Glacier Creek** to **Glacier Falls**, **Mills Lake**, and the connected and smaller **Jewel Lake**. From **Jewel Lake**, head toward **Lake Haiyaha**, which provides an incredible view of Hallett and Otis Peaks and the bowl in between. Return to the trailhead via Bear, Dream, and Nymph Lakes. Continue via shuttle or car to the **Sprague Lake** trailhead. This lovely lake has a level ADA accessible trail around its border. The trail also connects via a 20-minute walk to the Glacier Basin Campground.

Day 5: Start the day early and begin the trek on **Trail Ridge Road** over the **Continental Divide**. This congested road has several pullouts with terrific views. The apex of the road is the **Alpine Visitor Center**. The short **Alpine Ridge** summit trail extends to over 12,000 feet and provides a 360-degree view of the park. There are two visitor center buildings, each with shops and information, and there's a large café as well.

After the visitor center, begin the drive down to the Western Slope of the park. This is a more relaxed section, with less congested pullouts and fewer people. **Milner Pass** marks the **Continental Divide**. Stop here and hike one way or the other on the **Continental Divide Trail**. Also here is **Poudre Lake** and the **Ute Trail** that extends 4 miles back to the Alpine Visitor Center. Continue a steep descent and exit the park at the **Kawuneeche Visitor Center** into the Grand Lake area. This small lakeside town with ample lodging abuts the park and provides access to hiking trails and boating. Two terrific level hikes here are the 2-mile round-trip hike to **Adams Falls** or the 7.4-mile round-trip hike to **Cascade Falls**. Rental kayaks for use on Grand Lake are available from Mountain Paddlers and Grand Lake Marina.

See the appendix for useful lodging, camping, and activity contact information.

BLACK CANYON OF THE GUNNISON NATIONAL PARK

Several canyons of the American West are longer and some are deeper, but none combines the depth, sheerness, narrowness, darkness, and dread of the Black Canyon.

—Duane Vandenbusche, *Images of America: The Black Canyon of the Gunnison*

PAINTED WALL AND GUNNISON RIVER, BLACK CANYON OF THE GUNNISON
KRIS WICTOR/SHUTTERSTOCK

Located in southwest Colorado, Black Canyon of the Gunnison National Park sits on the very eastern edge of the Colorado Plateau as it abuts the Rocky Mountains. Carved by the raging Gunnison River about two million years ago, the canyon is now 2,700 feet deep (about half the depth of the Grand Canyon). The Black Canyon at its narrowest point is only 40 feet wide, and the lack of sunlight makes the canyon walls look black, with areas of the base of the canyon only getting sunlight about half an hour a day. Famous for its juniper trees, canyon-dwelling peregrine falcons, and native wildflowers, the national park protects 47 square miles, including 14 miles of the deepest and most rugged portion of the 48-mile Black Canyon.

Though this area was within the greater Ute territory, the Black Canyon itself was an inhospitable spot and mostly avoided by native peoples. The canyon was first mentioned in writing by surveyor Captain John Williams Gunnison in 1853 and was explored by teams of surveyors and engineers in the late 1800s and early 1900s as part of the effort to find westward rail expansion routes. Black Canyon of the Gunnison was named a national monument in 1933 and a national park in 1999.

SCHEDULING AND LODGING

The main park entrance at the south rim is open year-round, but the South Rim Road is closed from November through mid-April. The fishing and hiking that Black Canyon of the Gunnison is known for are best enjoyed in the summer, from mid-May through mid-October.

Though there is no lodging in the park, Montrose, Colorado, is about 20 minutes southwest of the South Rim entrance and offers numerous hotels. The **South Rim Campground** inside the park has about 30 sites, which can be reserved in advance from late-May through early September. This International Dark Sky Park is truly remote and delivers incredible night skies.

An insider secret about the park is the **Red Rock Canyon Lottery**. The Red Rock Canyon access trail travels from the South Rim to the Gunnison River on a shorter (3.4 miles) and more gradual (1,330 feet) path than other wilderness canyon hiking options. The lottery provides access to two back-country campsites and to 2 miles of Gunnison River frontage for world-class fishing. The lottery opens every December through March for the upcoming summer.

For the 1,500 people each year that visit the remote North Rim, there is the 13-site first-come, first-served **North Rim Campground**, accessed via 7 miles of unpaved road. For hard-walled lodging near the North Rim, the small town of Crawford is about 30 minutes east. There is no food service inside the park. Montrose has numerous grocery stores.

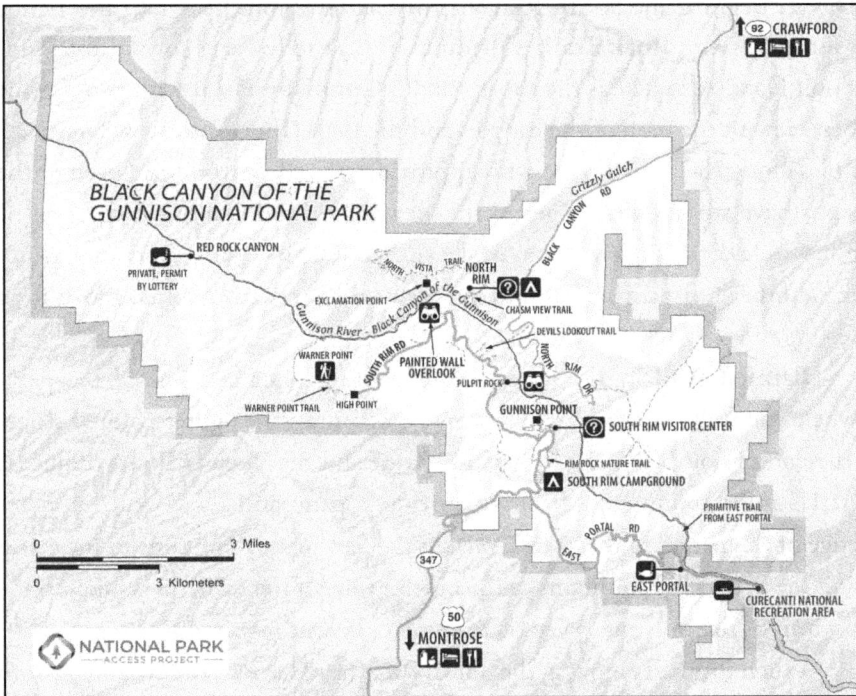

FISHING, RAFTING, ROCK CLIMBING

This remote region offers some of the best outdoor recreation in Colorado. Rock climbing on the sheer cliff walls is considered some of the best in the country. River rafting is offered west of the park in the Gunnison Gorge

National Conservation Area and can be arranged in Montrose.

The signature experience, though, is fly-fishing. The Gunnison River is designated a Gold Medal Water from 200 yards downstream of the Crystal Reservoir Dam near the park's southeast boundary. Only artificial flies and lures are permitted, and all rainbow trout are catch and release. Fishing licenses are available for sale in Montrose, and river access is via the East Portal Road.

THE TRIP

Day 1: Begin at the **South Rim Visitor Center**. From here, take the 1-mile round-trip **Rim Rock Trail**, providing southeasterly views toward the Gunnison Dam. Also here is the short walk to **Gunnison Point** with perhaps the best view in the park of the canyon and the river. The **South Rim Drive** is 7 miles along the canyon rim, with approximately 20 viewpoints. Seven of the stops have small walks to get to the viewpoints, and combined this will be a few miles of hiking/walking. Make sure to hike to **Pulpit Rock Overlook** for another terrific canyon and river view and also to **Devils Lookout** for a feeling of vertigo.

Painted Wall is one of the more photographed sections of the park, where the walls of the Black Canyon are striated with lighter-colored stone. The end of South Rim Road is **High Point** and the **Warner Point** trailhead. At 1.5 miles round trip, this hike provides a panoramic view of the western edge of the park and the river as well as the San Juan Mountains to the south and the West Elk Mountains to the north. (One of the wilderness hikes to the bottom of the canyon also starts from here. Permit required.)

When finished enjoying the South Rim, head back to the entrance booth and the turnoff to the park's **East Portal Road**. This steep dirt road with a 16 percent grade and hairpin curves is a nail-biter. Without a Red Rock Canyon trail permit, this is the only easy way to get down to the Gunnison River. Take a fishing rod and license, walk on the riverfront trail, and enjoy the canyon from a vantage point few get to see.

Day 2: It's about an hour and half clockwise, and two hours counter-clockwise, to the park's **North Rim** and some spectacular viewpoints. At the North Rim Campground is the 0.6-mile **Chasm Point Nature Trail** as well as the 3-mile round-trip **North Vista Trail** to **Exclamation Point**. Both trails are relatively level and provide incredible canyon views. From here, take the unpaved **North Rim Road** to various overlooks. This road was constructed by the Civilian Conservation Corps (CCC) and is listed on the National Register of Historic Places.

See the appendix for useful lodging, camping, and activity contact information.

MESA VERDE NATIONAL PARK

Your zeal and enthusiasm did more to arouse a militant sentiment in behalf of the preservation of the ruins than anything else.

—a note dated approximately 1901 from Senator Thomas Patterson of Colorado to Virginia Donaghe McClurg, head of the Colorado Cliff Dwellers Association and chief advocate, with Lucy Peabody, for creation of the national park

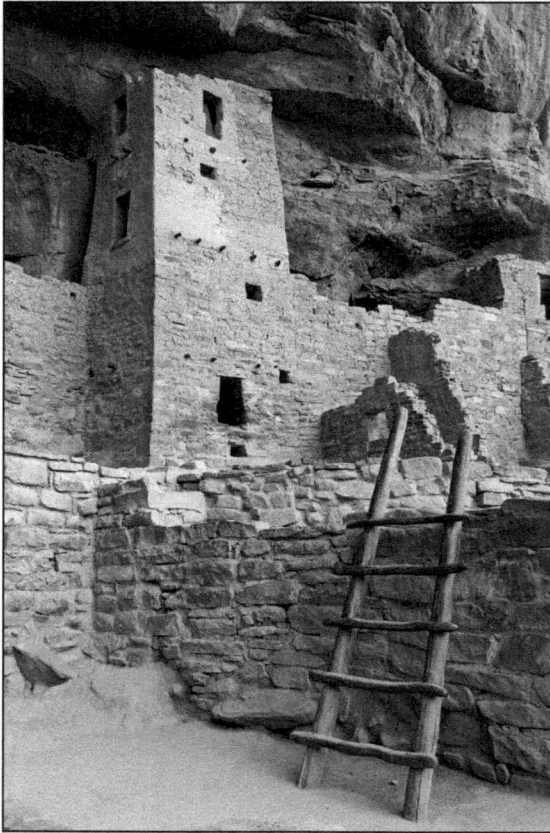

CLIFF PALACE, MESA VERDE NATIONAL PARK
BRYAN BRAZIL/SHUTTERSTOCK

This park contributes to our understanding of the lives of America's earlier people in a very special way. Mesa Verde, one of the richest archaeological areas in North America, was home to Ancestral Puebloans for the 600 years ending around 1300 when drought struck the region. Peak population was believed to be about 8,000 people in approximately the year 860. Mesa Verde's multistory sandstone brick-and-mortar cliff dwellings were built toward the end of this time, estimated around 1180 to 1270, indicating they were occupied for around 100 years.

The backbone of the park is Chapin Mesa, home to the park's largest dwellings, Cliff Palace and Balcony House. Though Cliff Palace was discovered in December of 1888 by cattle rancher Richard Wetherill, the broader area was brought to life by Swedish explorer and naturalist Gustaf Nordenskiöld, who documented the initial find with notes and photographs and was part of the group that identified more than 600 cliff dwellings in the canyons of Mesa Verde. The smaller but also important mesa on the park's western edge, Wetherill Mesa, is home to a compact collection of cliff dwellings and should not be missed.

The region is bordered by the Colorado and San Juan Rivers in what is now the Four Corners area where the states of Colorado, New Mexico, Utah, and Arizona meet. Mesa Verde is one of the highest sections of the Colorado Plateau, with an elevation ranging from 7,000 to 8,500 feet. The park was designated in 1906 by President Theodore Roosevelt, making it the seventh national park in the United States.

SCHEDULING AND LODGING

Far from a major airport, Mesa Verde is about four hours northwest of Albuquerque, six hours southeast of Salt Lake City, and seven hours southwest of Denver. In addition to proximity to the Colorado Plateau national parks Canyonlands and Arches, Mesa Verde is relatively close to two parks in the Rocky Mountains—Black Canyon of the Gunnison and Great Sand Dunes. At up to 8,500 feet, Mesa Verde can be cold until April, with May through

October the best time to visit and the window when ranger-led tours are available.

Near the visitor center and park entrance is the **Morefield Village Campground**, Morefield Camp & Grocery Store, and Knife Edge Cafe. With 267 campsites at Morefield, the campground accommodates both walk-in campers and advanced reservations. The long, winding road up onto Chapin Mesa brings visitors to the **Far View Lodge** and associated upscale Metate Restaurant (and more casual Far View Terrace Restaurant). Far View offers sweeping views of the Chapin Mesa and canyons below. Additional lodging is in Cortez, about 15 minutes west of the park entrance.

A NOTE ABOUT CLIFF DWELLING TOUR TICKETS

With advanced reservations, visitors have daily opportunities to see Balcony House and Cliff Palace. Tours of Long House on Wetherill Mesa, as well as tours of Mug House, Spring House, and Square Tower House, are offered frequently, though not necessarily daily.

700 YEARS TOUR

Available through park concessionaire Aramark, the 700-Years Tour is a half-day bus tour narrated by certified guides that provides an overview of Mesa Verde's history and offers short stops at sites spanning the 700-year history of the Ancient Puebloans. This tour includes a visit to Cliff Place and/or Balcony House with light hiking and presents a broader history of the area than the ranger-led tours. Private full-day tours are also available.

THE TRIP

Day 1: The **Mesa Verde Visitor and Research Center** is right before the main park gate. Stop here and get oriented, buy tickets for guided tours of the cliff dwellings, and purchase a snack at the grocery store in the nearby Morefield Village Campground. From here, head up to the **Chapin Mesa** to the cliff dwellings on the Scenic Drive. Stop first at the **Chapin Mesa**

Archeological Museum and the **Spruce Tree House**. This large cliff dwelling has an extensive viewing platform. Behind and above the dwelling is the 2.4-mile round-trip **Petroglyph Point** hike with views across Spruce Canyon to Wetherill Mesa. The hike connects with the 2.4-mile round-trip hike down into **Spruce Canyon**.

Continue on Mesa Park Loop Drive where the earlier finds—the **pit houses**—are located and where the geometrically perfect **Square Tower House** is found. The western section of Mesa Park Loop Drive is the eastern edge of Cliff Canyon. Here is the archaeologically important **Sun Temple** as well as various viewpoints of **Cliff Palace**.

From here, head to Cliff Palace Loop Drive to visit the two signature cliff dwellings—Cliff Palace and Balcony House. If tickets are not available, take the flat 1.2-mile round-trip **Soda Canyon Overlook Trail**, which looks down on Balcony House. End the time on Chapin Mesa with a visit to the **Far View Sites**. These stone buildings and village footprints were constructed almost a thousand years ago—before the cliff dwellings. They are eerily modern and fascinating.

Day 2: Start the day with the approximately 30-minute drive to the far southwest section of the park—**Wetherill Mesa**. The three-hour tour of **Long House** (with reservation), the second largest cliff dwelling in the park, is the highlight of this area. This intimate tour involves about 2.25 miles of walking as well as climbing stairs and ladders. Also here is the small **Badger House** community and the self-guided **Step House**. After heading down Wetherill and Chapin Mesas, stop at the **Montezuma Overlook** or take the 2-mile, round-trip, 150-foot elevation change **Knife Edge Trail** from the campground.

See the appendix for useful lodging, camping, and activity contact information.

GREAT SAND DUNES NATIONAL PARK

The sand-hills extended up and down the foot of the [Sangre de Cristos] about 15 miles, and appeared to be about 5 miles in width. Their appearance was exactly that of the sea in a storm, except as to color, not the least sign of vegetation existing thereon.

—from the journal of Zebulon Pike, 1807

GREAT SAND DUNES NATIONAL PARK
MIGUEL NAVROT/SHUTTERSTOCK

The Rocky Mountain Range has many subranges. One of the more spectacular is the Sangre de Cristo Mountains in southern Colorado. Great Sand Dunes National Park and Preserve totals about 150 acres of this area, of which about 20 acres is the dune field. Lying at the western base of the Sangre de Cristo Mountains, the dunes are in the beautiful San Luis Valley bounded on the west by another subrange—the San Juan Range. Primarily home to the Ute people, southern Colorado was explored by European settlers in the early to mid-1800s as part of the effort to find rail routes. Zebulon Pike, after whom Colorado's famous Pikes Peak is named, was one of the first people to describe the dunes.

Great Sand Dunes National Park has the tallest dunes in North America, rising from a base of 8,200 feet to a peak of 8,950 feet. Around 400,000 years ago, the dunes began forming from soil in a dry lakebed combined with sand and silt runoff from Medano and Sand Creeks. This soil, sand, and silt was whipped by wind against the Sangre de Cristo Mountains and settled into dunes, a process that continues to this day. Preservation of the area began in the 1920s, with national monument status achieved in 1932. Great Sand Dunes and a portion of the Sangre de Cristo Range were made a national park and preserve in 2004.

SCHEDULING AND LODGING

Located about four hours south of Denver and four hours north of Albuquerque, Great Sand Dunes National Park is remote. One of the iconic activities in the park is to play in Medano Creek's spring runoff. If this is something of interest, May and early June are the best times to visit. The park, with a low elevation of 8,200 feet, is cold during the long winter. In peak summer the sand can get as hot as 150 degrees.

While there is no hard-walled lodging in the park, near the entrance is the modest **Great Sand Dunes Lodge** and Oasis Restaurant. About 30 minutes southeast is the small town of Alamosa with many standard hotel brands. This is an International Dark Sky Park and a desirable camping destination. There are three camping options—the **Pinyon Flats Campground** at the entrance, backcountry camping in the dunes with a ranger-issued permit, and accessed by the 22-mile Medano Pass Primitive (four-wheel-drive) Road to the Point of No Return. Here there are 21 first-come, first-served sites—a great option for those who don't want to carry backcountry camping gear. This is a long, slow drive, taking up to several hours. If staying here, consider the Medano Lake hike, only accessible from this backcountry road.

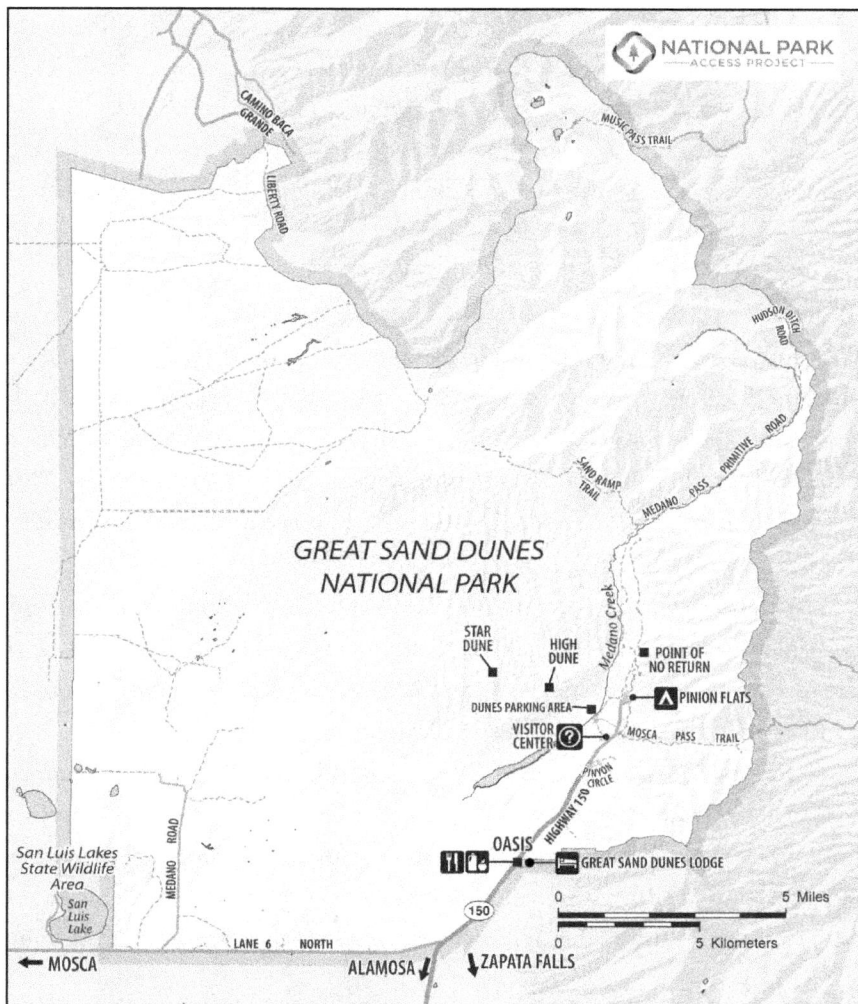

PETS

Great Sand Dunes National Park is one of the few national parks that lets you bring your dog on park trails and dunes. Dogs must be kept leashed at all times.

OUTSIDE THE PARK

The southwest corner of Great Sand Dunes National Park is pristine wetlands under the management of the Nature Conservancy and not accessible to the public. To get a feel for what the area is like, visit the San Luis State Wildlife Area at the park's southwest corner abutting the Conservancy land.

Also nearby is Zapata Falls. This slot-canyon-with-waterfall hike is a wonderful contrast to the dry sand dunes, with a trailhead not far south of the Great Sand Dunes Lodge and Oasis.

THE TRIP

Day 1: Just before entering the park, stop at the Great Sand Dunes Oasis for groceries for lunch and to rent a sand sled for the day. Once inside the park, start at the **Great Sand Dunes Visitor Center**. Then take the short Medano Creek Road to the Great Sand Dunes parking lot. In front are the dunes, with the 699-foot **High Dune** visible. Farther back in the dune field is the tallest dune in the park—**Star Dune** at 755 feet.

Medano Creek lies between the parking lot and the dune field, and plenty of gently sloping dunes make for acres of fun. Climbing High Dune to the top takes about two hours. Bring plenty of water and keep an eye on the parking lot, as the dune field can be disorienting.

After the dunes, find a shady lunch spot and then cross the road to the **Mosca Pass Trail**. This 6.5-mile, 1,500-foot elevation gain round-trip hike leads from the national park boundary near the trailhead into the national preserve. Extending from the valley floor through rock outcroppings and sparse forests to lush higher mountain meadows full of wildflowers and pine trees, this hike provides a perspective of both the dunes and the Sangre de Cristo Range. On the way down from Mosca Pass, hikers are treated to a view of the entire dune field.

See the appendix for useful lodging, camping, and activity contact information.

MONTANA AND WYOMING

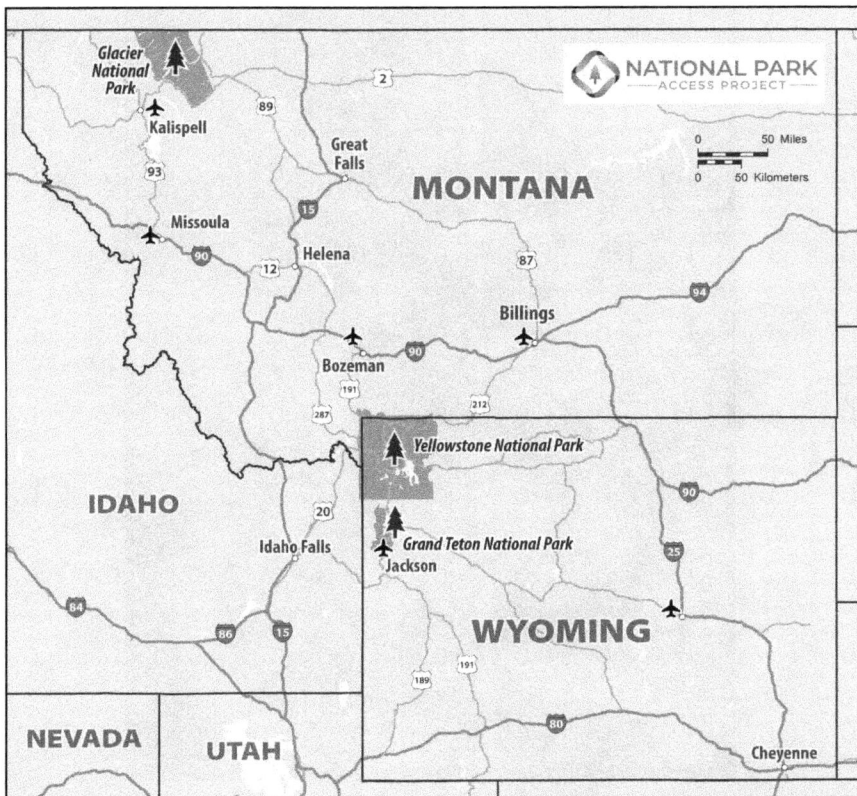

GLACIER NATIONAL PARK

Far away in Montana, hidden from view by clustering mountain-peaks,
lies an unmapped northwestern corner—the Crown of the Continent. . . .
Here is a land of striking scenery.

—George Bird Grinnell, *The Century Magazine*, 1901

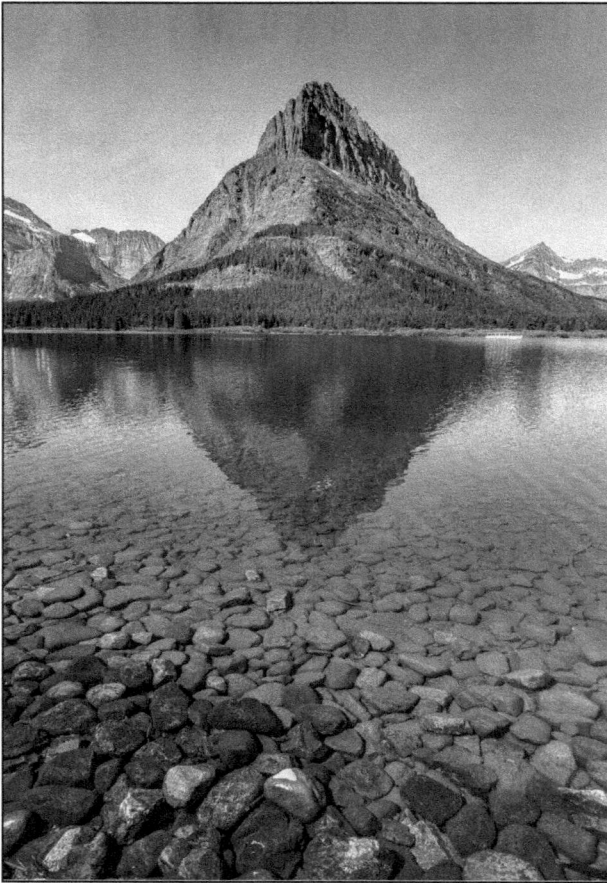

SWIFTCURRENT LAKE, GLACIER NATIONAL PARK
PUNG/SHUTTERSTOCK

Known as the "crown of the continent" for its jagged high-elevation peaks and gorgeous glacier-carved valleys, Glacier National Park is one of the most spectacular in the national park system. It's also one of the most difficult to visit due to its remote location and short season. The just over one-million-acre park is experiencing climate change. When established in 1910, Glacier National Park had around 150 glaciers; the number is now below 20. Diminishing glaciers impact the park's beautiful slate-blue glacier-fed lakes and rivers, which are found in few other places in the United States outside of Alaska.

Glacier National Park is within the long Rocky Mountain Range and includes three subranges—Clark, Lewis, and Livingston. The highest mountain in the park is Mount Cleveland at 10,479 feet, though most hiking trails top out at around 8,000 feet. The 50-mile Going to the Sun Road, built during the Great Depression, runs east–west through the park and provides access to many core attractions. The road's summit is the 6,646-foot-high Logan Pass on the Continental Divide. Glacier National Park has five main sections—West Glacier/Apgar, Lake McDonald, Saint Mary, East Glacier/Two Medicine, and Many Glacier/Swiftcurrent. Part of an International Peace Park with Canada's Waterton Lakes National Park, Glacier is connected to Canada via road from the Many Glacier area.

The Blackfeet Tribe made East Glacier home as long as 10,000 years ago, with a hub around the Two Medicine area. The large Blackfeet Reservation borders the park to the east, and the tribe remains active in park tourism. Fur trapping and westward exploration in the early 1800s put Glacier on the proverbial map, and rail access by the late 1800s meant the park would never again be remote. The Great Northern Railway from Chicago enabled construction of three of the park's historic lodges and still serves the park today as the Empire Builder connecting Chicago to Seattle with a stop in East Glacier. Congress first protected the area as a forest preserve in 1900, and by 1910 President William Taft signed a bill establishing Glacier as the tenth national park.

SCHEDULING AND LODGING

The easiest way to reach this remote park is to fly into Kalispell, Montana (Glacier Park International Airport), which is about 30 miles from the park's west entrance. A fun alternative is to book a sleeper car aboard the Empire Builder train. Rental cars are accessible from both the airport and the East Glacier train station. Glacier National Park has a short season, with the central Going to the Sun Road open from late June to mid-October. Most visitors see this park in the summer. Though the park is largely closed in the winter, off-season visitors will find year-round lodging in Kalispell and Whitefish as well as access to guided snowshoe, snowmobile, and cross-country skiing trips.

The park has some of the most spectacular and historic lodges in the national park system. Each of these lodges has access to dining and a market. Starting in West Glacier in the village of Apgar are the **Village Inn Motel**, located steps from Lake McDonald, and the **Apgar Village Lodge and Cabins** immediately behind the motel. Continuing on the Going to the Sun Road, the historic **Lake McDonald Lodge** has sweeping lakefront gardens with the less expensive **Motel Lake McDonald** nearby. On the eastern portion of Going to the Sun Road is Saint Mary Lake and the lake-facing **Rising Sun Motor Inn and Cabins**. And at the end of Going to the Sun Road is **Saint Mary Lodge**, which abuts the park boundary. To the south are the adjacent Two Medicine and East Glacier areas. The historic **Glacier Park Lodge** is here along with the Amtrak Empire Builder stop. The park's two northern lodges include the **Swiftcurrent Motor Inn** and the historic **Many Glacier Hotel** on Swiftcurrent Lake.

The park has 13 campgrounds, seven of which are located near the lodges. These include **Apgar** and **Fish Creek** in the Apgar area, **Sprague Creek** in the Lake McDonald area, **Rising Sun**, **Saint Mary**, **Two Medicine**, and **Many Glacier**.

BACKCOUNTRY LODGING

In 2017, a fire roared through the park and consumed the historic **Sperry Chalet**. This serviced 17-room backcountry lodge was built in 1913 and was rebuilt and opened to the public again in 2021. The difficult hike to the chalet is 6 miles one way with over 3,000 feet of elevation gain. This pristine backcountry lodge offers the reward of private rooms, breakfast, a packed trail lunch, and dinner, all under Montana's classic big sky. The park's other backcountry lodge, **Granite Park Chalet**, offers more limited service, allowing self-cook food and fresh linens to be reserved in advance. Accessed via Logan Pass and the famous 12-mile hike known as The Loop, this location is a challenge to reach. An outside pit toilet serves the location. Reservation requests for summer for both chalets open in January.

RED BUS TOURS, SHUTTLES, AND SUN TOURS

Iconic vintage red buses travel along the Going to the Sun Road and also to East Glacier and the Many Glacier/Swiftcurrent areas. The bus rides may be booked as shuttle transportation or as a professionally led tour with narration about park history, wildlife, and geography. Reservations are required in either case. Daily Sun Tours are operated by the Blackfeet Tribe from both West and East Glacier. These are half- or full-day tours amplifying the Native American elements of the park.

WATERTON LAKES NATIONAL PARK

Glacier and Alaska's Wrangell–St. Elias are the two national parks that share a border with Canada. Only Glacier, however, provides road access, with **Waterton Lakes National Park** about an hour-and-15-minute drive north of Many Glacier Hotel. Bring your passport and take advantage of this unique opportunity. See the historic **Prince of Wales Hotel** and take a boat ride on the **Waterton Shoreline Cruise** with a short stop at **Goat Haunt Mountain**. The parks were combined as an International Peace Park in 1932, though in practice the legal border remains.

GRIZZLY BEARS

An estimated 300 grizzly bears live in Glacier National Park. There has not been a recorded death by grizzly bear since the park opened in 1910. Keep distant from bears and all wild animals at all times.

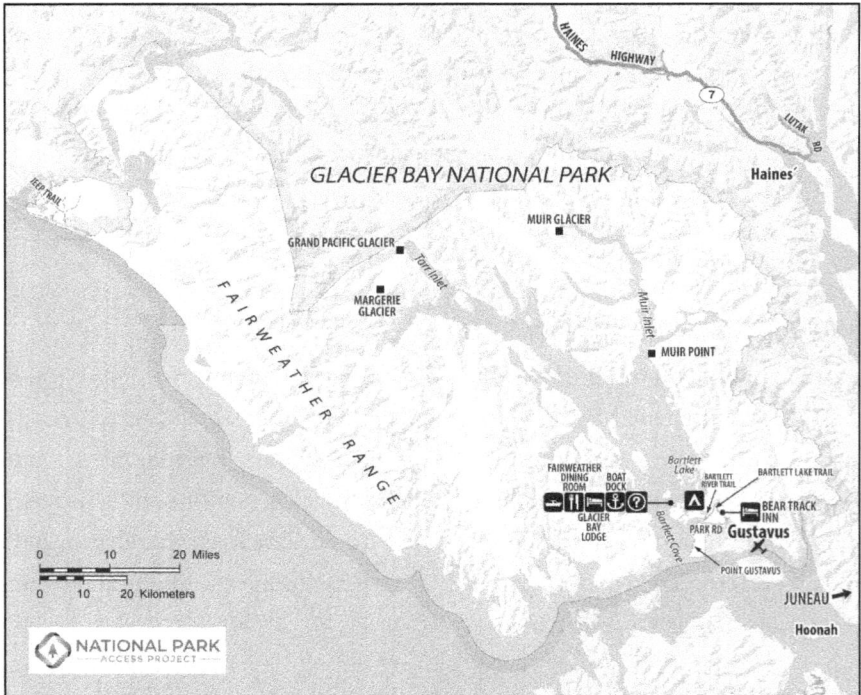

THE TRIP

Day 1: A visit to Glacier typically begins either in West Glacier or East Glacier. This description starts in the east. If coming from Kalispell, save time and for now avoid the Going to the Sun Road by taking Route 2 instead.

Enter the park at the Two Medicine Gate near the Two Medicine Ranger Station fronting **Two Medicine Lake**. This is a spectacular area surrounded by pristine, jagged mountains. Sightseeing is made easier by a boat ride operated about every other hour by Glacier Park Boat Company. Service runs from early June through early September; reservations are accepted. The top of the lake has a short trail to the beautiful **Twin Falls**. Return either via boat or by the 4-mile level lakefront hiking trails on either side of Two Medicine Lake. The path on the northern side of the lake is the **Dawson Pass/Continental Divide Trail** while the path on the south (**Two Medicine South Shore Trail**) includes the beautiful **Paradise Point.**

While here, consider hiking all or a portion of the **Scenic Point Trail**, with the trailhead near the ranger station. The full hike is 6.2 miles round trip with 2,350 feet of elevation gain, offering westward-only views. The summit (Scenic Point) provides views of the entire region, including of the high plains and the Blackfeet Reservation to the east.

Day 2: Head north from East Glacier on Highway 89 to the **Many Glacier** area. Once settled, enjoy the 3-mile level **Swiftcurrent Lake Nature Trail**. Another way to see Swiftcurrent Lake and the connected **Lake Josephine** is via the Glacier Park Boat Company, which operates boat trips leaving from Many Glacier Hotel about every hour and a half. Kayaks, canoes, and rowboats may also be rented.

Horseback riding is available from the Many Glacier area, Lake McDonald, and Apgar, with Many Glacier a beautiful spot for a guided tour. Full- and half-day riding options lead to **Cracker Lake** and **Cracker Flats** from the stables behind Many Glacier Hotel. This beautiful area in the shadow of Siyeh Mountain is not to be missed.

Day 3: Two of the best hikes in the park originate near the Many Glacier Hotel. These are **Grinnell Glacier** and **Iceberg Lake**. Each are full-day hikes, leaving from near the Swiftcurrent Motor Inn. The hike to Grinnell Glacier is 12 miles round trip with about 1,600 feet of elevation gain and can be shortened by 3.5 miles by taking the boat from Many Glacier Hotel to the head of

Lake Josephine. The full hike begins along the south side of Lake Josephine, delivering spectacular views of the lake and surrounding meadows. It extends to the glacier-fed Grinnell Lake and Upper Grinnell Lake to the Grinnell Glacier. Sightings of large animals like moose, bighorn sheep, and deer are common along the way.

The Iceberg Lake hike at 9.7 miles round trip with an elevation gain of 1,300 feet is to the north, departing from the Swiftcurrent Motor Inn. This hike extends through forests and alpine meadows to the small glacier-fed Iceberg Lake, which is surrounded by jagged mountains and the occasional mountain goat. The summits of both hikes are about 6,500 feet and are cold and windy even in summer.

Day 4: Travel south to the **Saint Mary Visitor Center** and after a stop, begin on the **Going to the Sun Road**. This classic road extends along the north shore of **Saint Mary Lake** and provides sweeping views. At the top of the lake is a parking lot accessing two waterfalls—**Saint Mary Falls** and **Virginia Falls**. The popular level hike to see both falls is 2.9 miles round trip. From here, continue on Going to the Sun Road to its peak—Logan Pass and the **Logan Pass Visitor Center**. Here, and also along the classic hike down to pristine **Hidden Lake**, visitors may see mountain goats grazing. At 5.4 miles round trip and 1,325 feet of elevation gain on the return leg, the Hidden Lake hike delivers the iconic scene of jagged mountains reflected in a near-perfect alpine lake.

Continue on the Going to the Sun Road toward **Lake McDonald**. The Lake McDonald area is a core section of the park. Not only is there lodging, camping, and dining, but Lake McDonald has swimming, lots of nearby hiking, and the Lake McDonald Corral. Not to be missed is a boat ride on the lake, with departures five times each day during peak season, including an evening boat ride. Canoes and kayaks may also be rented here.

Day 5: Near Lake McDonald is the beautiful **Trail of the Cedars** nature walk. This boardwalk stroll through 500-year-old cedars is a must. At its apex the walk connects with the **Avalanche Lake** hike at 4.5 miles round trip with 750 feet of elevation gain. This alpine lake is nestled among beautiful mountains and provides a perfect place to have lunch.

Head west to Apgar and the western edge of the park. The **Apgar Visitor Center** is here, along with access to a shallow section of Lake McDonald for swimming, boating, or as the site for iconic photographs of Glacier's tallest peaks reflected in Lake McDonald. Apgar also provides access to horseback riding and, from nearby West Glacier, rafting on the glacier-fed North Fork Flathead River.

**See the appendix for useful lodging, camping,
and activity contact information.**

YELLOWSTONE NATIONAL PARK

This is probably the most remarkable region of natural attractions in the world; and while we already have our Niagara and Yosemite, this new field of wonders should be at once withdrawn from occupancy, and set apart as [a] public National Park for the enjoyment of the American people for all time.

—Henry D. Washburn, surveyor general of Montana who headed the Washburn-Langford-Doane Expedition to explore what would become Yellowstone National Park

WOODEN BRIDGE OVER STEAMY TERRAIN, YELLOWSTONE NATIONAL PARK
MACIEJ BIEDOWSKI/SHUTTERSTOCK

America's first national park, Yellowstone holds a special place in the national park system. Located primarily in Wyoming, Yellowstone sits on the Yellowstone Caldera, a supervolcano formed about 600,000 years ago that measures around 35 by 45 miles, covering roughly the southwest third of the park. Because of the volcanic underpinning, Yellowstone stays warmer in the winter than the surrounding high plains, allowing for year-round support of abundant wildlife. Along with extensive geothermal attractions, visitors see bison, elk, deer, and a large variety of birds and small mammals. This diverse park has eight major areas: Mammoth Hot Springs, Roosevelt Camp, Lamar Valley, Grand Canyon of the Yellowstone, Hayden Valley, Lake Yellowstone, Old Faithful, and the West Yellowstone Geysers. The Rocky Mountain Range runs through the park, with two subranges, Washburn and Red Mountains, located entirely within the park.

Traces of human activity have been found dating back at least 11,000 years. The Kiowa people are known to have been present about 3,500 years ago and are ancestors to modern regional tribes, including the Shoshone. Native peoples and Western trappers converged in the early 1800s when westward explorers John Colter and William Clark went through the area. The 1871 Hayden expedition, though, was a defining moment for the park as we know it today. Geologist Ferdinand Hayden, photographer William Jackson, and artist Thomas Moran explored the area and brought back visual and physical evidence of the unique nature of the park. Soon after, almost 1.3 million acres was set aside and in 1872 President Ulysses S. Grant signed a bill naming Yellowstone the first national park.

Though Yellowstone's Grant Village honors the eighteenth president, it was President Theodore Roosevelt's 1903 visit to the park that brought the idea of Yellowstone into many United States homes. President Roosevelt stayed at what is now Roosevelt Camp, in rustic cabins similar to those still in place today.

SCHEDULING AND LODGING

Bozeman Yellowstone International Airport is about an hour and 45 minutes northwest of the park's north entrance. Yellowstone is open year-round, though in-park roads are open only from late May through early November. Eighty percent of the over four million annual visitors come during the summer months. Though the park has nine lodges, rooms sell out quickly in the summer. Consider the towns of Gardiner to the north and West Yellowstone to the west if lodging is needed outside the park.

In-park lodging is concentrated in six locations. These include the **Mammoth Hot Springs Hotel and Cabins** in Mammoth Hot Springs, the **Frontier** and **Roughrider** (camper) **Cabins** at Roosevelt Camp, **Canyon Lodge and Cabins** in Canyon Village, **Lake Yellowstone Hotel and Cottages** and **Lake Lodge Cabins** near Fishing Bridge on north Lake Yellowstone, the **Lodges at Grant Village** on south Lake Yellowstone, and **Old Faithful Inn**, **Old Faithful Lodge Cabins**, and **Old Faithful Snow Lodge** in Old Faithful Village. Of these, the Mammoth Hot Springs Hotel and Old Faithful Snow Lodge are open in the winter. Mammoth is accessible in the winter via private vehicle, while Old Faithful may be accessed only by snowmobile or park-provided snow coach.

There are 12 campgrounds inside Yellowstone with over 2,000 campsites. Campgrounds at **Grant Village**, **Canyon Village**, **Bridge Bay** (both RV and standard), and **Madison** accept advanced reservations. The remaining seven campgrounds are first come, first served. This includes **Mammoth Campground**, which is open year-round.

All villages have associated casual and formal dining and small grocery stores. At Roosevelt Camp, in addition to meal service at Roosevelt Lodge, there is a nightly Old West Cookout in Pleasant Valley, accessed via covered wagon or horseback ride. Advanced reservations are necessary. Grand Teton National Park is immediately south of Yellowstone and shares an entrance fee.

GEYSER AND ANIMAL SAFETY

At up to 500 degrees Fahrenheit, geysers and hot pots are likely fatal for those who get too close. Memorials are placed throughout the park noting deaths from interaction with hot water. Stay on the marked paths. Remain distant from wild animals and try to hike in groups of three or more.

FISHING

Yellowstone is full of rivers and lakes perfect for fishing during the June through October season; permit required. The famous Fishing Bridge area leading into Lake Yellowstone is thick with fish and also pelicans.

HORSEBACK RIDING

Stables are located at Roosevelt Camp and Canyon Village, with one- and two-hour rides offered in addition to the previously mentioned ride from Roosevelt Camp to Pleasant Valley for the cookout.

BOATING

Kayaks are available for rent from the Bridge Bay Marina near Fishing Bridge. From here, visitors may also reserve a one-hour boat ride on Lake Yellowstone. This guided trip leaves five times per day in peak season.

THE TRIP

Day 1: Enter at **Mammoth Hot Springs** near the park's northwest edge. This beautiful area has the world's largest collection of travertine hot springs. Begin at the **Albright Visitor Center** and historic **Fort Yellowstone** where ranger-led tours are frequent. From here, explore the hot springs via the 1.75 miles of boardwalk and extensive hiking trails.

Head east toward the **Tower-Roosevelt** junction. On the way is the beautiful **Wraith Falls** hike at under 1 mile round trip, with the descent providing views of the Gallatin Mountains to the north. Before the Tower-Roosevelt junction is Roosevelt Camp, including Roosevelt Lodge, associated cabins, and the covered wagon cookout dinner in nearby Paradise Valley.

Day 2: Located between Tower-Roosevelt and the park's little-used northeast entrance is the pristine **Lamar Valley**. Here and Hayden Valley are where herds of bison graze and wolves pace the distant tree line. Midway up

the valley, about an hour northeast of Roosevelt Camp, is the **Trout Lake** trailhead. This terrific hike is a 1-mile loop around the lake with views of Druid Peak and Mount Hornaday. After enjoying this easy and rewarding hike, head south toward Canyon Village.

HIKE MOUNT WASHBURN?

On the drive from Lamar Valley to Canyon Village, the base of the 10,223-foot Mount Washburn is on the left. One of three mountains in the park that have fire lookout towers, the summit provides a panoramic view of the park, including the Grand Canyon of the Yellowstone, Lake Yellowstone, and the distant Teton Range. With abundant wildflowers and wildlife, this is considered one of the best summit hikes in the park. The hike is more than a half-day commitment, offering two possible routes. The Dunraven Pass trail is 7 miles round trip with 1,500 feet of elevation gain, while the Chittenden Road Trail covers the same elevation in 6 miles round trip. Both hikes are considered strenuous and may have snow cover toward the top, even in peak summer.

At Canyon Village, begin at the **Canyon Visitor Education Center**. The **Grand Canyon of the Yellowstone** is the star of this section of the park. Famously photographed by Ansel Adams from **Artist Point**, the canyon has rim trails on both sides delivering amazing views. Though both the 3.8-mile **North Rim Trail** and the 2.2-mile **South Rim Trail** can be accessed from Canyon Village, there are parking lots on each side that serve the premier viewpoints. On the north side, North Rim Drive leads to **Inspiration Point**. From the road there are three parking lots, each with a short trail into the canyon. South Rim Drive serves the short **Uncle Tom's Trail** as well as Artist Point. The South Rim Trail parking lots also serve the **Wapiti Lake** and **Clear**

Lake Trails, which merge and provide a counterclockwise 4-mile level loop through small hot pots, lakes, and forests adjacent to the canyon, rejoining the canyon rim about 2 miles south of Artist's Point.

Day 3: Named in honor of geologist Ferdinand Hayden, the **Hayden Valley** is a prime location for wildlife viewing. Travel through Hayden Valley south toward Fishing Bridge. This area connects the Yellowstone River with **Lake Yellowstone**. Full of fish and home to the American white pelican, this is an iconic area of the park. Stop by the **Fishing Bridge Visitor Center** and from there take the short 0.7-mile **Pelican Creek Nature Trail** fronting the lake. For a slightly longer hike, drive a few miles east to the **Storm Point** trailhead. This beautiful 2.3-mile level loop trail leads you past **Indian Pond** and along the shores of Lake Yellowstone. As previously mentioned, both kayak rentals and one-hour boat trips are available from the Bay Bridge Marina.

Lake Yellowstone is a spectacular body of water. Younger than the park overall, at only about 150,000 years old, the lake is considered a caldera within a caldera. Underwater boiling water vents warm the lake, making it hospitable to fish and the pelicans that call the lake home. At its southwest corner is the **West Thumb Geyser Basin** with an extensive network of small hot pots, boardwalks, and views of underwater heat vents. Stop by the **West Thumb Information Center** while here.

Day 4: Old Faithful Village is considered by many to be the heart of the park. Here is the **Old Faithful Visitor Center** and the **Old Faithful Geyser**, which erupts around 20 times each day and can be viewed from surrounding bench seating. For those wanting a less crowded setting, walking trails extend gently beyond the geyser and through secondary but still amazing geothermal features. This boardwalk and trail system is the 4.6-mile **Upper Geyser Basin** and **Old Faithful Observation Point Loop Trail**. The core geothermal area at Old Faithful has an ancillary section, **Biscuit Basin** and **Mystic Falls**, which can be reached on foot or via car. The walk from Old Faithful crosses the Firehole River and passes more than 50 geothermal features on the way.

Day 5: The west side of Yellowstone from Old Faithful to Mammoth Hot Springs has numerous and unique geothermal features. To see and walk all the areas deserves a full day. From north to south, these features include:

- **Norris Geyser Basin:** The hottest geyser basin in Yellowstone, with water temperatures over 450 degrees. A winding 3-mile level trail is here.
- **Artist's Paint Pots Trail:** This area provides a 1-mile level loop trail through beautiful multicolored hot pots.
- **Firehole Canyon Loop Road:** The Firehole River offers wading and swimming in warmed water.
- **Lower Geyser Basin:** Home to approximately 100 geothermal features over 5 square miles, visitors see fumaroles, hot springs, geysers, and mud pots. This area has two access points—the **Fountain Paint Pots Trail** on one side of the Grand Loop Road and the Firehole Lake Drive on the other. Both areas offer parking and level walking trails of no more than 1 mile.
- **Midway Geyser Basin:** Home to some of the largest single hot springs in the world, including the **Grand Prismatic Spring**, which can be viewed via a 0.8-mile level loop trail.

**See the appendix for useful lodging, camping,
and activity contact information.**

GRAND TETON NATIONAL PARK

*The most remarkable heights in the great backbone of America are three
elevated, insular mountains which are seen at a distance of one hundred
and fifty miles, aptly designated as the Pilot Knobs,
known as the Three Tetons.*

—Alexander Ross, 1800s fur trader

MOULTON BARN, GRAND TETON NATIONAL PARK
KYLE SPRADELY/SHUTTERSTOCK

Located in northwest Wyoming, the Rocky Mountain Teton Range is famous in part because of the height of the central peaks at nearly 14,000 feet, combined with the lack of foothills. This dramatic protrusion of jagged mountains was caused by the Teton Fault and is made even more spectacular through reflection of the mountains on Jackson Lake. The highest of the central peaks, Grand Teton, measures 13,775 feet. Other major peaks in the range include Mount Owen, Teewinot, Middle Teton, and South Teton.

Long in the sights of preservationists, Grand Teton National Park was established in 1929 to protect the major peaks. The flatlands, though, centered around the Snake River, remained in private hands. In came national park patron John D. Rockefeller Jr., who acquired 33,000 acres around Jackson Hole and prepared to donate the land to the federal government. Resistance by locals delayed the transfer, but President Franklin D. Roosevelt ultimately used his individual authority under the Antiquities Act to accept the lands and create the Jackson Hole National Monument in 1943. Rancher rebellion ensued, and a 1950 compromise was reached to allow the expanded Grand Teton National Park but remove Wyoming as a place where the Antiquities Act could again be used. Between the park's northern border and Yellowstone National Park 10 miles to the north is the John D. Rockefeller, Jr. Memorial Parkway preservation land. The impact of this effort is a continuous preserved section from Jackson to the northern border of Yellowstone.

Though human history here dates back at least 11,000 years, the Shoshone are the native peoples more recently associated with the area. Fur traders began visiting in the early 1800s, followed soon thereafter by Mormon settlers migrating north from Salt Lake. Mormons and others took advantage of the Homestead Act of 1862, which allowed those with five years of continuous presence on land to achieve ownership of that land. Mormon Row, which at one time had 27 homesteaded residences, became part of Grand Teton National Park in the mid-1990s and was named to the National Register of Historic Places in 1997. The park as expanded measures 310,000 acres.

Grand Teton National Park is known for moose, some of the best fly-fishing in the world, gorgeous flatland hikes, difficult hikes to the central peaks, rafting on the Snake River, boating on Jackson Lake, and horseback riding.

SCHEDULING AND LODGING

Jackson has a regional airport about 15 minutes from the park entrance. In peak season, direct flights are available from around the country. For drivers, this is a long haul. The park is about 10 hours north of Denver, 6 hours east of Salt Lake City, and 4 hours south of Bozeman. Though most visitors come in the summer, fall foliage is spectacular, and the nearby Jackson Hole ski area, paired with the Nordic ski trails inside the national park, make this a fantastic winter destination. The main north–south road through the park is open year-round from Jackson to the Flagg Ranch Information Station.

Lodging in the park spans the range from rustic to grand. Moving north to south, the center of the park is **Colter Bay Village** with the **Colter Bay Cabins**, a café, laundry, grocery store, marina, and stables. **Jackson Lake Lodge**, an upscale option with sweeping views of the Teton Range, is to the southeast. **Signal Mountain Lodge** is modest, fronting Jackson Lake, and has a restaurant overlooking the water and the Teton Range. The high-end **Jenny Lake Lodge** is a bit farther south, and **Dornan's Spur Ranch Cabins** near Mormon Row rounds out the in-park lodging options. If these are full, consider the **Headwaters Lodge and Cabins at Flagg Ranch** outside the park in the John D. Rockefeller, Jr. Memorial Parkway area. All lodges have restaurants, and Jenny Lake Lodge has the only AAA four-diamond restaurant in the national park system.

The park has five campgrounds. Three of these are near the lodges, including **Colter Bay**, **Signal Mountain**, and **Jenny Lake**. Also, within the John D. Rockefeller, Jr. Memorial Parkway area is the **Headwaters Campground and RV Park** near the Headwaters Lodge. The two remote campgrounds include **Lizard Creek** on the north shore of Jackson Lake and **Gros**

Ventre at the far southeast section of the park. Yellowstone and Grand Teton share one entrance fee.

THE TRIP

Day 1: Start in the center of the park at Colter Bay Village. Begin at the **Colter Bay Visitor Center** and then enjoy the **Lakeshore Trail** along Jackson Lake. This 2-mile loop trail extends along the shore of a promontory, providing views of the Teton Range. Also here is the marina with canoes and kayaks available for rent on an hourly basis as well as the Jackson Lake Scenic Cruises departing throughout the day. Lunch options in Colter Bay include the Café Court as well as the Colter Bay General Store. After lunch, consider a horseback ride, offered from both Colter Bay or the nearby Jackson Lake Lodge. Advance reservations are recommended for these one- or two-hour rides. Another walking option from Colter Bay Village is the **Hermitage Point Trail.** Though a 10-mile loop, it's easy to walk just a portion of the level trail from the village along Jackson Lake before or after dinner.

Day 2: Signal Mountain Lodge provides boats for hire on an hourly basis, along with fishing gear and guides if needed. Boating the lake from here provides the closest wide-angle view of the Teton Range, along with great lake fishing. After boating and fishing, the Signal Mountain Lodge Store offers picnic lunch options. From here, drive 10 minutes south to the **Jenny Lake Visitor Center** on the small Jenny Lake just south of Jackson Lake. The **Inspiration Point** trailhead is accessed via a short boat ride or the 2-mile **Jenny Lake Trail**. Starting at the boat dock, the Inspiration Point Trail climbs just under 1 mile with 500 feet elevation gain. This is a popular and crowded hike but fun for families and with a terrific view at the top. For a longer hike, from Inspiration Point, keep going along the **Cascade Canyon Trail**. This trail extends deep into the Teton Range but can be hiked in any distance. This is a pretty hike through pristine backcountry, offering waterfalls and wildlife viewing.

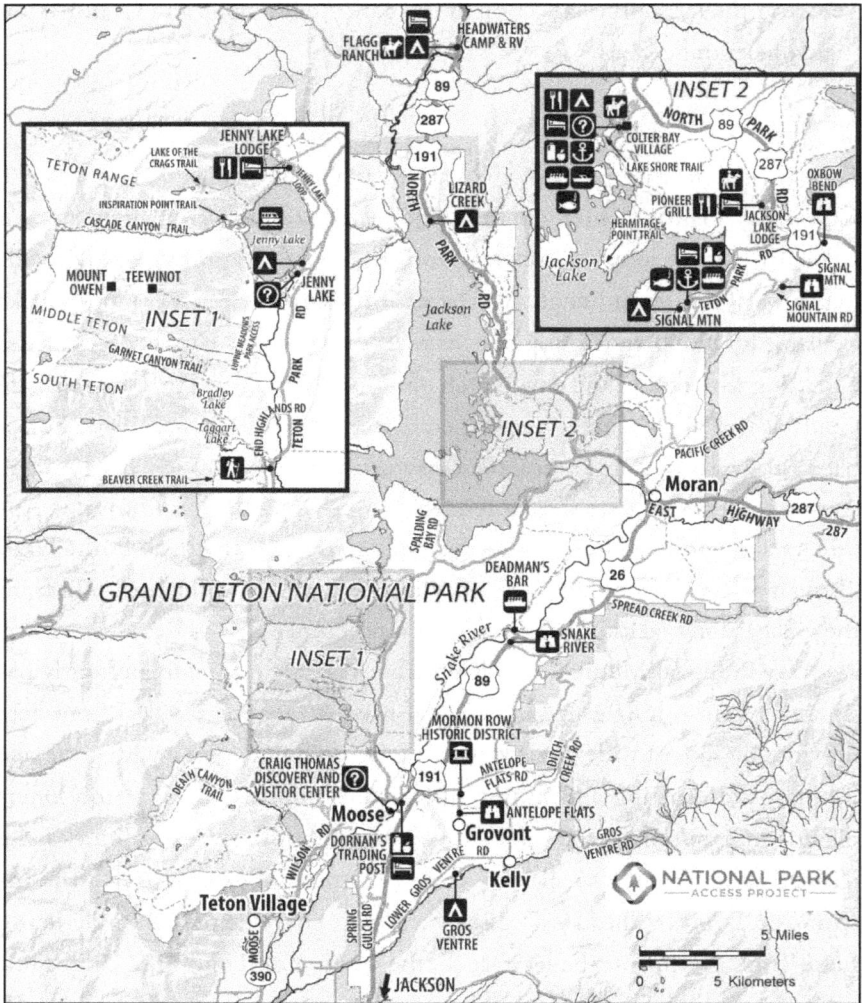

Day 3: The Snake River runs through the park, and a highlight for many is the 10-mile float between **Deadman's Bar** and **Moose Landing.** Numerous guide services run float trips in the park. For early birds, Solitude Float Trips offers a 6:00 a.m. float on weekdays. For the evening crowd, Triangle X Ranch offers a float with dinner, while Teton Whitewater, Grand Teton

Lodge Company, and Jackson Hole Whitewater all offer daytime and evening floats.

With the rest of the day, enjoy **Signal Mountain** and **Oxbow Bend**. A famous spot in the park, Signal Mountain provides views of the Teton Range and Jackson Lake to the west and the Gros Ventre Mountains to the east. There is a paved road to the top of Signal Mountain as well as a hiking trail that extends most of the way up the mountain before joining the road to the top. With so many world-class trails in this park, consider driving Signal Mountain. The round-trip drive, viewpoints, and short walks near the top will take less than an hour. From Signal Mountain, take the short drive to **Oxbow Bend.** This area with its iconic view of the Snake River and Mount Moran makes it the most photographed spot in the park. It's also a good place to see moose.

Day 4: Grand Teton is special in that it offers 8 miles of biking trails from the town of Moose to Jenny Lake as well as a separate 4-mile trip from Moose to the **Mormon Row** of historic and much photographed barns with the Teton Range in the background. The Mormon Row leg through **Antelope Flats** is 4 miles each way, with half on the main highway and the rest on a dirt road. Rent your own bicycles in Moose or arrange a biking tour. The small town of Moose is home to Dornan's Spur Ranch Cabins, a restaurant and general store. While here, visit the park's **Craig Thomas Discovery and Visitor Center**.

If energy remains for hiking, drive five minutes northwest of Moose to the **Taggart Lake** trailhead. This is one of the easier and most rewarding hikes into the lower elevations of the Teton Range. With a distance of 5.5 miles round trip and only 300 feet of elevation gain, this trail reaches both Taggart and Bradley Lakes and delivers beautiful backcountry scenery.

See the appendix for useful lodging, camping, and activity contact information.

TEXAS AND NEW MEXICO

BIG BEND NATIONAL PARK

The topography of Big Bend is so barren and jagged that America's astronauts in the 1960s took field trips to the park to prepare them for landing on the moon.

—John Jameson, from his 1996 book The Story of Big Bend National Park

WINDOW IN ABANDONED HISTORIC HOME OF J. O. LANGFORD,
BIG BEND NATIONAL PARK
JB MANNING/SHUTTERSTOCK

This massive national park measures 1,252 square miles, making it larger than the state of Rhode Island. Situated on the eastern edge of the Chihuahuan Desert in southern Texas, the park has diverse terrain. The Rio Grande River runs 118 miles along the park's entire southern border, through the Santa Elena, Boquillas, and Mariscal Canyons. Mexico sits on the other side of the river, creating a unique international travel opportunity for visitors. Big Bend National Park is the only United States national park to encompass an entire mountain range—the Chisos Mountains, with the 7,925-foot Emory Peak as the high point.

Established in 1935, the name Big Bend refers to the U-turn of the Rio Grande River around the park's southern border. The park is one of the less visited in the Lower 48 and has a thriving ecology, with over 1,200 species of plants and more unique species than any other national park. The park's geology is especially interesting, with rocks as old as 500 million years, sand dunes, areas that have been under a saltwater sea, and many fossils of petrified wood, turtles, crocodiles, and dinosaurs. Big Bend is perhaps most famous for the fossil of a *Quetzalcoatlus northropi*, a giant flying reptile with a 35-foot wingspan. Travelers have plenty of opportunities to learn about park geology and fossils at the park's four visitor centers.

SCHEDULING AND LODGING

Located about four and a half hours southeast of El Paso, three hours south of Midland, and almost six hours southwest of San Antonio, Big Bend National Park is one of the more remote, and therefore least visited, national parks in the United States.

Desert temperatures are unforgiving, and that is doubly true in Big Bend where desert and mountains combine for extreme hot and cold temperatures in the same day. Summer can be so inhospitable that the Castolon and Rio Grande Visitor Centers are closed from May through August. Enjoy Big Bend in the spring or fall.

The remote nature of the park, its size, and the location of attractions make staying in the park especially desirable. Chisos Basin hosts the park's single lodging option—**Chisos Mountains Lodge** (motel lodge, quaint stone cabins, restaurant, and market). Also here is the **Chisos Basin Campground** with 60 sites (40 may be reserved). The park's two other campgrounds are both on the Rio Grande River, including **Cottonwood** (in Castolon) with 24 first-come, first-served sites and **Rio Grande Village** (100 sites; 60 may be reserved). The park also offers a fairly extensive collection of rough dirt roads accessing designated backcountry camping sites. Big Bend National Park is an International Dark Sky Park and the darkest national park in the United States.

UNIQUE DANGERS IN BIG BEND NATIONAL PARK

In addition to extreme summer desert heat and harsh winter cold in the mountains, Big Bend is home to bears, mountain lions, and rattlesnakes. Hike in groups to limit your exposure to bears and mountain lions. To avoid rattlesnakes, hike in the middle of the trail. Due to Big Bend's long border with Mexico, Border Patrol agents are stationed on roads and throughout the park.

RAFTING THE RIO GRANDE THROUGH SANTA ELENA CANYON

This gorgeous raft trip adds an extra day to the journey. From the Santa Elena Canyon area, exit the park via the scenic Old Maverick Road to the historic ghost town of Terlingua and budget lodging at **Big Bend Motor Inn**. Outfitters that operate the one-day raft trips depart from Terlingua, some as early as 7:30 a.m. Rafts are put in at Lajitas and pulled out near Castolon before travelers are brought back to Terlingua around 5:15 p.m.

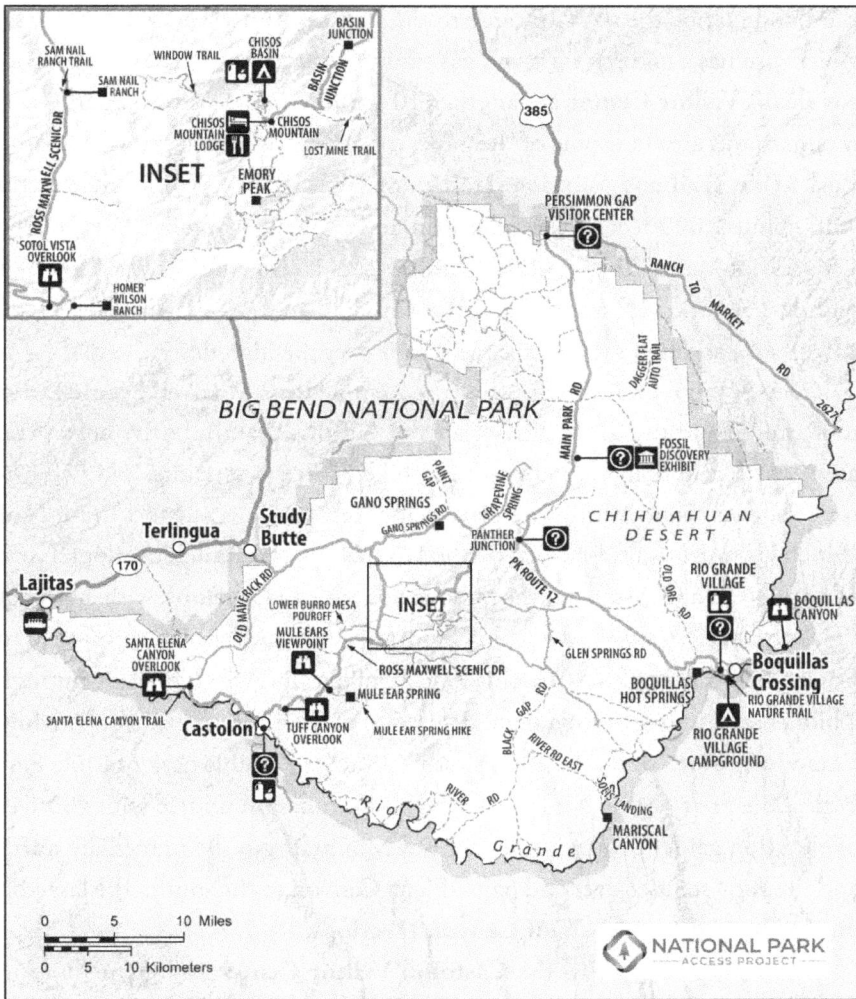

THE TRIP

Day 1: There are three main sections in the park—**Chisos Basin, Castolon/ Santa Elena Canyon**, and **Rio Grande Village**. Chisos Basin is the hub of the park and is easily accessed via the Panther Junction entrance. Not far before the Panther Junction entry point, stop at the **Fossil Discovery Exhibit**, an outdoor interpretive display of some of the major fossil finds in and near

Big Bend National Park. Continue to the **Panther Junction Visitor Center**, which also has a grocery store and gas station. The Chisos Basin and the **Chisos Basin Visitor Center** are another 10 winding miles into the park. This mountainous area has some of the park's most famous hiking trails, including **Lost Mine Trail** and **Window Trail**. Lost Mine Trail is 5 miles round trip with about 1,000 feet of elevation gain and provides sweeping views of the Chisos Mountains. The beautiful Window Trail is also 5 miles round trip, but with less elevation, and starting out downhill. Through "the Window," late-day hikers can often see an amazing sunset over the high desert.

Day 2: From Chisos Basin, take the 22-mile **Ross Maxwell Scenic Drive** to Castolon and the Santa Elena Canyon. Off this beautiful drive are several areas worth a stop, including two short hikes, three viewpoints, and two historic ranches. Shortly after the drive starts, the small and historic **Sam Nail Ranch** is on the right, followed by the **Homer Wilson Ranch** overlook (view of homestead and vista) and the famous **Sotol Vista Overlook** with a view of the entire western side of the park. Continuing, on the right is a cutoff road to **Lower Burro Mesa Pouroff**. This level 1-mile round-trip trail leads through a hidden box canyon with a high, dry waterfall (pouroff). Next, stop at **Mule Ears Viewpoint**, overlooking the nearly 4,000-foot double peak of Mule Ears Peaks. The pretty **Mule Ears Spring** hike, at 4 miles round trip with 400-feet of elevation gain, has views of the Chisos Mountains to the immediate north and the Rio Grande River and Santa Elena Canyon to the south. The last stop on the scenic drive is the **Tuff Canyon Overlook**.

After a short drive to the **Castolon Visitor Center** and camp store in abandoned-historic Castolon, continue to the end of the scenic drive at the **Santa Elena Canyon**. From here, the gentle **Santa Elena Canyon Trail** leads along the bank of the Rio Grande into the canyon. This short hike with stone stairs is considered one of the highlights of the park. From the hike's terminus, visitors may sit on stone outcroppings in the Rio Grande River and see far up the Santa Elena Canyon.

Day 3: From Chisos Basin, the drive to Rio Grande Village is about 45 minutes. Enjoy the **Rio Grande Visitor Center** and the 1-mile level **Rio Grande Nature and Overlook Trail** from the campground around a desert oasis pond and then through the desert to the Rio Grande River.

From the visitor center, take the short drive to the Boquillas area. If the border land port is open, with passport in hand, visitors can proceed through customs and hail a rowboat to Mexico to visit the Boquillas village. Once on the Mexican side, it's a short walk to the village, which has a small group of shops and cafés. Back on the US side, enjoy the **Boquillas Canyon Overlook**, with a view of the longest and deepest canyon in the park. The level yet barely defined 1.2-mile **Boquillas Canyon Trail** leads to the water's edge and the entrance to the canyon. End the day at the 105-degree **Hot Springs** on the edge of the Rio Grande River, accessed past the visitor center via a dirt road and a short hike.

See the appendix for useful lodging, camping, and activity contact information.

GUADALUPE MOUNTAINS NATIONAL PARK

J. C. Hunter has "by personal sacrifice and self-denial managed to keep this lovely [McKittrick] canyon in its original state."
—geologist Wallace Pratt, Senate Congressional Record, 1963

GUADALUPE MOUNTAINS NATIONAL PARK
LIFE ATLAS PHOTOGRAPHY/SHUTTERSTOCK

A fascinating element of some of the western national parks is that they were under water for millennia. Guadalupe Mountains National Park represents an exceptional example of a formerly underwater world. An inland sea extended north into Texas, bordered by what is now known as the Capitan Reef. This is the largest fossil reef in the world from the Permian Period, the last in the Paleozoic Era, about 250 million years ago. The park has the two tallest peaks in Texas—El Capitan at 8,085 feet and Guadalupe Peak at 8,749 feet. These are just the tips of the Permian coral reef that surrounded an approximately 10,000-square-mile shallow inland saltwater sea. The entire sea and reef were buried until around 12 million years ago when geologic activity pressed the 40-mile stretch known as the Guadalupe Mountains upward to approximately the range seen today.

Archaeologists date human activity in the park to about 12,000 years ago when foraging peoples made the area home. Later, Mescalero Apaches populated the region and came in contact with Spanish explorers around 1550. By 1890, the dominant land use was farming and ranching, and it is these historic buildings that the park has on view today. Preserved in 1966 and formally established as a national park in 1972, the park encompasses 135 square miles. It has over 80 miles of hiking trails, with spectacular canyons, waterfalls, and geological features. Activities in the park are concentrated around Pine Springs, where the high peaks are located, along with the nearby historic Frijole Ranch and McKittrick Canyon with its associated desert hiking. The park's remote northern entrance, Dog Canyon, is a two-and-a-half-hour drive from Pine Springs.

SCHEDULING AND LODGING

Located in the Chihuahuan Desert, Guadalupe Mountains National Park has hot and cold extremes. Open year-round, in the winter lows are in the thirties with highs in the fifties, while summer temperatures range from lows in the fifties to highs in the eighties. Though most people visit in the summer, spring and fall are beautiful and temperate.

The closest major airport is in El Paso, about two hours southwest of the park. This is also the airport most convenient to the adjacent Carlsbad Caverns National Park and, via a different route, to New Mexico's White Sands National Park. Midland International Air and Space Port provides a second access option and is between these parks and Big Bend National Park in south Texas.

There is no lodging here, though there are two campgrounds—**Pine Springs** and **Dog Canyon**. These campgrounds provide a combined 29 tent sites, first come, first served. There is one motel at the entrance to Carlsbad Caverns, **White's City Cavern Inn**, about 30 minutes north of Guadalupe's Pine Springs entrance. It offers motel-style rooms and is next to the Cactus Café, which serves breakfast, lunch, and dinner. Carlsbad, New Mexico, is another 30 minutes farther, with plenty of midpriced lodging, dining, and grocery stores.

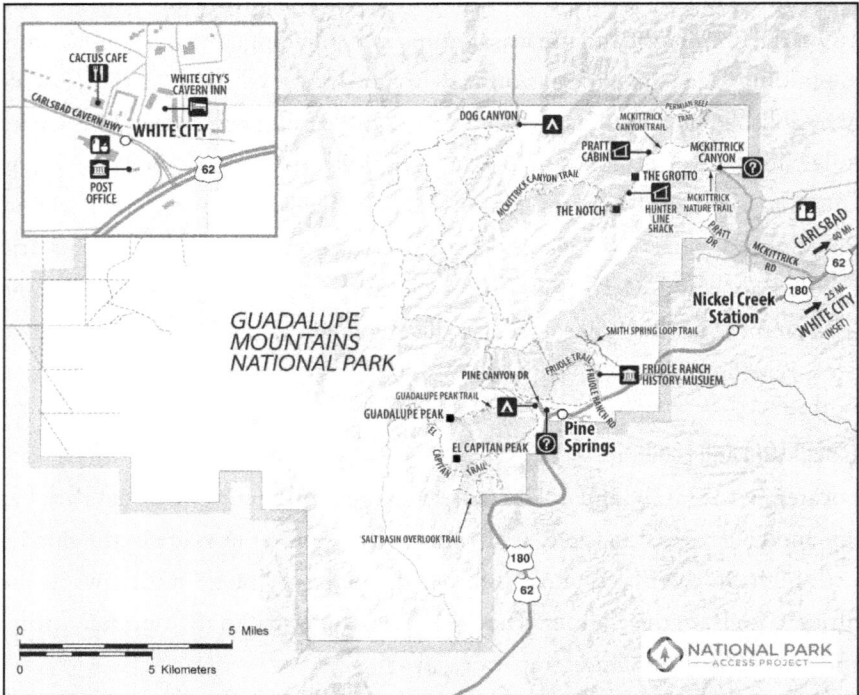

THE TRIP

Day 1: Begin at the small **Pine Springs Visitor Center** and get oriented. If planning to hike one of the high peaks, the trailheads are accessed here. The **Guadalupe Peak** hike to the **"Texas highpoint"** is 8.1 miles round trip with about 3,000 feet of elevation gain, steepest at the beginning. The summit provides views in every direction, in particular of the vast flatland that makes up this part of Texas.

After the big hike, take a short drive to **Frijole Ranch** with its historic ranch buildings and interpretive signage. The buildings are occasionally open for interior viewing. From here, the 2.4-mile level **Smith Spring Loop Trail** leads to a rare desert spring and through the spectacular scenery of the Chihuahuan Desert.

Day 2: About 20 minutes north of the Pine Springs entrance is McKittrick Canyon with a small parking lot and an information station that may have a ranger available. The highlight here is the **McKittrick Canyon Trail**. Though 10 miles round trip, there is a lot to see along the way, making the hike rewarding even if trekked in part. The historic **Pratt Cabin** is a flat 2.5 miles from the trailhead, and **The Grotto** rock caves also don't require much elevation gain. Only at the end is steeper hiking required to get to the **Hunter Line Shack** and "the notch" at the terminus where hikers are rewarded with views of McKittrick Canyon.

Another option is the 0.9-mile **McKittrick Nature Trail** with interpretive signage explaining the Permian geology. For a deeper geologic exploration, the **Permian Reef Trail** is also accessed from the parking lot. This trail is 8.4 miles round trip with 2,000 feet of elevation gain. The park has an electronic interpretive geology guide designed to pair with this hike.

**See the appendix for useful lodging, camping,
and activity contact information.**

CARLSBAD CAVERNS NATIONAL PARK

It's got all the cathedrals of the world in it, with half of 'em hanging upside down.

—Will Rogers, 1931 article "Mr. Rogers, On Mother's Day, Takes 'Ma for a 7-Mile Walk"

FAIRYLAND IN THE BIG ROOM OF CARLSBAD CAVERNS NATIONAL PARK
NAGEL PHOTOGRAPHY/SHUTTERSTOCK

Located in the southeast corner of New Mexico on the Texas border, Carlsbad Caverns National Park encompasses almost 50,000 acres and 120 known caves. The longest cave in Carlsbad Caverns, Lechuguilla Cave, is believed to be 140 miles long, though only 33 miles have so far been mapped by surveyors. This is also the deepest cave in the country, at over 1,600 feet below the earth's surface at its deepest known point. Other important caves in the park include Spider Cave at 3.5 miles long and Slaughter Canyon Cave at 2.5 miles.

Many features make Carlsbad Caverns unique. One of these is the "Big Room," the largest readily accessible limestone chamber in the country. Another special feature of Carlsbad is the way it was formed. Most caves are formed by rainwater slowly dissolving limestone, resulting in sinkholes, underground streams and rivers, and eventually cave systems. Carlsbad Caverns was formed differently. About five million years ago, hydrogen sulfide–rich water within the Capitan Mountains interacted with rainwater, dissolving limestone along fractures and folds. This process, known as speleogenesis, was completed about four million years ago and resulted in deeper caves than are typically found. In 1923, Carlsbad Caverns was designated a national monument by President Calvin Coolidge and became a national park in 1930. While here, take a cave tour (or two), learn about the 17 known species of bats in the park, hike some of the 50 miles of trails, and enjoy an exploration of the clear night sky.

SCHEDULING AND LODGING

Caves and hiking trails in the park can be enjoyed any time. Hundreds of thousands of Brazilian free-tailed bats live in Carlsbad Cavern from April through October. Bat enthusiasts may want to come in the spring to watch baby bats exit the caves for the first time. Park rangers run a free Bat Flight Program every evening from Memorial Day weekend through October at the Bat Flight Amphitheater at the natural entrance to Carlsbad Caverns, with start times varying based upon the time of sunset. Most evenings during this period the rangers also offer a Night Sky Program (Star Walk or Moon Hike). One day in July the park holds Dawn of the Bats. The spectacular flight of the bats is awe inspiring.

Carlsbad Caverns and Guadalupe National Parks are adjacent and share the same lodging and transportation options. The closest airport is El Paso International, with Midland (Texas) another option. **Whites City Cavern Inn** and the Cactus Café are located just before the entrance to the park, with additional lodging and dining in nearby Carlsbad. Within the park, there is a large café at the visitor center. The park does not have its own campground, though Guadalupe Mountains National Park Pine Springs Campground is about 20 minutes southwest.

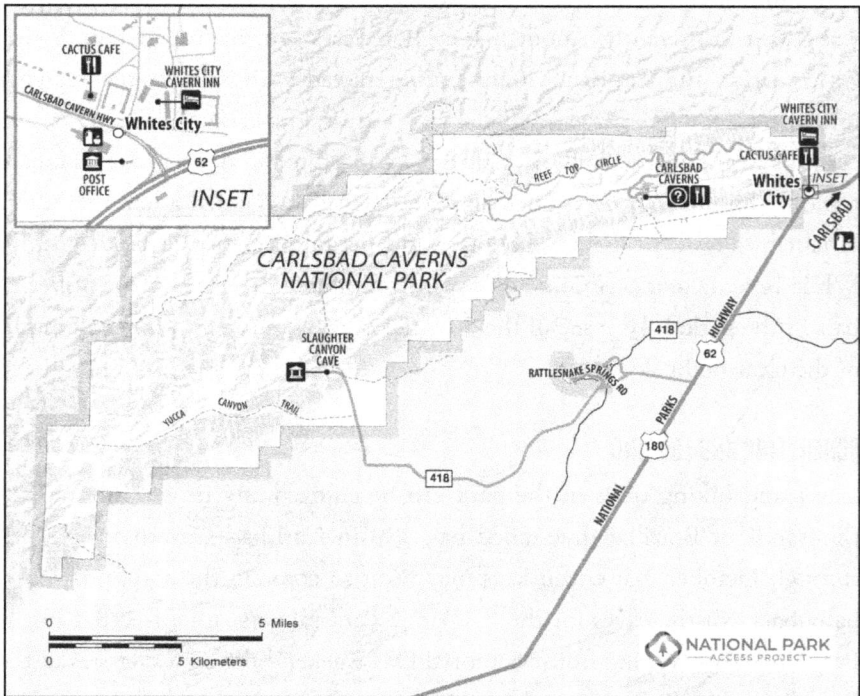

THE TRIP

Day 1: Start your trip at the **Carlsbad Caverns Visitor Center** and get oriented. Cave tour tickets are sold in advance online and also at the visitor center. There are currently five cave tours offered, in addition to the self-guided tour of the **Big Room** that takes about one and a half hours to walk the 1.25 miles of marked interpretive trails. All of the following tours are within Carlsbad Caverns' Lechuguilla Cave except the tour of Slaughter Canyon Cave.

- **Kings Palace:** Offered each morning, this tour lasts 90 minutes and covers 1 mile into the deepest portion of the cave, 830 feet below the desert surface.
- **Left Hand Tunnel:** Lasting two hours and covering 0.5 mile, this is an afternoon tour that is led by candlelight, a very special way to see the caves like they were originally explored.
- **Lower Cave:** Offered Saturday, Sunday, and two weekdays, this tour lasts three hours. It covers over 1 mile and offers an incredible diversity of cave formations. This tour is rated difficult due to 60 feet of ladder climbing and the need to walk backward stabilized by a rope.
- **Hall of the White Giant:** Offered twice per week, lasting four hours, and rated difficult due to the need to crawl in numerous areas.
- **Slaughter Canyon:** Offered once per week, this tour is the only opportunity to see the Slaughter Canyon Cave. This five-and-a-half-hour tour is considered moderately difficult. Highlights include the 89-foot-high Monarch column, the Christmas Tree crystal-decorated column, and the Chinese Wall rimstone dam.

One of the most popular aboveground activities in the park is the **Yucca Canyon Trail**. This 3.8-mile round-trip trail has a steep 1,500-foot elevation gain but accesses the top of a ridge providing expansive views of New Mexico into Texas. End the day with a ranger-led Bat Flight Program at the entrance to Carlsbad Caverns, followed by a Star Walk or Moon Hike.

See the appendix for useful lodging, camping, and activity contact information.

WHITE SANDS NATIONAL PARK

As dangerous a country as ever lay out of doors.

—attributed to writer Emerson Hough in 1931 when discussing the Tularosa Basin

WHITE SANDS NATIONAL PARK
JUDD IRISH BRADLEY/SHUTTERSTOCK

As one of the newer parks in the national park system, White Sands National Park is in its infancy regarding tourism. There is no lodging or serviced camping, and hiking trails are minimal. This area of New Mexico is home to some of the most cutting-edge space exploration research, and the park is sometimes closed due to nearby missile testing. In fact, the western half of the park is in cooperative use with the White Sands Missile Range located immediately to the north, while Holloman Air Force Base is to the northeast.

The San Andreas Mountains to the west and the Sacramento Mountains to the east form the Tularosa Basin in which the park is located. Measuring about 230 square miles, the park consists primarily of white sand dunes. Made of gypsum sand, the dunes are harder than traditional sand. This area was covered in sea water millions of years ago, and the gypsum is the old seafloor, whipped into dunes around 7,000 to 10,000 years ago, after the surrounding mountain ranges had settled into their current configuration. White Sands was named a national monument in 1933 and a national park in 2019.

SCHEDULING AND LODGING

Located an hour and half north of El Paso and three and half hours south of Albuquerque, this park is remote. The nearby town of Alamogordo, though, caters not only to national park visitors but also to those involved in the various space and defense activities in the area. Here there are many hotels and motels, along with the New Mexico Museum of Space History. The park offers hike-in backcountry camping via permit. Camping is not allowed on days of missile testing, and permits are only available directly from the visitor center. For reservable drive-in camping, try the **Oliver Lee State Park Campground** located about a half an hour east or the **Alamogordo/White Sands KOA** in Alamogordo.

Walking on white gypsum sand in August in the northern Chihuahuan Desert is not fun. Deaths in national parks are often caused by dehydration and exposure rather than animal encounters,. Four hikers have died in White

Sands National Park between 2015 and 2019 for these reasons. This park should be visited in spring or fall. A special bonus in fall is golden foliage on the park's cottonwood trees.

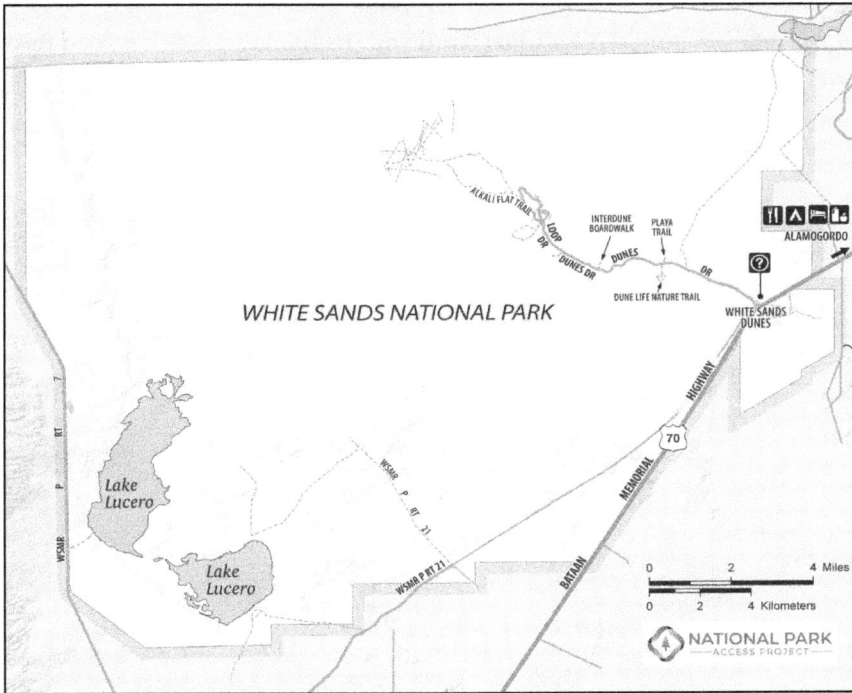

VISITING LAKE LUCERO DRY LAKE BED

The west half of the park is not accessible except by special permit (different from a backcountry camping permit). On eight Saturdays in the spring and late fall, visitors may purchase a ticket to a ranger-led hike to Lake Lucero, a mostly dry lake bed full of selenite crystals. Rangers will explain the park's geography and provide access to an area few people get to see.

THE TRIP

Day 1: The **White Sands Visitor Center** at the entrance to the park orients visitors to the geography, material, and cause of the white sand dunes. The

8-mile **Dunes Drive** accesses the gorgeous dunes, and five hiking options provide dunes access. The first of these is the 1-mile **Dunes Life Nature Trail** starting at the visitor center. From Dunes Drive, the half-mile **Playa Trail** and the half-mile **Interdune Boardwalk** both provide easy dunes-walking experiences. The 5-mile **Alkali Flat Trail** with its trailhead near the road turnaround is not flat but rather a three-hour walk up and down dunes, with the trail marked by three-foot-high orange metal stakes. This is the area where many hikers get into serious trouble from exposure and dehydration. If the full trail seems overwhelming, consider hiking part of the trail, starting on the left and traveling clockwise. The beauty of the expansive dunes and surrounding mountain ranges is evident from many places on this long trail. Off-trail driving, hiking, and biking is not advised in this park due to the nearby military installations.

**See the appendix for useful lodging, camping,
and activity contact information.**

DAKOTAS

WIND CAVE NATIONAL PARK

Have given up the idea of finding the end of Wind Cave.

—17-year-old Alvin McDonald, first known explorer of
Wind Cave's interior, 1890 diary

Bison bull grazing in Wind Cave National Park
H. Turner/Shutterstock

The Black Hills mountain range located in western South Dakota is home to the 199-mile Jewel Cave and its sister, the 150-mile Wind Cave. These caves are the second and third largest in the county (after Mammoth Cave in Kentucky). Make a point to see both cave systems while here and also enjoy Custer State Park and the Black Hills National Forest with its ponderosa pines, canyons, and grasslands. Covering almost 34,000 acres of surface area, Wind Cave National Park is a paradise for wildlife viewing. The eastern part of the park represents one of the last remnants of mixed-grass prairie that used to cover vast areas of the Great Plains. The park abounds with buffalo, pronghorn antelope, deer, elk, bobcats, and the rare black-footed ferret, which was reintroduced in 2008.

Wind Cave is considered one of the most complex maze caves in the world. The cave has unique features, especially its boxwork formation, a honeycombed calcite that hangs from the walls and ceilings. It's believed that as much as 90 percent of the world's boxwork is inside Wind Cave. Though there is about 150 miles of mapped cave, speleologists believe that only between 5 and 10 percent of the cave system has yet been found. In 1968, explorers found a series of cave lakes 500 feet below the surface. Part of the Madison Aquifer, this light- and photosynthesis-free environment nevertheless has at least 4,000 species of bacteria living in the cave pools. Wind Cave is the first subterranean area protected in the United States, designated in 1903 by President Theodore Roosevelt.

SCHEDULING AND LODGING

If flying into the area, Rapid City Regional Airport is about an hour and a half north of Wind Cave National Park and Denver International Airport is about five hours south. Daily tours of Wind Cave are offered year-round. With a constant temperature of 53 degrees Fahrenheit, the cave is chilly but not cold. South Dakota's Black Hills and grasslands can be unpleasant in the winter. Reliable temperatures above freezing occur between May and September, the peak months for visiting Wind Cave. Two special cave tours, Candlelight and Wild Cave, are only offered mid-June through early September.

Fifteen minutes north of Wind Cave is the town of Custer, along with Custer State Park, a wonderful destination in its own right and a gateway to Mount Rushmore. The town of Custer offers modest lodging, while the state park has four historic lodges as well as freestanding cabins available through **Custer State Park Resort**. There are campgrounds in Custer State Park with camper stores and restaurants nearby. For more rustic camping, the **Elk Mountain Campground** is within the Wind Cave National Park boundaries near the visitor center. In addition to the town of Custer and Custer State Park, the town of Hot Springs is located about 15 minutes south of Wind Cave.

CAVE TOURS

A highlight of the park is the two-hour ranger-led **Candlelight Tour** offered twice a day in the summer. For cave explorers, the park offers the four-hour **Wild Cave Tour** where visitors don caving gear and crawl through tight sections. Both these tours require advanced reservations (available by calling the visitor center a month or less before your trip). For the more casual traveler, Wind Cave offers daily first-come, first-served cave tours. The **Natural Entrance Tour** occurs about every 40 minutes; the **Garden of Eden** tour occurs three times per day, two hours apart; and the more strenuous **Fairgrounds Tour** is held about every 40 minutes. All tours feature the cave's famous boxwork.

HIKING CUSTER STATE PARK

Custer State Park's location immediately to the north of Wind Cave is in the core of the Black Hills and has hiking that captures the pine trees, rock spires, mountain lakes, and sweeping vistas of the area. The **Sylvan Lake** loop and trails into **Blue Bell Meadow** from **Legion Lake** are particularly nice.

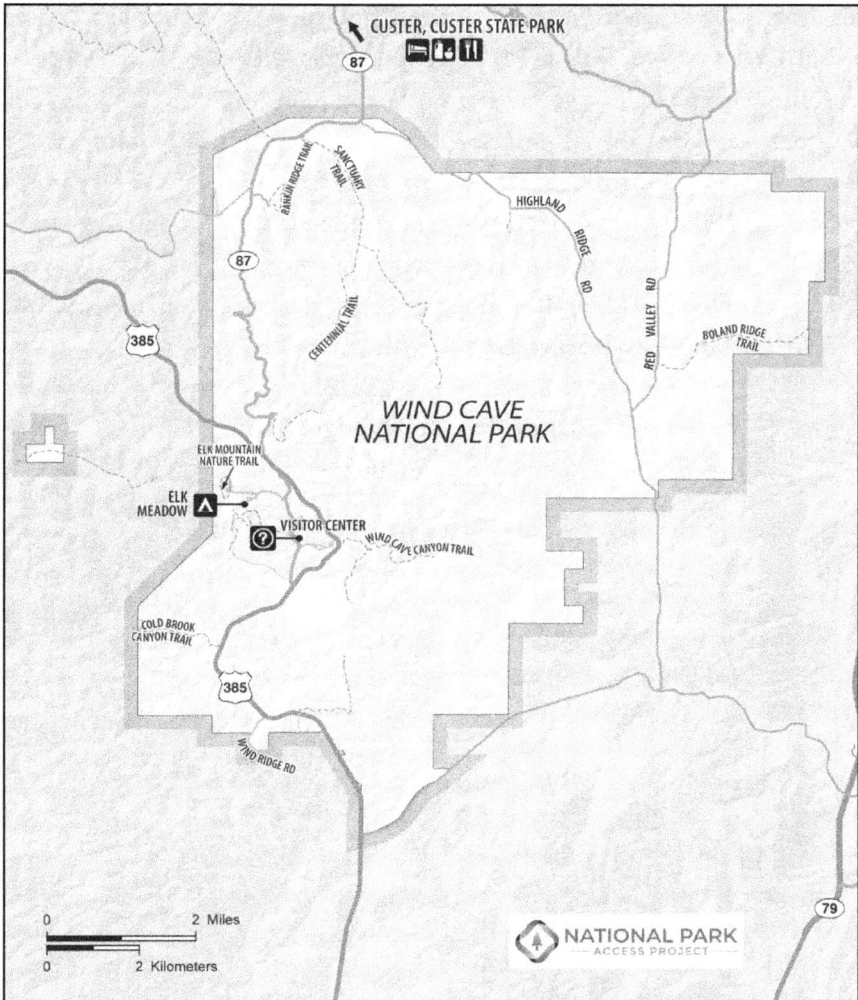

THE TRIP

Day 1: Pack a lunch and start the day at the hub of the park—the **Wind Cave Visitor Center**. Either procure cave tour tickets or prepare for your pre-arranged tour. All tours leave from the visitor center. Spend several hours in Wind Cave exploring boxwork, popcorn, frostwork, dogtooth spar crystals, flowstone, and other cave formations.

Most of the park's hikes are accessed from near the visitor center. The **Wind Cave Canyon Trail** at 3.8 miles round trip with only 200 feet of elevation change provides a good sense of the foothills of the Black Hills. For a shorter hike, access the 1.2-mile level **Elk Mountain Nature Trail** from the Elk Mountain Campground near the visitor center. The premier hike in the park is the **Boland Ridge Trail** at 4.8 miles round trip with 820 feet of elevation gain. Located at the far eastern and remote edge of the park, this area is ideal for seeing wildlife. If heading to or from Custer, stop and walk the 1-mile **Rankin Ridge Nature Trail**.

See the appendix for useful lodging, camping, and activity contact information.

BADLANDS NATIONAL PARK

The Bad Lands grade all the way from those that are almost rolling in character to those that are so fantastically broken in form and so bizarre in color as to seem hardly properly to belong to this earth.

—from the 1885 story "Hunting Trips of a Ranchman" by Theodore Roosevelt

BADLANDS NATIONAL PARK
ROB THOMAS MEDIA/SHUTTERSTOCK

Located east of the Black Hills in south central South Dakota, Badlands National Park has an interesting configuration. Surrounded by the largest protected mixed-grass prairie in the United States, the 600,000-acre Buffalo Gap National Grassland, the park is a mix of Badland buttes, pinnacles and spires, and gentle, rolling grass-covered hills. Though the park has 244,000 acres, over half of this (the Stronghold and Palmer Creek Units) is difficult to visit, located within the Lakota Pine Ridge Indian Reservation. The 111,000-acre North Unit on the other hand is home to the Badlands Loop Road, the Cedar Lodge and Campground, and the park's hiking trails. This is where most visitors spend their time.

Badlands National Park is known for the White River Badlands and their central feature: the 60-mile badland called The Wall. Consisting of eroded faces of stone, tens of millions of years in the making, the mystical Badlands are a unique feature of the northern Great Plains. The park is also home to what is believed to be the world's greatest fossil beds of large mammals. Skeletons of ancient camels, three-toed horses, saber-toothed cats, and giant rhinoceros-like creatures have all been found here. These animals are estimated to be 30 to 40 million years younger than the last known dinosaur. Badlands National Park is an active paleontological area, with a saber-toothed tiger skull found as recently as 2010. Today, visitors will likely see bison, which were reintroduced in the 1960s with a current herd of about 1,200, and other Great Plains large animals like big horn sheep, antelope, mule deer, and coyote.

Badlands National Park was designated in 1978 by President Jimmy Carter. This designation was the culmination of a land-acquisition gone bad. The US military purchased a portion of the Pine Creek Indian Reservation during World War II, with the tribe having the right to reacquire the land at a future date. The reacquisition never happened, and tensions between the government and the tribe grew. Allowing the combined three units to become a national park was a compromise, though many consider the national park land inside the reservation (Stronghold and Palmer Creek Units) to be an unresolved issue.

SCHEDULING AND LODGING

Harsh weather greets travelers to the Badlands during the long winter that can extend from October through April. The Ben Reifel Visitor Center at the park entrance is open from about April 15 to early October. The park's paleontology work is showcased each summer via the Fossil Preparation Lab, open from mid-June through mid-September, at the visitor center. The best time to visit Badlands is during the summer.

Within the park is the **Cedar Pass Lodge** (cabins and restaurant), and just outside the main gate is the **Badlands Inn**. Both are seasonal, with Cedar Pass having a longer reservation window of mid-April through mid-October. Though Badlands is not an International Dark Sky Park, it still has very low light pollution. Take the opportunity to camp under the stars at the **Cedar Pass Campground** or drive deep into the park to the **Sage Creek Campground** where car camping is permitted at one of 18 first-come, first-served sites. During many summer evenings, park rangers bring telescopes and give night-sky presentations at the Cedar Pass Campground Amphitheater. In July, learn even more about the night sky at the Badlands Astronomy Festival.

Located about one hour and 20 minutes east of Rapid City, Badlands National Park can be accessed from the north via Interstate 90 or from the south (between the North and Stronghold Units) via State Route 44. If coming from the north, groceries are available at the Badlands Trading Post. From the south, the Badlands Grocery Store is located in the small town of Interior outside the park gate.

EXPLORE THE STRONGHOLD UNIT

The **White River Visitor Center** is 55 miles southwest of the Ben Reifel Visitor Center at the southeast corner of the Stronghold Unit. Open from approximately Memorial Day to Labor Day, the center is staffed with rangers who can assist with planning a backcountry hike or overnight trip. There are no marked hiking trails in the Stronghold or Palmer Creek Units, and water sources are scarce. Badlands National Park is not a heavily visited US national park, and the Stronghold Unit receives only 10 percent of park visitors. This is a remote area. It is essential to register and plan the trip with a White River Visitor Center ranger. Call ahead to see if circumstances have temporarily closed the area to hikers.

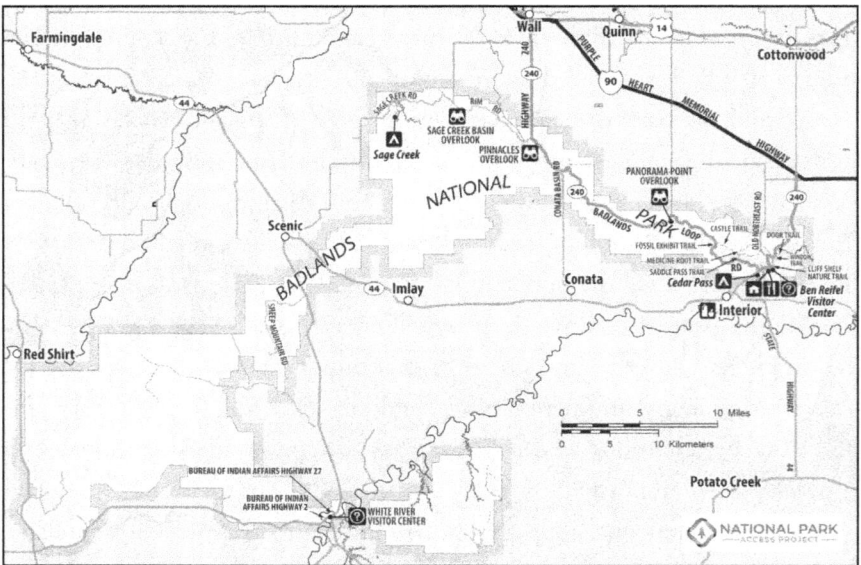

THE TRIP

Day 1: Pack a lunch and start the day at the **Ben Reifel Visitor Center**. If the season is right, enjoy visiting the paleontologists at the **Fossil Preparation Lab**. From the visitor center, the central trailhead parking lot is only a short drive up to **Cedar Pass**. Virtually all of the park's hiking trails may be accessed from here. The short hikes, including **Notch Trail** (1.3 miles round trip, 131 feet elevation change), **Window Trail** (0.2 miles round trip, 6 feet elevation change), and **Door Trail** (0.8 miles round trip, 36 feet elevation change) offer a variety of terrain and together provide 180-degree views to the park's north, east, and south toward the Pine Ridge Reservation and grasslands. The chalky white Badland soil can be baking hot, with the reflection almost blinding. Water and sunglasses are a must.

From the parking lot leading west is the 10.5-mile point-to-point **Castle Trail**. Cut the hike to 4.7 level miles by looping back to the parking lot via the **Medicine Root Trail**. This loop provides a wonderful diversity of views, including badlands, sparse woods, and fields of wildflowers growing out of almost nothing. After hiking, begin the Badlands Loop Road. This loop is U-shaped, from Cedar Pass to the Pinnacles entrance. From Pinnacles, the road continues as Sage Creek Road for another 13 miles to the end of the park. It's worthwhile to experience the full drive, including Sage Creek. There are about 15 viewpoints along the way, including **Pinnacles Overlook**, **Conata Basin Overlook**, and **Panorama Point** as well as the fascinating **Roberts Prairie Dog Town**. The full drive, including stops, can take between one and three hours. This area of the park is national wilderness and has no designated hiking trails. End the day at the Cedar Pass Lodge or Cedar Pass Campground and enjoy the open night sky.

See the appendix for useful lodging, camping, and activity contact information.

THEODORE ROOSEVELT NATIONAL PARK

Prairie-dogs are abundant . . . they are in shape like little woodchucks, and are the most noisy and inquisitive animals imaginable. They are never found singly, but always in towns of several hundred inhabitants; and these towns are found in all kinds of places where the country is flat and treeless.

—attributed to Theodore Roosevelt, president of the United States, 1901–1909

COTTONWOOD FOREST IN THEODORE ROOSEVELT NATIONAL PARK
SHARON DAY/SHUTTERSTOCK

This Great Plains park honors Theodore (Teddy) Roosevelt, the twenty-sixth president of the United States who served from 1901 to 1909 during the infancy of the national park system. As president he established three national parks: Crater Lake in Oregon, Wind Cave in South Dakota, and Mesa Verde in Colorado. He also helped establish the US Forest Service and set aside millions of acres as national monuments. Five national monuments named by President Roosevelt later became national parks, including Olympic in Washington, Grand Canyon and Petrified Forest in Arizona, and Pinnacles and Lassen Volcanic in California.

North Dakota, though, had a special place in Teddy Roosevelt's heart. In the fall of 1883, after the death of his wife and mother, Roosevelt traveled into what were then the Dakota Territories and purchased the Chimney Butte cattle ranch. The ranch had a Maltese cross as its cattle brand, becoming the namesake for Roosevelt's Maltese Cross residential cabin, a replica of which is now in the Theodore Roosevelt National Park South Unit. The following year he extended his holdings and purchased Elkhorn Ranch on the Little Missouri River, 30 miles northwest of Maltese Cross. After a few years in the area, Roosevelt returned to politics, a new marriage, and eventually the presidency. His last visit to the area was in 1896. Theodore Roosevelt National Park was established as a national memorial park in 1947 and was redesignated a national park in 1978.

The 110-square-mile park has three sections—the South Unit, the North Unit, and the small Elkhorn Ranch. While these sections are not connected, they all are surrounded by the 1,033,000-square-mile Little Missouri National Grasslands, resulting in a pristine rural Great Plains experience. The park, along with the national grasslands, preserves virgin and near-virgin prairie as well as the North Dakota multicolored badlands and extensive surface beds of petrified wood (located in the South Unit). At the time of Teddy Roosevelt this was buffalo country, and the animals were reintroduced into both units of the park between 1956 and 1962, with the park now boasting several hundred head. In addition, almost 200 species of birds call the park home, as do deer, elk, wild horses, coyotes, and of course prairie dogs.

SCHEDULING AND LODGING

This far north park is not near a major airport, so it's worth considering a combined trip with Badlands and Wind Cave National Parks, located about five hours to the south in South Dakota. In this case, flight access would be via Rapid City. Though the park is open year-round, both the North Unit and the South Unit have scenic drives that are partially closed in the winter. Closure is weather dependent and can happen in November or earlier, with temperatures staying below freezing through April. To make the most of this park, visit in summer, June through September. The North Unit is about 70 miles north of the South Unit. If including Elkhorn Ranch, the drive is about three hours between the two units.

The South Unit is bounded on the south by Interstate 94 with inexpensive hotels and motels lining the interstate along the park border. The small town of Medora has the highest concentration of lodging, as well as restaurants and shops. Inside the South Unit is the **Cottonwood Campground** (72 sites; half first-come, first served; half available for reservation). If camping, supplies are available at the Medora Convenience Store. There is no national park camping near the Elkhorn Ranch historic cabin sites, though the private **Elkhorn Campground** has sites for tents and RVs. In the North Unit, the **Juniper Campground** offers 27 first-come, first-served sites, and the small town of Watford City, about 15 minutes north of the North Unit, has numerous hotels and motels.

THE TRIP

Day 1: Begin the trip in the Painted Canyon area on the east side of the South Unit and outside the park's access gate. Here the **Painted Canyon Visitor Center** provides expansive views of the South Unit's Painted Canyon. Badland formations in this area are considered the most vibrant in the park, and the views are superior to most found on the park's scenic drives. The visitor center provides access to the 0.9-mile flat **Painted Canyon Nature Trail** and the 4.2-mile round-trip **Painted Canyon Trail**. This latter trail descends 400 feet into the Painted Canyon, but once on the bottom, the trail is fairly flat. Considered one of the top hikes in the park, visitors are treated to ubiquitous petrified wood and stunning multicolored badlands. The Painted Canyon Trail connects with other long trails throughout the park.

Head to Medora and the **South Unit Visitor Center**. Get oriented and visit the **Maltese Cross Cabin**, a replica of Theodore Roosevelt's first North Dakota holding. From Medora, enter the park and the 36-mile Scenic Loop Drive, with the Little Missouri River on the left. Stop first at **Peaceful Valley Ranch**, the only original homesite in the park, dating to about 1884. Theodore Roosevelt National Park has around 15 prairie dog towns, including several on the Scenic Loop Drive. A great place to see the prairie dogs is the dirt access road just past Peaceful Valley that leads to the **Lower Paddock Creek Trail**. This trail accesses an 11.5-mile loop through the heart of the badlands, but whether hiking or not, the start of the trail is thick with prairie dogs. Stand still for a few minutes and see hundreds of these curious animals.

Continue on the loop road. For a short 0.8-mile hike, stop at **Wind Canyon Trail** on the left. Proceeding on the loop drive, there are four more pullouts worth enjoying: the **Boicourt Overlook** and 0.3-mile trail, the **Buck Hill Lookout** with a 0.4-mile exploratory trail, the **Coal Vein Trail** at 0.8 miles, and the **Badlands Overlook**.

Day 2: Before heading out, pack a lunch and fill your vehicle with gas if going to **Elkhorn Ranch**. The ranch is about an hour north of Medora via dirt roads. There are no cabins or ranch buildings to view, but this isolated site with historic building foundations provides a sense of living in a very remote and, for much of the year, inhospitable place. It's worth the drive and visit.

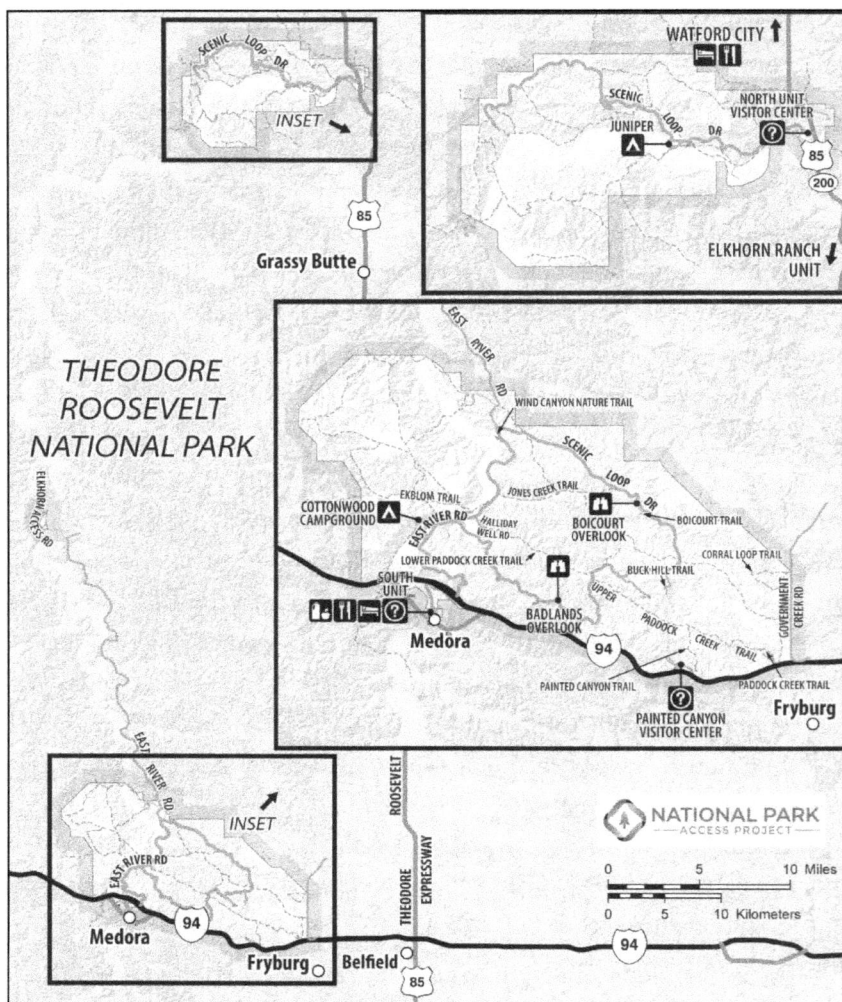

Another two-hour drive north leads to the **North Unit Visitor Center** and the 28-mile round-trip Scenic Loop Drive. There are a number of terrific hikes here, accessed from the scenic drive and connected to each other. A longer hike that connects almost all of them starts at Juniper Campground on the **Buckhorn Trail** toward the prairie dog towns. From here, take the **Caprock Coulee Nature Trail** and then circle around to the south to the

Achenbach Trail and back to the campground. This loop touches almost all the highlight hiking trails and is a mostly level 7.3 miles. At the end of the Scenic Loop Drive is the **Oxbow Overlook** looking out on the Little Missouri River and a 2.4-mile round-trip hike from here to **Sperati Point** for an even better view of the river and grasslands.

**See the appendix for useful lodging, camping,
and activity contact information.**

MINNESOTA AND MICHIGAN

VOYAGEURS NATIONAL PARK

We are against the park because: (1) It is impossible to preserve a country by flooding it with people—and if the park is successful, you will have people.

—Mr. and Mrs. Lane Peterson to the Voyageurs National Park subcommittee hearing, August 21, 1969

VOYAGEURS NATIONAL PARK
BLUEBARRONPHOTO/SHUTTERSTOCK

Encompassing 218,000 acres of land and water in northern Minnesota on the Canadian border, Voyageurs National Park offers over 500 islands and 655 miles of shoreline. Centered around the Rainy Lake Watershed that drains into Lake Superior through the Boundary Waters Wilderness, the national park divides its connected water bodies into four "lakes." The largest, Rainy Lake, is on the north side of the park, sharing a water boundary with Canada. The next largest, Kabetogama Lake, is separated from Rainy Lake by the park's major land body—the Kabetogama Peninsula (water access only). Moving east are two smaller lakes, Namakan and Sand Point.

From about 1700 to 1850 when fur trading was an important part of global commerce, *voyageurs*, or French fur traders, were active in this area known as the Voyageur Highway. Full of moose, gray wolves, loons, and beavers, this area is teeming with life. The park was authorized in 1975, and despite concerns expressed during congressional hearings regarding too many tourists, Voyageurs is one of the least visited national parks in the system.

SCHEDULING AND LODGING

Located about three hours north of Duluth, Minnesota, and four hours north of Minneapolis, this park takes some planning. Peak season is summer when the beautiful waterways can be enjoyed. Voyageurs National Park can be uncomfortably buggy through June, so if possible, plan to visit in July, August, or September. That said, if visiting Duluth in January, come on up. This is one of the northern US national parks that caters to winter visitors, with cross-country skiing and snowshoeing trails as well as a snowmobiling trail network.

While there is only one lodge in the park—**Kettle Falls Hotel** (and restaurant) on the Kabetogama Peninsula and only accessible by boat—there are many other wonderful waterfront options accessible by car. On the Ash River is the **Ash Trail Lodge** and the **Ash-Ka-Nam Resort and Lodge**. Both have small restaurants. Near the Rainy Lake Visitor Center and the Rainy Lake Boat Tour is **Thunderbird Lodge**, which provides hotel rooms, cabins, dining, moorage, boat rentals, and guide service. Between these two is the Lake Kabetogama Visitor Center, where there are many waterfront properties, most of which are loose collections of cabins, typically sharing a beach, dock, and sometimes with associated RV sites and/or campsites. A representative lodge is the **Pine Aire Resort** (cabins, lodge, and RV sites). There is one restaurant in the area: The Rocky Ledge Grill. The Gateway General Store is centrally located midway between the park's Ash River and Kabetogama sections. The busy town of International Falls near Rainy Lake has several grocery stores.

One of the International Dark Sky Parks, Voyageurs has some incredible camping options. Traditional serviced campgrounds don't exist inside the park boundaries, but the Kabetogama State Forest offers the lakefront 61-site **Woodenfrog Campground**, not far north of the Lake Kabetogama Visitor Center. The **Ash River State Forest Campground** is near the Ash River entrance. Voyageurs National Park is known for its campsites that all require access by boat. These campsites are divided into front-country (boat access, no additional hiking or canoeing) and backcountry (boat access, then hike or canoe to site). Both front-country and backcountry sites may be reserved through Recreation.gov.

RANGER-LED TOUR BOAT TRIPS

The park offers several summertime boat trips—from Rainy Lake Visitor Center and Lake Kabetogama Visitor Center. These include the full-day Kettle Falls Tour, the Grand Tour, the Life of the Lake Tour to the Harry Oveson Fish Camp, and the Ellsworth Rock Gardens tour. Advanced reservations are strongly encouraged.

BOATING, FISHING, WATER TAXIS, AND CANOEING IN VOYAGEURS NATIONAL PARK

With the exception of a few nice trails, most of the park activities require boat service. Lodges mentioned above and others rent small motor boats to guests and the public (boating license not required), and several offer guide service as well. Demand is high for independent boat trips so make reservations in advance.

For those planning the center-peninsula 9-mile Cruiser Lake Trail connecting Lost Bay on Kabetogama Lake to Anderson Bay on Rainy Lake, consider hiring a water taxi in advance. Border Guide Service has set-price water taxi service to major destinations in the park. If going this route, for an extra treat, once on the Kabetogama Peninsula, the national park has placed canoes in the backcountry available for rent on Recreation.gov. Canoes are concentrated in the lakes off Lost Bay (Shoepack, Elk, and Brown Lakes), and also in the more remote Chain of Lakes area.

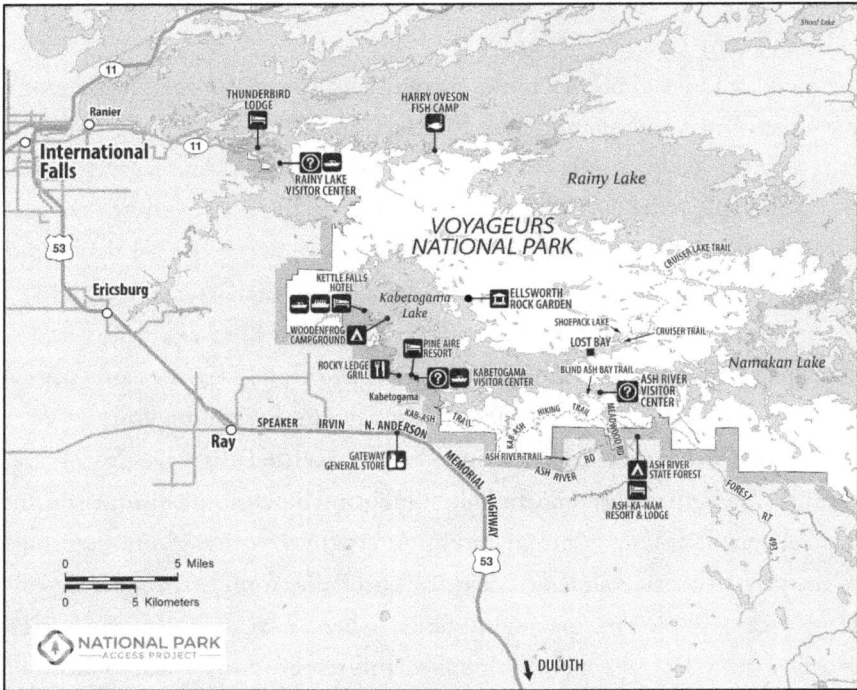

BRING A PROFESSIONAL MAP

Phone service can be spotty in the park, the battery can run dry, and a paper copy of the national park map will not do for a self-guided boat trip and hike on the Kabetogama Peninsula. If planning a peninsula adventure, make sure to have one or more waterproof, tear-resistant maps that are made specifically for wet environments. One option is the National Geographic Voyageurs Park and Paddle Routes Map Pack.

THE TRIP

Day 1: Start the trip near the Canadian border in International Falls with a visit to the **Rainy Lake Visitor Center**. Enjoy the full-size moose exhibit before embarking by boat on the **Grand Tour of Rainy Lake**. The short **Oberholtzer Trail** from the visitor center looks over beautiful **Black Bay**. End the day at the nearby Thunderbird Lodge and use the lodge kayaks for a jaunt in Rainy Lake.

Day 2: Drive about 45 minutes south and spend the day on Kabetogama Lake. The **Kabetogama Lake Visitor Center** is here, as is the option to join a ranger-led boat tour to **Ellsworth Rock Gardens**. Alternatively, rent a boat and explore the park's signature lakefront destinations, with the terraced Ellsworth Rock Gardens and **Lost Bay** being customary stops. At the head of Lost Bay is a dock accessing the 9-mile cross-peninsula **Cruiser Trail**. Hike a bit on this remote trail and end the day canoeing on **Elk Lake**, which can be accessed by walking from the dock along the shoreline. Day-use canoes at Elk Lake are available with an advanced reservation on Recreation.gov.

Day 3: The ranger-led boat trip to historic **Kettle Falls** leaves from Kabetogama. This trip allows time for light hiking and lunch at the historic inn and has the benefit of ranger interpretation. Alternatively, drive 25 minutes south to the park's historic **Ash River Visitor Center**, and from here the Kettle Falls Hotel boat will pick up overnight guests. A benefit of staying at the hotel is access to rented kayaks and motor boats. This remote area, which looks south into Canada, is at the separation point (Kettle Falls) between Namakan Lake and Rainy Lake. Visitors can access both lakes via kayak and Rainy Lake via motor boat. Regardless of whether a Kettle Falls visit is planned, enjoy the Ash River section, which hosts the park's major hiking trails accessible by car.

There are three trails here, with the first two, the 1.4-mile **Sullivan Lake Trail** and the 3.6-mile **Blind Ash Bay Trail**, providing a sense of the inland terrain as it interacts with the watershed. The third trail and the longest trail in the park is also here—the **Kab-Ash Trail** at around 25 miles. This is a wilderness trail, not maintained, but an interesting option for experiencing the Northwoods in their pristine state.

Day 4: If staying overnight at Kettle Falls Hotel, the boat returns to the Ash River Visitor Center around 10:30 a.m.

See the appendix for useful lodging, camping, and activity contact information.

ISLE ROYALE NATIONAL PARK

It is the moose and the wolf that make Isle Royale more than just another pretty place.

—Jeff Rennicke, from his 1991 book *Isle Royale: Moods, Magic, and Mystique*

ROCK HARBOR LIGHTHOUSE, ISLE ROYALE NATIONAL PARK
STEVEN SCHREMP/SHUTTERSTOCK

The largest island in Lake Superior at 45 miles long and 9 miles wide, Isle Royale is the farthest northwest sliver of Michigan. Situated at the mouth of the Boundary Waters watershed separating Minnesota and Canada, Isle Royale lies between Michigan's Upper Peninsula (Keweenaw Peninsula) and Ontario, Canada. Including the main island, about 400 smaller islands, and protected waters around the archipelago, the park measures 850 square miles.

First appearing on a map in 1744, the island became part of what is now the United States in 1783 as boundary lines were drawn between the United States and Canada. Actual possession of the island, though, was by the Ojibwa Tribe until 1843. The island was used by trappers and the Ojibwa for harvesting beaver from the mid-1700s to the mid-1800s, then for copper mining until around 1900. In 1931, President Herbert Hoover asked that a pristine northern wilderness be found for preservation, and in 1940 Franklin D. Roosevelt established Isle Royale as a national park. The park received a wilderness designation in 1976 and was named a UNESCO International Biosphere Reserve in 1980. Isle Royale, with about 20,000 visitors per year, is one of the least visited United States national parks.

Boasting 165 miles of hiking trails, this park is a paradise for those experienced in the outdoors. Portage canoes, kayak from island to island, or use the many water-transport services to curate a trip that combines hiking, paddling, and narrated boat tours. Formerly home to caribou until miners logged the island almost bare, the newer landscape supports wolves, moose, river otter, beaver, fox, and an abundance of year-round and migratory birds. Bring your binoculars.

SCHEDULING AND LODGING

Duluth, Minnesota, provides the closest airport to the park, with Minneapolis another hour south. The park is open from mid-April through mid-October, though winter-like weather can extend into May. Spring and summer happen in fast and furious fashion, with glorious summer recreation underway by June. Peak season in the park is the three weeks from mid-July through the first week in August. Isle Royale may be accessed by ferry or seaplane. Ferry access points are Grand Portage, Minnesota, two hours north of Duluth, and Houghton and Copper Harbor, Michigan, four and five hours north of Duluth, respectively. Seaplane access is from Houghton as well as Grand Marais, Minnesota. Four ferries work together using a staggered schedule. Each ferry has a slightly different purpose, servicing day trips, overnight trips, and mail/supply service.

The largest ferry, the *Ranger III*, departs from Houghton, while the smaller *Isle Royale* ferry departs from Copper Harbor. The *Voyageur II* and *Sea Hunter II* ferries depart from Grand Portage. All ferries leave in the early morning, requiring lodging near the ferry dock. In Grand Portage, consider the Grand Portage Casino, which has a lodge, RV park, and cabins. Houghton is larger, with many name brand hotels. Copper Harbor has a number of small lodging options, including the King Copper Motel on the waterfront. Nearby is the Fort Wilkins State Park Campground, also on the waterfront, and close to town restaurants and markets.

Once on the island, there are two villages. The main village of Rock Harbor is on the north side, while the small outpost of Windigo is on the south side. Within Rock Harbor is the smaller Snug Harbor which is the commercial hub of the park. **Rock Harbor Lodge** and restaurant are here, offering lakeside lodge rooms as well as duplex cottages with kitchenettes. In Windigo, the **Windigo camper cabins** may be reserved via the Rock Harbor Lodge website. Camping on the island is ubiquitous, though only the **Rock Harbor Campground** is near restaurant food service and the Rock Harbor Dock Store. All camping on the island, even in Rock Harbor, requires a reservation and permit. There are 36 campgrounds on this mostly road-free island, including many accessed only by boat. If planning a backcountry camping trip, the Houghton Visitor Center will provide backcountry permits.

WATER TAXI, GUIDED FISHING, BOAT RENTALS, AND *MV SANDY*
Rock Harbor Lodge operates a reservable water taxi with about 15 set-price

destinations to facilitate hiking and backcountry camping. The lodge also coordinates guided fishing trips on Lake Superior. The Snug Harbor Marina rents small motor boats for use in Rock Harbor, which is relatively narrow and about 11 miles long. Rock Harbor has approximately 10 docks with associated hiking trails and historic sites. Also available from the marina are canoes and kayaks. Finally, the *MV Sandy* tour boat offers one or two guided tours daily with interpretive commentary as well midtrip shore excursions.

PARTICIPATE IN THE 50-YEAR GRAY WOLF AND MOOSE STUDY OR VISIT THE SITE

Michigan Technological University (Michigan Tech) has been studying the population levels of gray wolves and moose on Isle Royale for over 50 years. This is the longest running predator-prey study in the world. Each year, members of the public may join in the population inventory by traveling at personal expense to Isle Royale for one of four weeklong backcountry expeditions. These trips require a donation to cover the cost of food and other operating expenses. Enjoy the backcountry with subject matter experts in this ultimate International Dark Sky Park. More information at IsleRoyaleWolf.org. If joining the study is not in the cards, rent a motor boat to traverse Rock Harbor. At the dock serving the Rock Harbor lighthouse and the historic Edisen fishing camp is the summer home of the wolf and moose study. If the researchers are present, they open the site to the public, offering a short lecture and exploration of wolf and moose skeletons.

TRAVEL TO WINDIGO

Experiencing Windigo on the island's southwest shore is easiest if traveling via ferry from the Grand Portage side. In this case, ferry service is direct. If traveling from Rock Harbor, visitors have several options, including seaplane and the *Voyageur II* mail/supply ferry. For walkers, the 40-mile Greenstone

Ridge Trail connects the two locations, and the Rock Harbor Lodge water taxi will deliver hikers to Malone Bay, about a 23-mile hike from Windigo.

THE TRIP

Day 1: Start your trip via ferry across Lake Superior. Approaching the island, the boat passes the distant historic **Rock Harbor Lighthouse** (built in 1855), travels through Rock Harbor, and docks in **Snug Harbor** where the Rock Harbor Lodge and campground are located. Enjoy the small **Rock Harbor Visitor Center** and get settled at your campsite or lodge. This peninsula extending from the main island provides an opportunity for about 10 miles of shoreline hiking. The main trails include the **Tobin Harbor Trail** on the west side of the peninsula, the **Rock Harbor Trail** on the east side, and the **Stoll Trail** on the north side leading up to the top of the peninsula at **Scoville Point**. Later, rent canoes or kayaks from the marina. Kayaks and canoes launch from the adjacent **Tobin Harbor**, full of diving, preening loons, and the occasional sea plane taking off or landing.

Day 2: Hiking the interior of this 45-mile road-free wilderness island is not easy to coordinate. The most straightforward hike requires a water taxi to **Daisy Farm**. Once at Daisy Farm, both the **Daisy Farm Trail** and the **Mount Ojibway Trail** lead up to Mount Ojibway with its observation tower providing distant views of the border between Minnesota and Canada, as well as Canada's Thunder Bay and extended coastline. From here, the **Greenstone Trail** (main trail down the center of the island) leads northwest to the other peak in the park – **Mount Franklin**. Though this peak is less distinct, views to the north are spectacular. From Mount Franklin, turn toward Rock Harbor and end the walk on the beautiful **Tobin Harbor Trail** which terminates near the Rock Harbor marina. The complete hike is a mostly level 10 to 11 miles.

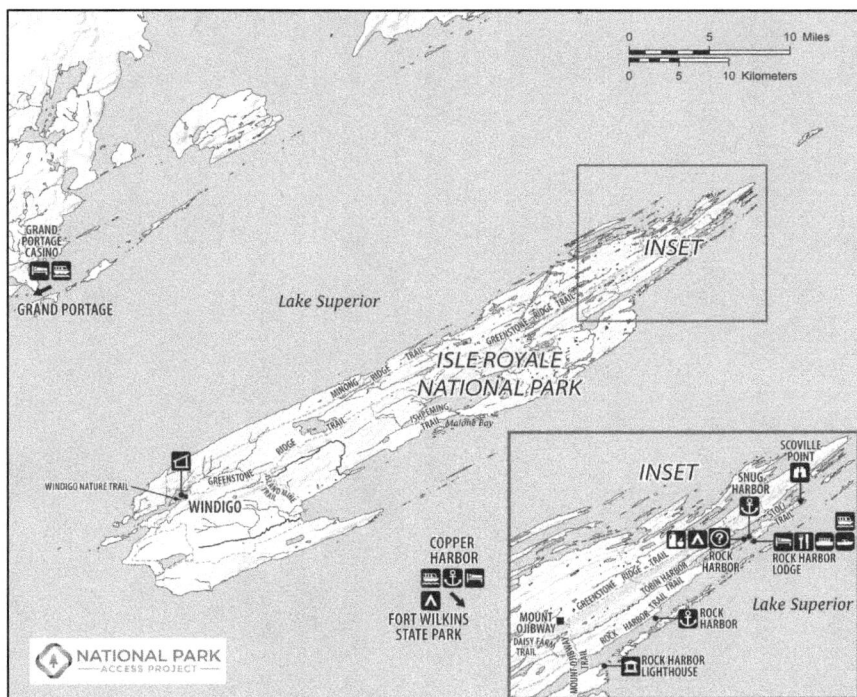

The *MV Sandy* operates from the Rock Harbor Lodge. Each day there are one or two separate tours in the morning, afternoon, or evening. Several cruises offer the opportunity to walk for a few miles as part of the excursion, potentially a substitute for the more ambitious Daisy Farm trip.

Day 3: Rent a motor boat and explore the many hikes and historic sites on Rock Harbor. From the interpretive walk on **Raspberry Island** to the park headquarters and loop hike on **Mott Island**, there is much to see. Make sure to include the historic Rock Harbor lighthouse museum and abandoned **Eidsen Fishery**. The base of the harbor at **Moskey Basin** offers a 4.4-mile round trip hike to **Lake Richie**.

**See the appendix for useful lodging, camping,
and activity contact information.**

MIDWEST

INDIANA DUNES NATIONAL PARK

We are prepared to spend the rest of our lives if necessary to save the dunes.
—English teacher Dorothy Buell,
a founder of the Save the Dunes Council, in 1952

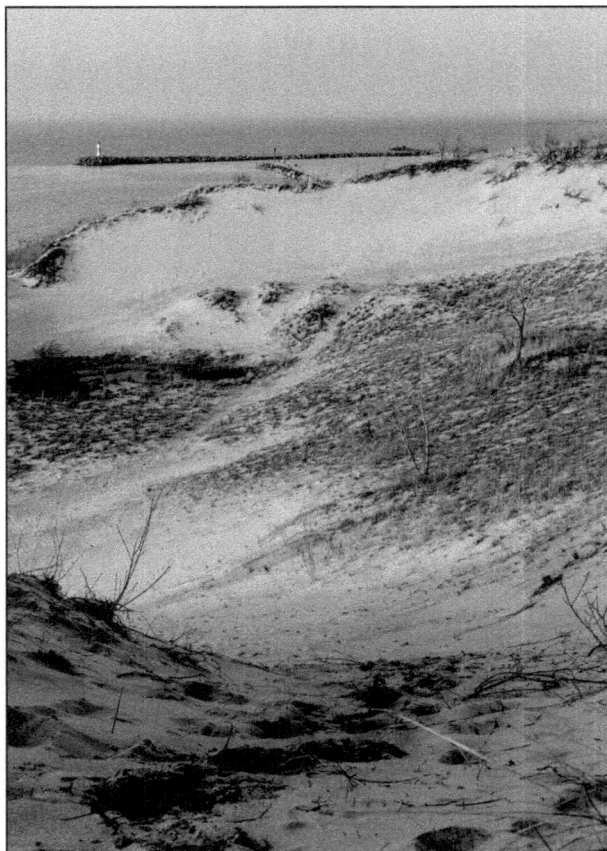

INDIANA DUNES NATIONAL PARK
KIRE MARINCESKI/SHUTTERSTOCK

Established in 2019, Indiana Dunes is the third newest national park. On the south shore of Lake Michigan, the park is on the Indiana-Illinois line, about an hour east of Chicago and an hour west of South Bend, Indiana. Surrounded by maritime and rail industry, the park does not feel remote but rather is an example of a protected area in the midst of development.

The dunes are a unique ecosystem including not only 200-foot-high sand formations but also forests, wetlands, bogs, swamps, and portions of virgin or near-virgin prairie. The park is believed to have over 1,100 unique plants and 350 species of birds in this important migratory waystation. Preservation efforts began around 1900, and the park was named a state park in 1926. Because this is a major industrial zone, preservation efforts were often viewed as impeding the progress of development and commerce. In the 1960s, the area was considered for either preservation land or an industrial port; it took a compromise at the national level to satisfy both the preservationists and the commercialists. In 1966 the park was named both a national lakeshore and the home of the future Port of Indiana, which is now within the national park boundaries. Also within the park boundaries are three lakeside residential developments and an active rail line serving both passenger traffic and the large US Steel operation nearby in both Gary and Portage, Indiana. Over time, Indiana Dunes grew to its present size of 15,000 acres with 15 miles of shoreline and 50 miles of hiking trails. Indiana Dunes State Park is nestled in the middle of the national park, adding another approximately 2,000 acres to the total size of preserved land and providing access to the tallest lakefront dunes in the area.

SCHEDULING AND LODGING

Though this is a shoreline park, Indiana Dunes need not be visited in the summer. In fact, if visiting Chicago, the Chicago South Shore and South Bend Railroad travels directly to the park, where it stops at four stations (the main stop is Dune Station). The park is open year-round, and though northern Midwest winters can be punishing, there is beauty here during all four seasons.

While there is no lodging in the park, the historic **DunesWalk Inn at the Furness Mansion** is just outside the park and a short walk from the Glenwood Dunes trailhead. This property has a remote check-in system and is not staffed. A larger option a few blocks from the park's historic Bailly Homestead is the pretty, half-timbered **Springhouse Inn**, breakfast included. In addition, the nearby small town of Chesterton has lodging options, along with restaurants and grocery stores. For campers, the park offers 67 campsites at the in-park **Dunewood Campground**, half of which may be reserved in advance. The **Indiana Dunes State Park Campground** is closer to the beach; reservations through Indiana State Parks. There are three small areas of private beach homes, including Ogden Dunes near the Port of Indiana, Dune Acres on the west side of the state park, and Beverly Shores at the park's east. Check home share sites for availability.

BOAT RIDES

Inland marinas with waterways to Lake Michigan are found in Portage and Michigan City, on the west and east side of the park respectively. Seasonal boat rides with a national park ranger have been offered through Harbor Country Adventures out of Michigan City, and private charters may be arranged from either marina.

THE TRIP

Day 1: Indiana Dunes National Park has two main sections of dunes—the national park area known as **West Beach** and the state park. The dunes inside the state park are larger, but the national park dunes are more varied. Start the day at the national park West Beach trails, where a parking lot serves all trailheads. The signature hike, **Dune Succession Trail**, begins with an impressive over-dune winding stairway leading from the parking lot through forests and dunes to the beautiful Lake Michigan shore. Two more trails also accessible from the parking lot lead along the shore of **Long Lake**. In total, the mostly level West Beach trails are just under 4 miles.

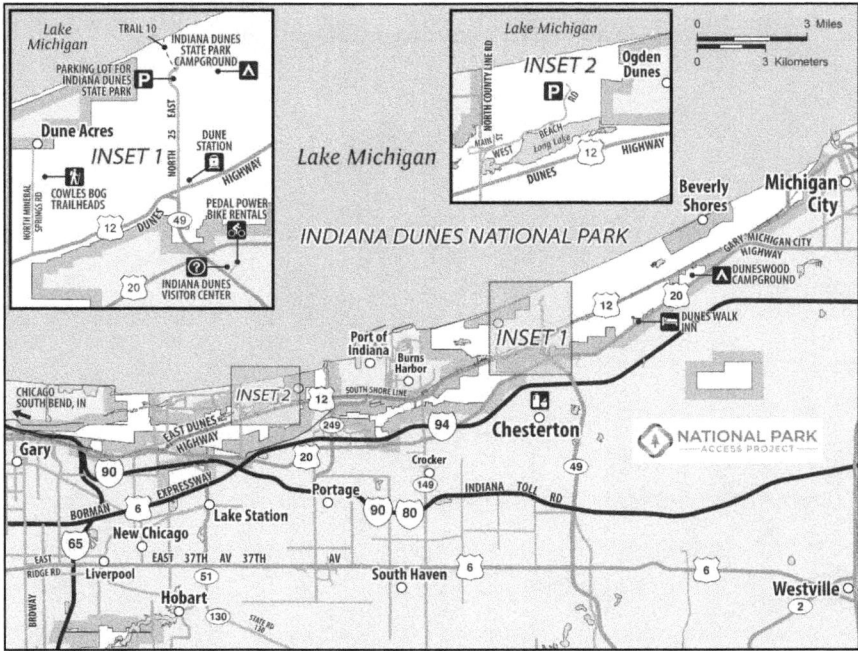

From here, head east to the fascinating **Bailly Homestead** and **Chellberg Farm** area, with historic buildings and hiking through deciduous forests on the 2-mile **Little Calumet River Trail**. A few miles east is the small **Indiana Dunes Visitor Center** and the seasonal **Pedal Power** pop-up bike rental shop next door. Though bicycles are not allowed on the hiking trails or the dunes, the park has plenty of lightly traveled roads, making this a nice way to spend a part of the day. Bike trail maps are available with rentals.

Near the visitor center is a top hike in the park—**Cowles Bog Trail**. This level 4.3-mile round-trip hike features the boggy wetlands near the shoreline and an abundance of unique plant and animal life. With the rest of the day consider a walk through the tall and pristine state park dunes (additional fee required) with their many hiking trails. The shoreline walk is **Trail 10**.

See the appendix for useful lodging, camping, and activity contact information.

GATEWAY ARCH NATIONAL PARK

[T]his little event, of France possessing herself of Louisiana . . . is the embryo of a tornado which will burst on the countries on both shores of the Atlantic and involve in its effects their highest destinies.

—President Thomas Jefferson in an April 1802 letter to Pierre Samuel du Pont regarding what would become the Louisiana Purchase

SAINT LOUIS ARCH IN GATEWAY NATIONAL PARK
TOM HILLMEYER/SHUTTERSTOCK

Renamed from Jefferson National Expansion Memorial in 2018, Gateway Arch National Park is viewed by some as not well aligned with the national park idea due to its small size at only 91 acres and its urban location. The park recognizes the strategic thinking of Thomas Jefferson in his desire to understand the full size and scope of what became the United States. His naming of explorers Lewis and Clark to undertake one of the greatest expeditions of all time was a major event in United States history. It led to the Louisiana Purchase and laid the geographic foundation for the contiguous United States. The Gateway Arch in Saint Louis is the memorial to this vision. Built in 1965 and renovated in 2018, the arch is 630 feet tall and is served by a high-speed elevator that accesses the observation area. The main floor and underground museum are also a must-see.

About 50 years after the Louisiana Purchase, Saint Louis would serve as the location for the most famous property rights trial of the 1800s, the Dred Scott case (1846–1857), where slavery was ultimately deemed legal on property rights grounds. One Civil War later, the United States remains an undivided union. The Old Courthouse where the Dred Scott case was heard is the second part of this park.

SCHEDULING AND LODGING

This urban park can be visited anytime, though the Gateway Arch is closed Thanksgiving, Christmas, and New Year's Day. There are over 7,000 hotel rooms in Saint Louis at many price ranges. Because the park is situated so close to downtown Saint Louis, there are no campgrounds.

Departing from near the Gateway Arch, riverboat cruises on the Missouri River operate from March through October. These trips, narrated by national park rangers, are offered on Saturdays and Sundays, and twice daily from Memorial Day through Labor Day.

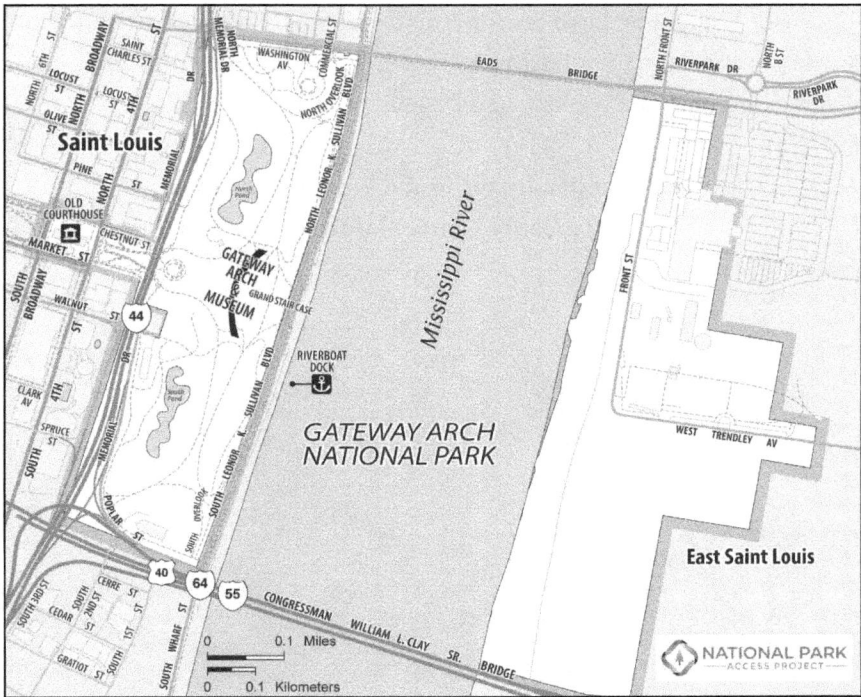

THE TRIP

Day 1: The **Gateway Arch**, riverboat, and documentary movie are ticketed and timed attractions. The Gateway Arch website sells combination tickets for the tram serving the top of the arch, the ranger-narrated riverboat ride, and the movie *Monument to the Dream* about the construction of the arch. The museum below the arch is free of charge. Renovated in 2018, the museum focuses on Thomas Jefferson and his vision for westward expansion as well as the role Saint Louis played in the growth of the nation.

The **Old Courthouse** is just across the Gateway Arch lawn and is an interactive museum with ranger-led talks and sometimes a mock trial. Check the website for activities planned the day you will visit. Even if nothing is scheduled, this fascinating building is worth your time. Exhibits explain the initial suit brought by Dred Scott for his freedom and the legal permutations that led to the Supreme Court viewing it as a property rights case and ruling against him. This case was one of the catalysts for the Civil War.

See the appendix for useful lodging, camping, and activity contact information.

CUYAHOGA VALLEY NATIONAL PARK

It's the Cuyahoga River that puts the cleave in Cleveland, separating East from Midwest, integration from segregation, a place that sees itself as America's westernmost Eastern city from a place that sees itself as the easternmost Midwestern city. The rest of the country sees it as neither, though it must be said that the rest of the country is perversely wont to misunderstand Cleveland.

—Mark Winegardner, author of *Crooked River Burning*

BRANDYWINE FALLS IN CUYAHOGA VALLEY NATIONAL PARK
MICHAEL SHAKE/SHUTTERSTOCK

One of the features of an evolving national park system is that some parks are not yet fully formed. Cuyahoga Valley National Park is one of them. Centered around the north-flowing Cuyahoga River, north of Akron and south of Cleveland, the park is bifurcated not only by the Cuyahoga River but by Interstates 80 and 271. Within the park, Riverview Road is separated from the Cuyahoga River by the Cuyahoga Valley Scenic Railroad Line and does not in fact provide a river view. The bridges over the river are constructed with solid concrete sides, again providing no view. This is a park where visitors need to be patient with the infrastructure, housing, and commercial buildings within the 33,000 acres. Rather than a driving trip, plan a walking and biking visit to best see and experience the Cuyahoga River and the fascinating associated history.

The relatively new visitor center focuses on the maritime history of the area, specifically on commercial riverboat traffic. The Erie Canal, completed in 1825, extended from the Atlantic Ocean to Buffalo, New York, and Lake Erie. Once in Lake Erie and the Cleveland area, there was not a way to connect the northern Midwest to the Erie Canal shipping corridor. Enter the Ohio and Erie Canal, completed in 1834 at a distance of 308 miles connecting Cleveland with Portsmouth, Ohio. The main part of the Ohio and Erie Canal ran between Akron and Cleveland via the Cuyahoga River Valley, with the earliest maritime traffic occurring around 1827. Canal traffic peaked in the 1850s, with the railroad becoming the commercial transport method of choice in the following decades.

In addition to the history of the Cuyahoga River, park visitors are provided with an excellent example of an upper Midwest deciduous forest, a vital bird migration corridor, and several important historic properties. Cuyahoga was designated a national recreation area in 1974 and became a national park in 2000.

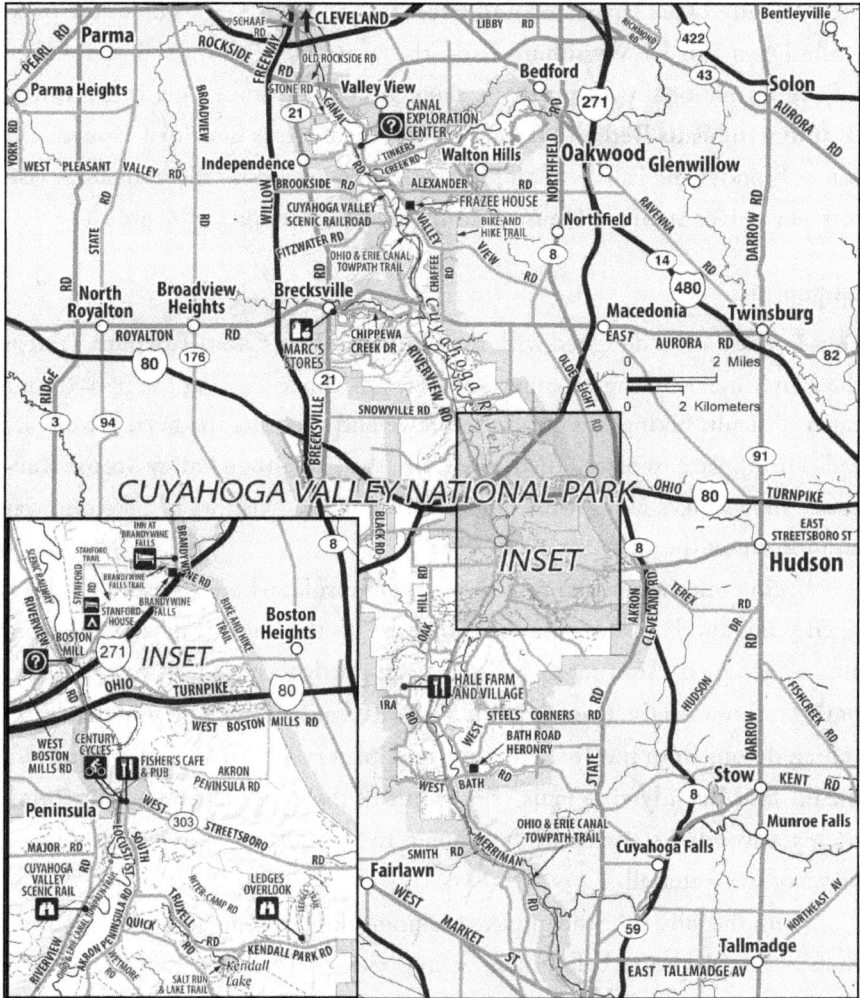

SCHEDULING AND LODGING

Cuyahoga National Park can be visited anytime. The flat valley trails are perfect for winter hiking or cross-country skiing (seasonal rentals available next to the Boston Mills Visitor Center), spring brings wonderful bird watching, summer is lush, and fall provides spectacular foliage. Because Cuyahoga is near major urban areas, visitors can stay anywhere. **Hampton Inn** and the pretty **Shady Oaks Farm Bed and Breakfast** are on the east side of the park, while **Days Inn by Wyndham** is on the west side. For those interested in staying on national park property, there are two options. One is the **Inn at Brandywine Falls Bed and Breakfast** and the other is **Stanford House**. The Inn at Brandywine Falls is quaint but restrictive regarding the hours that visitors can arrive. Stanford House is configured for occupancy by groups.

THE TRIP

Day 1: The park is designed with the **Ohio and Erie Canal Towpath Trail** as the centerline, running 20 miles north–south. Since viewing the park from a car is difficult, biking is a great alternative and prevents the need for outsize walks from place to place. The park's train, the **Cuyahoga Valley Scenic Railroad**, allows bikes along with their riders, enabling visitors to bike one way and return on the train.

Begin your visit in the tiny town of Peninsula, where Century Cycles is open year-round. Visitors may rent bicycles by the hour or day; reservations are not accepted. After renting a bike, head north about 2 miles on the **Towpath Trail** toward the **Boston Mills Visitor Center**. After enjoying the visitor center, detour from the Towpath Trail and head right for about a mile toward the 63-foot **Brandywine Falls**. This is one of the park's signature attractions; there's a wooden staircase leading down to the falls that provides beautiful views of the waterfall.

From the falls, take the unpaved hiking/biking trail to Stanford Road and then Stanford House before connecting back to Towpath. From here, bike about 4 miles to the **Pinery Narrows** and what many consider the prettiest 3 miles of the park. The next stop is the **Frazee House**, an 1820s Federal-style brick home that was one of the premier residences in the area at the time of its construction. Now on the National Register of Historic Places, Frazee House may only be viewed from the outside. Due to stabilization issues, it has been closed to the public since 2011.

Bike a final 2 miles to the **Canal Exploration Center**, featuring a canal lock that's been restored to its original 1905 condition. This river-slowing technology enabled riverboats on the Cuyahoga River to be spaced and was key to making commercial river traffic in Ohio economically powerful. After visiting the center, ride the train back to Peninsula. Consider a meal at the **Fisher's Café and Pub** in Peninsula.

Day 2: Cuyahoga National Park has 125 miles of trails, including the bike trail just described. Drive to **Kendall Park Road**, which is the hub of what many consider the best hiking in the park. Trails here are interconnected and accessed from the parking lots abutting the road. Some highlights are the **Ledges Overlook Trail** where hikers can view the Cuyahoga Valley while on a 2.2-mile level loop trail. On the opposite side of the road is **Kendall Lake** with the **Salt Run Trail** and **Lake Trail**, which combine to 4.3 miles. This is the largest lake in the park and is surrounded with beautiful trees, plants, and wildlife.

Stop for lunch at **Hale Farm and Village**, an outdoor living history museum with presenters in period costume from the mid-1800s, farm animals, an outdoor marketplace, and a café (no admission fee required to eat at the café or visit the marketplace). When finished, head south to one of Cuyahoga's two heron rookeries—**Bath Road Heronry** (located on Bath Road between Akron Peninsula and Riverside Roads). From March through May, hundreds of herons and their young are found here.

**See the appendix for useful lodging, camping,
and activity contact information.**

SOUTH

MAMMOTH CAVE NATIONAL PARK

On arriving at what is called the "Star-Chamber," our lamps were taken from us by the guide, and extinguished or put aside, and, on looking upwards, I saw or seemed to see the night heaven thick with stars glimmering more or less brightly over our heads, and even what seemed a comet flaming among them . . . Our conversation with Nature is not just what it seems.

—from the 1857 *Atlantic* article "Illusions" by Ralph Waldo Emerson

IN THE CAVE, MAMMOTH CAVE NATIONAL PARK
JOLOEE/SHUTTERSTOCK

Located in the Green River Valley of south-central Kentucky, Mammoth Cave National Park has 53,000 acres of surface area and is the world's longest known cave system with more than 400 miles explored and an estimated total size of 1,000 miles. The UNESCO World Heritage Site underground limestone cave extends well beyond the park's surface boundary. The basic geology of the cave includes a sandstone and shale cap at the surface through which water flows into and over limestone ridges. The leaks, called sinkholes, cause erosion and expanded caverns belowground, creating the Mammoth Cave system we see today.

There is evidence that thousands of years ago humans used the cave system for mineral extraction and burial preparation. Modern history of the cave begins around the time of the War of 1812 when saltpeter was extracted for use in gunpowder manufacture. Hyman Gratz purchased 200 acres of the surface and cave area for mining purposes in 1812, expanding his holdings the next year by 40 acres. Values fell after the war, and by 1839 the cave system was sold to John Croghan. Kentucky was a slave state until August of 1863, and part of Mr. Croghan's purchase included the slave Stephen Bishop. Mr. Bishop explored and gave tours of the cave, becoming such an expert that he created a map of Mammoth Cave in 1844 that became a primary map used by cave explorers for the next 40 years. By 1926, Mammoth Cave was authorized as a national park, pending assembling more land. The park was fully established in 1941 and dedicated in 1946 following the end of World War II.

SCHEDULING AND LODGING

The southeastern United States has some of the most forgiving weather in the world. Combine this with the steady temperature of the cave system and any time is a good time to visit Mammoth Cave National Park. Situated about an hour and a half from both Nashville, Tennessee, and Louisville, Kentucky, this park is easy to reach. There is one lodge in the park, **The Lodge at Mammoth Cave**, which has 20 motel-style rooms, associated cottages, and dining.

The park is surrounded by development, including Cave City and Park City, each with numerous hotels, dining, and grocery stores. Camping is abundant at Mammoth Cave with three campgrounds—**Mammoth Cave**, **Maple Springs**, and **Houchin Ferry**.

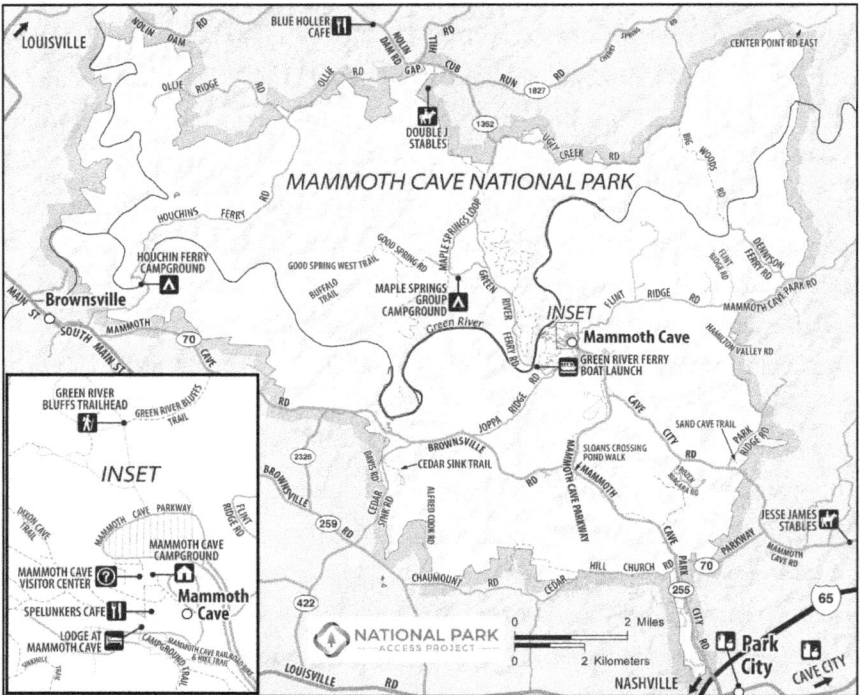

CAVE TOURS

Mammoth Cave National Park offers a number of cave tours. These vary in time of day, length, difficulty, and what is featured. If time permits, consider visiting over a few days with a combination of surface and cave activities. Cave tour tickets often sell out and may be purchased in advance and also at the visitor center. Wear comfortable nonslip shoes, and dress for cave temperatures of around 55 degrees Fahrenheit. Here is a summary of the cave tours:

- **Historic Tour:** Two-hour tour offered throughout the day. Focused on cave history and geology. A great way to start your visit.
- **Extended Historic Tour:** Popular two-and-a-half-hour morning tour including the full Historic Tour as well as River Styx and parts of other tours.
- **River Styx Tour:** Two-hour, 2.5-mile tour including all of the Historic Tour.
- **Domes and Dripstones:** Popular two-hour tour offered throughout the day. Includes Frozen Niagara and part of Grand Avenue.
- **Frozen Niagara:** A 75-minute tour with limited walking of no more than a quarter mile. See this as part of the Domes and Dripstones tour.
- **Violet City Lantern Tour:** Three-hour, 3-mile tour by lantern light leaving midafternoon. Includes parts of the Historic, Gothic Avenue, Star Chamber, and Mammoth Passage tours.
- **Mammoth Passage Tour:** A short tour of cave highlights.
- **Gothic Avenue:** Two-hour tour (portions of this tour seen on the Star Chamber, Historic, and Violet City tours).
- **Star Chamber Tour:** A two-and-a-half-hour evening tour.
- **Introduction to Caving Tour:** An opportunity to gear up and team build for three and a half hours of cave exploration. Saturdays and Sundays only.
- **Grand Avenue:** Four-hour, 4-mile tour includes Frozen Niagara and Domes and Dripstones.
- **Wild Cave:** Six-hour, 6-mile tour departing in the morning where visitors will see unique formations, free-climb cave walls, and crawl through tight spots. Adults only.

THE TRIP

Day 1: Start at the informative **Mammoth Cave Visitor Center** and get oriented. The Spelunker's Café is a great option for lunch. The **Green River**

Bluffs Trail system begins at the visitor center, with this 4.5-mile level loop trail providing a nice perspective of the Green River and the surrounding landscape. Return to the visitor center for an afternoon tour of Mammoth Cave, with the two-hour Domes and Dripstones tour being a great first foray.

Day 2: Spend the morning on a cave tour. The two-and-a-half-hour Extended Historic Tour is a nice option. When finished, exit the park via the Cedar Sink Road and stop on the way at the 1.8-mile level **Cedar Sink Trail**. Enjoy a classic southern lunch at the Blue Holler Café. No visit to Kentucky horse country is complete without a ride. The park has two stables on its border—Double J Stables and Jesse James Stables. Double J is located at the northeast corner of the park, offers two group rides each day, and provides access to remote trails. Reservations required for all rides. End the day with the nighttime Star Chamber tour.

Day 3: The **Green River** runs through the center of the park. Three outfitters—Cave Country Canoe, Green River Canoeing, and Mammoth Cave Canoe and Kayak—serve the park. They all operate trips in the morning. After lunch, enjoy an afternoon cave tour, perhaps the Violet City Lantern Tour.

See the appendix for useful lodging, camping, and activity contact information.

HOT SPRINGS NATIONAL PARK

"Four sections of land including said Hot Springs in 1832 [hot] springs, reserved for the future disposal of the United States [which] shall not be entered, located, or appropriated, for any other purpose whatsoever.

—legislation signed by President Andrew Jackson on April 20, 1832, marking what some believe to be the first national park

ENTRANCE TO THE GRAND PROMENADE, HOT SPRINGS NATIONAL PARK
GABRIELLE MOUSE/SHUTTERSTOCK

Though considered by most to be formally designated a national park in 1921, Congress preserved the Hot Springs Reservation in 1832, reflecting the importance of this area known for its 47 thermal springs with an average temperature of 143 degrees Fahrenheit. This congressional action is one of the first examples of preservation of land for public use and recreation and is understood as a historic precursor to the idea of the national park system.

Comprising 5,500 acres, the majority of Hot Springs National Park encompasses five low-lying mountains in the Zig Zag Mountains subrange of the larger Ouachita Range. The mountain names include Music, Sugarloaf, West, Indian, and Hot Springs. This last mountain is the source of the hot springs, which are believed to be more than 4,000 years old. The mountains support a combined 30 miles of hiking trails and are separated by the city of Hot Springs, which sits in the middle of the park and provides a full complement of services, including lodging and restaurants.

A park highlight is the eight-building Bathhouse Row, with the first bathhouse having opened in 1892 and the last completed in 1936. Each building has been modified and updated over this period. The bathhouses are named, with Fordyce serving as the park's visitor center. Of the remaining seven bathhouses, two—Buckstaff and Quapaw—are open to the public for thermal bathing. Of the remaining five, Maurice is currently closed. Lamar is used for park storage and office space, Superior has been licensed for use by Superior Brewery (the only brewery on national park land), Hale is now a hotel, and Ozark hosts the park's cultural center.

SCHEDULING AND LODGING

Located about an hour from Little Rock, Hot Springs National Park can be visited any time of the year. Though peak tourist season is summer, it's tough to be in Deep South summer heat while enjoying a dip in a hot spring. Try visiting in spring or fall during cooler temperatures. Lodging options in or abutting the park include **The Waters Hotel** across from Bathhouse Row,

Hotel Hale, and **Arlington Resort Hotel and Spa**. The park also has one 40-site campground, **Gulpha Gorge**, that accommodates both tent camping and recreational vehicles.

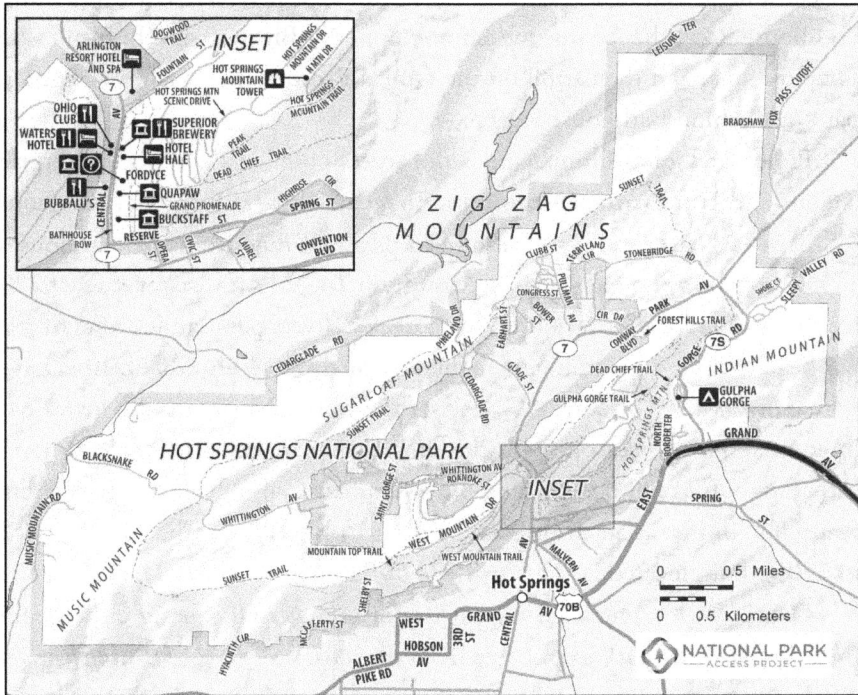

THE TRIP

Day 1: Spend the first day enjoying **Bathhouse Row**. Get oriented at the **Fordyce Visitor Center**, where frequent ranger-led tours showcase a large and preserved bathhouse and convey interesting information about the role of the bathhouses in health care in the early twentieth century. After a tour, make your way to either or both of the two open bathhouses—**Buckstaff** and **Quapaw**. Buckstaff is walk-in only (reservations not accepted), with arrival for the last treatment of the day no later than 2:45 p.m. Monday through

Saturday and 11:15 a.m. on Sunday. The most expansive service takes one hour and 45 minutes and is delivered in a private and semiprivate setting. Quapaw also offers a full suite of spa services and has a low-cost thermal pool for communal bathing. After a thermal springs experience, enjoy lunch on Bathhouse Row (the Avenue Restaurant, Superior Brewery, and Bubbalu's are some options) and then stroll on the **Grand Promenade**, the formal garden path just behind Bathhouse Row.

From the Grand Promenade is the access point to the trails leading up and around **Hot Springs Mountain**. These are easy trails through gorgeous southern deciduous forests. The summit is a half mile from the bathhouses and is topped by the **Hot Springs Mountain Tower**. An elevator reaches 220 feet higher, and the tower observation deck delivers panoramic views of the park and surrounding mountains. The **Hot Springs Mountain Scenic Drive** follows a similar path and also accesses the tower. Note that the tower has hours that vary by season, with the shortest being 9:00 a.m. to 5:00 p.m., extending until 9:00 p.m. during peak summer. Cap off the day by treating yourself to dinner at Superior Brewery or the famous Ohio Club (first opened in 1905), both located at the north end of Bathhouse Row.

Day 2: Pack a lunch for a great day of hiking and walking in beautiful forests. The entire park can be hiked via the loosely organized 9-mile **Sunset Trail**. This trail is a compilation of shorter trails, including the **West Mountain**, **Sugarloaf Mountain**, and **Stonebridge Road trails**. The terminus of this hike at Gulpha Gorge Campground connects with the back side of Hot Springs Mountain. The Sunset Trail is bifurcated by a number of roads and has sections that are within hearing distance of major highways. Though this hike is not a loop, ride-share services are available in Hot Springs for trailhead access.

Start the Sunset Trail hike at the top of West Mountain Summit Drive, where there is a parking lot and trailhead. From here, head west 2.8 miles along the West Mountain Trail to Blacksnake Road. After crossing the road, connect with the 2.6-mile Sugarloaf Mountain Trail to Cedarglades Road. Cross the road onto the 3.8-mile Stonebridge Road Trail that becomes the Sunset Trail as it terminates at the Gulpha Gorge Campground. From the campground, the **Dead Chief Trail** leads 1.4 miles back to Bathhouse Row.

See the appendix for useful lodging, camping, and activity contact information.

SOUTHEAST

SHENANDOAH NATIONAL PARK

If you drive to, say, Shenandoah National Park, or the Great Smoky Mountains, you'll get some appreciation for the scale and beauty of the outdoors. When you walk into it, then you see it in a completely different way. You discover it in a much slower, more majestic sort of way.
—Bill Bryson, *A Walk in the Woods*

BLUE RIDGE MOUNTAINS FROM STONY MAN MOUNTAIN,
SHENANDOAH NATIONAL PARK
JON BILOUS/SHUTTERSTOCK

Perhaps the most centrally located park to major population areas, the 200,000-acre long and narrow Shenandoah National Park encompasses the crest of the tallest ridge in the Blue Ridge Mountains of Virginia. For those accustomed to the rugged nature of the large western national parks, be prepared to find a different and gentler kind of beauty in Shenandoah. The park is known for its sweeping views to the west of the Shenandoah Valley, visible from two famous hiking trails (Stony Man and Hawksbill) and many roadside viewpoints.

With its proximity to Washington, DC, Shenandoah has a rich history of visits from political notables. The first national park, Yellowstone, was designated in 1906. This west-focused effort caused consternation among eastern preservationists who also sought a large national park. As pressure for a major eastern park was building, in 1929 President Herbert Hoover and First Lady Lou Henry Hoover purchased a 135-acre fishing camp on the eastern slope of the Blue Ridge Mountains known as Rapidan Camp. Press stories about Hoover's time entertaining dignitaries at the property helped build momentum for a larger park to be established in the area. The Hoovers gave the property to the Commonwealth of Virginia in 1932, and by 1935 President Franklin Delano Roosevelt established Rapidan Camp and additional land as Shenandoah National Park. The work transitioning private inholdings to national park land went on for many years and included acquiring the Skyland Resort, which still serves guests today. The Appalachian Trail extends through the entire length of the park and roughly parallels the famous ridgeline Skyline Drive.

SCHEDULING AND LODGING

Shenandoah's Swift Run Gap entrance is about 30 minutes from Charlottesville, Virginia, and about an hour and a half west of Washington, DC. The park has two lodges—**Big Meadows** and the historic **Skyland Resort** built in 1895. Skyland has sweeping views of the Shenandoah Valley, while Big Meadows is the park's hub. Both have on-site dining and a market. While the park is open year-round, the lodges and restaurants are open from mid-March through Thanksgiving.

Campgrounds include **Mathews Arm**, **Big Meadows**, **Loft Mountain**, and **Lewis Mountain**, with Lewis Mountain also offering reservable camper cabins. Except for Lewis Mountain, all campgrounds offer reservations in peak season and permit RVs. Camp stores are available at Big Meadows, Lewis Mountain, and Loft Mountain.

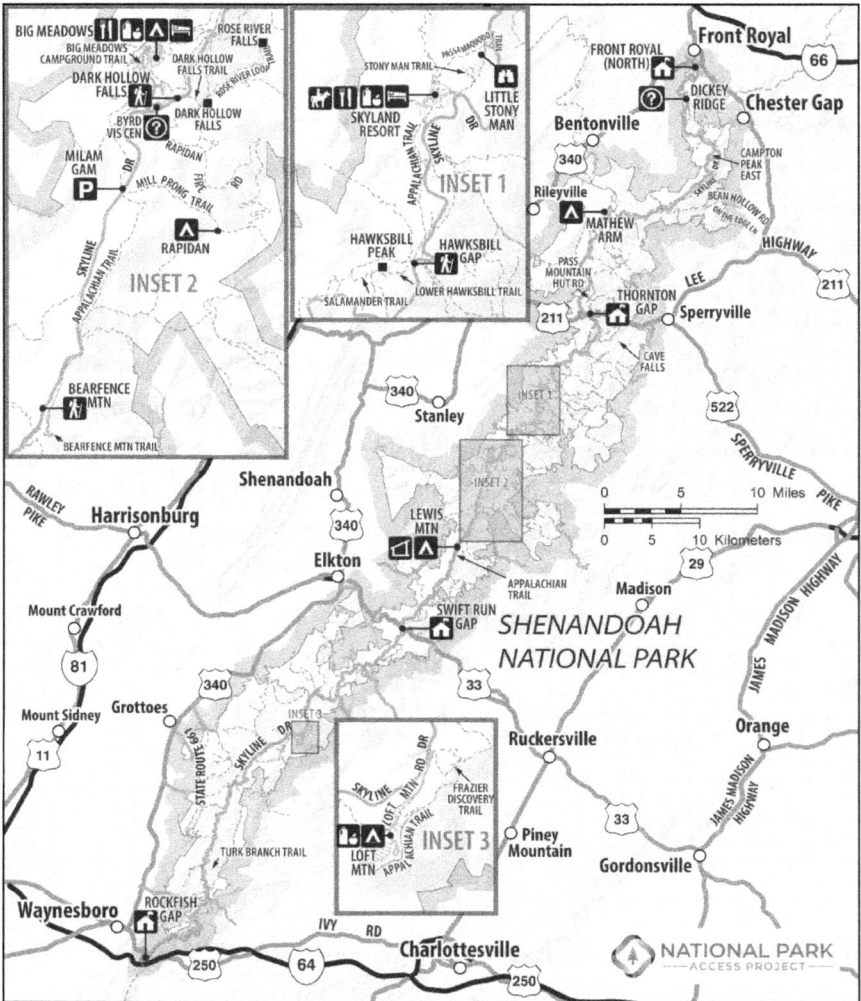

BACKCOUNTRY CABINS

The Potomac Appalachian Trail Club owns six backcountry cabins within the park that are reservable year-round.

DOGS AND HORSES

Dogs and horses are permitted in all areas of Shenandoah National Park.

THE TRIP

Day 1: This long and narrow park lends itself to starting at either the north or south section. To best get oriented, start in the north at the **Dickey Ridge Visitor Center** and the beginning of the 105-mile Skyline Drive. After the visitor center, drive south to Skyland Resort and the **Stony Man Summit Trail**. This trail leads to the second highest point in the park and provides sweeping views over the Shenandoah Valley and the towns of Luray and Stanley. In the near distance is Massanutten Mountain, with the George Washington and Jefferson National Forests in the far distance. Pair the summit hike with a section of the **Appalachian Trail** leading to the **Little Stony Man Overlook** and then walk back to the Skyland Resort via the rolling **Passamaquoddy Trail** with a near-continuous view over the Shenandoah Valley. This loop through stunning forests with panoramic views is about 4 miles and is one of the park highlights.

Between April and November, **Skyland Stables** offers between four and five one-hour horseback rides each day, reservations required. Enjoy a guided ride through some of the country's most ancient and beautiful deciduous forests.

Day 2: Head south to **Hawksbill Mountain**, the park's second major summit-view hike, accessed from the Hawksbill Gap parking lot. From here, there are two routes—a steep and direct version (Lower Hawksbill Trail) at 1.7 miles round trip and the **Appalachian Trail/Salamander Trail loop** on the ascent with the **Lower Hawksbill Trail** as the descent. This latter option is about 2 miles longer but provides views on the ascent and a much more gradual hike. Hawksbill Peak is the highest point in the park at 4,051 feet and provides 360-degree views of the Shenandoah Valley and the Blue Ridge Mountains.

From here, travel south to the center of the park and the **Big Meadows (Byrd) Visitor Center** and lodge. Pick up a picnic lunch at **Big Meadows Wayside Market** and enjoy it in **The Meadow**, which extends about a square half mile in front of the visitor center. When finished, try one of the more famous waterfall hikes in the park—**Dark Hollow and Rose River Falls**. The trailhead is just north of the visitor center, with the 3.7-mile hike extending down to Dark Hollow Falls and linking to the Rose River Falls Loop Trail.

Day 3: Park at the **Milam Gap** parking lot just south of Big Meadows. Across the street is both the Appalachian Trail heading right and the **Mill Prong Trail** heading left. Take the Mill Prong Trail, which will gently descend about 2 miles to President Hoover's **Rapidan Camp**. This is a pretty place for lunch, and in season you may be treated to a ranger tour of the several historic buildings.

After the hike, head south to the **Bearfence Mountain** trailhead for this easy 1-mile loop walk with terrific easterly views. Just south of here are the Lewis Mountain Cabins and camp store. The Swift Run Gap entrance station is another 10 miles south along Skyline Drive, with this entrance marking a dividing line between the park's larger northern section and its southern section centered around **Loft Mountain**. The Loft Mountain area has a campground, camper store, ranger station, and an extensive hiking system with panoramic views eastward. The easiest hike is the 1.2-mile **Frazier Discovery Trail**, which connects with the Appalachian Trail for the 3.7-mile round-trip **Loft Mountain loop hike** ending back at the parking lot. From here, Skyline Drive continues south to its terminus at **Rockfish Gap** and Interstate 64.

See the appendix for useful lodging, camping, and activity contact information.

NEW RIVER GORGE NATIONAL PARK

If they lived at the bottom of the hill, there was what we called a "local" used to run all the time up and down the river. And all of those coal camps, if you lived along the river at the bottom of the hill, you did most of your traveling by local train. It run every day and they could go to Thurmond or . . . Charleston. And that's the way most of them down there, if they wanted to go anyplace, did that.

—engineer Virgil Burgess regarding travel
by Kay Moor miners in the 1930s and 1940s

OLD COAL-MINING TOWN OF THURMOND, NEW RIVER GORGE NATIONAL PARK
RICK388/SHUTTERSTOCK

The newest United States national park, established in late 2020, New River Gorge is the first in West Virginia and expands the preservation of critical areas of the Appalachian Mountains. The north-flowing New River, at 53 miles long, created the largest gorge in Appalachia. Conservationists had long had their eye on the area, and in 1978 the National Park Service named the river and its banks a "National River." That preservation effort accelerated 10 years later, expanding federally owned land from 16,000 to 62,000 acres. The park and preserve as designated today has 72,000 acres, though only 7,000 acres are national park land. These noncontiguous national park areas include the Thurmond Historic District, the Grandview Overlook with a view 1,400 feet down to the New River, and the largest waterfall on the river—Sandstone Falls. The remainder of the park is national preserve where hunting is permitted.

New River Gorge National Park is oriented north–south, with the famous steel-arc New River Gorge Bridge a historic focal point connecting the small towns of Fayetteville and Lansing at the park's northern border. Hiking, rafting, and outdoor activity extends the full length of the river to the park's southern terminus in Hinton. In between is big and small game country; the park teems with white-tailed deer, otters, rabbit, fox, and black bear. The diverse forest is a birder's delight. Bald eagles, great blue herons, and peregrine falcons are some of the many bird species that call the park home. Though fishing and hiking are constant favorites, the park is known for its rafting and rock climbing. Renowned class III, IV, and V rapids are found here, along with some of the best rock climbing in the East.

The area has a vibrant history, with humans believed to be present at least 13,000 years ago and more recent tribal activity centered around the Algonquin, Iroquois, and Cherokee peoples. Today, visitors know West Virginia in part for coal mining, and history associated with the coal trade is central to the park, especially the Thurmond Historic District. Here the Thurmond Depot Visitor Center showcases the first two decades of the 1900s and the historic boomtown that existed to facilitate coal being shipped from the nearby mines around the country. Considered to have the richest coal veins in the state, Thurmond had the finest train stop, banks, and hotels in West Virginia. The town's remaining historic buildings are part of a walking tour offered by the Park Service.

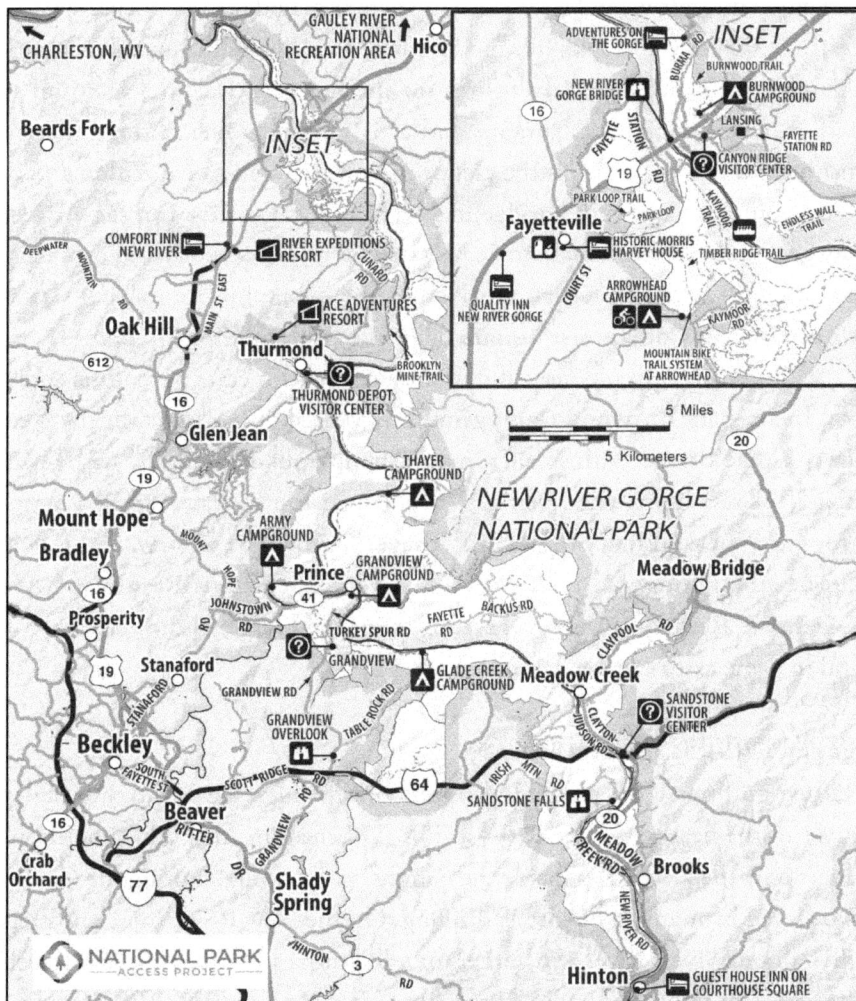

SCHEDULING AND LODGING

About an hour south of Charleston, West Virginia, New River Gorge is open year-round. The beautiful deciduous forest is showcased in the spring and especially the fall, though May through September is the peak time to visit and enjoy this rafting and rock-climbing paradise. Lodging is concentrated in Lansing, Fayetteville, Oak Hill, and Hindon, with all lodging outside the park boundaries. In Lansing, **Adventures on the Gorge** is a complete complex with cabins, camping, restaurants, and activities, including rafting. Though just outside the park, this is the closest option to a traditional national park lodge complex. Across the bridge in Fayetteville is **Quality Inn New River Gorge** and the five-room **Historic Morris Harvey House** bed and breakfast. In Oak Hill is the **Comfort Inn New River**, while in Hinton, the **Guest House Inn on Courthouse Square** offers rooms in multiple properties.

Camping is easy and beautiful in this usually temperate part of the country. The in-park **Burwood Campground** is located in Lansing near the New River Gorge Bridge, with smaller in-park campgrounds (typically with fewer than 10 sites) lining the river. Listed north to south, these smaller campgrounds are **Brooklyn**, **Stone Cliff**, **Thayer**, **Army**, **Grandview**, and **Glade Creek**. The rafting and biking centers **River Expeditions Resort** and **Ace Adventure Resort**, as well as Adventures on the Gorge, also offer camping and in some cases camper cabins.

RAFTING OUTFITTERS AND FLOAT OPTIONS

Rafting outfitters typically offer trips on both the New River and the Gauley River in the nearby Gauley River National Recreation Area. This book considers only the New River inside the national park, though rafting the Gauley is believed by many to be just as thrilling. On the New River, most outfitters offer a Lower New River trip, either for a full or partial day. This float travels through still pools and rapids rated from class II to class V. Also offered is the Upper New River option, a gentler float suitable for younger children.

Outfitters include the previously mentioned Adventures on the Gorge, Ace Raft, and River Expeditions.

CLIMBING GUIDES

With over 1,400 climbing routes in the park, it's worthwhile to experience what is considered some of the best rock climbing in the East. Guide services offer half- and full-day alternatives, and most prefer to offer a private guide to best meet the group skill level. Area guide services include New River Mountain Guides, Blue Ridge Mountain Guides, and Appalachian Mountain Guides.

MOUNTAIN BIKING

The Boy Scouts of America's 11,000-acre Summit Bechtel Reserve High Adventure Camp is adjacent to the west of New River Gorge National Park. Full of Boy Scouts for the entire summer, the National Park Service has utilized their service hours for the creation of 13 miles of mountain bike trails inside New River Gorge National Park. The Arrowhead Bike Farm and Trails complex is in the northwest section of the park, just south of Fayetteville. Providing bike rentals and guided tours, Arrowhead also offers The Handle Bar + Kitchen for an after-biking brew or bite.

THE TRIP

Day 1: Start your trip at the northern end of the park at the **Canyon Rim Visitor Center**. Viewing platforms showcasing the **New River** far below along with the looming **New River Gorge Bridge** ahead provide a terrific perspective of the whole area. For more views from the top of the gorge, head south about five minutes to the **Endless Wall Trail** leading in a mostly level 4.5-mile loop with views of the river, gorge sides, and sandstone rock faces filled with climbers. From here, head about 10 minutes across the New River to Arrowhead Bike Farm. Though the bike rental facility and restaurant are outside the park, the trails are mostly inside, with something for many ability levels. For hiking enthusiasts, near here is Kaymoor Road providing access to the steep 1.6-mile round-trip **Kaymoor Mines Trail** leading 900 feet down to the New River. End the day about a half an hour south in the **Thurmond Historic District**. The access road leads from Oak Hill down to the shore of the New River to the **Thurmond Depot Visitor Center** and the ranger-led or self-guided walking tour of Thurmond's historic buildings. If more energy remains, from the nearby Stone Cliff campground, the **Stone Cliff Trail** extends five miles round trip along the west shore of the New River.

Day 2: Start the day at the **Grandview Visitor Center** and the **Grandview** promontory with its spectacular views of the New River Gorge. From the visitor center is the spectacular **Grandview Rim Trail** extending north three miles round trip along the gorge rim to **Turkey Spur Rock**. The views from the trail are fantastic and feature much of the New River inside the national park boundaries. When finished, continue south to the **Sandstone Visitor Center** and the 1.1-mile level **Sandstone Falls Loop Trail**, which is about a 30-minute drive south. Perhaps enjoy lunch in the small village of Hinton, and then devote the afternoon to a guided rock-climbing adventure.

Day 3: Spend the last day rafting the New River.

**See the appendix for useful lodging, camping,
and activity contact information.**

GREAT SMOKY MOUNTAINS NATIONAL PARK

For the permanent enjoyment of the people.
—President Franklin D. Roosevelt,
dedicating Great Smoky Mountains National Park, 1940

CABIN IN GREAT SMOKY MOUNTAINS NATIONAL PARK
KEVIN E. BEASLEY/SHUTTERSTOCK

Covering 520,000 acres of the Smoky Mountains portion of the southern Appalachian Mountains, Great Smoky Mountains joins Yellowstone as one of two national parks spanning two states. Just under half of the park is in Tennessee while the remainder is in North Carolina. The storied Appalachian Trail runs through the middle of the park near the ridgeline of the range, one of the oldest on the planet. The region is the historic home of the Cherokee peoples and was settled in the 1700s by immigrants of European descent.

In the 1920s, after seeing the success of western national parks, residents of Knoxville, Tennessee, and Asheville, North Carolina, became interested in creating a national park in this area. The Smokies, though, had already been settled, with owned, leased, and homesteaded land standing in the way of an instant national park declaration. Instead, volunteer groups raised $5 million (about $75 million in current dollars) and the Laura Spelman Rockefeller Memorial Fund matched that $5 million. These dollars allowed private purchase of land, which was then transferred to Tennessee and North Carolina. The park was approved by President Calvin Coolidge in May of 1926, and the states completed the transfer of around 300,000 acres to the federal government by 1934. President Franklin D. Roosevelt formally dedicated the park in 1940.

Tennessee and North Carolina were concerned that a national park between their states would stifle commerce. As part of the transfer, the states required that there be no fees charged on Highway 441, which runs from Cherokee in North Carolina northwest to Gatlinburg in Tennessee. Though fees could technically be charged at smaller entrance roads into the park, there are currently no fee stations, and park access is free to all visitors. Great Smoky Mountains is the most visited national park in the country. In 2019, 12.5 million people visited Great Smoky Mountains, more than double the six million visits to the next most-popular park—Grand Canyon.

SCHEDULING AND LODGING
The park is open year-round, with summer and early fall popular times

to visit, though fall is spectacular in this heavily deciduous eastern forest. Nearby major metropolitan areas include Knoxville, Tennessee, and Asheville, North Carolina. Both have regional airports. The only lodging in the park is the steep-hike-in historic **LeConte Lodge**, open from mid-March through mid-November and serving breakfast and dinner to overnight guests staying in the seven cabins and three bunkhouses. Other lodging and food service is ample, with three park-abutting towns catering to travelers. In Tennessee, these include Gatlinburg (fun and crowded) and Townsend (pastoral), while in North Carolina the town of Cherokee provides plenty of hotel and dining options. If planning to visit Fontana Lake on the park's southwest side, the **Fontana Village Resort and Marina** is just outside the park boundaries.

There are 10 campgrounds in the park, serving various locations and interests. The largest is the 159-site **Cades Cove** in a picturesque valley in the southwest section of the park. Here you'll find a large camp store with bike rentals. Closer to the Sugarlands park entrance is **Elkmont** with 220 sites. Both campgrounds are open year-round and allow but do not require reservations. Smaller campgrounds, some seasonal, are found around the edge of the park. This large park has no food service inside the park boundaries. Remember to pack snacks and lunch, or purchase food at the Cades Cove Campground Store.

BIKING IN CADES COVE

The 11-mile Cades Cove Loop Road is closed for use exclusively by bicycles on Wednesdays and Saturdays before 10:00 a.m. between May and September. Bicycles are available for rent in Cades Cove, with rentals starting at 6:30 a.m. and often sold out by 7:30 a.m. Park bicyclists may share the road with cars the other five days. If car-free biking is important to you, consider camping either Tuesday or Friday night at Cades Cove, as the Cades Cove entrance does not open to cars until 8:00 a.m.

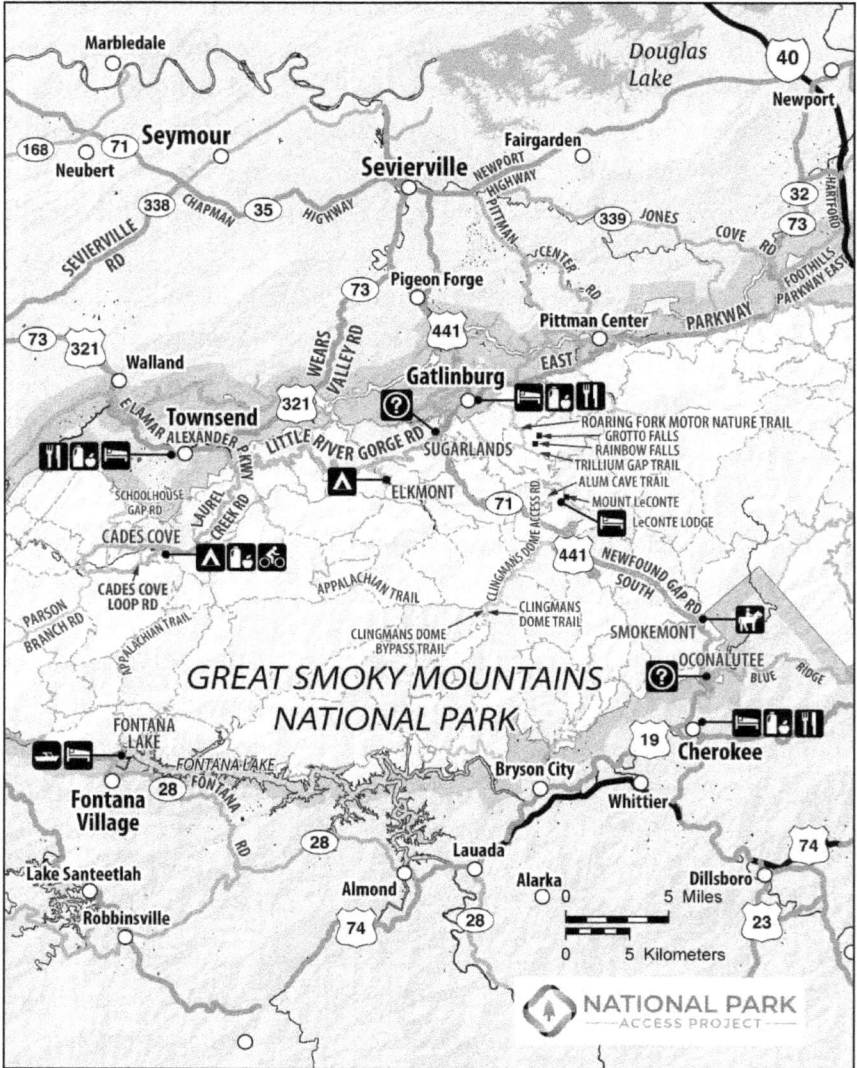

THE TRIP

Day 1: The park's main entrances are on Highway 441, entering from either Gatlinburg, Tennessee, or Cherokee, North Carolina. This trip description starts on the Gatlinburg side. The **Roaring Fork Motor Nature Trail**, one of the park's signature attractions, is accessed from Gatlinburg and does not connect to the rest of the park. Visit here first and enjoy the historic home-steads and farm buildings as well as beautiful hikes. Two hikes that stand out include the 5.5-mile round-trip **Rainbow Falls Trail** and the 2.6-mile round-trip **Trillium Gap Trail** to **Grotto Falls**.

When finished, enter the park and stop at the **Sugarlands Visitor Center**. After visiting, begin the approximately 45-minute winding drive on the Little River Road and then the Laurel Creek Road to **Cades Cove**. This pastoral valley surrounded by rolling mountains is a park highlight. The loop road around the valley has several pullouts to view and tour historic buildings. Take your time and stop at each one. About midway along the loop road is a turnoff to the **Abrams Falls** trailhead. This easy 5-mile round-trip hike to beautiful waterfalls with a swimming hole is a treat. After Cades Cove, either return to Gatlinburg on winding roads or exit the park at Highway 73, which leads to the small town of Townsend and, via a longer but less congested road, back to Gatlinburg.

Day 2: If planning to stay at LeConte Lodge, reverse this described order and visit Clingmans Dome first. Otherwise, begin the day at the **Alum Cave** trailhead and hike to the summit of **Mount LeConte**, the tallest mountain in the park at 6,593 feet. The Alum Cave Trail has two parking lots on New-found Road/441 (arrive early) and climbs 2,800 feet over 5.5 miles, offering diversity in views and plant life. The Mount LeConte summit provides one of the best views of the entire park.

After the hike, head to Newfound Gap and the road to **Clingmans Dome**. This man-made concrete circular observation platform is the actual high point of the park at 6,643 feet. From the parking lot, the walk to the observation tower is about half a mile on a paved footpath. Alternatively, immediately to the left of the paved path is a short trail (Clingmans Dome Bypass Trail) that connects with the Appalachian Trail. If you take this trail, turn right on the Appalachian Trail and walk a short distance to Clingmans Dome. From here, there are views of most of the mountains in the park as well as Fontana Lake in the distance.

Continue southeast toward the park exit at the **Oconaluftee Visitor Center**. The visitor center shares a site with the preserved multibuilding **Mountain Farm Museum**. Here visitors can go in the buildings and explore. This area is well worth your time. The town of Cherokee is about five minutes away.

Day 3: The vast and relatively empty east side of the park is a haven for horseback riders. Near the Oconaluftee Visitor Center is the **Smokemont Riding Stables**, which offers a 9:00 a.m. three-hour ride along the Oconaluftee River. If a riding enthusiast, start your day here.

After the ride, drive about an hour west to Fontana Lake. In the land acquisition for Great Smoky Mountains National Park, the north half of the 30-mile-long Fontana Lake became part of the national park, while the south half is part of the **Nantahala National Forest**. On the south side of the lake but near the national park boundary, the Fontana Village Resort provides boats for rent to explore the lake and fish. A short shoreline walk from the resort leads to the Fontana Dam and the national park **Lakeshore Trail**.

See the appendix for useful lodging, camping, and activity contact information.

CONGAREE NATIONAL PARK

What is our purpose in preservation, what can be served by hanging onto these pitifully small remnants of virgin forest land? . . . Why are we celebrating a Bicentennial? I hope not to just remind ourselves of past glory . . . So, also, should we celebrate and preserve the Congaree. For it could be, in its pristine wholeness, not only a reminder of the great forests which once existed, but also an inspiration for all of the American people.

—testimony of Sierra Club leader Ed Easton to the United States Congress, 1976

CYPRESS SWAMP, CONGAREE NATIONAL PARK
BROOKE CRIGGER/SHUTTERSTOCK

Located about 20 miles southeast of Columbia, South Carolina, and covering just over 26,000 acres, Congaree National Park preserves the largest tract of old-growth bottomland hardwood forest remaining in the United States. Abutting the Congaree River to the north, the park boundaries include the entirety of Cedar Creek as it feeds into the Congaree River. Congaree National Park preserves some of the tallest trees growing in a floodplain forest (notably loblolly pines), has cypress trees that are well over 500 years old, and provides one of the tallest temperate deciduous forest canopies remaining in the world.

The area is historically significant as the ancestral home of the Congaree Indians (decimated by smallpox in the 1700s) and as an area traversed by Hernando de Soto in the late 1500s. European settlers repeatedly tried to farm in the low-lying areas or swampland of South Carolina, including the Congaree, but timber harvesting ended up being the profitable land use in areas with floodplain or swamp-like bottomland. When lumber prices were high, cypress trees were harvested and floated down the Congaree River for shipment to points around the United States. Because of the wet and swampy soil in the Congaree, this area was less impacted by timber harvesting than others in the state and therefore better preserved. By 1950 there was a citizen movement for a formal preservation designation of this remaining old-growth forest, with the movement led in part by Harry Hampton. With others, Mr. Hampton was able to get the Congaree designated a national monument in 1976. The area became a national park in 2003.

SCHEDULING AND LODGING

Due to the hot, humid summer months, the best time to visit is in the spring and fall. Congaree National Park is one of only a few locations in the world where fireflies perform a synchronized mating dance, typically during several days in June. There can be over a thousand visitors a day during this time.

The main activities in the park—paddling Cedar Creek and hiking—can be done in one day. You'll want to spend the night either before or after your visit (or both) to enjoy this spectacular part of the country. Because Columbia is so close to the park entrance, it's easiest to select a hotel to suit your preferences within the city. Unfortunately, if you want to experience an outdoor-oriented lodge/hotel/motel, there really isn't a good choice. A few privately owned nearby cabins are available via home share sites, but the best way to be in the outdoors at Congaree is to camp. There are two campgrounds—**Longleaf** with 14 sites and **Bluff** with 6 sites—as well as backcountry camping via permit. Campground reservations open six months before your visit, and backcountry permits are available from the visitor center. Note that the Bluff Campground sites do not have vehicle access, requiring campers to carry in gear.

MULTIDAY PADDLE—CONGAREE RIVER BLUE TRAIL, CEDAR CREEK

A special activity for those with a few extra days is the Congaree River Blue Trail. Starting in Columbia and ending at the eastern end of Congaree National Park, this overnight paddle offered by Carolina Outdoor Adventures is great way to see the vast Congaree River. An alternative is to paddle the entire 20-mile Cedar Creek, which is entirely inside the park. This will include one overnight and can also be arranged via a guide service.

RANGER-LED ACTIVITIES

Congaree National Park offers about 30 days of ranger-led programs each year, primarily on Saturdays but also occasionally on Fridays. Options include guided hikes, walks, and canoe trips. Check the calendar for availability before your visit.

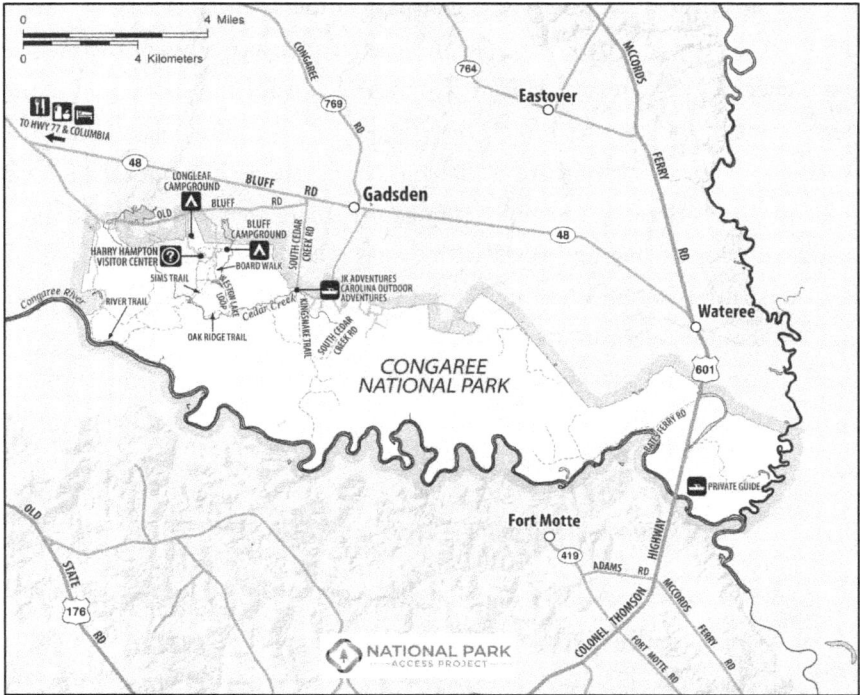

THE TRIP

Day 1: Cedar Creek is a slow-moving blackwater stream that runs through the heart of the park. Paddling the creek enables visitors to experience the cypress-tupelo swamp, floodplain forests, migratory and resident birds, aquatic animals, and possibly deer on the shore. Consider arranging the day based upon which river guide service you select. Each guide service offers different time slots. JK Adventures offers a three-hour paddle year-round daily at 9:00 a.m. with reservations available online. Carolina Outdoor Adventures offers infrequent trips on both weekends and weekdays, departing at either 10:00 or 11:00 a.m. These trips all include gear, a guide, and a downstream, then upstream paddle of Cedar Creek, starting and ending at the same point. This snake-and-bird-filled swamp is fascinating.

After paddling, spend time at the **Harry Hampton Visitor Center** near the park entrance and enjoy the lush 2.4-mile **Boardwalk Loop** through the old-growth forest. The boardwalk protects the delicate forest floor and saves hikers from swampy and wet soil. For the adventurous, though, hiking off the boardwalk is well worth the time. Almost empty of people, the off-boardwalk trails are raucous with bird calls. Home to loud owls and woodpeckers, hikers won't find quiet but will find peace. The most direct off-boardwalk trail is the **Sims Trail–Weston Lake Trail Loop** that in part parallels Cedar Creek and adds 3 level miles to the hike. From this core loop trail, longer trails extend into the old-growth forest.

See the appendix for useful lodging, camping, and activity contact information.

MAINE

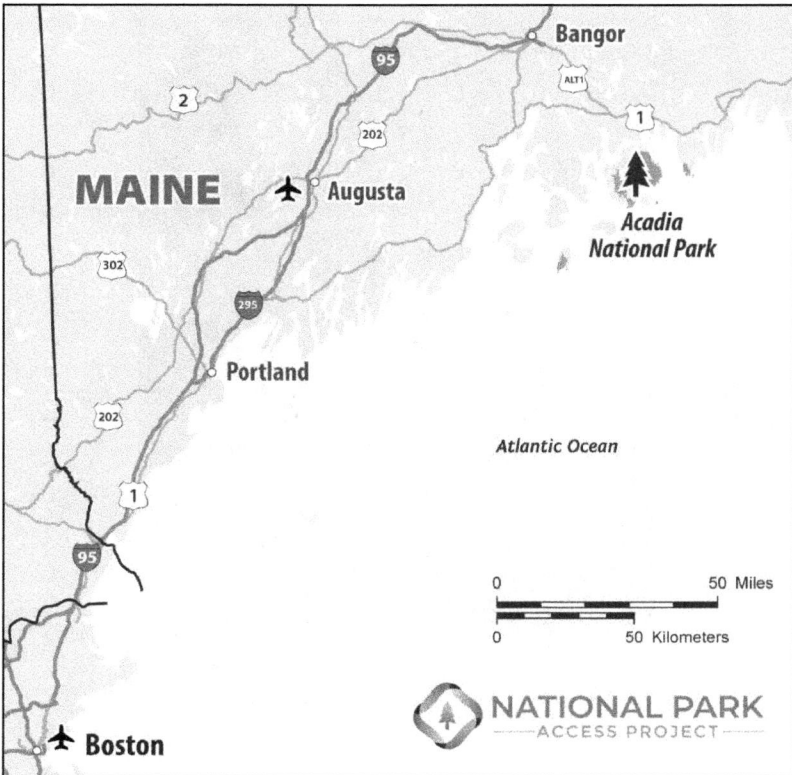

ACADIA NATIONAL PARK

Pursuing an old enthusiasm, [John D. Rockefeller] spent hours with surveyors and engineers in designing and constructing some sixty miles of roadways and bridges. In general, the purpose of his gifts to Acadia through the years was to make more accessible to visitors what he regarded "as one of the greatest views in the world."

—Nancy Newhall, from her 1957 book
A Contribution to the Heritage of Every American

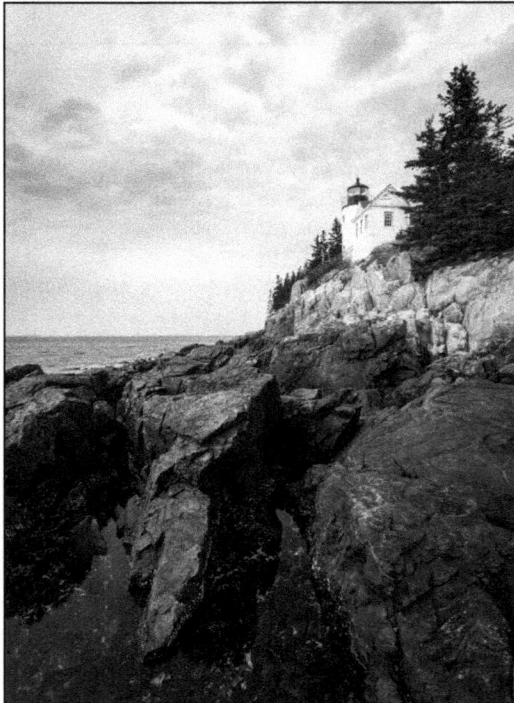

BASS HARBOR LIGHTHOUSE, ACADIA NATIONAL PARK
CLAYTON TOWNSEND/SHUTTERSTOCK

A central figure in the history of Acadia National Park is John D. Rockefeller. The first national park east of the Mississippi River, Acadia was established in 1916. Rockefeller funded the carriage roads and two gatehouses within the park from 1914 to 1940 as the park was developing. He loved the rocky outcroppings of the rugged Maine coast and had a large estate in the area (with incredible gardens still available to view). Because Mount Desert Island on which Acadia is primarily located was and is a fashionable spot to "summer," the park is intermixed with privately owned cottages and private roads. This can be frustrating or engaging. Take the latter view and embrace this feature by enjoying a Maine cottage rental and a Rockefeller garden tour to go with your Acadia visit.

The 49,052-acre park is split into three noncontiguous sections, with Mount Desert Island being the largest. Mount Desert Island is itself divided in half by Somes Sound, with most activities on the east side, including the carriage roads, Cadillac Mountain, most hiking, and the famous Sand Beach. The western section of Mount Desert Island is quieter, centered around the small village of Southwest Harbor. The two noncontiguous parts of the park include the Schoodic Peninsula about an hour and half drive or short ferry to the east and Isle au Haut accessed via an hour-and-a-half drive to the town of Stonington and then via a ride on a mail boat ferry.

SCHEDULING AND LODGING

Though the park is open year-round, most attractions are closed from October through April. Acadia National Park is best visited in the summer. There are two airports serving the park—Boston Logan International and Bangor International. The drive north from Boston is about six hours and east from Bangor is about two hours.

There is no national park lodging within the park boundaries, but summer cottages are available as home shares throughout Mount Desert Island. The town of Bar Harbor offers major hotels like **Hampton Inn by Hilton Bar Harbor** and the **Holiday Inn Bar Harbor Regency**, while Southwest

Harbor has smaller lodging options like the **Claremont Hotel**. There are two campgrounds on Mount Desert Island—**Blackwoods** with 300 campsites about 6 miles south of Bar Harbor, and **Seawall** with 150 campsites, about 4 miles south of Southwest Harbor. Both have a limited number of RV spots, and reservations are highly recommended during peak summer.

On the Schoodic Peninsula, camping is available at the **Schoodic Woods Campground** at the northern end of the national park boundary, and the **Winter Harbor Inn** is an option in Winter Harbor. Isle au Haut is accessed via ferry from Stonington, a tony and charming Maine village. If not staying on Isle au Haut, consider the **Inn on the Harbor** in Stonington. Camping on Isle au Haut is at the **Duck Harbor Campground**.

THE TRIP

Day 1: Just before entering Mount Desert Island from the north is the seasonal **Thomson Island Information Center**. Stop here or continue to the main **Hulls Cove Visitor Center**, just before Bar Harbor. Once oriented, drive a few more miles to downtown Bar Harbor and enjoy the village. Though not inside the national park, Bar Harbor is a hub for park-oriented attractions, including the Dorr Museum of Natural History with ocean-derived touch tanks and the Abbe Museum dedicated to the coastal Maine Wabanaki Alliance of Native American tribes. About 2 miles south is the Sieur de Monts Nature Center, the associated Wild Gardens of Acadia, and the precursor to the Abbe Museum.

The 57 miles of carriage roads in the park are closed to cars and are primarily used by bicyclists. Bicycles may be reserved in advance or rented in person at the Bar Harbor Bicycle Shop. The shop provides a comprehensive map, but a classic ride is the 4-mile trip from Bar Harbor to **Eagle Lake**, the largest lake in the park. The path leads along the east side of the lake to **Jordan Pond** and the historic **Jordan Pond House** offering lunch or afternoon tea and treats.

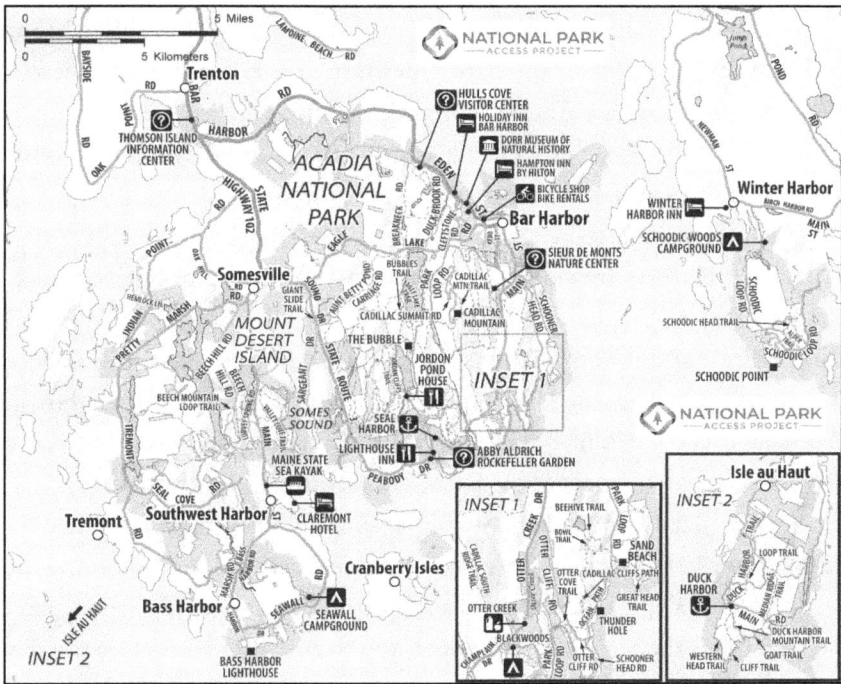

Day 2: Depart from Bar Harbor via car on the 27-mile **Park Loop Road** toward **Seal Harbor**, located just outside the park on the south coast of the main section of Mount Desert Island. Here is the **Abby Aldrich Rockefeller Garden**, one of the great formal gardens in the United States. Reservations, which open around June 1, are free of charge and highly recommended. Seal Harbor's **Lighthouse Inn Restaurant** is open for lunch, and the **Otter Creek Market** 2 miles east sells grocery items.

Continue on the Park Loop Road, stopping at the crashing waves of **Thunder Hole**, then on to the famous **Sand Beach**. There is a small parking lot serving the beach, the **Ocean Path Trail**, **Great Head Trail**, and **Beehive Trail**. The first two trails are short 1- to 2-mile ocean-facing paths that perfectly showcase the unique Maine coast. The Beehive Trail is also short but reaches a higher point with better views. Just north of the beach is **Great Head** with oceanfront walking trails. With the remainder of the day, finish the Park Loop Road and end with a drive to the summit of **Cadillac Mountain**, the highest point in the park. The summit offers panoramic views of the park and the ocean. There are numerous hiking trails up the mountain, including the ocean-facing 7.5-mile round trip **Cadillac Mountain South Ridge Trail**, which begins just south of Otter Creek.

Day 3: The less visited half of Mount Desert Island centered around **Southwest Harbor** provides an opportunity to experience the calm of a Maine summer. On the way, stop for the short 1.2-mile **Beech Mountain Loop Hike** that summits Beech Mountain, provides views in every direction, and descends overlooking Long Pond. Enjoy lunch in Southwest Harbor and then take a two- or four-hour kayak tour through Maine State Sea Kayak. After dinner, enjoy sunset at the iconic **Bass Harbor Lighthouse.**

Day 4: Bar Harbor offers a daily 45-minute ferry to **Winter Harbor**, with **Schoodic Point** then accessible via a two-hour walk or a short bus ride on the **Island Explorer Shuttle**. This beautiful, remote, and rugged area of the park offers the one-way **Schoodic Loop Scenic Road** as well as the short **Schoodic Head Trail**. If planning to continue on to Isle au Haut, consider skipping the ferry and driving an hour and a half from Bar Harbor to Schoodic Point instead. From here, the classic Maine village of Stonington, gateway to Isle au Haut, is another hour-and-45-minute drive.

Day 5: Remote **Isle Au Haut**, with a beautiful shoreline, hiking trails, and no services is a classic Maine destination. The Isle au Haut mail boat offers same-day ferry service to and from the island in the summer months, from mid-June through early September. Pack a lunch and take the 10:00 a.m. ferry to Isle au Haut, arriving at 10:45 a.m. at Isle au Haut town and around 11:00 a.m. at Duck Harbor. Get off at Duck Harbor and enjoy a loop hike on the **Duck Mountain Trail**, then along the **Goat Trail, Cliff Trail**, and **Western Head Trail**. This loop trail should take about four hours, in time for the 4:00 p.m. ferry back from Duck Harbor back to Stonington.

See the appendix for useful lodging, camping, and activity contact information.

FLORIDA AND
US VIRGIN ISLANDS

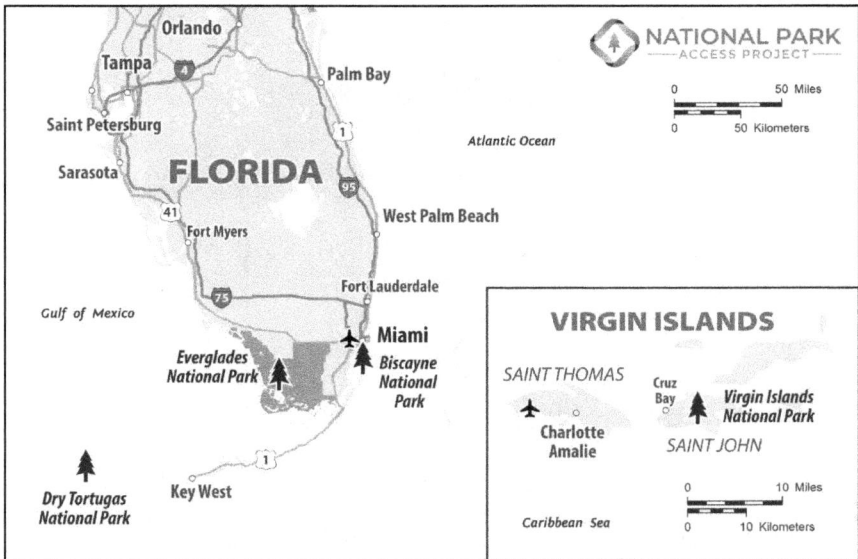

EVERGLADES NATIONAL PARK

The miracle of the light pours over the green and brown expanse of saw grass and of water, shining and slow-moving below, the grass and water that is the meaning and the central fact of the Everglades of Florida. It is a river of grass.

—Marjory Stoneman Douglas, from her 1947 book *The Everglades: River of Grass*

PINE GLADES LAKE, EVERGLADES NATIONAL PARK
BETH RUGGIERO-YORK/SHUTTERSTOCK

Located in southwest Florida, Everglades National Park is the largest tropical wilderness in the United States. Measuring about 730 square miles of exposed land and 1,620 square miles underwater, this is the third largest national park in the Lower 48 states, surpassed only by Death Valley and Yellowstone. Florida's land has been dredged and developed and has had water rerouted for hundreds of years. The Everglades represents 20 percent of the original wetlands that covered the state. Author Marjory Stoneman Douglas, who in 1947 wrote *River of Grass*, advocated in the middle of the twentieth century against further draining the Everglades watershed for development. She was arguably the park's most effective champion. Visitors throughout Florida see her legacy, represented by plans to restore part of the original water flow from Lake Okeechobee in central Florida to the Everglades. The park had been set aside in 1934 for preservation, and national park status was formally granted in 1947.

The Everglades, teeming with life, are home to over 360 species of birds, 300 species of fish, 140 species of trees, 40 species of mammals, and 5,000 species of insects. Big animals include the elusive panther, the charming manatee, and the ubiquitous but endangered American crocodile. One animal, the Burmese python, is invasive and has in recent decades wreaked havoc on the balance of species. Believed to have been introduced by people releasing pet snakes, the python has decimated small animals and caused the rabbit, for example, to be almost nonexistent in the park. Snake-removal specialists have been hired to cull the pythons, and there are occasional python capture events open to the public.

Everglades National Park has two entrances, one on the west (Naples/Fort Myers) side and one on the east (Miami) side. A paved road through the park and the adjacent Big Cypress National Preserve connects the two sides and takes about two and a half hours to drive.

SCHEDULING AND LODGING

The Everglades has a long wet season extending from mid-April through mid-November. During this time most tours are not in operation and many national park services are closed. Peak visitation is during the mid-November through mid-April period, or the even narrower window of January and February, which is prime birding season.

Abundant lodging is available in Homestead near the park's east entrance. In Everglade City, near the west entrance, the **Ivey House** is within walking distance of the few restaurants in the area. The two national park campgrounds are both on the park's east side. **Flamingo Campground** has platform tents with canvas walls, and both Flamingo and the nearby **Long Pine Key Campground** offer standard camping for both tents and RVs.

WILDERNESS WATERWAY

For the adventurous, there is also a connecting water path between the two sides of the park. The Wilderness Waterway extends through the Ten Thousand Islands that make up the barrier between the Atlantic Ocean's Gulf of Mexico and the Everglades wetland. Crossing the waterway takes 8 to 10 days via canoe or kayak, though outfitters concentrated on Chokoloskee Island on the park's west side offer shorter two- and three-day trips including only part of the waterway. For do-it-yourselfers, the park offers reservable backcountry permits and camping sites through Recreation.gov, including in the famous chickees. These special sleeping platforms with bug-netting walls were used by the Seminole people when they populated the Everglades area in the 1700s and 1800s. It's an understatement to note the mangrove-created islands can be confusing. If traveling without a guide, bring GPS and a waterproof nautical map.

BOAT TRIPS

Boat trips are offered from both Flamingo and Everglades City/Chokoloskee Island. From Flamingo, national park vendor Flamingo Adventures provides a backcountry tour into the brackish-water mangroves and the eastern edge of the Wilderness Waterway as well as a saltwater tour on Florida Bay. These trips are each a few hours and provide narrated tours of very different environs.

From Everglades City/Chokoloskee Island, national park vendor Everglades Adventures (same owner as Flamingo Adventures) provides a 90-minute narrated excursion into the salt waters of the Wilderness Waterway.

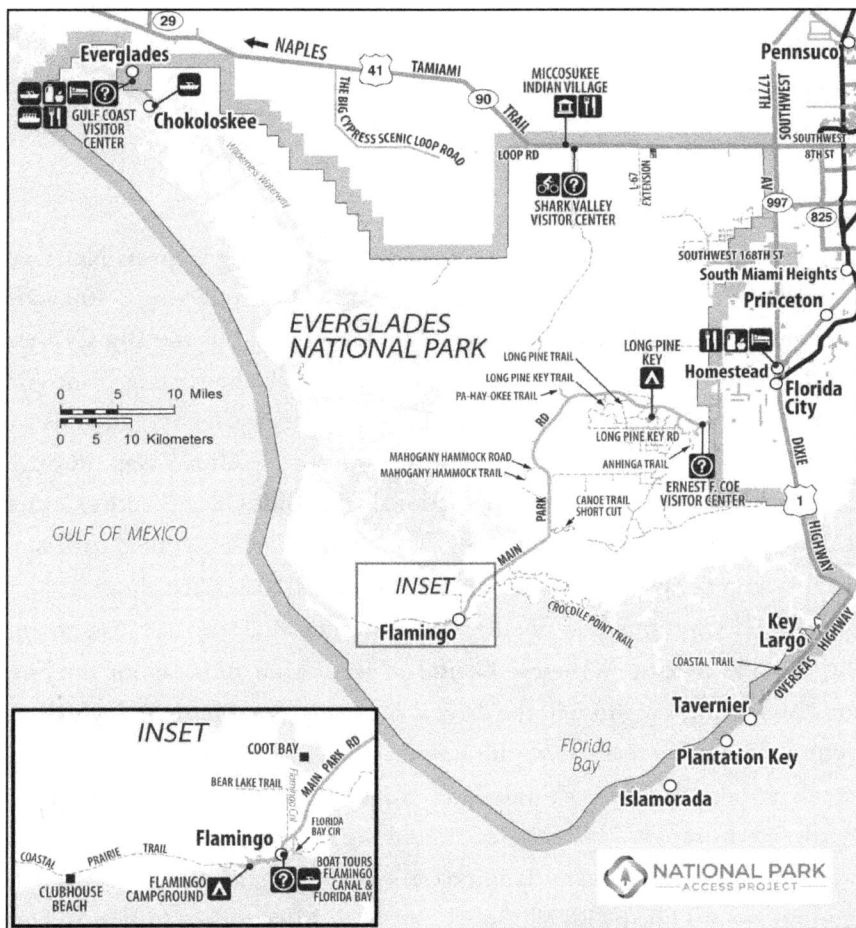

For those seeking longer and more custom options, the western section of the park has a lot to offer, especially for kayakers. The Turner River offers extensive brackish water mangrove terrain and large mid-everglade ponds for kayaking and pole-boat tours. The East River hosts a large rookery for nesting herons, double-crested cormorants, brown pelicans, and ibis, while numerous man-made canals provide kayak access to clusters of mangrove-lined water paths. Chokoloskee Island's marina is entirely in salt water, with boat trips leaving from here that extend well into the Wilderness Waterway and often include the option to kayak around islands far from shore. Outfitters operating from Everglades City/Chokoloskee Island include Everglades Adventures, Shurr Adventures, and Everglades Area Tours.

THE TRIP

Day 1: Starting on the park's west side, a visit to the **Big Cypress National Preserve** on the way to the Everglades is worthwhile. Protecting 2,400 acres of cypress trees, the preserve has no dry hiking trails, but the **Big Cypress Bend Boardwalk** offers a short, elevated boardwalk showcasing plant and animal life in this lush cypress grove. Bald eagles, osprey, herons, and ibis are thick here, with alligators lining the tributary waters. After a walk through the cypress, head to the Everglades National Park **Gulf Coast Visitor Center** at the southern tip of Everglades City. From here, take the national park vendor boat trip or arrange for a private boat tour, both described above.

Day 2: Continue east on the Tamiami Trail/Highway 41. Stop at the **Big Cypress Swamp Welcome Center** to learn a bit more about this vast area. About midway through the drive is the Everglades **Shark Valley Visitor Center**. Tram rides to an observation tower are available here, along with bike rentals to bike the same 15-mile level route through the central Everglades **Shark River Slough**. This dense section of the Everglades is thick with birds, fish, sawgrass, and, at the midpoint observation tower, an overstory tree canopy and swamp filled with alligators. The small **Miccosukee Indian Village** across the street from the visitor center is an option for lunch.

Continuing east, exit the Big Cypress National Preserve and travel south to Homestead and the east entrance to the park at the **Ernest F. Coe Visitors Center**. Just past here is one of the highlights of the park, the **Anhinga Trail**. This short boardwalk trail over ponds and wetlands is teeming with anhinga birds, fish, and alligators. From here, it's not far to the longest hiking trail in the park, the **Long Pine Trail**, extending from the Long Pine Key Campground to **Pine Glades Lake**. Technically with over 7 miles of hiking, the National Park Service does not maintain the trail, making the easily navigable portion either the few miles from the campground or the short walk from the main park road to the lake.

Day 3: Take the main park road from the Ernest F. Coe Visitor Center approximately 45 minutes to its terminus in Flamingo at the **Flamingo Visitor Center** and marina. Here boat trips are offered that travel south into the open waters of **Florida Bay** and north up the mangrove-lined **Flamingo Canal** into **Coot Bay** near the eastern terminus of the Wilderness Waterway. Both of these boat trips are worthwhile, with guides explaining two very separate ecosystems. After boating, consider hiking part of the waterfront **Coastal Prairie Trail**, a 3.2-mile unmaintained round-trip hike to **Clubhouse Beach**. On the way out of the park, pull out on two short interpretive trails including **Mahogany Hammock** and **Pa-hay-okee**.

See the appendix for useful lodging, camping, and activity contact information.

BISCAYNE NATIONAL PARK

*Today, with great pride, we come here to add an area that is every bit as
important as these others—the Biscayne National Monument. I think
this is a unique treasure. I am going back to see it. I can't wait until I do.
It will give our people almost 200,000 acres of islands and their adjoin-
ing bay and ocean waters, and they are all brimming with tropical plant
and animal life.*

—remarks by President Lyndon B. Johnson declaring
Biscayne a national monument, 1968

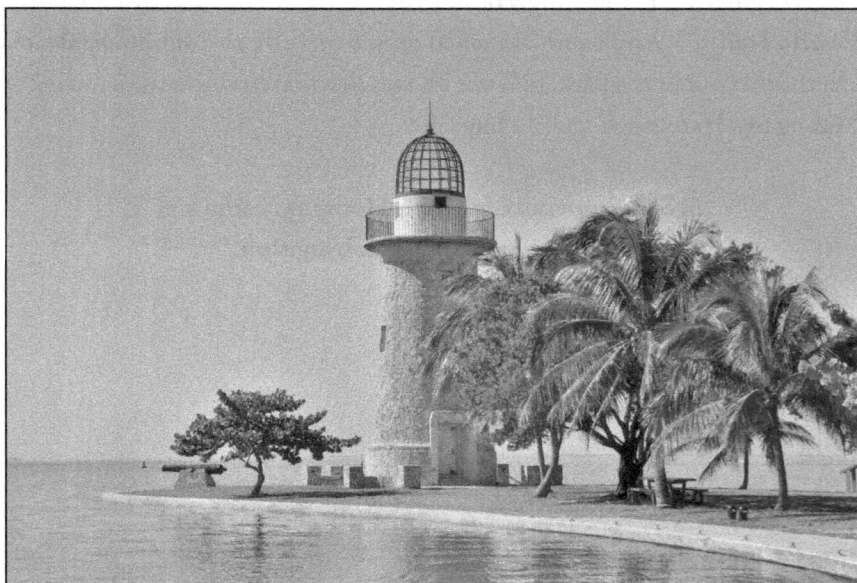

BOCA CHITA KEY LIGHTHOUSE, BISCAYNE NATIONAL PARK
AREND TRENT/SHUTTERSTOCK

East of Everglades National Park and south of Miami lies Biscayne National Park, which is 95 percent underwater and encompasses much of Biscayne Bay. This national park of mangroves, shallow bays, barrier keys, and barrier reefs measures around 180,000 acres with an average water temperature of approximately 80 degrees Fahrenheit. The Florida Keys, of which this park is a part, make up the one of the largest and longest coral reefs in the world. Biscayne protects immense areas of mangroves as well as sea grass on the delicate shallow bay bottom. The park has barrier keys, or islands, including Boca Chita Key, the larger Elliot Key, and Adams Key. Each has a marina or boat dock for day use. Biscayne was established as a national monument in 1968 and a became national park in 1980.

The park extends past the barrier keys into the Atlantic Ocean, and it's here where world-class scuba diving and snorkeling is located. Believed to have over 50 shipwrecks of various sizes, the Maritime Heritage Trail includes six major wrecks. Of these, three are suitable only for scuba diving and three are shallow enough for snorkelers. Coral reefs for snorkeling are found in the Hawk Channel east of the keys, with a reef system also located in the northern section of the park's bay. In addition to the keys, outer reefs, and shipwrecks, the edge of the bay is lined with mangroves, while its base is full of sea grass. This combination is a perfect home for the park's manatees and manta rays.

Not part of some mapped park boundaries, but still part of Biscayne National Park, is the historic village of Stiltsville. Accessed via a tour from Key Biscayne, which is connected via road to Miami, this attraction makes sense to see at the start or end of a Biscayne National Park tour. The National Park Service transferred management and restoration of the seven historic elevated wood Stiltsville homes to the Stiltsville Trust in 2003. Since that time, due to hurricanes and fundraising pressures, the houses have fallen further into disrepair and currently none are open to the public. The tour of the exterior of the Stiltsville homes is via boat with a guide.

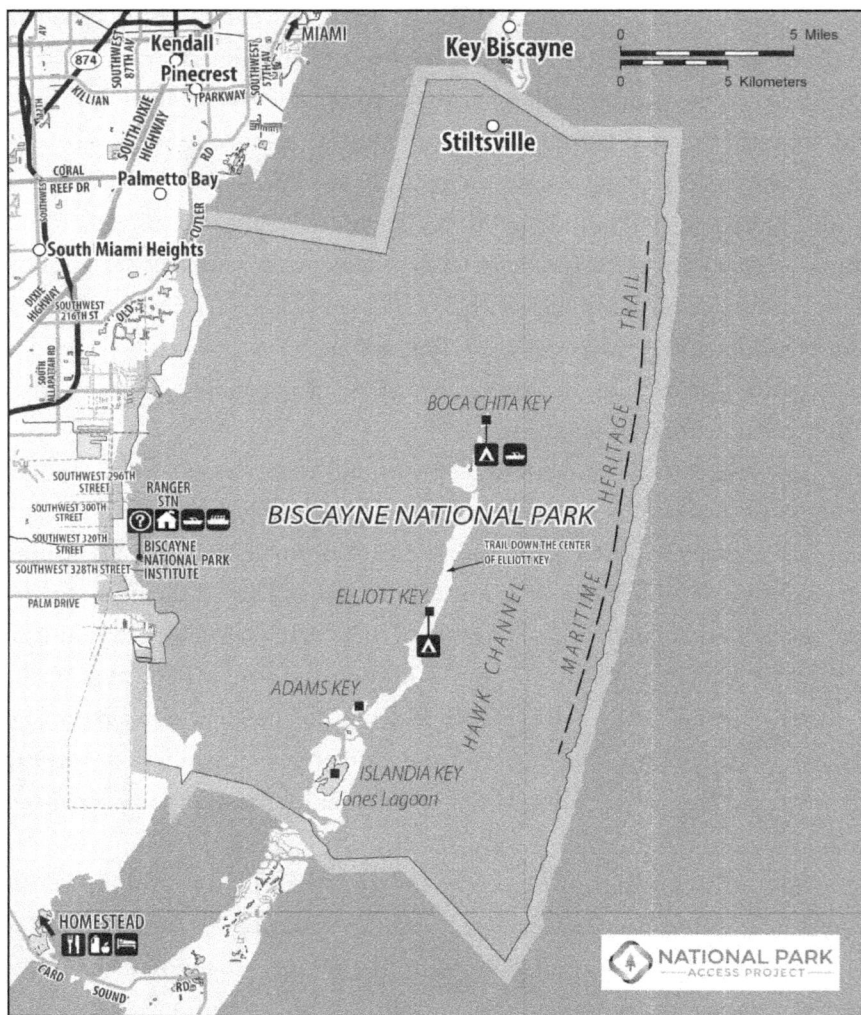

SCHEDULING AND LODGING

Biscayne may be enjoyed anytime, though spring and summer bug season is so intense that the keys are effectively closed. Peak season is from October through April when the migratory birds are plentiful and the water is still warm enough for enjoyable boating, swimming, snorkeling, and diving.

Though there is no lodging in the park, Biscayne is just east of the city of Homestead and south of Miami. On the islands, the park offers both **Boca Chita Key Campground** and **Elliott Key Campground**. From May 1 through September 30, there is no cost to camp due to the intensity of bugs. There is a small store at the visitor center with limited snacks. Grocery stores and restaurants are abundant in this densely populated area.

BOATING

Biscayne National Park Institute is the outfitter and tour guide serving the park. Both campgrounds are accessed only by boat, and the institute will either arrange for fee-based boat service or provide visitors with contact information to self-arrange a boat ride. The trip described below includes various boat trips, each with an interpretive guide. Biscayne National Park Institute also offers rented kayaks for self-guided exploration and can arrange for a captained larger boat for a custom itinerary. This park is almost all underwater, and boating is necessary to fully appreciate all Biscayne has to offer.

THE TRIP

Day 1: Homestead Bayfront Park is home to the **Biscayne National Park Ranger Station**. Start here and learn a bit more about the park. The **Biscayne National Park Institute** operates numerous and changing programs. An example is a morning snorkeling tour of one of the shallow **Maritime Heritage Trail** sunken ships, followed by a shoreline kayak trip in the afternoon.

Day 2: The institute runs two full-day tours. One is a sailing trip back and forth to either Boca Chita or Elliott Key, and the other is a tour that incorporates paddling in **Jones Lagoon** on the southern **Islandia Key**; lunch on Adams, Elliott, or Boca Chita Key; and snorkeling in the bay or outer reefs. These trips last from 10:00 a.m. to 4:30 p.m.

Day 3: The two-hour guided tour of the historic village of **Stiltsville** departs from the **Crandon Park Marina** on **Key Biscayne** located just outside Miami. Tours are offered Friday, Saturday, and Sunday at 10:00 a.m.

and 1:00 p.m. with an additional Saturday afternoon trip from 4:00 to 6:00 p.m. While on Key Biscayne, consider a waterfront lunch at Boater's Grill or Lighthouse Café at the tip of the key.

See the appendix for useful lodging, camping, and activity contact information.

DRY TORTUGAS NATIONAL PARK

[Billy Bones's] stories were what frightened people worst of all. Dreadful stories they were about hanging, and walking the plank, and storms at sea, and the Dry Tortugas, and wild deeds and places like the Spanish Main.

—from *Treasure Island* (published in 1882) by Robert Louis Stevenson

FORT JEFFERSON, DRY TORTUGAS NATIONAL PARK
CHRIS LaBASCO/SHUTTERSTOCK

Located at the maritime crossroads between the Gulf of Mexico, the western Caribbean, and the Atlantic Ocean, Dry Tortugas became important on navigational maps. The explorer Juan Ponce de Leon is believed to have named Dry Tortugas in 1513 when he encountered the islands in his travels. The word *tortugas* means "turtles" in Spanish, and the term "dry" means that there is no source of fresh water. Seafarers welcomed the knowledge that the islands presented a source of food. Dry Tortugas National Park is 70 miles west of Key West and is considered the westernmost of the Florida Keys. It is most affordably accessed via a daily high-speed ferry from Key West. Float-plane and charter boat service is also available.

Dry Tortugas National Park consists of seven keys. The high-speed ferry accesses Garden Key, where Fort Jefferson and the campground is located. Garden Key is connected via a sand bridge to Bush Key, which is in turn connected to Long Key. These three keys operate as a single destination. Three additional small keys are Hospital Key, Middle Key, and East Key, none of which are much visited. The seventh and westernmost key, Loggerhead, is about 3 miles from Garden Key and is accessed via private vessel. To properly visit Loggerhead, boaters must first register at Garden Key.

Birding is a reason many people visit Dry Tortugas National Park. Famed naturalist and painter John James Audubon came to Dry Tortugas in 1832 to paint some of the island's 300 species of migratory birds. Visitors have the chance to see cormorants, brown pelicans, black-bellied plovers, ruddy turnstones, royal terns, and so many more. Migration peaks in April through mid-May. Unfortunately, Bush Key (which provides access to Long Key) is off limits from April through September due to nesting terns and noddies. If birding, bring long-distance binoculars, and stand at the start of the land bridge. With a powerful-enough lens, views of thousands of nesting birds should be the reward. The majority of the park, or 64,700 acres, is underwater. The shallow water makes for warm swimming and abundant coral reefs for snorkeling and has plenty of shipwrecks for scuba diving.

SCHEDULING AND LODGING

Most visitors to Dry Tortugas come for the day, and a long day it is, checking in to the *Yankee Freedom III* desk at 7:00 a.m. and arriving back into Key West via ferry at around 5:30 p.m. Lunch is provided, and snacks are for sale. About half of these 10 travel hours are spent on the water. Overnight visitors may use one of the 11 campsites at the **Garden Key Campground** without a reservation; overflow spots are also available. Kayak Kings Key West rents kayaks for single or multiday use and provides drop-off and pick-up service to the ferry. Kayakers will need a boat permit from the National Park Service. If purchasing food for an island overnight, Fausto's Food Palace grocery store is open from 7:30 a.m. to 8:00 p.m. the day before departure. Key West has plenty of hotel space as well as multiple campgrounds.

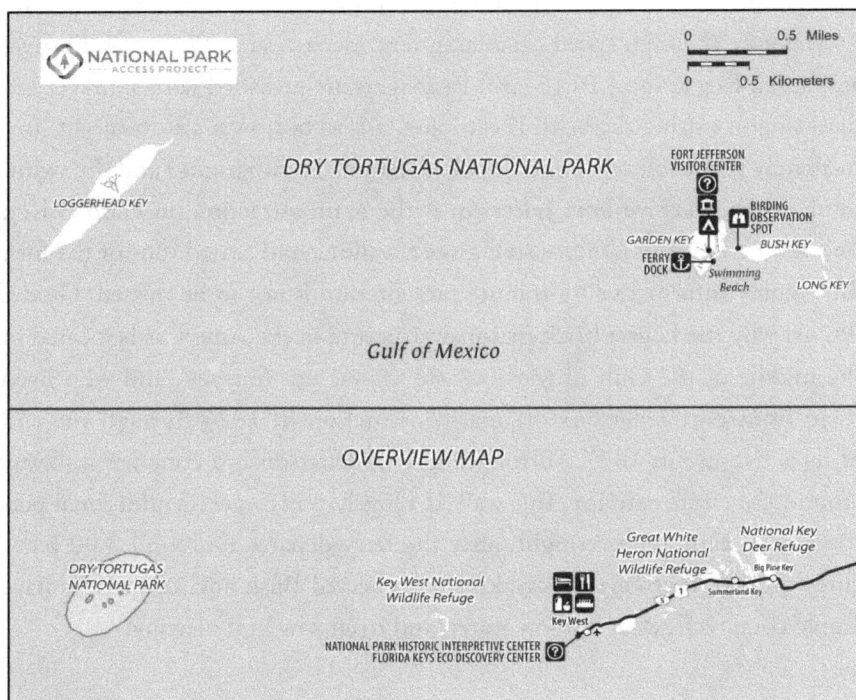

THE TRIP

Day 1: From Miami, **Key West** is a four- to five-hour drive. Perhaps the most famous of the Florida Keys, Key West retains the "old Florida" vibe. Beautiful public beaches line the south shore, the **Duval Street district** provides fun shopping and restaurants, and the **Ernest Hemmingway House** is a must-see. Dry Tortugas National Park does not have a traditional visitor center, and the park instead outsources to three information providers. There is a bookstore on the island and two interpretive exhibits in Key West. The first exhibit, the **Dry Tortugas National Park Historic Interpretive Center**, is near the ferry dock and has a scale replica of Fort Jefferson. This is also known as the **Bight Interpretive Center**. The second is the **Florida Keys Eco Discovery Center** operated in part by the Office of National Marine Sanctuaries and in part by the National Oceanic and Atmospheric Administration. Both are free to visit.

Day 2: The high-speed catamaran ferry departs at 8:00 a.m. and arrives at Garden Key around 10:15 a.m. Passengers are provided with snorkels and masks upon exiting the boat. If camping, ask to borrow a set overnight. Immediately to the left of the ferry dock is the small campground and the swimming beach. Massive **Fort Jefferson** is the main attraction on Garden Key. The *Yankee Freedom III* ferry staff gives a walking and seated tour of the fort. This highly informative 45-minute presentation is not to be missed. Guides discuss why the largest brick masonry structure in the Americas is located in the middle of the Gulf of Mexico, why it was not finished, and who lived there from Fort Jefferson's original construction in 1824 through the end of its active use in 1877. Surrounding Fort Jefferson is a concrete walkway around the entire exterior. This walk is a lovely way to get an additional perspective. If camping overnight, after the ferry departs at around 3:00 p.m., enjoy a quiet afternoon of kayaking. Connected Bush and Long Keys have ample coral reefs, clear shallow water, and front row bird viewing.

Day 3: The ferry returns to Key West around 3:00 p.m., providing campers almost an additional full day to swim, snorkel, kayak, bird, and explore Fort Jefferson.

**See the appendix for useful lodging, camping,
and activity contact information.**

US VIRGIN ISLANDS NATIONAL PARK

There I found very many islands, filled with innumerable people, and I have taken possession of them all for their Highnesses, done by proclamation and with the royal standard unfurled, and no opposition was offered to me.

—from the letters of Christopher Columbus to King Ferdinand and Queen Isabella of Spain regarding his 1492 voyage where he landed on certain Caribbean Islands

SEA TURTLE, US VIRGIN ISLANDS NATIONAL PARK
MICHAEL BVI/SHUTTERSTOCK

In addition to the 50 states, the US has five populated territories: Puerto Rico and Guam (both added in 1898), the US Virgin Islands (1917), American Samoa (1959), and the Northern Mariana Islands (1975). Each territory has its own history and culture, and part of the fun is experiencing the unique nature of these places that feel like part US and part foreign country.

There are around 7,000 large and small islands in the Caribbean Sea. The US Virgin Islands include some of the larger islands—Saint Thomas, Saint Croix, and Saint John as well as Water Island and around 50 smaller islets and cays. The US Virgin Islands National Park is located on Saint John. Nearby and accessed via ferry from both Saint Thomas and Saint John are the British Virgin Islands, including the larger islands of Tortola, Virgin Gorda, Jost Van Dyke, and Anegada as well as 32 smaller islands.

Inhabited at least since the middle of the first century BCE by native tribes (in particular the Taino Indians), the Virgin Islands and other Caribbean islands became involved in sugar production and the associated slave trade in the mid to late 1600s. What are now the US Virgin Islands were controlled by Denmark from the late 1600s until the US territorial acquisition in 1917.

SCHEDULING AND LODGING

Hurricane season extends from June through November and peaks from August through October. The warmest waters outside of hurricane season are from April through June, and this is prime tourist season in Saint Thomas and Saint John. From Miami there are frequent direct flights into Saint Thomas, most landing in the afternoon. If time constraints make catching the last ferry to Saint John too challenging, consider staying in one of the many hotels in Charlotte Amalie, the capital of the US Virgin Islands, or in charming Red Hook near the ferry dock. In Red Hook, a relaxed lodging option is **Two Sandals by the Sea Inn** or the waterfront **Secret Harbor Beach Resort** with a public beach and snorkel gear available for rent. On Saint John, midrange lodging includes **Saint John Inn**, **Cruz Bay Boutique Hotel**, and **Estate Lindholm**, while expensive resorts include **Gallows Point Resort** in

Cruz Bay and **The Westin**. The US Virgin Islands National Park operated lodging and camping at **Cinnamon Bay**. This area was damaged in 2017 by Hurricane Maria and has been under construction, with reopening currently planned in 2022. There are no other formal campgrounds on the island.

THE ROCKEFELLERS AND CANEEL BAY

The Rockefeller family has been instrumental in the expansion of the national park system, with major land gifts in Acadia National Park, Grand Teton National Park, and the US Virgin Islands National Park as well as monetary gifts toward land acquisition in Great Smoky Mountains National Park. Laurance Rockefeller, having granted a large tract of land in 1942 to the federal government for Grand Teton National Park using his Jackson Hole Trust, again used the trust to acquire about 5,000 acres on Saint John. In 1959 he donated this land to the federal government, and the park was approved that same year. The park has since grown to 12,500 acres, including about 7,000 acres of land and 5,500 acres underwater. At the time of Rockefeller's 1959 land grant, he held back a small area, Caneel Bay and Resort, for future transfer. The machinations and intrigue behind the effort to prevent or accelerate the transfer of this land to the National Park Service represent an ongoing substory in the park, with transfer currently expected by 2023.

CELL SERVICE

Many cell phone carriers treat the US Virgin Islands as a foreign country. For American visitors, either be prepared to live with whatever lodging-based wireless service is provided or purchase international service for the trip.

RENTED VEHICLE, TAXI SERVICE, AND PUBLIC TRANSPORTATION

The airport in Saint Thomas is on the opposite side of the island from the ferry to Saint John. Taxi service is ubiquitous both from the airport to the ferry dock and also on Saint John. This is the easiest option, though access to some of the more remote Saint John beaches is limited if traveling via taxi.

For those who decide to rent a car, a ferry berth will need to be reserved separately. Driving on Saint Thomas and Saint John is on the opposite, or left, side of the road consistent with the United Kingdom, while rented cars are American-style with the driver on the left. Roads are congested, narrow, and poorly maintained. If renting a car, come prepared for an adventure. Once on Saint John, a developing-country style taxi/bus service is in place with pickup trucks lined with rear bench seating continuously circulating on the main roads of the island. Hail the pickup truck, hop on, and hop off at your destination, paying only for the distance traveled.

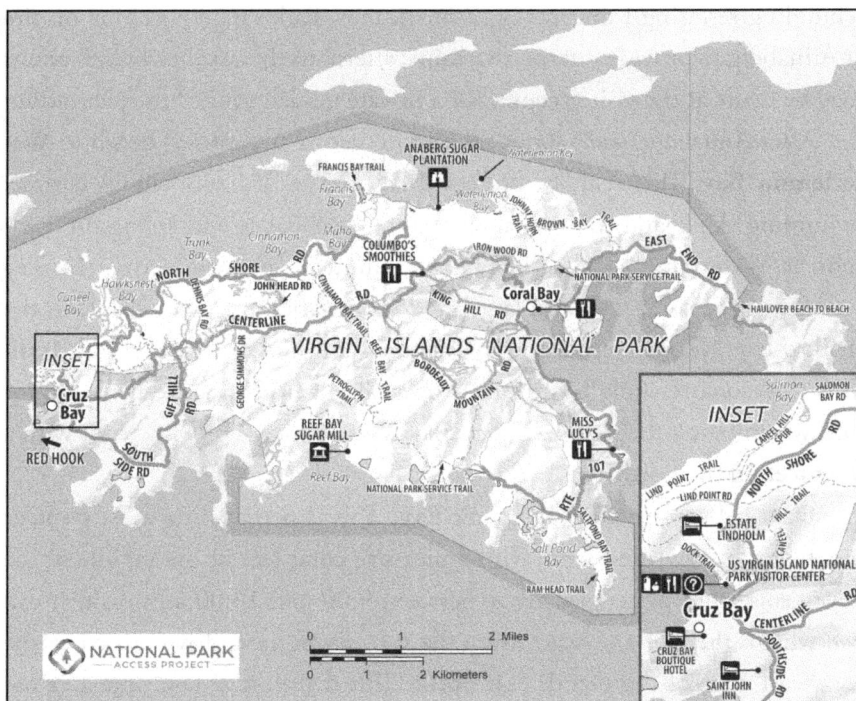

THE TRIP

Day 1: Take the ferry from Red Hook to **Cruz Bay**, the hub of Saint John. Begin at the small **US Virgin Island National Park Visitor Center** and from there take the **Lind Point Trail** to **Salmon Bay** and on to **Caneel Bay**. Both of these bays offer nice beaches and snorkeling, with lunch available for purchase from the Caneel Bay outdoor concession stand.

Depart Caneel Bay and drive or taxi about half an hour to the northern tip of Saint John and the **Annaberg Sugar Plantation**, the largest sugar plantation ruins on the island. Learn about the flow of people through the US Virgin Islands—from the early Taino Indians to Dutch sugar traders to West African sugar plantation slaves to United States ownership of the island and now to the next round of population turnover following the devastation and rebuilding resulting from the 2017 hurricanes. Park rangers may be on site at Annaberg to provide interpretive tours; alternatively, advanced reservations may be made at the visitor center for a private guided tour of the plantation.

After Annaberg, walk about 20 minutes along the (rocky) beach to **Waterlemon Bay**. This shallow, protected bay has terrific snorkeling. If time, swimming skills, and stamina allow, a tour de force of snorkeling on Saint John is **Waterlemon Cay**. About a 45-minute swim from shore, this key boasts pristine coral reefs and larger and more varied fish than visible in the shallow bay. Near Watermelon Bay is Francis Bay and the **Francis Bay Trail**. This three-quarter-mile boardwalk loop trail is considered the best area for bird watching on the island. Francis Bay is also a nice snorkeling spot with a long reef on the north side.

Day 2: Begin the day at **Trunk Bay**. This is perhaps the most popular beach and bay on the island, with a nice-size coral reef in the middle of the bay. Cruise ship passengers arrive between 9:00 and 10:00 a.m., which can overwhelm the reef and scare away the fish. From here, drive or taxi to the southeast edge of the island, **Salt Pond**. This dry almost desertlike area has perhaps the most popular short hike on the island—**Ram Head**. This trail, just over a mile each way, includes the walk downhill to the beach, a short cutoff to Salt Pond, and then a walk along the promontory culminating at Ram Head. Once finished, enjoy snorkeling in **Salt Pond Bay**. Considered by some to be the best snorkeling in Saint John, the water here is shallow and very clear, making the sea life vivid and easy to see. After snorkeling, enjoy lunch at Miss Lucy's, an island favorite.

Head back toward **Maho Bay**. Frequented by the locals, Maho Bay is large, shallow, and right on the main road. It's also home to families of sea turtles that swim quite close to snorkelers. A must for the young and young at heart. End the day at the large and less protected **Cinnamon Bay**. The parking lot here accesses both the bay and a short interpretive loop trail through sugar-refining ruins.

Day 3: Spend the morning on dry land, hiking the longest trail in the park—the 4.4-mile round-trip **Reef Bay Trail** with about 1,200 feet of elevation change. Leading to the **Reef Bay Sugar Mill** ruins, this center-island trail can be hiked in part. After the hike, stop by Columbo's Smoothies for a cold treat and head back to Cruz Bay and the ferry to Saint Thomas.

**See the appendix for useful lodging, camping,
and activity contact information.**

HAWAII AND AMERICAN SAMOA

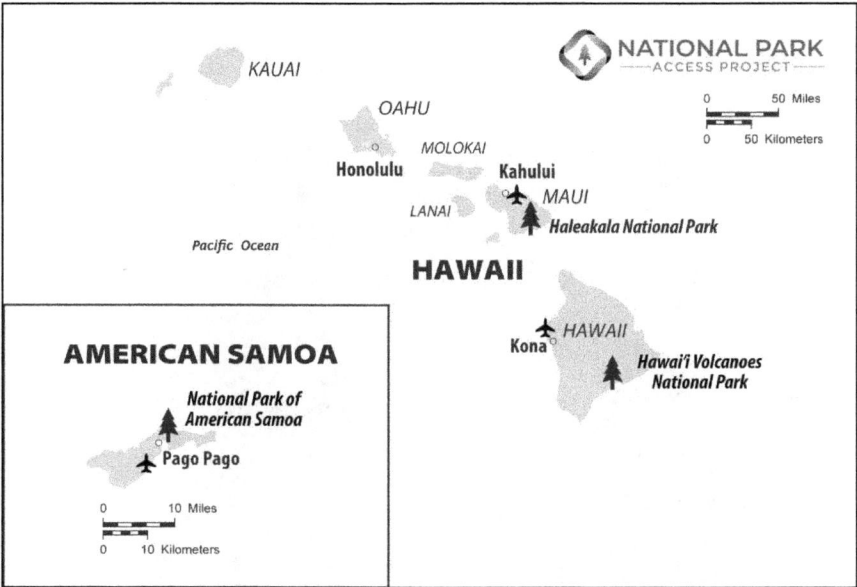

HALEAKALA NATIONAL PARK

It is the sublimest spectacle I ever witnessed.

—American writer Mark Twain, upon seeing sunrise from the Haleakala crater rim in 1866 while a special correspondent for the *Sacramento Union* newspaper

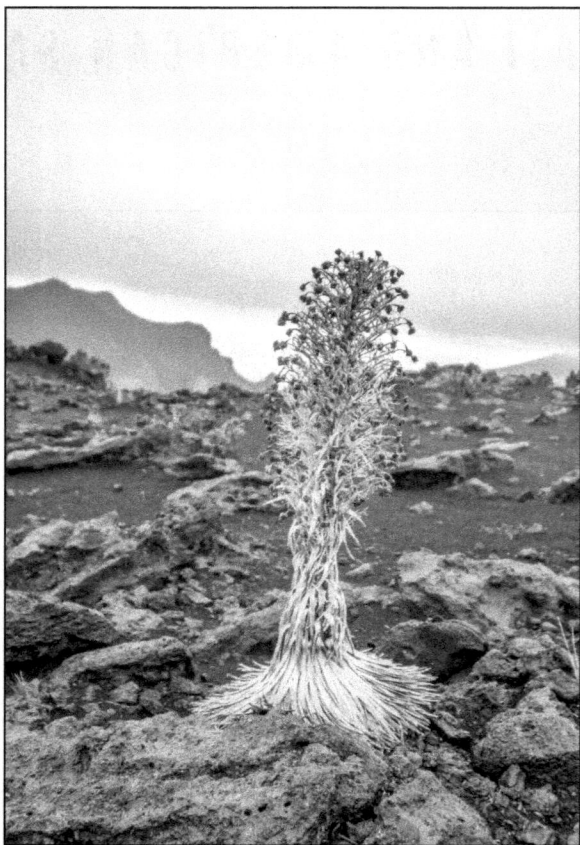

Hawaiian silversword just after bloom, Haleakala National Park
Marki260423/Shutterstock

The volcanic Hawaiian Island chain is showcased on the island of Maui, which is centered around two volcanic mountains—West Maui Mountain and Haleakala. The peak of the Hawaiian Island chain at over 10,023 feet, the volcano mountain of Haleakala translates as "the House of the Sun" or "the House Built by the Sun" and is possibly the largest dormant or near-dormant volcano in the world. Spectacular sunrise views from the crater rim are legendary, so much so that visitor demand exceeds the supply of parking spaces, making reservations required for sunrise viewing. Haleakala's summit temperatures are unforgiving, dropping below freezing and above 80 degrees in a single day. With over 30 miles of hiking, the volcano crater basin provides rare terrain and incredible views.

While Haleakala National Park is known for the volcano summit, this part of Maui also hosts one of the island chain's most spectacular rain forests. A small portion of the rain forest is within the national park boundaries in the area of Kipahulu. The Hana Highway leading from Haleakala's crater road to the villages of Hana and Kipahulu is world renowned for its lush beauty. Make this drive, and stay in Hana or Kipahulu during part of your trip. In total, Haleakala National Park measures more than 30,000 acres, and though formally established in 1961, it was originally preserved in 1916 at the urging of Thomas Jaggar as a result of his scientific work at the Hawaiian Volcano Observatory.

SCHEDULING AND LODGING

Hawaii's temperate climate makes every month a good month for a visit. If a goal is seeing the sunrise from the Haleakala summit, late December and early January have the latest sunrises, just after 7:00 a.m. The Haleakala summit is about an hour from Maui's Kahului Airport.

There is no lodging in the park, but there are two campgrounds. **Hosmer Grove** is located at 7,000 feet elevation on the road up to Haleakala near the entrance gate and may be a good option for sunrise seekers, while **Kipahulu Campground** is located near the ocean and the town of Hana. In this vacation paradise, hotels, inns, and private home rentals are ubiquitous. For those who want to be close to the volcano, the small **Kula Lodge** is near the entrance. Though there is no food service at the crater rim, the village of Kula has small restaurants and a gift shop with snacks. A few miles south of Kula is the Morihara Store selling grocery items.

HALEAKALA OBSERVATORIES

The University of Hawaii Institute for Astronomy operates a large observatory complex at the peak of Haleakala. This fascinating series of buildings and massive telescopes is not open to the public, but the website links to outside groups that operate occasional tours and lectures.

THE TRIP

Day 1: If planning a sunrise summit, get up before the crack of dawn and head to the park with permit in hand. From the park entrance gate, it's another half an hour to the summit.

Once parked, head 0.4 miles up from the parking lot on the **Pa Ka'oao Trail**, where there are fabulous views as the sun rises over Hawaii. The **Haleakala Visitors Center** opens at 8:00 a.m., providing information about the volcano's formation, rock types, wind speeds, and temperature ranges. The classic Haleakala hike extends into the crater on the **Sliding Sands Trail (Keonehe'ehe'e Trail)**, which runs from the parking lot into the crater, through the hard pack desert and cinder cone volcano vents, to its terminus at the **Kapalaoa Cabin**. The full hike is a pretty tough 11.5 miles round trip and can take up to 10 hours. The good news is that the hike can be shortened to almost any length, and many of the amazing views are available from several points on the trail. Offshoots to the summits of various volcano vents offer a different perspective. While hiking, keep a lookout for the famous Haleakala silverswords, a low plant that can live up to 90 years before flowering once and then dying. These endangered plants are only found on Haleakala.

Day 2: The east side of Haleakala National Park is about a two-hour drive on the spectacular **Hana Highway**. Leave time to stop at **Twin Falls**, the **Hana Lava Tubes**, and the **Wai'anapanapa State Park** with its black sand beaches.

The village of Hana is a historic seat of power on the Hawaiian Islands and a key area of historic territorial battles. About 45 minutes past Hana is **Kipahulu**. From the **Kipahulu Visitors Center** is the short **Seven Sacred Pools Oheo Gulch** loop trail extending 0.6 miles through lush vegetation, freshwater pools, a waterfall, and along the oceanfront. This is a classic hike in this part of the park, showcasing the lush greenery on top of visible hardened lava flows. After this walk, take the other well-known hike in this area, **Makahiku Falls**, with a terminus at **Waimoku Falls**. This 4-mile round-trip hike gains 650 feet with a spectacular bamboo forest at the midpoint.

**See the appendix for useful lodging, camping,
and activity contact information.**

HAWAI'I VOLCANOES NATIONAL PARK

[At the crater, the Hawaiian guides] turned their faces toward the place where the greatest quantity of smoke and vapor issued, and, breaking the ['ohelo] branch they held in their hand in two, they threw one part down the precipice, saying: Oh, Pele, here are your branches; I offer some to you; Some I also eat.

—1823 notes, missionary Reverend William Ellis,
believed the first white visitor to Kilauea

LAVA FLOWING INTO THE OCEAN, HAWAI'I VOLCANOES NATIONAL PARK
LAUREN K GC/SHUTTERSTOCK

The "Big Island" of Hawaii is the largest of the Hawaiian Islands. Hawai'i Volcanoes National Park measures 325,000 acres and includes parts of two volcanoes: Mauna Loa ("Long Mountain") and Kilauea ("Spewing"). Mauna Loa, which last erupted in 1984, is the largest mountain in the world when measured to its underwater base. The Kilauea volcano has been the most active in the Hawaiian Island chain and is one of the youngest at between 300,000 and 600,000 years old. Visitors come to the park to view lava in Kilauea's Halema'uma'u Crater, to see slow-moving active lava flows, and to witness lava pour directly into the sea. In 2018, Kilauea experienced a major eruption that spewed ash 30,000 feet in the air, collapsed 2,000 feet of the crater's summit, and destroyed around 700 homes. Extensive earthquakes plagued the area. The park was closed for about 130 days as a result of the eruption, and a famous landmark, the Thomas A. Jaggar Museum, was irreparably damaged. Since the eruption, lava has been less visible.

The Hawaiian Islands are believed to have been first inhabited about 1,500 years ago by Polynesian explorers, and the park has extensive archaeological evidence of ancient peoples, including thousands of petroglyphs. Hawai'i Volcanoes was named a national in 1916, making it the eleventh national park in the system. The United Nations has designated the park both an international biosphere reserve and a World Heritage Site.

SCHEDULING AND LODGING

Any time is a good time to visit Hawai'i Volcanoes National Park. Hawaiian Island weather changes little from month to month, and volcanic activity can happen anytime. The Big Island's main villages are the dry, sun-kissed Kona and the rainier Hilo. Volcanoes National Park is about 45 minutes south of Hilo and about two and a half hours southeast of Kona, where Ellison Onizuka Kona International Airport is located.

Lodging in the park has recently been renovated following damage caused by the 2018 eruption. Near the rim of the Kilauea Caldera is the upscale historic **Volcano House** hotel (originally built in 1846) with 33 rooms, two restaurants, and shops. Staying here provides a front-row seat as the sun sets over the caldera. The nearby **Namakanipaio Campground** has campsites and recently refurbished camper cabins. Reservations are accepted up to 18 months in advance. The gateway village of Mauna Loa/Volcano Village has small inns and rooms available on home share sites. Hilo offers extensive lodging at many price points.

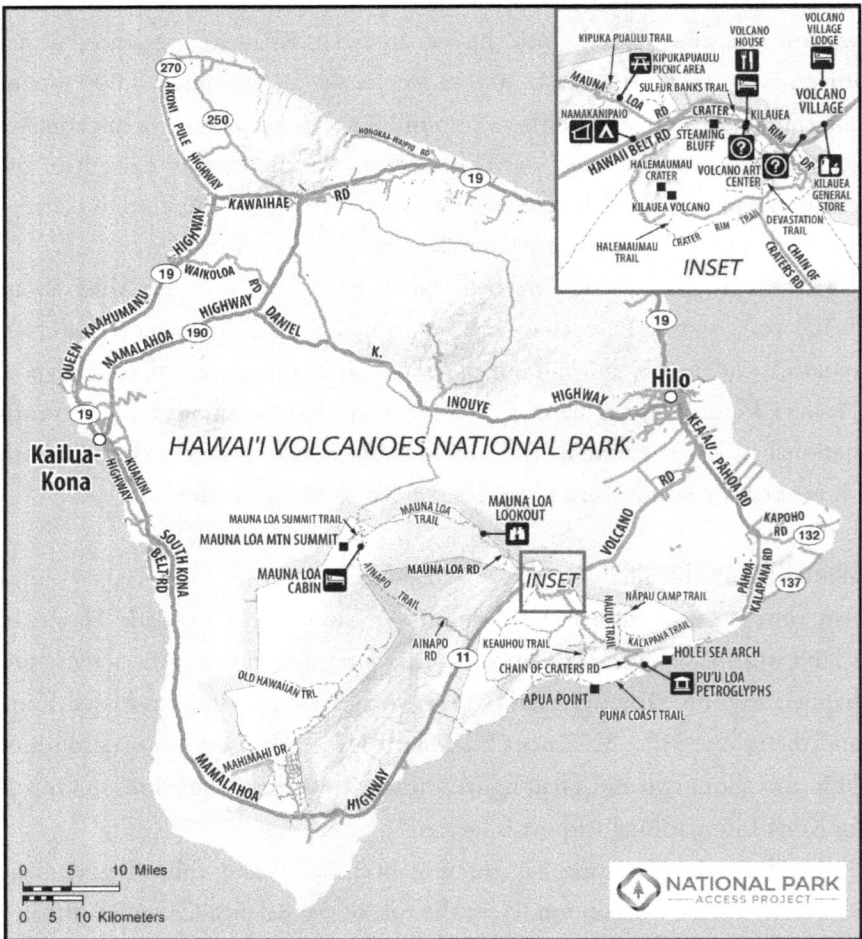

THE TRIP

Day 1: Coming from Kona or Hilo, enter the park and stop at the **Kilauea Visitor Center**. When finished, enjoy the 2-mile level loop trails that lead to the **Steam Vents**, **Steaming Bluff**, and **Sulphur Banks**. This spectacular area provides a boardwalk over hot soil hospitable only to rare plants. The steam and sulfur are otherworldly. Also accessed from the visitor center is the **Crater Rim Trail** along the rim of the Kilauea crater. The trail extends 1 mile in each direction and provides incredible and diverse views of the inside of the crater.

After the walks and perhaps lunch at the visitor center or Volcano House, drive on **Crater Rim Drive**, heading left. Just past the midpoint, the **Volcano Art Center Gallery** is on the right. Continue, turning left onto **Mauna Loa Road**. Stop at the **Kipukapuaulu Picnic Area** and from here begin the 1.2-mile level **Kipukapuaulu (Bird Walk) Trail**, which leads through some of the oldest tropical forests on the island, interspersed with hardened lava flow from the Mauna Loa eruption. After the walk, continue up the road to its terminus. There's a picnic area and lookout here. The Mauna Loa summit trail begins here.

Day 2: From the Kilauea crater rim, pack a lunch and begin driving the 20-mile **Chain of Craters Road** to the ocean. Right at the beginning is the **Puʻu Puaʻi** parking lot that connects with **Devastation Trail**. This short 1-mile walk shows the recovery from the 1959 eruption of Kilauea. The Chain of Craters Road passes by many of the park's named craters, with plenty of spots to stop and view them. As the road nears the ocean, on the left will be the *Puʻuloa* **Petroglyphs**, with over 20,000 Hawaiian petroglyphs believed to date from around 600 years ago. The walk through this area is a level 1.4 miles round trip. From here, the nearby terminus of the road leads to the **Holei Sea Arch**, lava fields, the crashing ocean surf, and the **Puna Coast Trail** along the oceanfront. At 3.1 miles each way, this exposed hardened-lava trail leads to **Apua Point**.

SUMMITING 13,250-FOOT MAUNA LOA

The top of the Mauna Loa Lookout Road is the beginning of the Mauna Loa summit hike. Segmented in two, with the first section 7.5 miles and the next 9.5 miles, the full hike is 34 miles round trip with 6,500 feet of elevation gain, or about 400 feet per mile. There are two backcountry cabins: Red Hill Cabin at the summit of **Puʻuʻulaʻula** at mile 7.5 and Mauna Loa Cabin at the summit of Mauna Loa, 9.5 miles later. These bare-bones unheated cabins sleep around 25 people and require backcountry permits. For those with less time and better fitness, Ainapo Road leads to the 15-mile round-trip Ainapo Trail, with 1,000 feet of elevation gain per mile. The Halewai Cabin is 2,000 feet into this hike at 8,000 feet elevation and is managed by the state rather than the National Park Service. A hike of Mauna Loa requires extensive planning and the correct gear for both safety and enjoyment.

See the appendix for useful lodging, camping, and activity contact information.

NATIONAL PARK OF AMERICAN SAMOA

As the traveler who has once been from home is wiser than he who has never left his own doorstep, so a knowledge of one other culture should sharpen our ability to scrutinize more steadily, to appreciate more lovingly, our own.

—Margaret Mead, from her 1928 book *Coming of Age in Samoa*

SAMOAN BEACH, NATIONAL PARK OF AMERICAN SAMOA
SHOT BY SHELDON/SHUTTERSTOCK

Of the 63 national parks, this is the only one with "national park" at the start of the park's name. Perhaps this reflects the inevitable tension regarding oversight and sovereignty of an island area 6,000 miles from the US mainland. Or possibly it reflects the fact that this park is not owned by the United States. In 1993, Samoan chiefs granted a 50-year land lease to the United States. The Samoan islands are Polynesian, with the western islands having been a sovereign nation since 1962. Before that, they were controlled by New Zealand, Germany, and in earlier centuries by Polynesian tribes.

American Samoa consists of five islands and two atolls, with the main islands including Tutuila, Ofu, and Ta'u, all of which host a section of the national park. Similar to Puerto Rico, American Samoa became a United States colony or territory in phases between 1900 and 1904, with full ratification in 1929.

With under 5,000 visitors per year, this park competes with Alaska's Gates of the Arctic, Lake Clark, and Kobuk Valley for least-visited national park. A lightly developed tropical paradise and the only US national park south of the equator, the National Park of American Samoa reminds visitors of a bygone era.

SCHEDULING AND LODGING

While temperatures are balmy year-round, the islands are driest in June, July, and August, making these months ideal for a visit. Pago Pago on the island of Tutuila is the territory's main city, with round-trip flights provided by Hawaiian Airlines out of Oahu a few times per week. The five-hour flight departs Oahu in the late afternoon, arriving around 9:30 p.m., while the return flight is a red-eye. Based upon flight schedules, the typical visit includes three nights and three days on the island. The National Park of American Samoa offers no lodging within the park boundaries, and camping is prohibited. However, the national park staff will provide references for a stay in a private home, or "homestay." There are also three hotels on the island: **Sadie's by the Sea**, **Tradewinds**, and **Sadie Thompson Inn**.

It's difficult to travel to other American Samoan islands from Tutuila. There's an eight-hour ferry from Tutuila to the island of Ta'u that leaves every few weeks. While primarily a cargo run, the boat offers around 20 passenger berths. After the ferry arrives in Ta'u, private fishing boats may be hired for transport to the nearby island of Ofu. There have been island-hopping flights in the recent past between Tutuila and Ta'u , but none are running at this time. Given these challenges, this itinerary focuses only on the island of Tutuila. Cash is king on American Samoa and may be needed to go on a hike, walk on a beach, or eat at a restaurant. Remember to bring strong bug spray, as both Zika and dengue fever are found on the island. And bring your snorkeling gear.

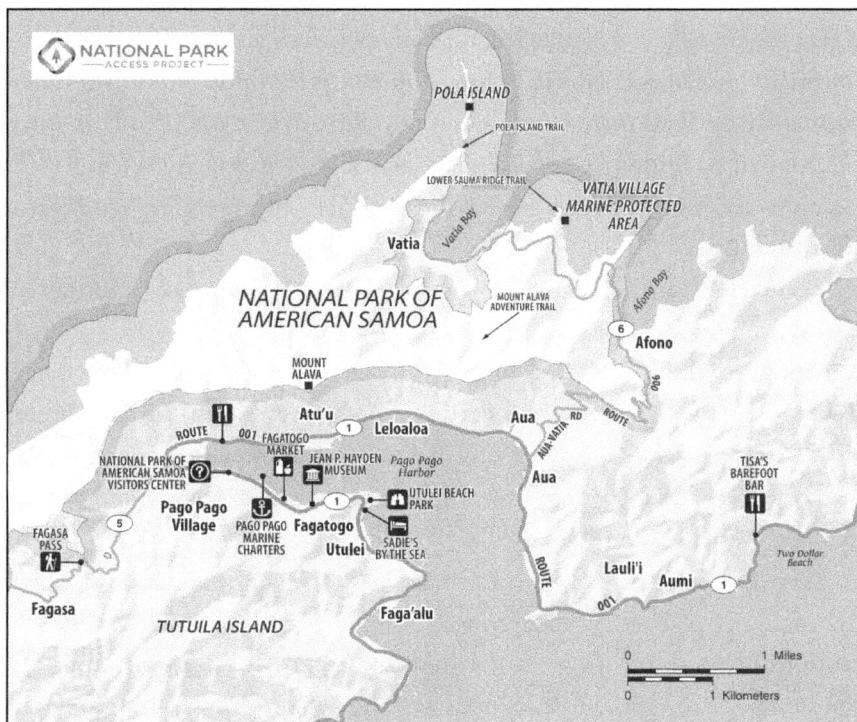

OUTSIDE EXPERTISE

American Samoa has been closed to tourism for several years due to Covid-19. This section relies upon interviews with visitors who experienced the National Park of American Samoa prior to the closure, as well as on-island vendors and national park staff. Tourism flights are anticipated to resume in 2022.

THE TRIP

Day 1: After an oceanside breakfast in this rustic Polynesian paradise, make your way to the **National Park of American Samoa Visitor Center**, which is open from 8:00 a.m. to 4:30 p.m. on nonholiday weekdays. Plan to spend some time here determining trails, mountains, and beaches to visit. Consider beginning with the scenic coastline drive on the national park's one road, Route 6, to the seaside village of Vatia. Once here, drive to the end of the road where there's a short 0.1-mile trail to the beach with a view of the small, uninhabited Pola Island. On the return, stop for the 0.4-mile round-trip **Lower Sauma Ridge Trail** that leads to the south side of Vatia Bay. This is an interpretive trail with informational signage and some archaeological features. Its terminus has a view of Pola Island and overlooks the **Vatia Village Marine Protected Area**.

While heading back to the town center, instead of turning right toward Pago Pago Harbor, turn left, shortly arriving at Tisa's Barefoot Bar, an iconic island restaurant and a great spot for lunch. A short distance farther is **Two Dollar Beach**. This pristine private beach requires cash admission, sells snacks, and provides access to great coral reefs for snorkeling. Look for American Samoa's famous coconut crabs. Return to Pago Pago Harbor and to snorkeling at **Utulei Beach Park**.

Day 2: Spend part of the day on the park's major hike—**Mount Alava**. The national park is centered around Mount Alava, at 1,600 feet, and its foothills down to the ocean to the west and north. There are two routes to the summit—the Mount Alava Trail and the Mount Alava Adventure Trail. Start hiking the Mount Alava trailhead at Fagasa Pass, 1.2 miles past Pago

Pago. This 7-mile round-trip hike leads into the American Samoan forest with nonbiting fruit bats, birds, and plenty of bugs. Hikers are rewarded with a summit view of the entire island and on the descent can connect with the Mount Alava Adventure Trail.

A trip to American Samoa is not complete without a few cultural diversions. Spend the afternoon at the Fagatogo Market in Pago Pago trying traditional taro-based foods and fresh fish. Or enjoy the **Jean P. Haydon Museum** of Samoan culture in the town center. At sunset, make your way to the **Fagetele Bay Trail** with its terrific ocean views.

Day 3: The National Park of American Samoa includes 13,500 acres over three islands. Of this, 4,500 acres are underwater. Consider hiring a charter boat for the day through Pago Pago Marine Charters. Charter operators take clients fishing, to remote beaches, and to snorkeling or diving in the **Fagatele Bay Marine Sanctuary/National Marine Sanctuary of American Samoa**. After a great day on the water, fly back to Hawaii on the red-eye.

See the appendix for useful lodging, camping, and activity contact information.

ALASKA

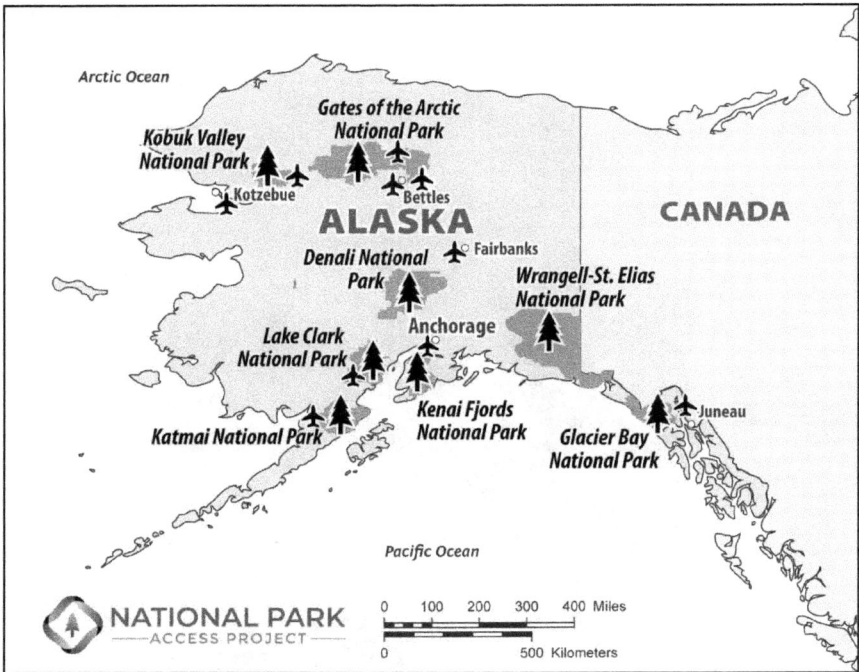

GLACIER BAY NATIONAL PARK

Glacier Bay is undoubtedly young as yet. Vancouver's chart, made only a century ago, shows no trace of it, though found admirably faithful in general. It seems probable therefore, that even then the entire bay was occupied by a glacier of which all those described above, great though they are, were only tributaries . . . that this whole system of fjords and channels was added to the domain of the sea by glacial action is to my mind certain.

—*John Muir, from his 1915 book Travels in Alaska*

GLACIER BAY NATIONAL PARK
STILL IN MOTION/SHUTTERSTOCK

Situated on the northwest edge of Alaska's Inside Passage, Glacier Bay is visually spectacular. The Fairweather Mountains serve as a backdrop to the long Glacier Bay and its apex, the Tarr Inlet. The park has over 1,000 glaciers, including 16 tidewater glaciers, four of which calve into the ocean.

There are few better places to see the impacts of climate change than Glacier Bay. Though historically used by the Tlingit peoples for hunting and fishing, around 300 years ago glaciers expanded, covering Glacier Bay and its northern inlets. Explorers, including Captain James Cook in 1778 and Captain George Vancouver in 1794, observed mostly a massive glacier, with a small inlet and limited shoreline. Around 100 years later, the 1879 visit of naturalist John Muir witnessed a transformed landscape, with the glacier having retreated more than 30 miles and travel possible up the bay to what is now Muir Point. By 1916 the ice had melted to expose the Tarr Inlet, and over the next 100 years the ice retreated significantly farther to the extent that three of the seven tidewater glaciers, including the Muir Glacier, no longer calve. In Alaska today, almost all glaciers are shrinking and thinning, including those in Glacier Bay.

Glacier Bay National Park and Preserve encompasses around 580,000 acres, most of which is wilderness. The park was first preserved in 1925 by President Calvin Coolidge through creation of the Glacier Bay National Monument. Along with most of the other Alaskan national parks, Glacier Bay was made a national park in 1980 by President Jimmy Carter. The park has only a few marked trails around Bartlett Cove, and most visitors spend their time sightseeing this large park from a boat.

NATIVE PEOPLES AND ALASKA NATIONAL PARKS

Approximately one in five Alaskans is of Native American or Native Alaskan descent, the highest percentage of any US state. Following Alaska statehood in 1959, concerns existed regarding native claims to land not already federally protected for conservation. The Alaska Native Claims Settlement Act of 1971 gave Native Alaskans 44 million acres, or about 10 percent of the state.

This was partly a financial settlement related to potential revenues from oil and gas extraction. In addition to this settlement land, native lands are found throughout Alaska, and Alaskan national parks interact with native lands and peoples in ways that national parks located elsewhere do not, particularly with regard to perpetual access.

In 2020, Glacier Bay National Park acquired 150 acres in Berg Bay on the western shore of Glacier Bay. Historically tribal land, native peoples had been forced south due to glacier expansion. Known as the Chookanheeni site, the acquisition agreement granted permanent access to the federally recognized 1,200-member Chookaneidi clan. These types of arrangements are not uncommon in Alaskan national parks.

SCHEDULING AND LODGING

Though Glacier Bay National Park is open from May through September, most travelers visit in July or August when transportation options are greatest. Starting in mid-June, Alaska Airlines provides daily service between Juneau and Glacier Bay's hub village of Gustavus. Alaska Seaplanes and other smaller Juneau-based carriers operate the 30-minute flight between Juneau and Gustavus year-round. The Alaska Marine Highway (ferry) serves the four-hour Juneau to-and-from Gustavus route throughout the year, with summer sailings typically twice per week.

Glacier Bay Lodge, inside the national park on Bartlett Cove, provides transportation from the nearby airstrip and ferry dock. Recently refurbished and with an on-site restaurant, the lodge is a nice and comparatively affordable choice. A more upscale option is the private **Bear Track Inn**, which offers curated daily activities including private boating and kayaking trips. The **Bartlett Cove Campground** is near Glacier Bay Lodge and is first come, first served. Note that there is no grocery store in Gustavus. If camping, bring all of your own food, and come prepared with bear-safe food storage. Additionally, lodge dining is open to campers.

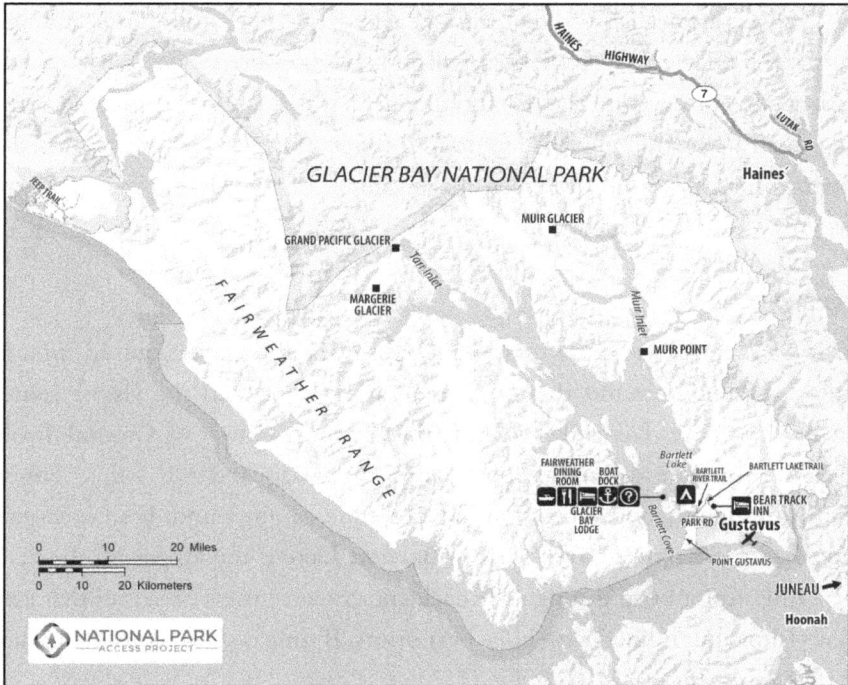

COASTAL BROWN BEARS AND BLACK BEARS

Glacier Bay Lodge and its associated campground are situated on and near miles of shoreline, backed by dense forest. The coastal brown bear is found throughout the park along the coastline, and black bears are found in the forests.

BOATING AND KAYAKING

A daily boat tour including lunch leaves from Glacier Bay Lodge and travels through the park to the Tarr Inlet and its two tidewater glaciers—Grand Pacific and Margerie. This is the most efficient way to see the water-facing portion of the park, and the operator, Glacier Bay Lodge and Tours, is the only vendor with permission to sail into Tarr Inlet.

Kayaks are available to rent from Glacier Bay Lodge. With prior arrangement, the Glacier Bay Tour Boat will provide one-way service for kayakers, either taking them into the bay for a longer kayak back to the lodge or picking them up as the tour boat returns to the lodge. While kayakers miss the opportunity to see the Tarr Inlet, the advantage of a long and peaceful kayak trip may be a fine tradeoff.

THE TRIP

Day 1: Travelers are likely to arrive in Gustavus in the afternoon in time to enjoy the hikes around the lodge and campground and the visitor center in Bartlett Cove. Easy hikes include the 0.5-mile **Tlingit** or **Coastal Trails** (leading opposite directions, both along the coast) and the 1-mile **Forest Trail** through the forest between the lodge and campground. If adventurous and fast, the **Bartlett River Trail** to **Bartlett Lake** is the longest in the park at 9 miles round trip through the backcountry wilderness on a trail that sees few visitors but is lined with huge bear prints. If time is short, consider hiking only part of this trail.

Day 2: Breakfast early and board the **Glacier Bay Boat Tour** at 7:30 a.m. Enjoy a ranger-narrated tour of the bay; see calving glaciers, whales, seals, sea lions, arctic birds, mountain goats, and bears on the shore; and so much more. Return from the trip for a walk on the beach and dinner at the lodge.

Day 3: The ferry leaves Gustavus at 1:30 p.m. Alaska Seaplanes schedules flights throughout the day, and Alaska Airlines has a late-afternoon departure. Spend this day kayaking, either with a guide or independently. Bartlett Cove and nearby Lester and Young Islands are teeming with sea otters, harbor porpoises, sea lions, seals, bald eagles, and birds galore. Whales are visible in the distance. Kayak reservations are strongly recommended.

**See the appendix for useful lodging, camping,
and activity contact information.**

DENALI NATIONAL PARK

Alaskans as a general rule try to be law abiding in everything except hunting, and in that they think they have a perfect right to game—and wherever they want it. . . . confiscation would have a tendency to keep wrongdoers out of the park.

—first park superintendent Henry P. Karstens, advocating for a regulation requiring prospectors and miners to keep a record of game killed so he could judge if they were hunting only when truly necessary, as Congress intended

MOUNT DENALI SUNRISE REFLECTED IN WONDER LAKE, DENALI NATIONAL PARK
JOSEPH SOHM/SHUTTERSTOCK

Located in central Alaska about four hours north of Anchorage, this massive national park pays homage to its central feature—Mount Denali. The high point of the 600-mile Alaska Range, Mount Denali is the highest point in North America. A visually stunning mountain that rises from its 2,000-foot base to its 20,310-foot peak, Denali is a mile taller from base to summit than the 29,000-foot Mount Everest. Often behind clouds during summer travel season, the mountain lures visitors to spend days at key vantage points waiting for a peek.

Though over six million acres in size, the majority of Denali National Park is wilderness. There is one road, the 92-mile Denali Park Road, with only the first 15 miles accessible by private car. Mount Denali is not easily visible until around mile 50, requiring visitors to take advantage of one of the several bus trips into the park. The end of the park road is an old mining village, Kantishna, and the location of the backcountry airstrip and privately owned backcountry lodges. Just before Kantishna is what many consider the heart of the park—Wonder Lake. This beautiful backcountry lake reflects the Alaska Range in its surface and is surrounded by gorgeous alpine tundra.

The Denali area has a long history of human activity, especially as a summer native hunting ground for caribou (still ubiquitous today) and later a location for fur trappers and gold miners. Named a national park in 1917 (under the Mount McKinley National Park Act), the park sees around 600,000 visitors each year.

SCHEDULING AND LODGING

The main park visitor center is open from mid-May through mid-September, and the best time to visit is the peak June through August period. Denali is about four hours north of Anchorage via Route 3 (cars and buses) or via the Alaska Railroad's Denali Star Train (standard or premium "dome" option). Once in the base village of Denali Park, there are ample hotels and motels as well as camping. Denali Bluffs Hotel in Denali Village is a midpriced option, and its sister property, Grand Denali Lodge, offers dining and a café. Denali

Park Village has numerous restaurants at many price points. The park's major campground, Riley Creek, is across the street and adjacent to the visitor center, while the Savage River Campground is inside the park at the end of the 15-mile open-access portion of the park road. For campers and hikers, the Denali General Store is open until 10:00 p.m. Other than the restaurant at the main visitor center, there is no food sold inside the park.

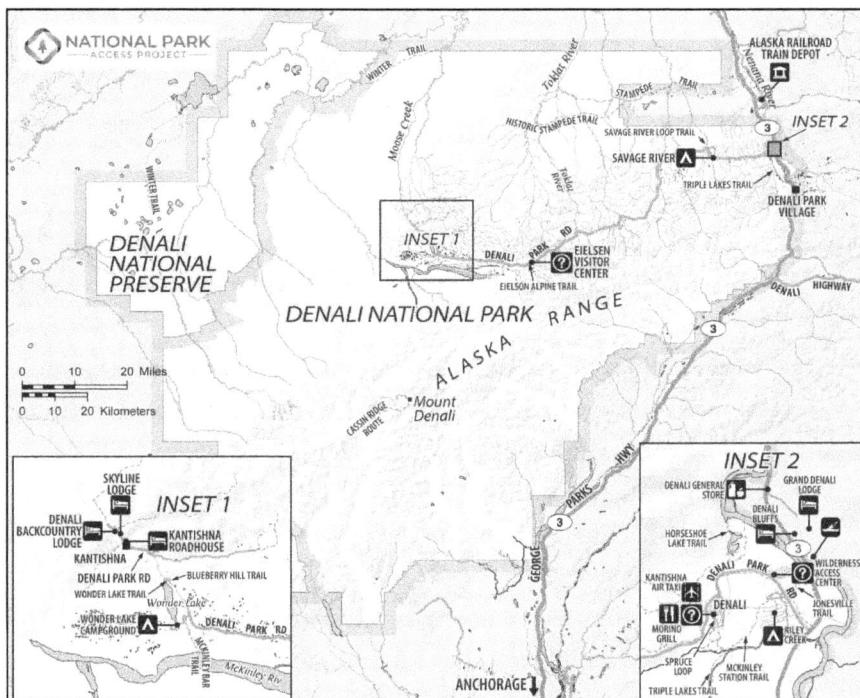

Because of the time needed to reach the Park Road terminus, it's worthwhile to spend a few nights in the backcountry, near Kantishna. The bus schedule results in a near requirement to stay at least two nights. There are four privately owned backcountry lodges: **Denali Backcountry Lodge**, **Skyline Lodge**, **Kantishna Roadhouse**, and the premium **Camp Denali** and **North Face Lodge**. The lodges typically provide or rent bicycles and fishing gear, sell transit bus tickets, share hiking directions, and either sell packed lunches or let you make your own. For campers, the **Wonder Lake Campground** is about 6 miles from the end of the Denali Park Road. This is a beautiful campground with access to Wonder Lake, Reflection Pond, views of the Alaska Range, and a nearby path to the McKinley River. It's also in grizzly bear territory, with bears occasionally found in the area.

BUS SERVICE IN DENALI

Denali National Park offers four bus-access options, described below. Though advanced reservations are strongly suggested, tickets for the tours, and also the transit bus, may be obtained in person at the Wilderness Access Center next to the Denali Visitor Center.

- **Kantishna Experience:** A full-day activity to the park road terminus that takes about 12 hours round trip and includes lunch. This narrated comfortable motor coach ride provides the best overview of the park.
- **Tundra Wilderness Tour:** To Stony Hill Scenic Overlook around 60 miles into the park. Considered one of the best places to see and photograph Mount Denali.
- **Denali History Tour:** To the Teklanika River and the Primrose Hill viewpoint, about 30 miles into the park. This tour is focused on park history.
- **Transit Bus:** A green school bus, without ranger or naturalist. Operates along the full park road with four formal stops, though it may be hailed by hikers and others on demand.

FLIGHTSEEING AND AIR TAXI

The Denali Park Road is quite distant from the glaciated mountains that form such an important part of the park. Flightseeing companies fill this void, taking visitors on aerial tours of the mountains and sometimes even landing on a glacier. The park website has approved flightseeing vendors. In addition, there is one air taxi service, Kantishna Air Taxi, approved to land at the backcountry airstrip and ferry visitors back and forth. Air taxis don't land on glaciers but do fly near enough to the mountains that visitors can clearly see the glorious glaciated terrain.

THE TRIP

Day 1: Begin at the large and well-organized **Denali Visitor Center**. This complex has a restaurant (Morino Grill), sled dog demonstration, and the nearby Wilderness Access Center. Enjoy the visitor center before catching the shuttle bus for the short ride to the **sled dog presentation program** that runs three times per day in June, July, and August. After seeing the dogs and the visitor center, consider a nearby hike. From the visitor center, the 2.5-mile level loop **Horseshoe Lake Trail** is the closest option. **McKinley Village**, 7 miles to the south, provides access to the level 1.5-mile **Oxbow Loop Trail** and the signature **Triple Lakes Trail**. Though this trail extends 9 miles from the Denali Visitor Center to McKinley Village, hikers can start at McKinley Village and go the much shorter distance to the first lake.

Day 2: Transit buses depart from the Denali Bus Depot near the visitor center. The transit bus will stop on demand, but there's not much to do until the **Eielson Visitor Center** at around mile 62, which is one of the first places where visitors can see Denali on a clear day. From Eielson, the **Eielson Alpine Trail** to Thorofare Ridge provides even bigger views. This 2-mile round-trip trail is steep with 1,000 feet of elevation gain. Return to the bus and travel the rest of the way to either Wonder Lake Campground or a backcountry lodge. The midpriced lodges are close together near **Moose Creek**, which is a nice place for an evening walk.

Day 3: If not camping at Wonder Lake, the lake is 6 miles from the backcountry lodges, accessible by bicycle or transit bus. The far end of Wonder Lake closest to the lodges has a short 1-mile loop trail, the **Blueberry Hill Trail**, that leads to the lake and a small dock. There isn't a trail around Wonder Lake, so this is one of the best ways to sit on the lakeshore and view the distant peaks. Continue along Denali Park Road and Wonder Lake to the famous **Reflection Pond** of Ansel Adams photography fame. When Mount Denali is visible, this pond perfectly reflects the mountain, yielding one of the most iconic images of the park. Head along the park road to the entrance road to the Wonder Lake Campground at the top of the lake. From the entrance road, and before the campground, is the **McKinley Bar Trail**, a level 4.6-mile out-and-back trail to the **McKinley River**. This trail has magnificent views of the Alaska Range, and depending upon the time of year, its terminus at the McKinley River showcases the river's roaring silt-filled glacier runoff. If biking, keep going on Park Road for an increasingly impressive view of the Alaska Range.

Day 4: Returning on the transit bus provides the opportunity to view wildlife and stop anywhere. All buses stop at the caribou-rich **Toklat River** (about mile 50) for a restroom break. Once back in Denali Village, consider an afternoon of rafting the **Nenana River** that runs along the east side of Denali National Park. Numerous guide services offer trips ranging from a few hours to a full day.

**See the appendix for useful lodging, camping,
and activity contact information.**

KENAI FJORDS NATIONAL PARK

[A location] that combined the quiet dignity of the primitive forest with the excitement of the ever-changing ocean.

—Rockwell Kent, believed to be the first American artist to paint Kenai Fjords, from his writings in *Wilderness: A Journal of Quiet Adventure in Alaska* (1920)

ORCA WITH CALF IN RESURRECTION BAY, KENAI FJORDS NATIONAL PARK
MICHAEL ROSEBROCK/SHUTTERSTOCK

Kenai Fjords National Park preserves the glacier-carved northwest portion of the land fronting the Gulf of Alaska. This includes the glaciated Kenai Mountains and its primary feature, the 700-plus-acre Harding Icefield. About 30 glaciers flow from the nearly mile-thick Harding Icefield, including the Exit Glacier, which is the easiest to visit. The Harding Icefield continuously pushes the glaciers toward the Gulf of Alaska. This movement of glaciers, from the peaks to the oceans, results in dramatic fjords accessed via boat where six tidewater glaciers calve and flocks of birds hunt the disrupted fish. Also in the park are smaller islands and peninsulas extending into the Gulf of Alaska that serve as migration and nesting areas for a large number of birds. It's estimated that nearly 200 separate species of birds are found in Kenai Fjords National Park at some point in the year.

At just over 600,000 acres, Kenai Fjords is the smallest Alaskan national park. The ancestral home of the Athabaskan people, the term Kenai in Athabaskan means "flat land." It's hard to square this definition with the geography. Kenai in Inuit means "black bear," so perhaps this is the better translation.

To the immediate west of the park is Resurrection Bay. Park travel is centered around the bay, with ferries, tour boats, and kayak trips traveling through it to reach the long Kenai Fjords shoreline. Full of whales, sea otters, harbor seals, nesting puffins, and so many other species, Resurrection Bay is an integral part of the Kenai Fjords experience. Along with most of the other Alaskan national parks, Kenai Fjords was formally established in December of 1980 by President Jimmy Carter.

SCHEDULING AND LODGING

South of Anchorage by two hours via the Seward Highway and four hours via the Alaskan Railroad, Kenai Fjords is the easiest national park to access in Alaska. The trip is lovely, traveling along the Turnagain Arm of the Cook Inlet and through the village of Portage. Though the park is open year-round, services are fully open only in June, July, and August, with limited operation in May and September. If hiking the Harding Icefield, it's best to visit in July and August when the trails are clear.

Heading south from Anchorage, it makes sense to begin at Exit Glacier. The park's single campground is located here—the 12-site **Exit Glacier Campground** near the glacier's base. Lodging just outside the park is along the Seward Highway at its interchange with Exit Glacier Road. **Seward Windsong Lodge** and **Exit Glacier Lodge** are here, with the **Best Western Plus Edgewater** and **Hotel Seward** in nearby downtown Seward on Resurrection Bay. There are many restaurants at varying price points. There's also a nice campground in downtown Seward—**Harbor Side Campground**. Groceries are available at the **Seward Marketplace** between the Exit Glacier turnoff and downtown Seward.

For those with more time and resources, the **Kenai Fjords Glacier Lodge** inside the park fronting Aialik Bay is a splurge. Accessed via floatplane or boat, the lodge offers a classic curated Alaska experience, with fishing, boating, wildlife trips, kayaking, and more. For a similar but more affordable experience, try Fox Island, accessed via ferry from Seward. Though not inside the national park boundaries, the **Fox Island Wilderness Lodge** provides a taste of the Alaskan lodge experience.

HARDING ICEFIELD HIKE

This 10-mile round-trip hike from the Exit Glacier area gains 3,800 feet and is cold enough toward the top to warrant warm hiking gear even in the summer. The park's nonmarine animals are here, including mountain goats, moose, wolverine, black bear, and many more. This hike is a signature activity in the park, and if time does not allow the full trek, consider going partway on the trail to Marmot Meadows.

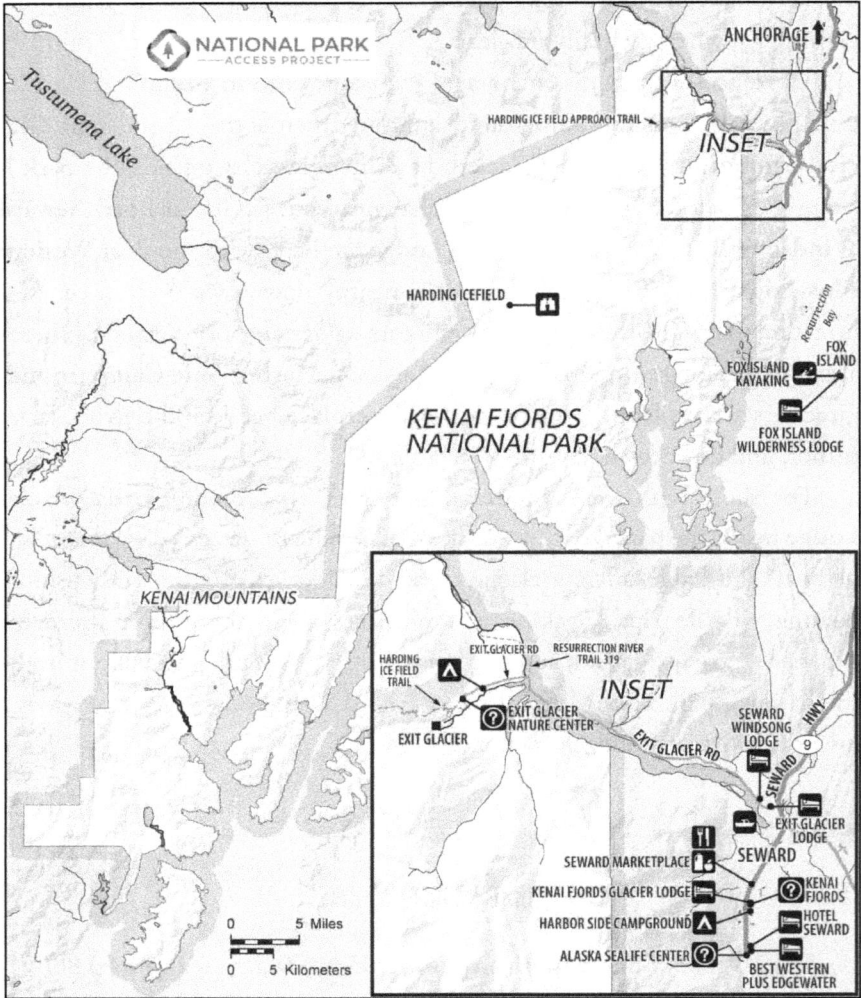

FLIGHTSEEING

Floatplanes and small aircraft may be hired from Seward, allowing expansive views of the entire park, its many tidewater glaciers, and the Harding Icefield.

COMMERCIAL BOAT TOURS OF THE FJORDS

Most visitors reserve space for a daylong boat trip that features Resurrection Bay, one or two fjords with tidewater glaciers, and the small rock outcroppings full of migratory birds. These tour options are described below.

THE TRIP

Day 1: Start at **Exit Glacier** with its **Nature Center** and trail systems. Hiking is the main activity here. Start with the level **Glacier View Loop Trail** that leads along the Exit Glacier runoff (the **Outwash Plain**). The blue/green/brown rushing water is a fantastic sight. The Glacier View Loop Trail connects with the **Harding Icefield Trail** and the **Glacier Overlook Trail**. Take this second trail to the foot of the glacier. It continues in a loop format with offshoots to get closer to the glacier. Combined, this is about a 2-mile hike with around 300 feet of elevation gain.

Descend from Exit Glacier and take the Harding Icefield Trail even if not planning on the full hike. Head up through gorgeous forests about a mile and a half, gaining about 1,200 feet, to **Marmot Meadows** and another portion of the Exit Glacier. The full hike can take three or four hours and transitions from temperate to cold. It's worth a call to see if there's a ranger-led hike to Marmot Meadows. If so, this is a wonderful way to learn about the forest, glacier, and ice field. If ending the day in Seward, consider visiting the **Alaska SeaLife Center**, which can be open as late as 9:00 p.m. in the summer. Home to a rehabilitation program for walruses rescued by fishing boats, this building has marine life not seen in most parts of the United States.

Day 2 and 3: Two companies offer boat tours—Major Marine and Alaska Collection. Boat trips can be booked in advance or through walk-up dockside ticket booths. Here are the standard tours:

- **Wildlife and Natural History Cruise:** Travel around **Resurrection Bay**, including lunch or dinner on **Fox Island**. Most operators allow this trip to have some flexibility in the departure, return, and whether you have lunch or dinner. Some combinations allow a good amount of time on Fox Island. Total boat time is around five hours.

- **Six-Hour Cruise:** Boat in Seward's Resurrection Bay, see islands and a tidewater glacier, and have lunch or dinner on the boat. Varying departure times.

- **Nine-Hour Cruise to Northwestern Fjord:** This long boat ride sails to the calving glaciers in Northwestern Fjord and to the migratory bird habitat islands along the way. Lunch is served on board. This trip includes everything from the six-hour cruise and provides more whale-watching time in Resurrection Bay.

To see almost everything, spend one day on Fox Island and one day viewing the Northwestern Fjord, seabird habitat, and whales.

See the appendix for useful lodging, camping, and activity contact information.

KATMAI NATIONAL PARK

Bears are not companions of men, but children of God, and His charity is broad enough for both . . . Yet bears are made of the same dust as we, and breathe the same winds and drink of the same waters. A bears days are warmed by the same sun, his dwellings are overdomed by the same blue sky, and his life turns and ebbs with heart-pulsings like ours and was poured from the same fountain.
—ATTRIBUTED TO JOHN MUIR

BROWN BEAR WITH SALMON, KATMAI NATIONAL PARK
GUDKOV ANDREY/SHUTTERSTOCK

At the top of Alaska's lower left tail known as the Alaskan Peninsula, Katmai National Park encompasses over four million acres of pristine wilderness. The park is known for its brown bears. Physically similar to grizzly bears, the bears of Katmai feast on king salmon migrating up the Brooks River and Brooks Falls during the months of July and August. Visitors to Katmai come to see the bears during this brief window, with bear viewing centered around the Brooks River as it feeds into Naknek Lake. From here, visitors can also see the other major highlight of the park—the Valley of Ten Thousand Smokes. The site of a 1912 volcanic eruption, the valley and surrounding peaks have been considered active volcanoes since 1900.

Katmai National Park was designated a national monument in 1918 and became a national park in 1980 as part of the Alaska National Interest Lands Conservation Act. Native peoples were in the area for thousands of years, disrupted in the 1760s by Russians who discovered the Katmai region as part of the sea otter trade. Russia was the major outside influence until Alaska was sold to the United States in 1867. As the area was progressively preserved, it became known for fishing and tourism. Hunting is not permitted in Katmai.

SCHEDULING AND LODGING

To reach Katmai, the most affordable option is to take a one-hour commercial flight on Alaska Airlines or Ravn Air from Anchorage to King Salmon. From here, travelers can take a Katmai Air floatplane into Brooks Camp, the park's hub. Many visitors tie Katmai and Lake Clark National Parks together. In this case, carriers that provide service to both parks include Lake and Penn Air, Lake Clark Air, and Rust's Flying Service. Though the Brooks Camp season is from June 1 through mid-September, most visitors come between mid-July and mid-August when the bears are feeding.

The park's hub, Brooks Camp, has a small main dining building surrounded by 16 cabins, with the complex called **Brooks Lodge**. Reservations at the cabins are allocated via lottery based upon entries received the year prior. During the month of July, all guests are limited to a three-night stay. Visitors need at least two nights to see the bears, experience world-class fly-fishing, and enjoy the Valley of Ten Thousand Smokes. Lodging is also available in King Salmon with daytime access to the park via floatplane. The **Brooks Campground**, secured by an electronic fence, is located near Brooks Lodge. Camping reservations open each January, with campers able to eat meals at Brooks Lodge with advanced reservations.

A NOTE ABOUT PRIVATE LODGES

Within Katmai National Park are four additional private lodges. **Grosvenor Lodge** on Lake Grosvenor sleeps 6 people. Its sister property, **Kulik Lodge** near Kulik Lake, sleeps 27. **Enchanted Lake Lodge** on Nonvianuk Lake sleeps 12, and **Royal Wolf Lodge** on the Nonvianuk River sleeps 12. These are primarily fly-fishing lodges accessed via floatplane from King Salmon. Visitors can request that the trip include a day of fishing the Brooks River and a stop at the bear-viewing platform at Brooks Falls.

KATMAILAND, INC.

Katmai National Park has partnered with Katmailand, which operates numerous tours within the park. Visitors may wish to hire a guide to walk between bear-viewing platforms and explain bear genders, ages, and habits such as mating, rearing of young, and fishing. Between Brooks Camp and the viewing platform there are plenty of people and rangers, though bears do also share the pathway. It's not unwise to have a guide. Katmailand also provides fly-fishing experiences, ranging from fishing the Brooks River at Brooks Camp to all-day floatplane fly-fishing excursions. Finally, through Katmailand, visitors may reserve tickets for the full-day ranger-led bus tour of the Valley of Ten Thousand Smokes.

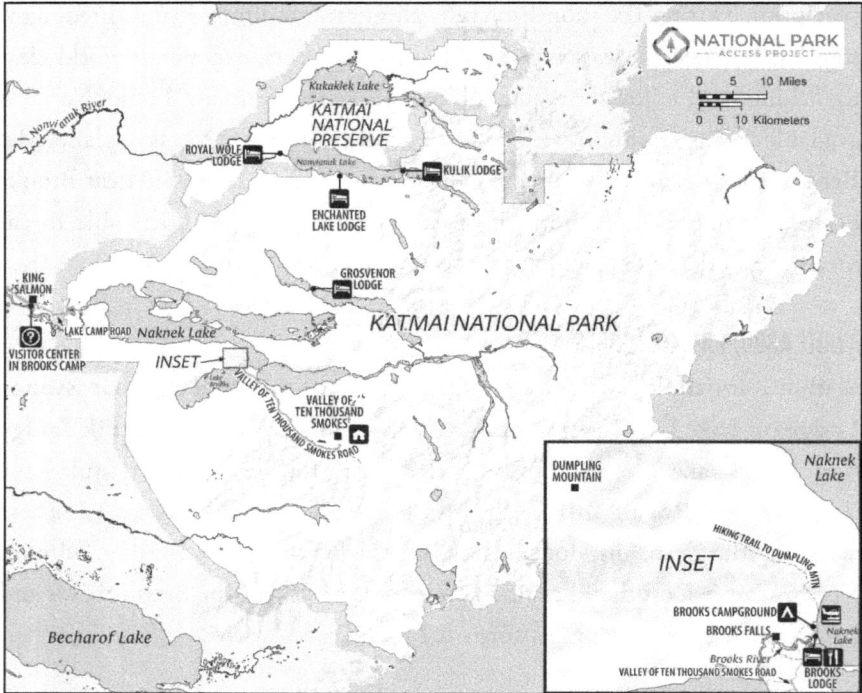

THE TRIP

Day 1: It's a short one-hour flight from Anchorage to King Salmon and another 30 minutes into **Brooks Camp**. Once at Brooks, visitors attend a bear safety lecture given by a ranger before the approximately 1-mile level walk to the **Brooks Falls Viewing Platform**. This is one of two bear-viewing platforms, the other located at the mouth of the Brooks River. When the salmon are running, the rangers limit each visitor's time on the platform. Bears, for better or worse, can also be seen along the hiking path, along the riverfront, and on the lake shoreline.

    Day 2: Take advantage of some of the best fly-fishing in the world. The Brooks River mouth has numerous places to fish for a few hours. Alternatively, enjoy a daylong floatplane excursion to fish in more secluded areas of the park. From Brooks Camp is the park's longest formal trail, the **Dumpling**

Mountain Trail at 8.2 miles round trip with 2,400 feet of elevation gain. The first half mile of this hike is along the beautiful lakefront where huge bear footprints line the sand.

Day 3: The daily seven-hour ranger-led bus tour to the **Valley of Ten Thousand Smokes** takes visitors to the site of the largest volcanic eruption of the twentieth century. The eruption blew the top off Mount Katmai and lasted for 60 hours, spreading debris for hundreds of miles. The drive is 20 miles each way, with the destination including lunch and an optional 2.6-mile round-trip narrated hike. Though more difficult to coordinate, an aerial tour of the Valley of Ten Thousand Smokes may be added to private flights from Lake Clark National Park or from King Salmon.

See the appendix for useful lodging, camping, and activity contact information.

LAKE CLARK NATIONAL PARK

Think of all the splendors that bespeak Alaska. Glaciers, volcanoes, alpine spires, wild rivers, lakes with grayling on the rise. Picture coasts feathered with countless seabirds. Imagine dense forests and far-sweeping tundra, herds of caribou, great roving bears. Now concentrate all these and more into less than one percent of the state—and behold the Lake Clark region, Alaska's epitome.

—John Kauffmann, conservationist

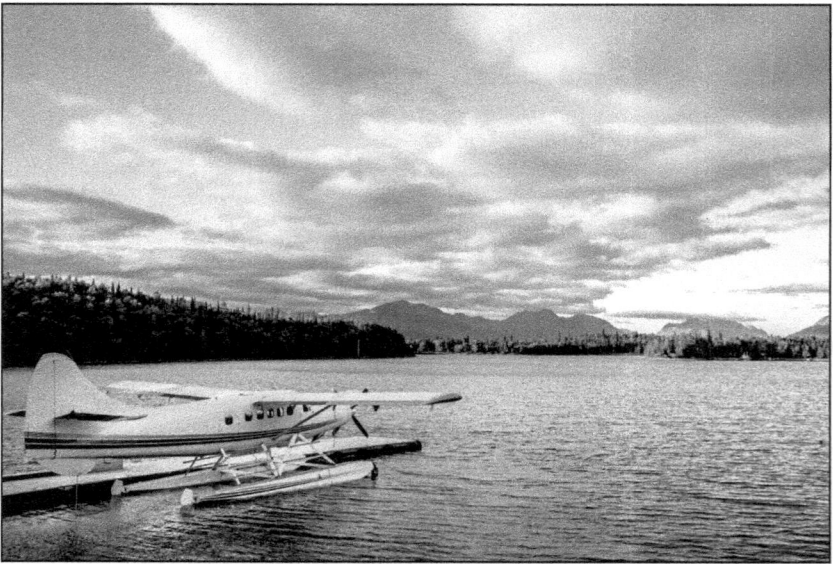

PORT ALSWORTH, LAKE CLARK NATIONAL PARK
COMBAT VET PHOTOGRAPHY/SHUTTERSTOCK

Located in southwest Alaska just north and west of the top of the Alaskan Peninsula, Lake Clark National Park and Preserve encompasses over four million acres of pristine wilderness. It was proclaimed a monument in 1978 and established as a national park in 1980 by the Alaska National Interest Lands Conservation Act. Lake Clark National Park has it all, from coastline on the Cook Inlet to the high peaks of the Neacola and Chigmit Mountains, including the volcanic Mount Redoubt at 10,197 feet. Lake Clark itself is the sixth largest lake in Alaska, at 42 miles long and 5 miles wide. It provides habitat via the Kvichak River for up to three million salmon that migrate from Bristol Bay into Lake Clark each year and also for grayling, trout, and many other fish that make the lake home year-round.

The area offers powerboating, kayaking, fly-fishing the tributaries, deep-water lake fishing, and sightseeing via floatplane. In addition to the inland Lake Clark, the national park has two other marquee areas—Crescent Lake near Mount Redoubt and Silver Salmon Creek on the coastline feeding directly into the Cook Inlet. Silver Salmon Creek is home to coastal brown bears. This is a wildlife photographer's paradise.

SCHEDULING AND LODGING

Lake Clark's season is from mid-June through mid-September, with July and August the peak months. Unfortunately, this is a pretty tough park to see, as there are no roads and only about 10 miles of formal hiking trails. The easiest way into Lake Clark National Park is via plane from Merrill Field in Anchorage across the Chigmit Mountains into Port Alsworth on Lake Clark's Hardenburg Bay. Lake Clark Air is owned by the Farm Lodge and runs multiple trips per day, and other carriers such as Lake and Penn Air and Rust's Flying Service also work well. Once in Port Alsworth, private fishing guides and floatplanes shuttle visitors to see the sights.

There is no grocery store in Port Alsworth and the town is dry. The airlines permit travelers to bring alcohol for their stay in Port Alsworth, though it may not be consumed in public areas or dining halls. There are four lodges here, including **The Farm Lodge**, **Alaska Fishing Unlimited Lodge** (a fishing package is required as part of the stay), the small **Wilder House Bed and Breakfast** (lunch and dinner not provided), and **Chulitna Lodge** (not dry) across Lake Clark from Port Alsworth (transportation provided). Camping is allowed anywhere in the national park without a permit. **Tulchina Adventures** in Port Alsworth offers platform tents with mosquito-netting sides as well as a hard-walled camper cabins.

Silver Salmon Creek fronting the Cook Inlet is the park's less visited area, accessed via plane from Anchorage (Lake and Penn Air) and from Soldotna on the Kenai Peninsula (Natron Air). There are two all-inclusive lodges here: **Alaska Homestead Lodge** and **Silver Salmon Creek Lodge**. These lodges offer stays as short as one day. The final area of the park with lodging is at Crescent Lake. The high-end **Redoubt Mountain Fishing Lodge** is here, accessed via floatplane from Anchorage, with plane travel coordinated in part by the lodge.

FISHING IN LAKE CLARK NATIONAL PARK

This is the kind of place where even people who have never cast a line can be successful. Teeming with all kinds of fish from lake dwelling to stream feeding to salmon that are simply on a starvation run to spawn and die, there is something for everyone. If planning to fish on your own, bring gear and a license. Guided trips provide all necessary gear, with last-minute licenses for sale at the intermittently open Farm Lodge kiosk.

SAMARITAN'S PURSE IN PORT ALSWORTH

Visitors will see in Port Alsworth the large Tanalian Bible Camp and private waterfront cabins occupied by individuals and couples attending Operation Heal Our Patriots for returning veterans. These are both projects of the Franklin Graham organization Samaritan's Purse.

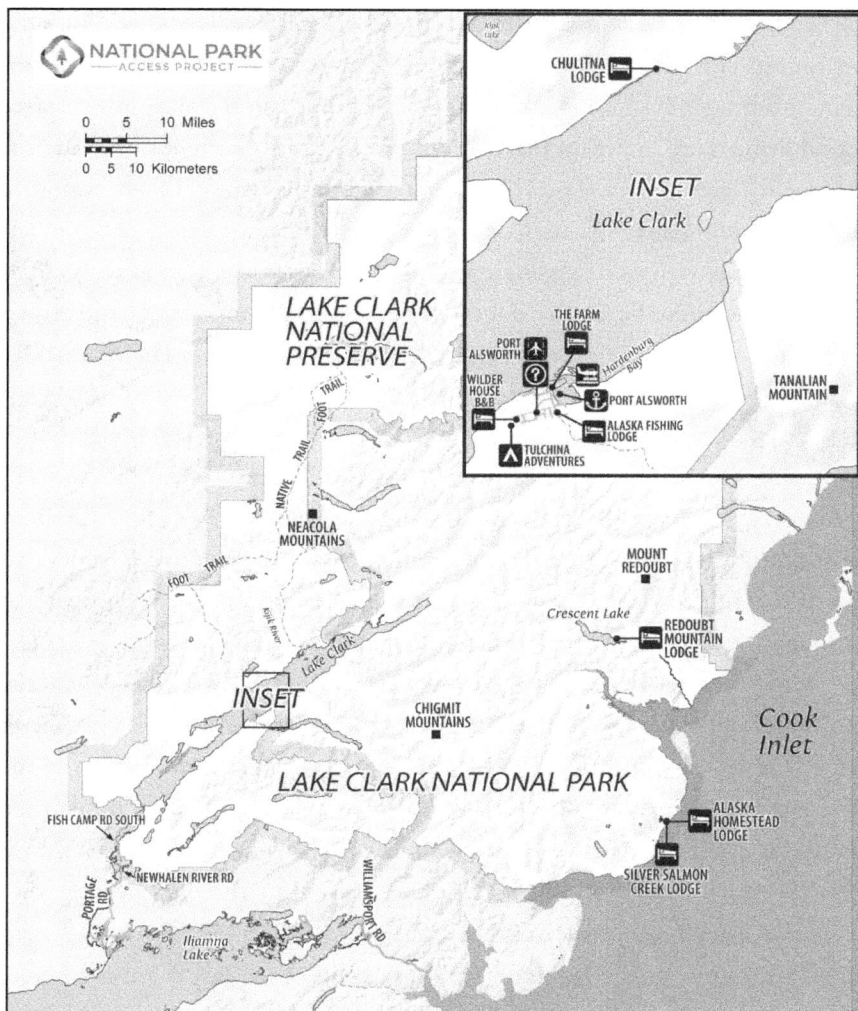

THE TRIP

Day 1: It's a short one-hour flight from Anchorage to Port Alsworth, leaving plenty of time to hike the area. It's worth packing trail food even if staying at a lodge, as the first meal served will be dinner. Once in Port Alsworth, begin at the **Port Alsworth Visitor Center**. Though a fairly empty room, the visitor center is often staffed by experienced rangers and at times a park historian. From here, begin one of the two marked hikes in the area—the **Beaver Pond Loop Trail**. Start on the **Falls and Lake Trail** that loops back to Port Alsworth via the Beaver Pond Trail for a total of 3.7 miles. The extension to **Kotrashibuna Lake** via **Tanalian Falls** adds 1.6 miles for a total of 5.3 miles. The moderate trail gains elevation gradually and provides a good representation of the gorgeous and varied terrain. Even in high summer, the tilted trees and short alpine tundra flowers make it easy to imagine how harsh the area is in the winter.

Day 2: Options for seeing the **Lake Clark** and fishing run the gamut in price and distance from Port Alsworth. Tulchina Adventures rents kayaks and a motorized fishing skiff. For self-guided trips, consider the nearby **Tanalian River** and its multiple tributaries, and the more distant **Kijik River** across the lake. Guided fishing trips may be arranged with relatively short notice through the Farm Lodge.

Day 3: To get a broader sense of the area, spend a day on the tough hike up **Tanalian Mountain**. The summit overlooks Port Alsworth and Lake Clark as well as the Chiglit Mountains between Lake Clark and Anchorage and the Neacola Mountains across Lake Clark. The Neacola Mountains represent the southern end of the Alaska Range, which extends up to and past Mount Denali. An 8.3-mile round-trip hike that begins on the easy Beaver Pond Trail, the **Tanalian Mountain hike** climbs from 650 to 3,900 feet above sea level, with most of the elevation gain occurring in the last 2.5 miles before the summit. From almost every point the views are amazing. Mountain goats peacefully graze near the top, and hikers look down on the procession of small planes taking off and landing at Port Alsworth.

See the appendix for useful lodging, camping, and activity contact information.

WRANGELL-ST. ELIAS NATIONAL PARK

Honorable Mike Gravel, State of Alaska. Dear Mike, As you are well aware, the Wrangell Mountains were taken in the federal land grab called the Antiquities Act. Included in the Wrangell–St. Elias Park was my exclusive guiding area on the Sanford River.

—letter written in Anchorage, Alaska, in July 1979 by guide Ron Hayes to his congressmember Mike Gravel and read on the US Senate floor

HISTORIC HARDWARE BUILDING IN MCCARTHY,
WRANGELL-ST. ELIAS NATIONAL PARK
MIRAGES.NL/SHUTTERSTOCK

The largest park in the US national park system, Wrangell–St. Elias measures over 13 million acres, nearly six times the size of Yellowstone National Park. It extends from the Pacific Ocean at sea level to Mount St. Elias at 18,008 feet. Established as a national monument and World Heritage Site in 1979 and a national park in 1980, the park preserves nine of the highest peaks in the United States, including Mount Wrangell, which is one of the largest active volcanoes in North America. Four major mountain ranges converge here, including the Wrangell, St. Elias, Chugach, and the eastern part of the Alaska Range. This mountainous area has three important glaciers. At 80 miles long, the Nabesna Glacier (extending to the north of the park) is the longest valley glacier in the world. The Hubbard Glacier is the world's longest tidewater glacier, and the Malaspina Glacier is the largest piedmont glacier in North America. Unfortunately, park access for the typical traveler is not designed to feature these glaciers.

Though a majestic, sweeping park, its remote location makes for limited access. Gratitude for the park's road service goes to the Kennecott Copper Company. A source of abundant copper in the late 1800s, the McCarthy and Kennecott areas were developed, mined, and exhausted of productive copper by the mid 1930s. Guided recreation and preservation efforts began not long afterward, with the national park service currently focused on preserving the iconic red copper mill buildings that so often showcase this park.

SCHEDULING AND LODGING

While the park is technically open year-round, roads are open and clear from around mid-June to mid-September. The easiest and least expensive way to visit the park is to rent a car/SUV and drive from Anchorage. About four hours east of Anchorage is Copper Center, Alaska, and the Wrangell–St. Elias Visitor Center. The Copper River of Copper River salmon fame surrounds the park on its west side and separates the visitor center from the park. Once in or near Copper River, visitors can head north on State Route 1 (toward the Nabesna Glacier) or south on State Route 4 (toward McCarthy). For a first visit, the majority of people head south, which provides access to McCarthy, the historic Kennecott mine, and the Kennecott and Root Glaciers. A bit south of Copper River is the town of Chitina. From here, travelers can fly into McCarthy via Wrangell Mountain Air. Flights are also available from Anchorage direct to McCarthy on Thursday and Saturday. Most visitors, though, drive past Chitna and into the park using a rough dirt road connecting Chitna and McCarthy. This drive takes about two hours.

The largest concentrations of lodging are in Copper Center and McCarthy. Princess Cruise Lines operates **Copper River Princess Wilderness Lodge** for their own patrons, but outside parties can reserve available rooms. A smaller rustic option is the **Old Town Copper Center Inn and Restaurant**. There are two campgrounds in Copper Center—**King for a Day** and **Salmon Grove**. Within McCarthy, the upmarket option is the historic **Kennicott Glacier Lodge** a few miles from McCarthy village (shuttle service provided; meals included), with the **Ma Johnson's Hotel** and the **Kennicott River Lodge** located in the McCarthy village center. Camping in McCarthy is at the **Glacier View** or **Base Camp** campgrounds. Groceries are available at the Mountainview Gas and Grocery in Copper Center and at the McCarthy Store and Bakery in McCarthy village. Both McCarthy and the nearby village of Kennicott have restaurants.

GUIDE SERVICES, HIKING, MINE TOURS, RAFTING

Wrangell–St. Elias is massive and remote. Without advance planning, it can feel overwhelming to try to take advantage of what the area has to offer. Large wildlife and minimally marked trails only amplify the challenge. Guide services are plentiful in and around the park. In Copper Center, Copper River Guides provides half- or full-day fishing trips, while in McCarthy, St. Elias Alpine Guides leads hikes and historic tours of the Kennecott Copper Company mine. Also in McCarthy, McCarthy River Tours and Outfitters offers rafting trips and other guide services.

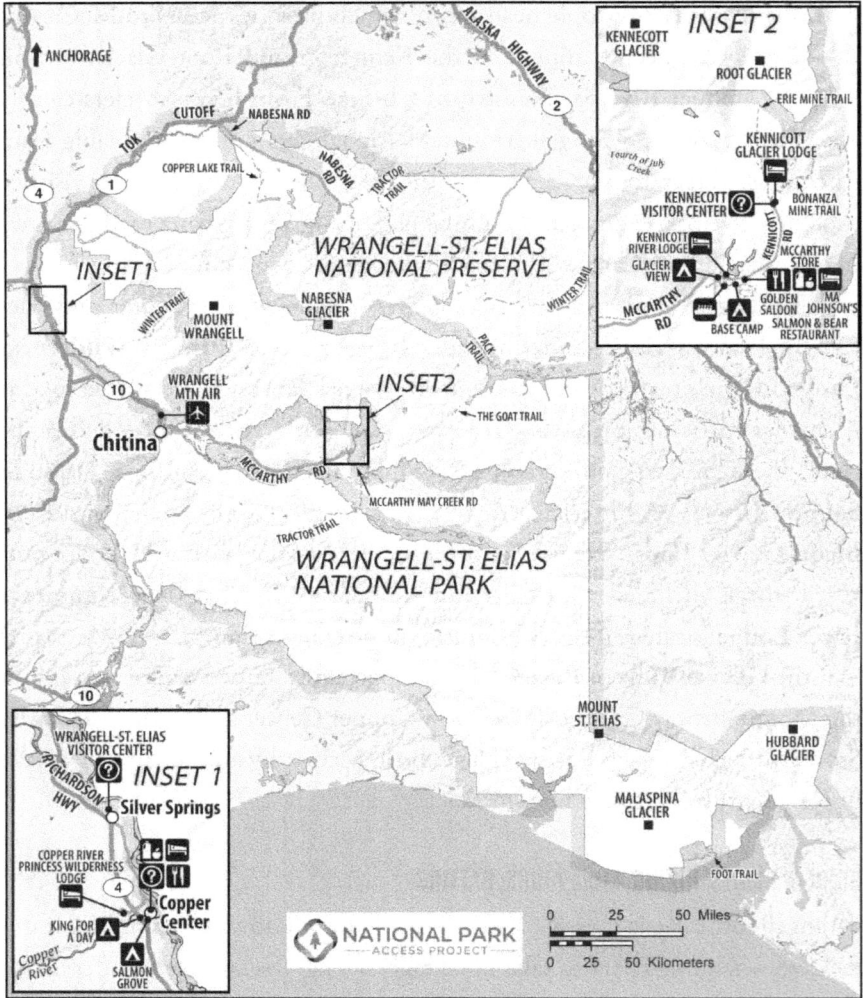

THE TRIP

Day 1: After a morning drive to Copper Center, stop at **Wrangell–St. Elias Visitor Center**. Here enjoy the half-mile **Copper River Bluffs Trail** with views over the Copper River to the Wrangell Mountains. In the afternoon, get to know one of the most famous rivers in Alaska by floating or fishing the Copper River. Fish from shore (with a license) or use a guide service that will take you to the productive fishing holes. Copper River Guides is able to semi-customize a float or fishing trip.

Day 2: McCarthy is a two-hour drive from Copper Center or a short flight from Chitina. While in McCarthy, rent crampons and buy snacks at the McCarthy Store and Bakery and then catch the fee-for-service Wrangell Mountain Transport shuttle to Kennecott, about 5 miles up the road. If staying at the Kennicott Glacier Lodge, shuttle transportation is provided. Stop at the **Kennecott Visitor Center** and get oriented to the **Kennecott Copper Company mine** history and the interior spaces currently open for public viewing. There is an extensive walking tour of the many historic mine buildings that can take several hours. For a curated experience, St. Elias Alpine Guides has a special permit to operate interior mine tours. Use the rest of the day to see one of the glaciers that crown the Wrangell Mountains. Though the brown dirt-like Kennicott Glacier is visible from the Kennicott Lodge, viewing the more stunning Root Glacier requires a hike. The Root Glacier is accessed via the **Root Glacier/Stairway Icefall Trail** which begins just past the mine buildings and provides a short, 4-mile round trip option only to the Root Glacier, or a longer 6.5-mile alternative to the Stairway Icefall. On the hike enjoy views of some of the park's signature peaks—Mount Blackburn, Regal Mountain, and Donaho Peak. Once at the Root Glacier, hikers see the Root and Kennicott glaciers meet and can walk onto the Root Glacier ice sheet. Hiking beyond the Root Glacier to the Stairway Icefall involves entering a remote area with frequent bear sightings and a rough trail.

Day 3: River water full of glacial silt reflects the light in a unique way. Take advantage of the guide services in McCarthy to experience rafting glacier water in the lake created by the **Kennicott Glacier** and its runoff into the **Kennicott River** just past McCarthy. McCarthy River Tours and Outfitters operates these excursions.

See the appendix for useful lodging, camping, and activity contact information.

KOBUK VALLEY NATIONAL PARK

[T]he most isolated wilderness I would ever see.
—John McPhee, referencing the Kobuk Valley in his
1976 book *Coming into the Country*

CARIBOU CROSSING KOBUK RIVER, KOBUK VALLEY NATIONAL PARK
T.M. URBAN/SHUTTERSTOCK

Located 25 miles above the Arctic Circle, Kobuk Valley National Park preserves 1.8 million acres. Its central features are the Kobuk River and the arctic sand dunes. The Kobuk River begins in Gates of the Arctic National Park as runoff from the Arrigetch Peaks, traveling southwest over 300 miles to the Hotham Inlet on the Chukchi Sea. The Kobuk River forms the approximate southern boundary of the park, with the Baird Mountains portion of the Brooks Range comprising the northern (and much larger) section.

The core of the park from a tourist perspective is its southeast corner. Here is a gorgeous section of the Kobuk River as well as the caribou migration hub Onion Portage and the famous arctic sand dunes. These dunes are separated into three dune fields—the Great Kobuk Sand Dunes, Little Kobuk Sand Dunes, and the Hunt River Dunes. The 25-square-mile dunes are most accessible at the park's southeast corner, rising 100 feet above the surrounding landscape. Created from rock pulverized from retreating ice thousands of years ago, these dunes are among the northernmost in the world. The park is wilderness area, with no roads and no designated trails. All access in the summer is via plane.

Though the park is full of large wildlife, including moose, wolf, and bear, the quintessential park animal is the caribou. Around 500,000 caribou migrate south in late September and north in mid-April and cross the Kobuk River around Onion Portage, which has been named a National Historic Landmark District. This is the largest crossing of its kind in North America. Native Inupiat people have harvested caribou in this area for at least 9,000 years and still live in and near the park. Though most United States national parks are strategically focused on providing recreation opportunities, this park's greater focus is on preserving access for native peoples. The park's name, Kobuk, is an Inupiat word meaning "big river." Kobuk Valley was named a national park in 1980 as part of the Alaska National Interest Lands Conservation Act.

SCHEDULING AND LODGING

Almost all of the 10,000 annual visitors to Kobuk arrive during the summer. It's tempting to try to catch the April or September caribou migration, but weather above the Arctic Circle can be impractically cold during all but peak summer months. Though most of Kobuk Valley is temperate with a high of 70 and low of 50 degrees Fahrenheit in July, the heat absorption by the dunes can make hiking them uncomfortably hot, with recorded temperatures as high as 100 degrees.

The easiest way to get to Kobuk Valley is to fly from Anchorage to Kotzebue. This small 3,000-person village is a hub native community as well as a central location for the fishing, petroleum, and northwest Alaska tourism industries. Once in Kotzebue, visitors decide whether to flightsee with touchdown in the park or fly into the 96 percent native village of Ambler (dry/alcohol-free) and stay at **Kobuk River Lodge.** This lodge is a small multi-purpose building, including a family home, the main grocery store for the village, and a lower-level room with two bedrooms, a living room, and a bathroom shared with grocery store staff. This lower level is for lodge guests, and represents the only lodging in Ambler. The lodge and grocery owner is also the chef and river guide, offering a full-day rafting trip into the park and a guided hike to the dunes. Bering Air provides regular flights to the village of Ambler. For flightseeing trips, Golden Eagle Outfitters offers flights that in a single day allow visitors to see both Kobuk Valley and Gates of the Arctic National Parks.

NO ITINERARY DESCRIPTION

For those without extensive backcountry expertise, it is not practical to attempt an unguided trip into Kobuk Valley National Park. The park has no road access or marked trails, and is rarely visited by park rangers. The trip descriptions here discuss the various ways to see the park with vendors or guides. If attempting an unguided trip, work with the rangers in Kotzebue who can help make the visit successful.

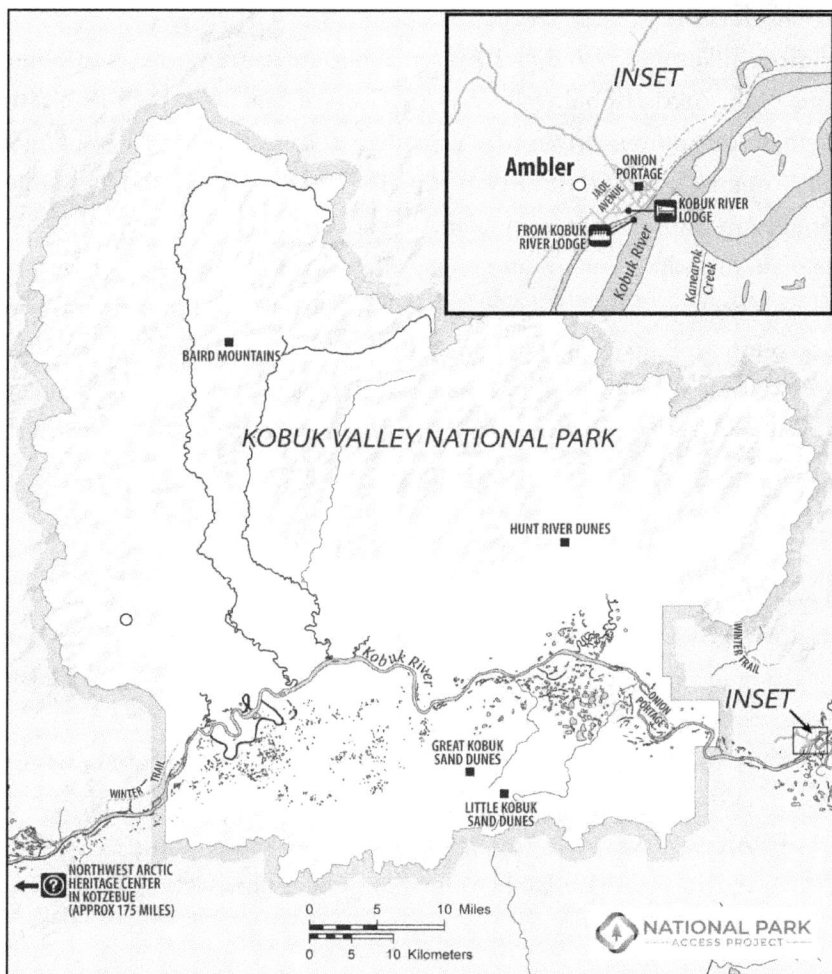

NORTHWEST ARCTIC HERITAGE CENTER

The park headquarters and visitor center is the **Northwest Arctic Heritage Center** in Kotzebue, directly across the street and an easy walk from the airport. Here, visitors find rangers, bear canisters for loan, and a museum about the arctic ecosystem and Inupiaq culture. Kobuk Valley National Park is not patrolled by rangers.

RAFTING THE KOBUK

Outfitters like Arctic Wild and Alaska Alpine Adventures offer a combined Gates of the Arctic/Kobuk Valley trip, including a float down the **Kobuk River**. These are outfitter-driven trips with a preset itinerary. Arctic River Guides will customize a Kobuk River float trip. The Kobuk River Lodge and Onion Portage Adventures, both in Ambler, offer rafting trips of varying lengths into the park, including as short as one day. These trips on the Kobuk River pass **Onion Portage**. The guided trip from Kobuk River Lodge includes trail-free backcountry hiking to the **Great Kobuk Sand Dunes**. This hike takes about three hours and covers four miles of rough and boggy terrain. Enjoy lunch at the massive sand dune and explore bear and moose footprints on the sand. Onion Portage Adventures will customize a longer trip, including camping on the Kobuk River bank.

BACKCOUNTRY HIKING

River travel is a certain kind of vacation and is not for everyone. For those preferring to travel on foot, here are some guides that serve Kobuk Valley for hiking trips:

- Alaska Wilderness Expeditions/Golden Eagle Outfitters Air Taxi (Kotzebue) provides custom trips.
- Arctic Treks Adventures (Fairbanks) provides preset trips.
- Arctic Wild (Fairbanks) provides preset trips, including combined Gates and Kobuk.

See the appendix for useful lodging, camping, and activity contact information.

GATES OF THE ARCTIC NATIONAL PARK

The view from the top gave us an excellent idea of the jagged country to-ward which we were heading. The main Brooks Range divide was entirely covered with snow. Close at hand, only about ten miles to the north, was a precipitous pair of mountains, one on each side of the North Fork. I bestowed the name Gates of the Arctic on them.

—explorer Robert Marshall in 1930

ANAKTUVUK PASS AIRSTRIP, GATES OF THE ARCTIC NATIONAL PARK
LUNASEE STUDIOS/SHUTTERSTOCK

GATES OF THE ARCTIC NATIONAL PARK

At 7,500,000 acres, Gates of the Arctic is just slightly smaller than Alaska's Wrangell–St. Elias and is the second largest US national park. Established in 1980 as a far north wilderness refuge, the park has no roads or hiking trails. Gates of the Arctic is entirely above the **Arctic Circle** and encompasses much of the 700-mile Brooks Range, which extends from Canada to the Chukchi Sea. Six major rivers run through the park, including the Alatna, John, Kobuk, Noatak, North Fork of the Koyukuk, and Tinayguk. The park's tallest peak is Mount Igikpak at 8,500 feet. Though a select few visitors attempt major summits in the park, most of the 10,000 annual visitors walk the valleys and enjoy fishing and boating the pristine waterways.

Tribal homelands extend into various areas surrounding the park, with the largest of these villages, Anaktuvuk Pass, home of the Athapaskan and Inupiat peoples. Archaeological finds inside the park indicate people have been living in and around the Brooks Range for at least 13,000 years. Native peoples then and now feast on the abundant caribou, with the park home to the 320,000-strong Western Arctic and Teshekpuk Caribou Herds. Also plentiful are moose, Dall sheep, musk ox, grizzly bear, black bear, wolf, wolverine, fox, and millions of migratory birds.

Modern exploration was first recorded in 1930 by outdoor enthusiast and conservationist Robert Marshall. His writings about the park, including the name Gates of the Arctic, raised awareness of the area by the still young national park movement. President Jimmy Carter in his Alaska land preservation effort named the park a national monument in 1978 and signed its national park declaration in December of 1980. The combined and mostly adjacent Gates of the Arctic National Park and Preserve, Kobuk Valley National Park and Preserve, Arctic National Wildlife Refuge, and Noatak National Preserve protect around 50 million acres of arctic land. The term Gates of the Arctic refers to two mountains - Frigid Crags (5,500 feet) and Boreal Mountain (6,650 feet). These mountains rise on either side of the North Fork Koyukuk River on the park's eastern side.

SCHEDULING AND LODGING

Though Gates of the Arctic is open year-round, most travelers visit in the summer months. The hottest month here is July, with an average temperature of 51 degrees. Snow starts mid-August in parts of the park and can happen anytime.

Wright Air provides air service from Fairbanks to Bettles, Coldfoot, and Anaktuvuk Pass on the park's north side. From Bettles, Brooks Range Aviation and the Bettles Lodge both offer flightseeing trips into the park, while Coyote Air operates flightseeing out of Coldfoot. Though Bettles is not accessible by road in the summer, the Dalton Highway is about eight miles to the east. The winter freeze allows for construction of a snow-road, enabling Bettles businesses to bring in cars and other heavy equipment.

Lodging includes **Bettles Lodge** in Bettles, **Coldfoot Motel and Campground** in Coldfoot, and **Nunamiut Corporation Kitchen and Motel** in Anaktuvuk Pass. All camping inside the park is backcountry via permit, with no designated campsites.

NO ITINERARY DESCRIPTION

It is not practical to attempt an unguided trip into Gates of the Arctic National Park. The park has no road access or marked trails, is rarely visited by park rangers, and is rugged in the extreme. The trip descriptions here discuss the various ways to see the park with vendors or guides. If attempting an unguided trip, work with the rangers in Kotzebue, Bettles, or Coldfoot who can help make the visit successful.

GUIDE SERVICES

For those planning on one-day flightseeing with a touchdown, vendors include Brooks Range Aviation, Coyote Air, Bettles Lodge, and Golden Eagle Outfitters. Longer private guided trips are also available. These trips typically meet in Fairbanks, fly to one of the three main villages, and then fly into the park. Itineraries include the easier base camp with hiking and fishing option and the more difficult air drop in one location, with pick-up in another. Some outfitters with experience in Gates of the Arctic backcountry adventure include the following:

- Alaska Alpine Adventure (Anchorage) provides preset trips.
- Arctic River Guides (Fairbanks) provides custom trips.
- Arctic Treks Adventures (Fairbanks) provides preset trips.
- Arctic Wild (Fairbanks) provides preset trips including combined Gates and Kobuk.
- Expeditions Alaska (Anchorage) provides preset trips.

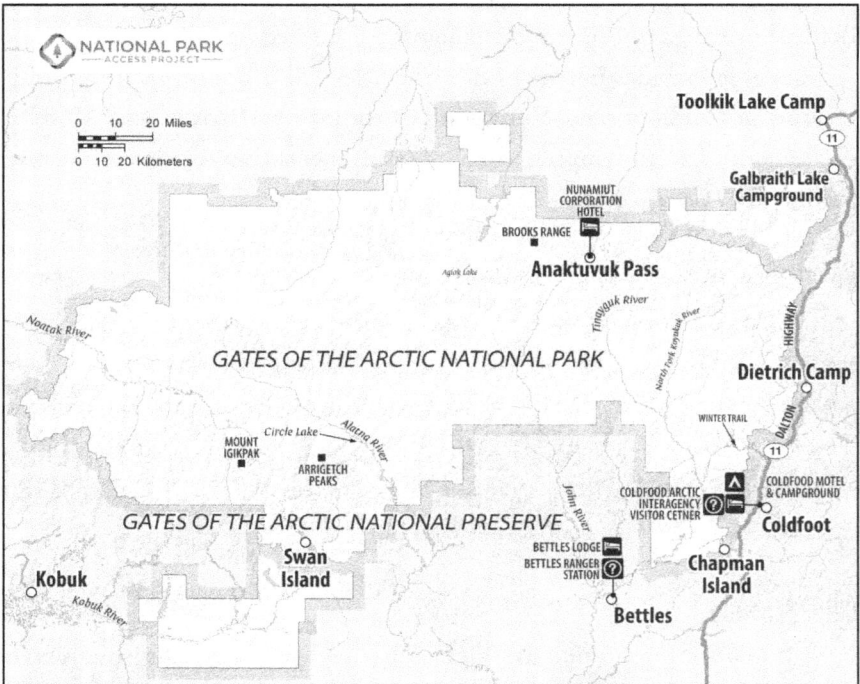

SAMPLE MULTI-DAY TRIPS

For those not flightseeing, a typical longer trip includes, from Bettles, a drop at **Walker Lake** and a multi-day raft trip down the **Kobuk River** with an exit at the native village of Ambler, just before Kobuk Valley National Park. Also from Bettles, another option is a drop and pick up at **Circle Lake** near the **Arrigetch Peaks** and **Alanta River**. Here visitors access abundant hiking and water sports using inflatable kayaks or rafts. Moving to the north of the park, from Anaktuvuk Pass, visitors get dropped and picked up at **Agiak Lake** for abundant alpine hiking, or raft the **John River** south through the park, exiting via a float plane pick up out of Bettles. Another water transit option includes a raft trip from Anaktuvuk Pass to the **North Fork Koyukuk River** which travels south between the two mountains comprising the **Gates of the Arctic.** This trip also terminates in Bettles.

SAFETY AND RANGER REGISTRATION

Those not using a guide service must register with a ranger at Bettles, Coldfoot, or Anaktuvuk Pass. Travelers will be required to certify proficiency in backcountry survival, including the ability to take care for your own life and that of your travel partners. There is no cell phone service here.

BIG GAME HUNTING

Gates of the Arctic is divided into the national park and the national preserve. Big game hunting is allowed (with an Alaska hunting license) in the preserve. Various outfits offer fly-in guided caribou hunting excursions.

See the appendix for useful lodging, camping, and activity contact information.

ACKNOWLEDGMENTS

THANK YOU TO THE many people who reviewed chapters of this book, tested trip suggestions, and provided insider tips. Special thanks to Oscar Pontiff, who proofread chapters and ensured accurate contact information for lodges, campgrounds, and providers of in-park activities. Paul Hein and Chris Hein of Topographics LLC in Saratoga Springs, New York, created the wonderful maps. Kirkus Editorial, a subsidiary of Kirkus Media LLC, in New York, New York, copy edited the manuscript. Megan Katsanevakis of Hue Creative in Charleston, South Carolina designed the cover and the interior layout.

APPENDIX

INCLUDED HERE IS ONLINE contact information for lodging, camping, visitor centers, grocery providers, and activities in and around the parks. A phone number is included in the rare cases where a URL is not available. Campgrounds that do not require reservations are not listed.

ACADIA

Lodging and dining outside the park

Bar Harbor and Southwest Harbor

Camping inside the park

https://www.recration.gov/

Seawall, Blackwoods

Duck Harbor, Schoodic Woods

Visitor Center

https://www.nps.gov/acad/planyourvisit/basicinfo.htm

Hulls Cove Visitors Center

Gardens

https://www.gardenpreserve.org/abby-aldrich-rockefeller-garden

Abby Aldrich Rockefeller Garden

Bike Rental

https://barharborbike.com/

Bar Harbor Bicycle Rental

Kayaking

https://www.mainestatekayak.com/

Maine State Sea Kayak

AMERICAN SAMOA

Lodging and dining outside the park

https://sadieshotels.com/

Sadie's by the Sea

Sadie Thompson Inn

https://tradewinds.as/

Tradewinds Hotel

Visitor Center

https://www.nps.gov/npsa/planyourvisit/basicinfo.htm

National Park of American Samoa Center

Boat Charter

https://pagopagomarinecharters.com/

Pago Pago Marine Charters

ARCHES

Camping inside the park

https://www.recration.gov/

Devils Garden

Visitor Center

https://www.nps.gov/arch/planyourvisit/hours.htm

Arches Visitor Center

Fiery Furnace Hike Pass

https://www.recration.gov/

BADLANDS

Lodging and dining in the park

https://www.cedarpasslodge.com/

Cedar Pass Lodge

Badlands Inn

Camping inside the park

https://www.cedarpasslodge.com/campground

Cedar Pass Campground and RV Park

Visitor Centers

https://www.nps.gov/thingstodo/visit-ben-reifel.htm

Ben Reifel Visitor Center

White River Visitor Center: 605-455-2878

Grocery/Markets

http://badlands-grocery.edan.io/

Badlands Grocery

BIG BEND

Lodging and dining in the park

https://www.chisosmountainslodge.com/

Chisos Mountain Lodge

Camping inside the park

https://www.recreation.gov

Chisos Basin, Cottonwood, Rio Grande Village

Visitor Centers

https://www.recreation.gov

Chisos Basin Visitor Center

Castolon Visitor Center

Grocery/Markets

Basin Convenience Store: 432-477-2292

Rafting

https://visitbigbend.com/river-trips/

Visit Big Bend

https://www.bigbendrivertours.com/

Big Bend River Tours

BISCAYNE

Lodging and dining outside the park

Greater Miami

Visitor Center

https://www.nps.gov/bisc/planyourvisit/basicinfo.htm

Dante Fascell Visitor Center

Boat Tours and Stiltsville

https://www.biscaynenationalparkinstitute.org/

BLACK CANYON OF THE GUNNISON

Lodging and dining outside the park

Montrose, Crawford

Camping inside the park

https://www.recration.gov/

South and North Rim Campgrounds

Visitor Center

https://www.nps.gov/blca/planyourvisit/visitorcenters.htm

South Rim Visitor Center

Red Rock Canyon Permits

https://www.nps.gov/blca/planyourvisit/redrockinfo.htm

BRYCE CANYON

Lodging and dining inside the park

https://www.brycecanyonforever.com/

Lodge at Bryce Canyon

Lodging and dining outside the park

https://www.bryceviewlodge.com/

Bryce View Lodge

Camping inside the park

https://www.recration.gov/

Sunset

Visitor Center

https://www.nps.gov/brca/planyourvisit/tourvisitor.htm

Bryce Canyon Visitor Center

Canyon Trail Rides

https://www.canyonrides.com/bryce-canyon-horseback-riding/

CANYONLANDS

Lodging and dining outside the park

Moab

Camping inside the park

https://www.recreation.gov/

Needles Campground (Willow Flat: walk in)

Visitor Centers

https://www.nps.gov/cany/planyourvisit/hours.htm

Island in the Sky Visitor Center

Needles Visitor Center

Bike Rentals

https://chilebikes.com/

Chile Pepper

https://poisonspiderbicycles.com/

Poison Spider

https://www.rimcyclery.com/
    Rim Cyclery

CAPITOL REEF

Lodging and dining outside the park

https://brokenspurinn.com/
    Broken Spur Inn

https://capitolreefresort.com/
    Capitol Reef Resort

Camping inside the park

https://www.recration.gov/
    Fruita

Visitor Center

https://www.nps.gov/care/planyourvisit/basicinfo.htm
    Capitol Reef Visitor Center

CARLSBAD CAVERNS

Lodging and dining outside the park

https://whitescitynm.com/
    Whites City Cavern Inn

Visitor Center

https://www.nps.gov/cave/planyourvisit/visitor-center.htm
    Carlsbad Caverns Visitor Center

Cave Tours

https://www.recreation.gov/
    Kings Palace, Left Hand Tunnel, Lower Cave,
    Hall of White Giant, Slaughter Canyon

CHANNEL ISLANDS

Lodging and dining outside the park

https://www.ihg.com/holidayinnexpress/hotels/us/en/ventura/vntnd/hoteldetail

   Holiday Inn Express and Suites Ventura Harbor

https://www.marriott.com/hotels/travel/oxrfp-four-points-ventura-harbor-resort/

   Four Points by Sheraton Ventura Harbor

Camping outside the park

https://www.parks.ca.gov

   McGrath State Campground—Greater Ventura

Camping inside the park

https://www.recreation.gov/camping/campgrounds/232498

   Scorpion Ranch Campground

Visitor Centers

https://www.nps.gov/chis/learn/news/scorpion-ranch-visitor-center.htm

   Channel Islands Visitor Center in Ventura

   Scorpion Ranch Visitor Center

Ferry Serving Channel Islands

https://reserve.islandpackers.com

   Island Packers Cruises

Kayak Reservations

http://cikayak.com/kayak-rentals/

   Channel Islands Kayak Center Reservations

https://www.islandkayaking.com/

   Channel Islands Adventure Company

CONGAREE

Lodging and dining outside the park

   Columbia

Camping inside the park

https://www.recreation.gov

  Bluffs

  Longleaf

Visitor Center

https://www.nps.gov/cong/planyourvisit/hours.htm

  Harry Hampton Visitor Center

Kayak Trips

https://www.carolinaoutdooradventures.com/cedar-creek

  Carolina Adventures

https://jkadventureguides.com/

  JK Adventure Guides

CRATER LAKE

Lodging and dining inside the park

https://www.travelcraterlake.com/lodging-camping

  Crater Lake Lodge

  Mazama Village Cabins

Camping inside the park

https://www.travelcraterlake.com/lodging-camping

  Mazama Village Campground

Visitor Centers

https://www.nps.gov/crla/planyourvisit/visitorcenters.htm

  Rim Visitor Center

  Steel Visitor Center

Grocery/Markets

https://www.travelcraterlake.com/things-to-do/shopping-supplies/#mazama-village

  Mazama Village Store

Boat Trips

https://www.travelcraterlake.com/things-to-do/boat-tours/wizard-is-land-tours

    Wizard Island Boat Tours

CUYAHOGA

Lodging and dining inside the park

https://www.conservancyforcvnp.org/experience/plan-your-visit/re-treats-lodging/

    Stanford House

https://www.innatbrandywinefalls.com/

    Inn at Brandywine Falls

Visitor Center

https://www.nps.gov/cuva/boston-mill-visitor-center.htm

    Boston Mill Visitor Center

Bike Rentals

https://www.centurycycles.com/about/peninsula-pg2844.htm

    Century Cycles

Train Ride

https://www.cvsr.org/

    Cuyahoga Valley Scenic Railroad

DEATH VALLEY

Lodging and dining inside the park

https://deathvalleyhotels.com/

    Stovepipe Wells and Furnace Springs Campgrounds

https://www.oasisatdeathvalley.com/

    Oasis at Death Valley

    Ranch at Death Valley

https://www.panamintsprings.com/

    Panamint Springs Resort

    Camping inside the park

https://www.recreation.gov

    Black Rock, Cottonwood

    Indian Cove, Jumbo Rocks

Visitor Center

https://www.nps.gov/thingstodo/visit-the-furnace-creek-visitor-center.htm

    Furnace Creek Visitor Center

Grocery/Markets

    Stovepipe Wells Grocery Store

DENALI

Lodging and dining inside the park

https://www.alaskacollection.com/lodging/denali-backcountry-lodge/

    Denali Backcountry Lodge

https://www.katair.com/skyline-lodge/

    Skyline Lodge

https://www.kantishnaroadhouse.com/

    Kantishna Roadhouse

Camping inside the park

https://www.reservedenali.com/

    Wonder Lake, Savage River, Riley Creek

Visitor Centers and Sled Dogs

https://www.nps.gov/dena/planyourvisit/the-denali-visitor-center.htm

    Denali Visitor Center

    Eielson Visitor Center

Air Taxi

https://www.katair.com/

    Kantishna Air Taxi

DRY TORTUGAS

Lodging and dining outside the park

Key West

Visitor Center

https://www.nps.gov/drto/planyourvisit/visitor-centers.htm

Eco Discovery Center

https://www.drytortugas.com/

Yankee Freedom Ferry

Kayak Rentals

https://www.kayakkingskeywest.com/rentals/

EVERGLADES

Lodging and dining outside the park

Everglades City

Homestead

Camping inside the park

https://www.recreation.gov

Flamingo Campground

Long Pine Key Campground

Visitor Centers

https://www.nps.gov/ever/planyourvisit/visitorcenters.htm

Gulf Coast Visitor Center

Shark Valley Visitor Center

Ernest F. Coe Visitor Center

Boat Tours

https://flamingoeverglades.com/

Flamingo Adventures

https://evergladesadventures.com/

Everglades Adventure Kayak and Eco Tours

GATES OF THE ARCTIC

Lodging and dining outside the park

http://bettleslodge.com/
> Bettles Lodge

https://www.coldfootcamp.com/
> Coldfoot Motel and Campground

https://nunamiut-corporation-camp-kitchen.business.site/
> Nunamiut Corporation Kitchen and Motel

Visitor Center

https://www.nps.gov/gaar/planyourvisit/index.htm
> Bettles Ranger Station and Visitor Center

Flightseeing

https://brooksrange.com/

Brooks Range Aviation

https://flycoyote.com/
> Coyote Air

GATEWAY ARCH

Lodging and dining outside the park

> Saint Louis

Visitor Centers

https://www.gatewayarch.com/buy-tickets/
> Gateway Arch Museum: Arch, Museum, Boat

https://www.nps.gov/jeff/planyourvisit/och.htm
> Old Courthouse

GLACIER

Lodging and dining inside the park

https://www.glaciernationalparklodges.com/lodging
> Village Inn at Apgar, Lake McDonald Lodge
> Rising Sun Motor Inn, Many Glacier Hotel

Swiftcurrent Motor Inn

https://www.glacierparkcollection.com/lodging

Apgar Village Lodge and Cabins, St. Mary Lodge

Glacier Park Lodge, Motel Lake McDonald

Backcountry Lodges

http://www.sperrychalet.com/reservations.php

Sperry Chalet

https://www.graniteparkchalet.com/reservations.html

Granite Park Chalet

Camping inside the park

https://www.recreation.gov

Apgar, Fish Creek, Sprague Creek, Rising Sun

Saint Mary, Two Medicine, Many Glacier

Visitor Centers

https://www.nps.gov/glac/planyourvisit/visitor-centers.htm

Saint Mary, Apgar, Logan Pass Visitor Centers

Grocery/Markets

https://parkcafeandgrocery.com/park-grocery

Park Grocery

Horseback Riding

https://www.swanmountainglacier.com/

Swan Mountain Outfitters

Bus Tours

https://www.glaciernationalparklodges.com/red-bus-tours

Red Bus Tours

https://www.glaciersuntours.com/

Sun Bus Tours

GLACIER BAY

Lodging and dining inside the park

https://www.visitglacierbay.com/

Glacier Bay Lodge

Camping inside the park

https://www.nps.gov/glba/planyourvisit/campground.htm

Bartlett Cove

Visitor Center

https://www.nps.gov/glba/planyourvisit/visitorcenters.htm

Glacier Bay Visitor Center

Glacier Bay Boat Tour

https://www.visitglacierbay.com/

Glacier Bay Boat Tour

Kayak Rentals

https://glacierbayseakayaks.com/day-trips/one-day-kayak-adventure

Glacier Bay Sea Kayaks

GRAND CANYON

Lodging and dining inside the park—South Rim

https://www.visitgrandcanyon.com/

Yavapi Lodge and RV Park

https://www.grandcanyonlodges.com/lodging/

Bright Angel Lodge, Thunderbird Lodge

El Tovar Hotel, Kachina Lodge, Maswik Lodge

Lodging and dining inside the park—North Rim

https://www.grandcanyonforever.com/

Grand Canyon Lodge North Rim

Camping inside the park

https://www.recreation.gov

Mather Campground South Rim

North Rim Campground

https://www.nps.gov/grca/planyourvisit/backcountry-permit.htm

Indian Gardens

Phantom Ranch

Visitor Center

https://www.nps.gov/grca/planyourvisit/visitorcenters.htm

   Grand Canyon Visitor Center

Grocery/Markets

Canyon Village Market and Deli: 928-638-2262, ext. 27

Rafting

https://www.riveradventures.com/

   Wilderness River Adventures

GRAND TETON

Lodging and dining inside the park

https://www.gtlc.com/lodges

   Jackson Lake Lodge, Jenny Lake Lodge, Colter Bay Village

   Headwaters Lodge and Cabins at Flagg Ranch

https://www.signalmountainlodge.com/

   Signal Mountain Lodge

https://dornans.com/

   Dornan's Spur Ranch

Camping inside the park

https://www.recreation.gov

   Colter Bay, Signal Mountain, Jenny Lake

Visitor Center

https://www.nps.gov/grte/planyourvisit/visitorcenters.htm

   Jenny Lake and Colter Bay Visitor Centers

Grocery/Markets

https://www.gtlc.com/dining/the-general-store-colter-bay-village

   General Store at Colter Bay Village

Rafting

https://trianglex.com/river-trips/

   Triangle X

https://grand-teton-scenic-floats.com/
> Solitude

https://www.tetonwhitewater.com/
> Teton Whitewater

https://www.jhww.com/
> Jackson Hole Whitewater

Bike Rentals

https://dornans.com/
> Dornans

GREAT BASIN

Lodging and dining outside the park

https://www.stargazernevada.com/
> Stargazer Inn

https://www.whisperingelms.com/
> Whispering Elms

Camping inside the park

https://www.recreation.gov/
> Baker Creek, Grey Cliffs, Upper & Lower Lehman Creek

Visitor Center and Lehman Cave Tours

https://www.nps.gov/grba/planyourvisit/lehman-caves-tours.htm

GREAT SAND DUNES

Lodging and dining outside the park

http://www.gsdlodge.com/
> Great Sand Dunes Lodge

Camping inside the park

https://www.recreation.gov
> Pinon Flats Campground

Visitor Center

https://www.nps.gov/grsa/planyourvisit/visitor-center.htm

Great Sand Dunes Visitor Center

Grocery/Markets and Sand Surfboard Rentals

http://www.greatdunes.com/

Great Sand Dunes Oasis

GREAT SMOKY MOUNTAINS

Lodging and dining inside the park

http://www.lecontelodge.com/

LeConte Lodge

Camping inside the park

https://www.recreation.gov

Cades Cove, Elkmont

Visitor Centers

https://www.nps.gov/grsm/planyourvisit/visitorcenters.htm

Cades Cove, Oconaluftee

Sugarlands, Clingmans Dome

Grocery and Bike Rentals

https://cadescovetrading.com/

Cades Cove

Horseback Riding

http://smokemontridingstable.com/

Smokemont Riding Stables

GUADALUPE MOUNTAINS

Lodging and dining outside the park

https://whitescitynm.com/

Whites City Cavern Inn

Visitor Center

https://www.nps.gov/gumo/planyourvisit/visitorcenters.htm

Pine Springs Visitor Center

McKittrick Canyon Visitor Center

HALEAKALA

Lodging and dining outside the park
https://kulalodge.com/
  Kula Lodge

Camping inside the park
https://recreation.gov
  Hosmer Grove, Kipahulu

Visitor Center
https://www.nps.gov/hale/planyourvisit/hours.htm
  Haleakala, Kipahulu

Grocery/Market
Morihara Store Kula: 808-878-2502

Sunrise Pass—Haleakala Volcano
www.recreation.gov

HAWAI'I VOLCANOES

Lodging and dining inside the park
https://hawaiivolcanohouse.com/
  Volcano House

Camping inside the park
https://hawaiivolcanohouse.com/?page_id=976
  Namakanipaio Campground and Camper Cabins

Visitor Center
https://www.nps.gov/havo/planyourvisit/kvc.htm
  Kilauea Visitor Center

Grocery/Markets
Kilauea General Store, Volcano: 808-967-7555

HOT SPRINGS

Lodging and dining inside the park
https://www.hotelhale.com/

Hotel Hale

Lodging and dining outside the park

https://thewatershs.com/

Waters Hotel

https://www.arlingtonhotel.com/

Arlington Resort Hotel and Spa

Visitor Center

https://www.nps.gov/hosp/learn/historyculture/fordyce-bathhouse.htm

Fordyce Visitor Center and Museum

Bathhouses

https://www.buckstaffbaths.com/

Buckstaff

https://www.quapawbaths.com/

Quapaw

INDIANA DUNES

Lodging and dining outside the park

http://www.duneswalkinn.com/

DunesWalk Inn at the Furness Mansion

https://springhouseinn.com/

Springhouse Inn

Camping inside the park

https://www.recreation.gov

Dunewood Campground

Visitor Center

https://www.nps.gov/indu/planyourvisit/idnlvc.htm

Indiana Dunes Visitor Center

ISLE ROYALE

Lodging and dining inside the park

https://www.rockharborlodge.com/

Rock Harbor Lodge

Ferries

Ranger III from Michigan: 906-482-0984

https://www.isleroyale.com/

Isle Royale Ferry from Copper Harbor, MI

https://www.isleroyaleboats.com/

Voyageur II and *Sea Hunter III* from Grand Portage, MN

Kayak Rentals

https://www.rockharborlodge.com/rock-harbor-marina

Isle Royale Boat Tours on the MV Sandy

https://www.rockharborlodge.com/sightseeing-schedule

Visitor Center

https://www.nps.gov/isro/planyourvisit/hours.htm

Houghton Visitor Center

Grocery/Markets

https://www.rockharborlodge.com/gifts-and-supplies

Dockside General Store

Water Taxi

https://www.rockharborlodge.com/water-taxi

JOSHUA TREE

Lodging and dining outside the park

https://www.joshuatreeinn.com

Joshua Tree Inn

https://www.marriott.com/hotels/travel/psptn-fairfield-inn-and-suites-twentynine-palms-joshua-tree-national-park/

Fairfield Inn and Suites Twentynine Palms

Camping inside the park

https://www.recreation.gov

Black Rock, Cottonwood

Indian Cove, Jumbo Rocks

Visitor Centers

https://www.nps.gov/jotr/planyourvisit/visitorcenters.htm

   Oasis Visitor Center

   Joshua Tree Visitor Center

Guided Tours

https://www.recreation.gov/ticket/facility/tour/1040

   Keys Ranch

KATMAI

Lodging and dining inside the park

https://katmailand.com/brooks-lodge-lottery/

   Brooks Lodge Lottery

Visitor Centers

https://www.nps.gov/katm/planyourvisit/visitorcenters.htm

   King Salmon Visitor Center

   Brooks Camp Visitor Center

Valley of Ten Thousand Smokes Tour

https://katmailand.com/katmai-national-park/valley-of-ten-thousand-smokes/

   Brooks Lodge

   Sport Fishing

https://katmailand.com/sport-fishing/

   Brooks Lodge

KENAI FJORDS

Lodging and dining outside the park

https://www.sewardalaskalodging.com/

   Exit Glacier Lodge

https://www.bestwestern.com/en_US/book/hotels-in-seward/best-western-plus-edgewater-hotel/propertyCode.02016.html

   Best Western Edgewater Hotel

Visitor Centers

https://www.nps.gov/kefj/planyourvisit/visitorcenters.htm

    Kenai Fjords National Park Visitor Center

    Exit Glacier Nature Center

Resurrection Bay and Fjords Boat Tours

https://www.alaskacollection.com/day-tours/kenai-fjords-tours/

    Kenai Fjords Tours

https://majormarine.com/all-cruises/

    Major Marine Tours

KINGS CANYON

Lodging and dining inside the park

https://www.visitsequoia.com/lodging

    John Muir Lodge and Grant Grove Cabins

    Cedar Grove Lodge

Lodging and dining outside the park

https://www.mslodge.com/lodging

    Montecito Sequoia Lodge

Camping inside the park

https://www.nps.gov/seki/planyourvisit/campgrounds.htm

    Azalea Campground (Grant Grove)

    Moraine, Sentinel, Canyon View, Sheep Creek (Cedar Grove)

Visitor Centers

https://www.nps.gov/seki/planyourvisit/visitorcenters.htm

    Kings Canyon Visitor Center

    Cedar Grove Visitor Center

Grocery/Markets

https://www.visitsequoia.com/shop/grant-grove-market

    Grant Grove Market

KOBUK VALLEY

Lodging and dining outside the park

http://www.kobukriverlodge.com/

  Kobuk River Lodge

Visitor Center

https://www.nps.gov/kova/planyourvisit/northwest-arctic-heritage-center.htm

  Northwest Arctic Visitor Center

Rafting

http://www.kobukriverlodge.com/

  Kobuk River Lodge

https://www.onionportagealaska.com/

  Onion Portage Adventures

Flightseeing

https://alaskawildernessexpeditions.com/

  Golden Eagle Outfitters

LAKE CLARK

Lodging and dining in Port Alsworth

https://www.thefarmlodge.com/

  The Farm Lodge and Lake Clark Air

Camping in Port Alsworth

https://www.tulchinaadventures.com/port-alsworth

  Tulchina Adventures

Visitor Center

https://www.nps.gov/lacl/planyourvisit/hours.htm

  Port Alsworth Visitor Center

Flightseeing and Fishing

https://www.thefarmlodge.com/

  The Farm Lodge

LASSEN VOLCANIC

Lodging and dining inside the park

https://lassenlodging.com

    Drakesbad Guest Ranch

    Manzanita Lake Camping Cabins

Lodging and dining outside the park

http://hatcreekresortrv.com

    Hat Creek Resort and RV Park

https://highlandsranchresort.com

    Highlands Ranch Resort

https://thevillageatchildsmeadow.com

    The Village at Childs Meadow

Camping inside the park

https://www.recreation.gov

    Southwest, Manzanita Lake, Warner Valley

Visitor Centers

https://www.nps.gov/lavo/planyourvisit/visitorcenters

    Kohm Yah-mah-nee Visitor Center

    Loomis Museum

Grocery/Markets

https://www.nps.gov/lavo/planyourvisit/goodsandservices.htm

    Manzanita Lake Camper Store

Horseback riding and fishing

https://lassenlodging.com/drakesbad

    Drakesbad Guest Ranch

MAMMOTH CAVE

Lodging and dining inside the park

https://mammothcavelodge.com/

    The Lodge at Mammoth Cave

Camping inside the park

https://www.recreation.gov

Mammoth Cave, Maple Springs, Houchin Ferry

Visitor Center

https://www.nps.gov/maca/planyourvisit/mammoth-cave-visitor-center.htm

Mammoth Cave Visitor Center

Cave Tours

https://recreation.gov

Over 10 unique tours

Canoe and Kayak Tours

https://www.cavecountrycanoes.com/

Cave Country Canoe

http://mammothcavecanoe.com/

Green River Canoeing

Horseback Riding

http://www.doublejstables.com/

Double J Stables

https://kentuckyactionpark.com/attractions/

Jesse James Stables

MESA VERDE

Lodging and dining inside the park

https://www.visitmesaverde.com/lodging-camping/far-view-lodge/

Far View Lodge

Camping inside the park

https://www.visitmesaverde.com/lodging-camping/morefield-camp-ground/

Morefield Campground

Visitor Centers

https://www.nps.gov/meve/planyourvisit/meve_vc.htm

Mesa Verde Visitor and Research Center

https://www.nps.gov/meve/planyourvisit/museum.htm

Chapin Mesa Archeological Museum

Grocery/Markets

https://www.visitmesaverde.com/lodging-camping/morefield-camp-ground/

Morefield Campground Store and Knife Edge Cafe

Ranger-Led Cliff Dwelling Tours

https://recreation.gov

Cliff Palace, Balcony House, Long House

Mug House, Square Tower House, Spring House

700 Years Tour of Park Archaeology

https://www.visitmesaverde.com/tours/700-years-tour/

MOUNT RANIER

Lodging and dining inside the park

https://mtrainierguestservices.com/accommodations

Paradise Inn

National Park Inn

Sunrise Day Lodge (dining only)

Camping inside the park

https://www.recreation.gov

Cougar Rock Campground

Ohanapecosh Campground

Visitor Centers

https://www.nps.gov/olym/planyourvisit/visitorcenters

Henry M. Jackson Visitor Center

Ohanapecosh Visitor Center

Sunrise Visitor Center

Grocery/Markets

https://mtrainierguestservices.com/longmire-general-store

Longmire General Store

NEW RIVER GORGE

Lodging and dining outside the park

https://adventuresonthegorge.com/lodging/

Adventures on the Gorge Cabins

https://www.qualityinnnewrivergorge.com/en/

Quality Inn New River Gorge

Visitor Center

https://www.nps.gov/neri/planyourvisit/visitorcenters.htm

Canyon Rim Visitor Center

Thurmond Visitor Center

Sandstone Visitor Center

Bike Riding

https://arrowheadbikefarm.com/

Arrowhead Bike Farm

Rafting

https://raftinginfo.com/

River Expeditions

Climbing

https://www.newriverclimbing.com/

New River Mountain Guides

NORTH CASCADES

Lodging and dining outside the park—Ross Lake Area

Totem Trail Motel: https://totemtrail.com/reserv

Buffalo Run Inn: http://buffaloruninn.com

Lodging and dining inside the park

http://www.rosslakeresort.com/accommodations

Ross Lake Resort

https://lodgeatstehekin.com/accommodations

North Cascades Lodge at Stehekin

https://www.silverbayinn.com

Silver Springs Inn

http://stehekinvalleyranch.com

Stehekin Valley Ranch

https://stehekinpastry.com

Stehekin Pastry Company

Camping inside the park

https://www.recreation.gov

Newhalem, Colonial Creek, Gorge Lake

Goodell Creek, Purple Point, Stehekin

Visitor Centers

https://www.nps.gov/noca/planyourvisit/visitorcenters.htm

North Cascades Visitor Center (Ross Lake Area): 206-386-4495

Golden West Visitor Center (Chelan/Stehekin Area): 509-699-2080

Market/Kayak/Red Bus

https://lodgeatstehekin.com/plan-your-trip/stehekin-activities

Lodge at Stehekin

Ferry

https://ladyofthelake.com

Lake Chelan Ferry: 509-682-4584

OLYMPIC

Lodging and dining inside the park

https://www.olympicnationalparks.com/lodging

Log Cabin Resort (kayaks)

Lake Crescent Lodge (kayaks)

Sol Duc Hot Springs Resort (hot springs)

Lake Quinault Lodge (kayaks)

https://www.thekalalochlodge.com

Kalaloch Lodge

Camping inside the park

https://www.recreation.gov

Kalaloch

Sol Duc Hot Springs RV Park and Campground

Visitor Centers

https://www.nps.gov/olym/planyourvisit/visitorcenters.htm

Olympic National Park Visitor Center

Hurricane Ridge Visitor Center

Hoh Rain Forest Visitor Center

Grocery/Markets

Fairholme General Store: 360-928-3020

Thriftway Grocery Store: 360-374-6161

Northshore Grocery: 360-288-2458

Kayaks and Hot Springs

https://www.olympicnationalparks.com/

PETRIFIED FOREST

Visitor Centers

https://www.nps.gov/pefo/planyourvisit/visitorcenters.htm

Painted Desert Visitor Center

Rainbow Forest Visitor Center

Café/Market/Painted Desert Inn Museum

https://petrifiedforesttrading.com/painted-desert-diner-menu/

Painted Desert Diner

PINNACLES

Camping inside the park

https://www.visitpinnacles.com

    Pinnacles Campground

Visitor Center and Store

https://www.nps.gov/olym/planyourvisit/visitorcenters.htm

    East Pinnacles Visitor Center and Book Store

REDWOOD

Lodging and dining near park boundaries

https://elkmeadowcabins.com

    Elk Meadow Cabins

https://www.requainn.com

    Historic Requa Inn

https://www.ihg.com/holidayinnexpress/hotels/us/en/klamath

    Holiday Inn Express Klamath

https://www.hiouchimotel.com

    Houchi Motel

Camping inside the park

https://www.reservecalifornia.com/CaliforniaWebHome

    Jedediah Smith, Mill Creek, Elk Prairie, Gold Bluffs

Visitor Centers

https://www.nps.gov/redw/planyourvisit/visitorcenters

    Thomas H. Kuchel Visitor Center

    Prairie Creek Visitor Center

    Jedediah Smith Visitor Center

    Hiouchi Visitor Center

Grocery/Markets

    Orick Market: 707-488-2120

    Woodland Villa Market: 707-482-2081

    Shoreline Deli and Market: 707-488-5761

Tall Trees Trail Permit

https://www.nps.gov/redw/planyourvisit/talltreespermits

ROCKY MOUNTAIN

Lodging and dining near park boundaries

https://www.stanleyhotel.com/

    Stanley Hotel

https://ymcarockies.org/lodging/

    YMCA of the Rockies

https://www.esteswildwoodinn.com/

    Wildwood Inn

https://www.westernriv.com/

    Western Riviera Lakeside Lodge

Camping inside the park

https://www.recreation.gov

    Longs Peak, Glacier Basin, Moraine Park

    Aspenglen, Timber Creek

Visitor Centers

https://www.nps.gov/romo/planyourvisit/visitorcenters.htm

    Beaver Meadows, Alpine, Fall River Visitor Centers

    Kawuneeche Visitor Center

https://www.visitestespark.com/partners/advertising/visitor-center/

    Estes Park Visitor Center

Horseback Riding

http://rockymountainhorserides.com/

    Glacier Creek Stables

SAGUARO

Visitor Centers

https://www.nps.gov/sagu/planyourvisit/visitor-center-information.htm

    Red Hills Visitor Center

Rincon Visitor Center

Arizona Sonora Desert Museum

https://www.desertmuseum.org/

SEQUOIA

Lodging and dining inside the park

https://www.visitsequoia.com/lodging/wuksachi-lodge

Wuksachi Lodge

Lodging and dining outside the park

https://www.mslodge.com/lodging

Montecito Sequoia Lodge

https://www.silvercityresort.com

Silver City Mountain Resort

Camping inside the park

https://www.recreation.gov/camping/campgrounds

Lodgepole Village Campground

Platform Tent Lodging in Backcountry

https://www.sequoiahighsierracamp.com

Sequoia Bearpaw Meadow High Sierra Camp

Visitor Centers

https://www.nps.gov/seki/planyourvisit/visitorcenters.htm

Lodgepole Visitor Center

Foothills Visitor Center

Giant Forest Museum

Grocery/Markets

https://www.visitsequoia.com/shop/lodgepole-market

Lodgepole Village Grocery Store

Crystal Cave Tour Reservations

https://www.recreation.gov/ticket/facility/251898

SHENANDOAH

Lodging and dining inside the park
https://www.goshenandoah.com/lodging
- Skyland Resort
- Big Meadows Lodge

Camping inside the park
https://www.recreation.gov
- Mathews Arm
- Big Meadows
- Loft Mountain
- Lewis Mountain

Visitor Centers
https://www.nps.gov/shen/planyourvisit/visitorcenters.htm
- Dickey Ridge Visitor Center
- Harry Byrd/Big Meadows Visitor Center

Grocery/Markets
https://www.goshenandoah.com/activities-events/shopping
- Big Meadows Wayside

Horseback Riding
https://www.goshenandoah.com/activities-events/horseback-riding

THEODORE ROOSEVELT

Lodging and dining near park boundaries
https://www.wyndhamhotels.com/americinn/medora-north-dakota
- AmericInn by Wyndham in Medora

Camping inside the park
https://www.recreation.gov
- Cottonwood Campground

Visitor Centers
https://www.nps.gov/thro/planyourvisit/visitorcenters.htm
- North Unit Visitor Center

South Unit Visitor Center
Painted Canyon Visitor Center

US VIRGIN ISLANDS
Lodging and dining outside the park
http://twosandals.com/
Two Sandals by the Sea—Red Hook
https://stjohninn.com/
Saint John Inn
http://hotelcruzbay.com/accommodations.html
Hotel Cruz Bay
Visitor Centers
https://www.nps.gov/viis/planyourvisit/visitorcenter.htm
Rainy Lake Visitor Center
Cruz Bay Visitor Center
Ferry to Saint John
https://www.vinow.com/travel/virgin-islands-ferry-schedules/stjohn/
VI Now
https://www.varlack-ventures.com/ferryservices
Varlack Ventures

VOYAGEURS
Lodging and dining inside the park
https://www.kettlefallshotel.com/
Kettle Falls Hotel
Lodging and dining outside the park
http://www.ashtraillodge.com/
Ash Trail Lodge
http://www.pineaire.com/resort-sketch.html
Pine Aire Resort
https://thunderbirdrainylake.com/lodging/

Thunderbird Lodge
Camping outside the park
https://www.dnr.state.mn.us/state_forests/
Visitor Centers
https://www.nps.gov/voya/planyourvisit/visitorcenters.htm
Rainy Lake Visitor Center
Kabetogama Lake Visitor Center
Ash River Visitor Center
Grocery/Markets
https://www.gatewaygeneral.com/
Gateway General Store
Water Taxi
https://www.voyageursoutfitters.com/
Voyageurs Outfitters

WHITE SANDS

Camping outside the park
https://koa.com/campgrounds/alamogordo/
White Sands/Alamogordo KOA
Visitor Center
https://www.nps.gov/whsa/planyourvisit/visitorcenterpr.htm
White Sands Visitor Center
Lake Lucero Tour
https://www.nps.gov/whsa/planyourvisit/lake-lucero-tour.htm

WIND CAVE

Lodging and dining outside the park
https://custerresorts.com/lodges-and-cabins/
Custer State Park Lodges
Visitor Center
https://www.nps.gov/wica/planyourvisit/guidedtours.htm

Wind Cave Visitor Center
Cave Tours and Camping
First come, first served at visitor center

WRANGELL-ST. ELIAS
Lodging and dining inside the park
https://www.kennicottlodge.com/
Kennicott Glacier Lodge
https://majohnsonshotel.com/
Ma Johnson's Hotel
Visitor Center
https://www.nps.gov/wrst/planyourvisit/copper-center-visitor-center.htm
Copper Center Visitor Center
Guided trip of Kennecott historic mine buildings and guided hiking
https://www.steliasguides.com/
St. Elias Alpine Guides
Rafting Outfitters
https://raftthewrangells.com/
McCarthy River Tours

YELLOWSTONE
Lodging and dining the park
https://www.yellowstonenationalparklodges.com/
Mammoth Hot Springs Hotel and Cabins
Roosevelt Camp Frontier and Roughrider Cabins
Lake Yellowstone Hotel and Cottages and Lake Lodge Cabins
Lodges at Grant Village
Old Faithful Inn, Lodge Cabins, and Snow Lodge
Camping inside the park
https://www.recreation.gov

Grant Village, Canyon Village, Bridge Bay, Madison

Visitor Centers

https://www.nps.gov/yell/planyourvisit/visitorcenters.htm

Old Faithful, Canyon, Fishing Bridge, Grant Visitor Centers

Grocery/Markets

https://www.yellowstonevacations.com/dining-shopping/yellowstone-general-stores

Horseback Riding

https://www.yellowstonenationalparklodges.com/adventure/wild-west-adventures/saddle-up/

Boat Rides

https://www.yellowstonenationalparklodges.com/adventures/water-adventures/

Covered Wagon Cookout

https://www.yellowstonenationalparklodges.com/adventure/wild-west-adventures/old-west-dinner-cookout/

YOSEMITE

Lodging and dining inside the park

https://www.travelyosemite.com/lodging

Wawona Hotel, Yosemite Valley Lodge

The Ahwahnee, White Wolf Lodge

Platform Tent Lodge with Vehicle Access

https://www.travelyosemite.com/lodging

Tuolumne Meadows Lodge

Curry Village

Platform Tent Lodging in Backcountry

https://www.travelyosemite.com/lodging/high-sierra-camps

May Lake, Glen Aulin, Sunrise, Merced Lake, Vogelsang

Camping inside the park

https://www.recreation.gov

Upper/Lower/North Pines

Wawona, Bridalveil Creek, Porcupine Flat

Visitor Centers

https://www.nps.gov/places/000/yosemite-valley-visitor-center.htm

Yosemite Valley Visitor Center and Museum

Wawona Visitor Center

Tuolumne Meadows Visitor Center

Big Oak Flat Visitor Center

Mariposa Grove Museum

Grocery/Markets

Pioneer Gift and Grocery at Wawona: 209-375-6574

Yosemite Lodge Gift Shop: 888-413-8869

Village Store in Yosemite Valley: 209-372-1253

Crane Flat Gas and Grocery in Tuolumne Meadows

ZION

Lodging and dining inside the park

https://www.zionlodge.com/

Zion Lodge

Camping at the park entrance

https://www.recreation.gov/

Watchman, South

Visitor Centers

https://www.nps.gov/zion/planyourvisit/visitorcenters.htm

Zion Canyon

Kolob Canyons

www.ingramcontent.com/pod-product-compliance
Lightning Source LLC
Chambersburg PA
CBHW072040020426
42334CB00017B/1342